Naturalism in Question

Naturalism in Question

EDITED BY
MARIO DE CARO
AND
DAVID MACARTHUR

HARVARD UNIVERSITY PRESS

Cambridge, Massachusetts

London, England   2004

Copyright © 2004 by the President and Fellows of Harvard College
All rights reserved
Printed in the United States of America

Library of Congress Cataloging-in-Publication Data

Naturalism in question / edited by Mario De Caro and David Macarthur.
  p. cm.
Includes bibliographical references and index.
ISBN 0-674-01295-X
1. Naturalism. I. De Caro, Mario. II. Macarthur, David.

B828.2.N375 2004
146—dc22   2003067631

Acknowledgments

We hope that this book is one of the more welcome products of our age of globalization. It was projected when we were working in the United States, and prepared when we had returned to Australia and Italy, respectively. Its contributors are drawn from three continents.

Many institutions and people have helped us during its preparation. The initial idea for the book was conceived in Somerville and Cambridge, Mass., in some memorable conversations at Pamplona Café, the Someday Café, and Toscanini's. The idea took shape in the stimulating environment of the Philosophy Department at Tufts University, two members of which are owed our deepest gratitude. Erin I. Kelly's kindness, generosity, and tireless willingness to offer help have been invaluable. And Stephen L. White's enthusiasm and wise counsel, over innumerable conversations and correspondences, kept our spirits up and the project on track.

We are grateful to the original publishers for permission to reproduce the following papers: Barry Stroud's "The Charm of Naturalism" (Chapter 1), published in *Proceedings of the American Philosophical Association* 70 (1996): 43–55; John McDowell's "Naturalism in the Philosophy of Mind" (Chapter 5), published in German in *Neue Rundschau* 110 (1999): 48–69; and Donald Davidson's "Could There Be a Science of Rationality?" (Chapter 8), published in *International Journal of Philosophical Studies* 3 (1995): 1–16.

For their support and advice at crucial stages in the project we would like to thank Jody Azzouni, Stanley Cavell, Mark Colyvan, Richard Moran, Huw Price, and Hilary Putnam. In addition, we would like to acknowledge the valuable support of our colleagues at Università Roma Tre and Macquarie University, Sydney, respectively; in particular, Rosaria Egidi, Giacomo Marramao, Peter Menzies, and Nick Smith.

We would also like to acknowledge Lindsay Waters, the Editor for Humanities at Harvard University Press. In Socratic fashion, Lindsay acted as midwife for this project. His enthusiasm, editorial skills, and resourcefulness helped see the book into print in its present form.

Finally, we would like to warmly thank our partners, Giulia and Catherine. For two years they have sweetly tolerated the inconveniences of living with an editor of a book whose coeditor lived two oceans and ten time zones away. We are ever grateful for their love and encouragement. This book is dedicated to them.

Contents

Naturalism in Question

Introduction: The Nature of Naturalism

MARIO DE CARO AND DAVID MACARTHUR

*T*HE CRITICAL CONCERN of the present volume is contemporary naturalism, both in its scientific version and as represented by newly emerging hopes for another, philosophically more liberal, naturalism.[1] The papers collected here are state-of-the-art discussions that question the appeal, rational motivations, and presuppositions of scientific naturalism across a broad range of philosophical topics. As an alternative to scientific naturalism, we offer the outlines of a new nonreductive form of naturalism and a more inclusive conception of nature than any provided by the natural sciences. Our authors collectively believe that holding scientific naturalism up for philosophical scrutiny and challenging its misconceptions is of the first importance both for understanding ourselves and our place in the world, and also for the future direction of philosophy itself.

Instead of presenting an unwieldy for-and-against anthology, we decided that since scientific naturalism is the current orthodoxy, at least within Anglo-American philosophy, it would be more fruitful to collect papers that are critical of that orthodoxy and aim at constructively reforming it. We have restricted ourselves to authors broadly within the analytic tradition of philosophy. Partly this is a matter of the sheer magnitude of undertaking to compare the attitudes of the analytic and continental traditions to the sciences; partly it is because we believe that the

1

fate of analytic philosophy is more closely aligned with the fate of contemporary or scientific naturalism.

Eleven of the fourteen articles collected here are new papers, most by distinguished philosophers written especially for this anthology. Three have previously appeared in print. The papers by Donald Davidson and Barry Stroud are reproduced here on the grounds that they are seminal discussions of scientific naturalism that are relatively difficult to find. Davidson's paper, however, is accompanied by an original afterword. John McDowell's paper, which clarifies and amplifies some key themes of *Mind and World* (1994), has previously only appeared in German.

In Section I, we first turn to consider the background and central themes of *scientific* naturalism before briefly summarizing some of the main lines of criticism presented by the papers collected here. In Section II, we provide some indication of the ways in which our authors provide a road map, outlining some positive theoretical directions for philosophy after scientific naturalism. The volume can usefully be thought of as providing the beginnings of a more liberal or pluralistic form of naturalism.

I. Scientific Naturalism: Some Themes

An overwhelming majority of contemporary Anglo-American philosophers claim to be "naturalists" or to be offering a "naturalistic" theory of a key philosophical concept (say, knowledge) or domain (for example, ethical discourse).[2] Naturalism has become a slogan in the name of which the vast majority of work in analytic philosophy is pursued, and its preeminent status can perhaps be appreciated in how little energy is spent in explicitly defining or explaining what is meant by scientific naturalism, or in defending it against possible objections.

For the few who do take the trouble to explain naturalism, perhaps the most familiar definition is in terms of the rejection of supernatural entities such as gods, demons, souls, and ghosts.[3] However, the category of the supernatural is no clearer and no less controversial than the category of the natural. As John Dupré notes in the present volume, it is no good simply to identify the supernatural with the immaterial, since there are many immaterial things that we are perfectly happy to countenance: for example, concepts and numbers. In philosophy, the idea of the supernatural is often associated with theism and Cartesian dualism. But it is hard to see how this idea of the supernatural can help to provide a satisfactory understanding of contemporary scientific naturalism. Although naturalism may once have been primarily understood in terms of the rejection of the Judeo-Christian God or the immaterial soul, the most pressing questions about naturalism now arise in areas of philosophy other than theology, and the great majority of philosophers of mind have long since abandoned Cartesian dualism.[4]

Apart from being used to refer to the denial of the existence of God or to indicate the rejection of the dualism of mind and body, the term "naturalism" is also commonly used to mark one's acceptance of a scientific philosophy, or to denote the attempt to "naturalize" some allegedly contentious entities or concepts, and in various other ways as well. The papers by Hilary Putnam and John McDowell both suggest that the major battles in contemporary metaphysics concern the status of the normative: one side claiming it as a *sui generis* aspect of nature, and the other side treating such a conception as supernatural, and so reducing norms to something nonnormative, on a more restrictive, scientific conception of nature. In this debate also, both "naturalism" and "supernaturalism" are contested terms, and there is no neutral understanding of either to settle the dispute.

It is a philosophical commonplace that "Naturalism means many different things to many different people."[5] When one considers this widely varied usage it seems plausible that at least part of the attraction of naturalism depends upon a tendency to vacillate between uncontentious and contentious senses of the term. This has led to a situation in which one might despair of finding any unified doctrine(s) lying beneath the various claims made on behalf of naturalism. And this, in turn, fosters a sense that "naturalism" is a hopelessly portmanteau term without any discernible core meaning and, as such, not a particularly suitable candidate for philosophical examination.

Nonetheless, in spite of its complexity and ambiguity, we believe that there is a substantial core conception of naturalism that underlies a great deal of current philosophical thought. While it may not be possible to capture everything philosophers now associate with the term "naturalism," there are, we believe, two core themes—although there are, of course, real and apparent disagreements about how they are to be understood in detail. These two important and characteristic themes of naturalism are:

1. *An Ontological Theme:* a commitment to an exclusively scientific conception of nature;
2. *A Methodological Theme:* a reconception of the traditional relation between philosophy and science according to which philosophical inquiry is conceived as continuous with science.

In order to distinguish this kind of naturalism from other, or older, versions, let us call it *scientific* naturalism. Now let us consider each of its themes in turn.

1. The Ontological Theme: A Scientific Conception of Nature

Schematically, the first theme is a commitment to a scientism that says not only that modern (or post-seventeenth-century) natural science provides *a* true picture of nature but, more contentiously, that it is the *only* true picture.[6] Wilfred Sellars expresses its animating spirit in his remark that "science is the measure of all things, of what is that it is, and of what is not that it is not."[7]

Perhaps the most common reason cited in favor of this view is some version of what might be called the "Great Success of Modern Science Argument." It argues from the great successes of the modern natural sciences in predicting, controlling, and explaining natural phenomena—outstanding examples of which are mathematical physics and Darwin's theory of evolution—to the claim that the conception of nature of the natural sciences is very likely to be true and, moreover, that this is our *only* bona fide or unproblematic conception of nature. It is the latter claim that earns scientific naturalism the label of "scientism."

The acceptance of an exclusively scientific conception of nature is what leads to the demand for the various projects of naturalizing the mind and its contents (involving, say, ethical values, colors, and numbers)[8] that dominate contemporary research in metaphysics. Projects of naturalization have typically been conceived as substantive semantic projects in which the concepts of apparently nonnatural discourses must be: 1) reduced or reconstructed in terms of naturalistically respectable posits—that is, the posits of the natural sciences; or 2) treated as useful fictions; or 3) construed as playing a nonreferential or nonfactual linguistic role; or 4) eliminated altogether as illusory manifestations of "prescientific" thinking.

The highly revisionary aims of most naturalization projects is an indication of the fact that, by and large, scientific naturalists tend to adopt a narrow or restrictive conception of what constitutes legitimate natural science: at a minimum, physics, or more plausibly, physics and also chemistry and biology.[9] In so doing, they draw a (no doubt controversial) line between science proper and other kinds of rational inquiry such as history or art criticism. The substantive conception of natural science they presuppose has complex roots, but two discernible influences are a con-

tinuing allegiance to the in-principle unity of the sciences and the appeal
of a strong version of physicalism.

In the recent past, it is significant that the terms "naturalism" and
"physicalism" have often been used interchangeably.[10] Part of the reason,
as John Dupré's paper explains, is that the Great Success of Science Argument has been thought to provide grounds for physicalist monism: the
thesis, as Armstrong explains it, "that the world contains nothing but the —
entities recognized by physics."[11] And this is no doubt related both to
the idea of the unity of the sciences and to the tradition of privileging
physics as our paradigm of a natural science.[12]

However, it is worth noting that there is no consensus about there
being one master conception of scientific nature. This reflects the fact
that there is dispute about the unity and scope of the sciences, even *within*
the scientific naturalist camp. Not surprisingly, then, scientific naturalism
is not identical to physicalism. Although every physicalist[13] (in Armstrong's sense) is committed to scientific naturalism, not every scientific
naturalist is a physicalist. On a pluralist conception of science, a scientific
naturalist might think there are entities such as acids or predators or
phonemes that chemistry or biology or experimental psychology commits
him to that are not (reducible to) physical entities, and that, consequently,
the explanations of, say, biology are not reducible, even in principle, to
the explanations of physics.

Of course, some philosophers understand physicalism otherwise, as a
supervenience claim, namely that all nonphysical properties (such as
mental and aesthetic properties) supervene on physical properties.
Whether this is something that all scientific naturalists must accept depends upon how supervenience is understood, a highly controversial matter.[14] Yet however it is understood, most physicalists also assume that the
nonphysical is (in some strong but hard-to-define sense) dependent on,
and determined by, the physical but not vice versa. Although many may
find the idea of a nonreductive physicalism appealing,[15] these further
commitments seem to inexorably push physicalism in the direction of
various forms of reductionism.[16]

There is a long-standing and quite general problem in distinguishing
science proper from other forms of critical inquiry. In both the analytic
and the continental traditions there has been much dispute, for instance,
about whether the so-called "human and social sciences," including intentional psychology, sociology, and anthropology, are really autonomous
and legitimate sciences in their own right like physics, chemistry, and
biology.[17] Most scientific naturalists tend to answer "no" to this question;
more liberal naturalists, such as the writers included in this anthology,

would instead say "yes" on the grounds that the limits of the "scientific" are broader, and looser, than the orthodoxy suggests.

2. The Methodological Theme: The Continuity of Philosophy and Science

The second scientific naturalist theme involves a major reconception of the traditional relation between philosophy and science. Traditional philosophy attempted to establish a priori, and once for all, the presuppositions, extent, and limits of knowledge and reality. It bore a foundational relation to the enterprise of scientific inquiry. In Cartesian and Kantian thought, for example, philosophy provides the epistemological and metaphysical foundations for the natural sciences.[18]

Over the past four centuries since the beginnings of the scientific revolution, there has been a gradual but relentless reversal of the roles of philosophy vis-à-vis science as we find in, say, Descartes's "First Philosophy." Hume took a decisive step toward scientific naturalism in severely restricting the scope of a priori knowledge to the relation of ideas, in adopting an ironic and cautious agnosticism, and in advocating a new "science of Man,"[19] whose guiding ideal is to regard the human as simply a part of nature, not set over against it.[20]

Scientific naturalism is, as Quine elegantly puts it, the "abandonment of the goal of a First Philosophy prior to natural science."[21] Abandoning First Philosophy involves two related ideas: 1) the denial of philosophy's traditional authority—philosophy can no longer claim to be the master discipline that sits in judgment of the claims of the natural sciences; and 2) the denial that the results of philosophy play a foundational role with respect to the sciences.

In fact, scientific naturalists defend an even stronger claim, namely that "philosophy is continuous with the natural sciences."[22] What this adds to the rejection of First Philosophy is the idea that philosophy has no autonomy with respect to the sciences. Philosophy, on this conception, *is* science in its general and abstract reaches.

3. Some Common Forms of Scientific Naturalism

The ontological and methodological themes can come apart, in principle. An ontological scientific naturalist need not subscribe to the methodological theme, since one might believe in a scientific conception of nature on distinctively philosophical grounds. However, a methodological scientific naturalist will presumably endorse the ontological theme on the ground that scientific inquiry has ontological presuppositions and implications.

It is also worth noting that we can also define a semantic version of naturalism that presupposes a prior commitment to the ontological version. Here, then, are the three influential types of naturalism:

i) The *ontological scientific naturalist*[23] holds that the entities posited by acceptable scientific explanations are the *only* genuine entities that there are.[24] A weaker version holds that scientific posits are the only unproblematic (or nonqueer)[25] entities that there are.

ii) The *methodological (or epistemological) scientific naturalist*[26] holds that it is *only* by following the methods of the natural sciences—or, at a minimum, the empirical methods of a posteriori inquiry—that one arrives at genuine knowledge. A weaker version holds that the methods of the natural sciences are the only unproblematic methods of inquiry. On this view scientific knowledge is the only unproblematic (or unmysterious) kind of knowledge that there is, thus provisionally allowing for nonscientific knowledge in some loose or practical sense.

iii) The *semantic scientific naturalist*[27] holds that the concepts employed by the natural sciences are the *only* genuine concepts we have and that other concepts can only be retained if we can find an interpretation of them in terms of scientifically respectable concepts. A weaker version holds that such concepts are the only unproblematic concepts we have. (Note that this kind of naturalism *might* be defended on a priori conceptual grounds, although it will be under considerable internal pressure to abandon such methodology.)

Of course, scientific naturalism tends toward a global doctrine, committed to all of these versions together, on the basis of the scientific aspiration for a complete and exhaustive explanation of all phenomena. There are many ways of further refining and elaborating the present understanding of scientific naturalism involving, for example, different ways of accounting for such things as values, numbers, meanings, or modalities—all very problematic in the eyes of the scientific naturalist. Rather than explore these matters here, we have left it to each author to articulate a conception of scientific naturalism that fits broadly with our characterization while also suiting their own dialectical purposes.

At this point we must briefly mention the controversy surrounding the a priori. It is clear that scientific naturalists, indeed naturalists of all stripes, reject the traditional (that is, unrevisable) a priori. Nonetheless, it is worth noting that one might give up the traditional a priori yet retain a notion of revisable a priori truths. That is, one might still think that conceptual analysis remains possible, so long as a priori claims about meanings are admitted to be empirically defeasible.[28] Yet from the perspective of strict scientific naturalism, even this will seem an unstable half-way position.[29]

4. Scientific Naturalism and the Analytic Tradition

The nineteenth-century positivism of Comte, Mill, Spencer, Mach, and others was a commitment to the idea that scientific knowledge is the only knowledge there is and that philosophical method is nothing other than scientific method. Although science and philosophy of science had been growing in importance since the scientific revolution, the positivists were, in effect, the first fully fledged scientific naturalist movement.

It is an important fact about analytic philosophy that its founders strongly attacked scientific naturalism, even as they called for a scientific philosophy. Frege and Wittgenstein notoriously rejected the positivists' psychologism in the philosophy of logic. And together with Russell and the Logical Positivists, they believed that "Philosophy aims at the logical clarification of thoughts"[30] by way of logical or conceptual analysis. Early analytic philosophers believed that philosophy could investigate logic, or elucidate the structure of knowledge or the nature of our concepts, a priori without any help from the empirical sciences.

Russell's hopes for a "scientific philosophy" must be understood in the light of a widespread confidence that philosophy is fundamentally distinct from science and that philosophy is authoritative over its own domain of logic. Analytic philosophers followed Russell in hoping that by employing modern methods of logical analysis "philosophy would thus achieve something like the status of a science,"[31] not in becoming science but in adopting a method that, like science, is "co-operative and cumulative."[32]

No one is more important in undermining this early analytic conception of the relation of philosophy and science than W. V. Quine. His attack on the analytic/synthetic distinction and the possibility of traditional a priori truths dismantled the presuppositions of the logical analysis of language or concepts that was central to the "Linguistic Turn."[33] Quine's naturalization of epistemology[34] undermined the last vestiges of First Philosophy and strongly endorsed the continuity between philosophy and science.[35] Today, many scientifically minded analytic philosophers think there is no theoretical alternative to full-blown scientific naturalism.

Although it comes in various kinds and strengths, scientific naturalism is now *the* philosophical orthodoxy within Anglo-American analytic philosophy—a phenomenon signaled by the title of a recent centennial article, "The Naturalists Return."[36] It seems fair to say that the fate of analytic philosophy is now, in large part, tied to the fate of scientific naturalism. This conjecture seems to be borne out by the fact that a growing number of analytic philosophers of the late twentieth and early twenty-first century have been drawn to increasingly reductive (some might say militant)[37] forms of scientific naturalism—those that depend upon very restrictive conceptions of natural science and (scientific) nature.

5. Criticisms of Scientific Naturalism

It must be emphasized that what is at issue here is not respect for the results of the natural sciences.[38] This is an attitude every sane philosopher can be expected to have. Scientific naturalism involves the much stronger claim that science is, or ought to be, our *only* genuine or unproblematic guide in matters of method or knowledge or ontology or semantics.

The criticisms of scientific naturalism presented here cluster around four main topics: 1) the self-consistency of scientific naturalism; 2) naturalist accounts of mind; 3) naturalist accounts of agency; and 4) reductive attitudes to normativity, especially in the ethical and aesthetic domains. Due to considerations of space, we have not been able to cover all the topics that one might hope to cover in a full treatment of naturalism. In particular, several important topics, including religion, mathematics, and logic, have received little or no attention here. In spite of this, we have managed to cover a large range of issues that have the combined virtues of being topical and of central philosophical importance.

In order to give some sense of the directions the papers take and of their mutual affinities, we shall now briefly summarize some of their main lines of criticism. In the next section we will try to indicate how our authors provide some positive directions for philosophy *beyond* the scientific naturalist orthodoxy.

I) THE SELF-CONSISTENCY OF SCIENTIFIC NATURALISM

The papers in Part I of this book all question the scientific naturalists' own understanding of science. As we have seen, the projects of naturalization of contemporary metaphysics depend upon a restrictive conception of nature that, in turn, is based on a restrictive conception of science.

Barry Stroud's "The Charm of Naturalism" is an excellent piece to open the volume, as it provides a very useful survey of the difficulties facing scientific naturalism in a number of different areas. Stroud argues that the scientific naturalist who attempts to reduce or eliminate colors, values, and meanings is at least required to make sense of the *content* of our beliefs about colors, values, and meanings—something that a restrictive conception of nature does not seem to allow one the resources to do.

John Dupré's "The Miracle of Monism" argues that naturalism's commitment to a minimal empiricism is at odds with the scientific naturalist tendency to endorse physicalist monism and reductionism. These two doctrines are supported by what are, paradoxically, supernatural myths about the unity of science and the completeness of physics. They represent a form of First Philosophy that the consistent naturalist is committed to reject.

In "The Content and Appeal of 'Naturalism,' " Hilary Putnam criticizes Quine's distinction between unproblematic first-grade and problematic second-grade conceptual systems and its philosophical legacy in the work of Richard Boyd, Simon Blackburn, Bernard Williams, Peter Railton, Jerry Fodor, Stephen Leeds, and David Lewis. In so doing he makes room for the possibility of "conceptual pluralism": the view that ethical statements, statements of meaning or reference or counterfactuals—indeed most of the statements denigrated as second-grade by naturalists—are bona fide forms of rational discourse, governed no less than scientific statements, by norms of truth and validity.

In "Naturalism Without Representationalism," Huw Price attempts to demonstrate a paradoxical feature of scientific naturalism. He argues that contemporary scientific naturalism is really an object naturalism concerning how to "place" various objects (for example, values, numbers, and meanings) within the-world-as-studied-by-science. Price shows that these placement problems presuppose, independently of the empirical study of language, metaphysically substantial conceptions of reference and truth. He argues that a *subject naturalism*, which concerns itself first and foremost with questions about our *use* of linguistic terms and expressions, places important constraints on object naturalism. From this linguistic perspective, object naturalism seems insufficiently naturalistic by its own lights.

II) SCIENTIFIC NATURALISM AND THE MIND

Scientific naturalists typically conceive nature as a causally closed spatiotemporal structure governed by efficient causal laws—where causes are thought of, paradigmatically, as mind-independent bringers-about of change or difference. It is assumed that human beings can be fully understood in terms of finding how they fit into this larger causal structure.

The papers of Part II explore whether such an account could do justice to the normative character of intentional states, reasons, and concepts.

John McDowell's paper, "Naturalism in the Philosophy of Mind," traces our modern philosophical obsessions concerning the mind and its intentional states to a *restrictive naturalism* that identifies nature with the realm of law as developed by modern science. On this conception rational and normative items are made to seem supernatural and must be either eliminated or reduced. By way of an examination of some ideas of Ruth Millikan, McDowell proposes a different *liberal naturalism*—inspired by Aristotle—according to which reasons, values, and meanings are conceived as *sui generis* but natural items on the basis of the actual character and role of thinking, knowing, and evaluating in our lives.

In "Naturalism and Skepticism," David Macarthur argues that scientific naturalism is committed to what he calls *a causal model of experience*. According to this conception, there is an (efficient) causal gap between the mind and the world that invites unanswerable skeptical problems. Macarthur shows that by overlooking or rejecting the intimate relation between belief and reason-giving, naturalists such as Quine, Goldman, and Strawson are unable to defuse the skeptical threat that naturalism naturally invites. This undermines one of the main arguments in its favor, namely that scientific naturalism is supposed to earn the right not to have to answer the skeptic.

Akeel Bilgrami reflects on the thought that intentional states are essentially normative in "Intentionality and Norms." He argues that this implies their irreducibility to physical states *and* that intentional states *cannot* be dispositions as scientific naturalists tend to suppose. Intentional states such as beliefs are *commitments*, and one can have a commitment to thinking something without being so disposed. Since this conclusion seems to be at odds with the widely held thesis that the intentional supervenes on the physical, Bilgrami wonders whether this thesis is, perhaps, a naturalistic prejudice.

According to Donald Davidson in "Could There Be a Science of Rationality?" psychological concepts are characterized by normative, holistic, and externalist elements that cannot be reduced—whether nomologically or definitionally—to the concepts of the hard natural sciences. Yet, notwithstanding the failure of reductionism, our psychological concepts are indispensable for understanding human thought and action.

III) SCIENTIFIC NATURALISM AND AGENCY

In Part III the authors challenge the idea that action or freedom can be reductively accounted for in terms of the causal worldview of scientific naturalism. For instance, naturalists typically try to explain agency by reducing action to behavior caused by some belief-desire pair. Jennifer Hornsby's paper, "Agency and Alienation," criticizes this conception as defended by David Velleman. She argues that the belief-desire model of psychology provides an impoverished account of human motivation. *Pace* Velleman, it cannot be corrected by simply *adding* other mental states and events as further causes of actions. She goes on to show that the naturalistic picture does not have the resources to adequately capture an agent's doing something intentionally.

Mario De Caro ponders the fact that a growing number of philosophers argue that human freedom is incompatible with both causal determinism and causal indeterminism, and that, for this reason, free will is either an illusion or a complete mystery. In "Is Freedom Really a Mystery?" he shows that these arguments only appear compelling if one assumes a scientific ontological naturalism, especially one taking the form of physicalist monism. He argues that on an alternative pluralist view, skepticism about free will loses much of its appeal.

Stephen L. White's paper, "Subjectivity and the Agential Perspective," concerns the difference between the normal agent and a "passive subject" who agrees with us about all the natural facts, but who finds the idea of action *unintelligible*. White appeals to this example to address a question that is logically prior to the increasingly common claim that freedom is an illusion: the question What, if freedom is an illusion, is it an illusion *of*? White sees analogies between this question and those raised by recent work on the meaning of evaluative terms and on the perceptual phenomenology of evaluative experience. And he suggests that reductive, naturalistic accounts of agential concepts face the same difficulties as their counterparts in metaethics. White goes on to propose an alternative account that is antireductionist and that grounds the meaning of agential terms in a richer conception of visual experience than the currently entrenched camera metaphors allow.

IV) ETHICAL AND AESTHETIC NORMATIVITY

Although the issue of the ineliminability and irreducibility of normativity is a leitmotif of this entire volume, in Part IV we consider how ethical and aesthetic normativity cannot be adequately accounted for in a scientific naturalist setting that denies the existence of the relevant *sui generis* norms.

When we turn to consider the contemporary philosophical debate on personal identity, we find that it, too, is dominated by scientific naturalists who only disagree as to *which* natural facts constitute personal identity:

whether they are psychological (Lockeans) or biological (animalists). In "A Nonnaturalist Account of Personal Identity," Carol Rovane offers an alternative *normative* analysis of personal identity that is "nonnatural" insofar as what constitutes personal identity are not natural facts, but rather the products of effort and will. Persons can, and sometimes do, choose and strive to redraw the boundaries that distinguish them from one another, allowing for the possibility of group persons containing many human beings and multiple persons within a single human being.

In her paper "Against Naturalism in Ethics," Erin I. Kelly considers current scientific naturalist theories that see morality as aiming to reach intersubjectively justifiable norms and that attempt to account for morality without relying upon evaluative concepts. Kelly argues that these theories inevitably fail to appreciate the ineliminable normative content of ethics. No set of empirical facts can adequately account for the role that substantive moral reasoning plays in our attempts to reach a reasonable consensus about moral norms.

Stanley Cavell's contribution, originally written to appear as a postscript to "The *Investigations'* Everyday Aesthetics of Itself," provides a profound reading of Wittgenstein's remarks on nature and the natural history of the human. Cavell discerns an intimate relation between human nature and the normativity of judgment, the capacity of one's words to speak for others and others for oneself, perhaps in new or better ways.

II. Some Directions for a New Naturalism

No doubt there will be those who will be strongly inclined to characterize these criticisms of scientific naturalism as forms of antinaturalism. But that would be to take a stand on the very issue in question, namely, who has the right to the key terms of "naturalism" and "nature." It is important, in considering this question, to recall that what is at issue in this volume is *scientific* naturalism, not anything that might properly deserve the title of "naturalism." Although no one here wants to deny that core scientific descriptions of nature are very likely to be true, what *is* in question is whether they provide us with our *only* conception(s) of nature, or the only conception(s) we need.

After Quine's widely influential work, it is an important fact that almost all philosophers—including those who oppose scientific naturalism— want to claim for themselves the title of "naturalism." All sides can agree that this represents a major shift in philosophy's conception of itself and of its relation to the sciences, even if there is disagreement about how to understand the nature of this shift. Nowadays very few philosophers will want to claim that philosophy has any special domain—whether the study of knowledge, language, concepts, being, or whatever—that is *wholly* independent of the findings of the best current scientific theories. Nor would they claim that philosophy can dictate to the sciences from a higher position of authority. As Quine puts it, where the sciences are concerned, there is now no higher tribunal than science itself.

The rejection of First Philosophy can be regarded as a minimal sense of "naturalism" that even the authors of the present volume subscribe to. It is widely acknowledged that philosophy can no longer claim for itself its traditional foundational status, something that has led Richard Rorty to say that we should simply "[cease] to worry about the autonomy of philosophy."[39] However, it is precisely the issue of autonomy around which the hopes for a new naturalism turn, as we shall explain below.

Apart from being united with scientific naturalists in this negative conception of naturalism, most of our authors hope for a new, more substantive, *nonscientistic* naturalism distinct from the scientific (or, better, scientistic) naturalism that is currently so influential. In this spirit, John Dupré has endorsed "pluralistic naturalism," Jennifer Hornsby, "naive naturalism,"[40] John McDowell, a "liberal naturalism,"[41] and Barry Stroud, a "more open minded or expansive naturalism."[42] Although the ways in which our authors conceive of this alternative differ in emphasis and detail, they share four general features:

1. The papers represent a shift in philosophical focus from concern with nonhuman nature to *human* nature, where this is conceived as a historically conditioned product of contingent forces. This shift is evident in a greater concern to accurately describe, in Cavell's phrase, "the full panoply of things" as they figure in our experience or language.[43] All the papers acknowledge a descriptive task, a concern to accurately map our actual responsiveness to norms, our actual uses of language, or the actual nature of our commitments—even in spite of our tendencies to reflectively distort our lives in thought.

2. A nonreductive attitude to normativity in its various guises runs through the volume. One of the primary motivations for scientific naturalism is what Putnam calls "a horror of the normative." *Sui generis* norms are stigmatized as supernatural and in need of "naturalization." The contributors to the present volume all want to question this project and to argue that *sui generis* norms need not be understood as supernatural, mysterious, or queer. Some of our authors are even happy to include them as genuine aspects of

nature, on a broader conception than we are currently familiar with.

3. Another important theme running through the volume is the need for a new self-image for philosophy after scientific naturalism. As a start, it is important to distinguish the rejection of First Philosophy from the stronger claim that philosophy is continuous with the sciences. Although all of our authors accept the former, most (though not all) reject the latter, favoring a conception of philosophy as, at least in some areas and respects, autonomous from scientific method, if by this we mean autonomy from specialized data-collection, experiments, expert opinion, and so on. Here there is a need to distinguish what anyone knows as a master of their native language, the realm of what Wittgenstein called "the ordinary," from scientific knowledge. Furthermore, on this new conception, the results and authority of philosophy (insofar as it has any authority) do not depend upon the support of any specific scientific findings. Of course, we do not want to deny that such findings may provide the impetus to philosophical reflection, or that they may help to undermine one's philosophical conclusions.

4. Finally, all the authors in this volume share a pluralist conception of the sciences—and not only in the limited sense accepted by some scientific naturalists who admit that chemistry and biology are irreducible to physics. Our authors are happy to concede that science has no essence and that the very idea of a sharp division between what is scientific and what is not is highly questionable. Indeed, the *ideal* of the unity of the sciences is an unrealized and unrealizable dream. The point is not just that there is no single method or set of methods that is properly called *the* scientific method, but, more than this, that there is no clear, uncontroversial, and useful definition of science to do the substantial work scientific naturalists require of it.[44]

This point is particularly relevant with regard to the status of the human and social sciences. To acknowledge their legitimacy as sciences inevitably involves commitments to prima facie irreducible normative items such as values, reasons, and meanings; and these are, of course, among the very items that are typically candidates for naturalization! Thus we return again to the important question of whether scientific naturalism is self-consistent. The papers by Putnam, Dupré, Price, Stroud, and De Caro all provide good reason to doubt whether scientific naturalism is

naturalistic enough *by its own lights*, and to convict its restrictive
conceptions of science, knowledge, and reality as further instances of First Philosophy that it ought, in all consistency, to
jettison.

Moreover, in general, this pluralistic attitude conveys a radical
mistrust of the typical strategies adopted by scientific naturalists
to solve philosophical dilemmas by pursuing naturalization projects. The papers collected here discuss such issues as intentionality, agency, freedom, meaning, reference, rationality, and personal
identity in the belief that all attempts to reduce, eliminate, or re-
conceive these concepts in terms of supposedly more scientifically
legitimate notions do not just fail—they entirely miss the kind of
importance that these notions have in our lives and experiences.

However, although the authors of this anthology share these fundamental
views, they diverge in other respects. This should be no surprise. This
volume is not intended to be a manifesto for *one* new paradigm for naturalist philosophy to supplant the old scientific naturalism. Our pluralism
extends to philosophy itself: in our view, there is no unifying philosophical method, nor any single right way of *understanding* what philosophy
is or does.

Nonetheless, since we have provided criticisms of scientific naturalism
it seems worthwhile to add a brief sketch outlining one possible alternative conception of philosophy. The following remarks are controversial
and are not intended to be representative of the authors of this volume
as a whole. They are offered simply as an example of *one* way we might
think about philosophy after scientific naturalism.

The question is this: What is the role and authority of philosophy if
it is not to be identified with that of the sciences? This is the question
that is urgently raised by the papers collected here. They make clear that
we must find some more positive conception of philosophy beyond the
rejection of its traditional pretensions.

One suggestion is that a good model for the authority of philosophy
is not science but criticism, say, the criticism of art or literature or morality or the distinctive activity of making sense of each other—at least
on a certain understanding of these activities.[45] In all these cases there is
a question of getting something right, of better or worse judgment, of
support by reasons and claims to truth, without all (or even most) disagreement being explicable as a matter of ignorance or error or irrationality. Like a good art critic, a good philosopher must excel at knowing
when and how to enter reasons in support of her claims, something that

can only be successful if she is attentive to circumstance, style, presentation, and rhetorical force.[46] As the history of philosophy amply demonstrates, philosophical reasoning, like criticism, cannot guarantee agreement on pain of irrationality.

Agreement in philosophy, like agreement in aesthetics or morality, is an ideal that, despite being constantly strived for, is in fact rarely attained. It is thus very different from the guaranteed agreement in logic, mathematics, or (core) science, which exists only through the *exclusion* of subjectivity. The absence of guaranteed agreement in philosophy is an indication that agreement is achieved through the *inclusion* of subjectivity.[47] The philosopher, on this understanding, is someone who does not discount her individuality but attempts to master it in ways that become an example to others: by speaking for herself as honestly and accurately as she can, she discovers that she can speak for others, as well.[48]

Partly because philosophy cannot count on agreement, engaging with the threat of skepticism remains a perennial task of philosophy. Indeed Cavell, Macarthur, and Stroud are inclined to think of philosophy and skepticism as internally related. This attitude is in stark contrast to the confident dismissal of skepticism characteristic of scientific naturalism. This dismissive attitude also demonstrates a striking difference of opinion about the place of history in philosophy, since the history of modern philosophy is in no small measure the history of its "refutations" of skepticism. Often scientific naturalists give the impression of thinking that philosophy began with Quine, and that to read earlier texts is to leave philosophy behind for the study of the history of ideas. The new naturalism, alternatively, finds its sense of itself and its problems in readings or interpretations of its history.

Philosophy is at an important crossroads. Scientific naturalism exhorts us to purify our methods, knowledge, ontology, and concepts from their allegedly prescientific errors and impurities. When purified, philosophy becomes science. The present volume makes a strong case for an alternative conception. The new directions for philosophy after scientific naturalism earn the title of naturalism by, in one direction, extending the notion of nature beyond scientific nature to fully include the various aspects and normative dimensions of human nature, and in another, by reinterpreting the rejection of philosophy's foundationalist aspirations and its traditional claims to authority. One can accept that there is no First Philosophy while still affirming the possibility of the autonomy of philosophy, even in spite of an acknowledgment that the distinction between science and philosophy is one that is constantly being renegotiated.[49]

I
SCIENCE AND REALITY

1

The Charm of Naturalism

BARRY STROUD

I WANT TO MAKE some very general observations on what many see and applaud as a broadly "naturalistic" turn in recent philosophy. There seems little doubt at first glance that there is such a thing, at least judging from what many now *call* what they are doing. Something known as "epistemology naturalized" has been with us for some time. Or at least a recommendation to that effect was made some time ago.[1] More recently we have been encouraged in such enterprises as "naturalized semantics," "naturalizing belief," and even more generally, "intentionality naturalized." And now there is the even more general project (why not go all the way?) of "naturalizing the mind" (the title of a delightful recent book).[2] I have even seen something called "naturalizing responsibility." And there are no doubt many other efforts at "naturalization."

Is there more to all this than just a trendy label? What, if anything, is behind it? Is it something distinctive and new? And if so, is it a good thing? These questions are not easy to answer. The idea of "nature," or "natural" objects or relations, or modes of investigation that are "naturalistic," has been applied more widely, at more different times and places, and for more different purposes than probably any other notion in the whole history of human thought. The earliest turn toward naturalism that I have heard of was in the fifth century B.C. And they seem to have been happening every so often ever since.

When we look at this most recent enthusiasm for what its proponents

21

call "naturalism," I think we find that, whatever they are excited and optimistic about, it is not naturalism as such. With two exceptions that I will mention in a moment, I think there is nothing in naturalism alone that is sufficiently substantive to be philosophically controversial. What is usually at issue is not whether to be "naturalistic" or not, but rather what is and what is not to be included in one's conception of "nature." That is the real question, and that is what leads to deep disagreement. And as far as I can see, those disagreements are not themselves to be settled by what can be recognized as straightforwardly "naturalistic" means. So one thing that seems not to have been "naturalized" is naturalism itself. If it were, the resulting naturalistic view of the world might be impressively comprehensive and illuminating, and superior to views of other kinds, but if it had those virtues it would have them on its own merits, not simply because it is an instance of something called "naturalism."

"Naturalism" seems to me in this and other respects rather like "World Peace." Almost everyone swears allegiance to it, and is willing to march under its banner. But disputes can still break out about what it is appropriate or acceptable to do in the name of that slogan. And like world peace, once you start specifying concretely exactly what it involves and how to achieve it, it becomes increasingly difficult to reach and to sustain a consistent and exclusive "naturalism." There is pressure on the one hand to include more and more within your conception of "nature," so it loses its definiteness and restrictiveness. Or, if the conception is kept fixed and restrictive, there is pressure on the other hand to distort or even to deny the very phenomena that a naturalistic study—and especially a naturalistic study of human beings—is supposed to explain. The source of these two conflicting movements of thought is what I want to illustrate.

But the first thing to do with naturalism, as with any philosophical doctrine or "ism," is to ask what it is against. What does the so-called "naturalistic turn" turn away from, or deny? Here we have to distinguish two aspects of naturalism. There is naturalism as a view of what is so, or the way things are, or what there is in the world. And there is naturalism as a way of studying or investigating what is so in the world. A naturalistic study of human beings would study and understand them in relation to the rest of nature. Obviously, what you think the natural world is like will have an effect on how you investigate the things in it, and what you think is the best way to understand them. The two aspects of naturalism are connected.

Under the first aspect, as a doctrine about what is so, or what there is, naturalism says that there is nothing, or that nothing is so, except what holds in nature, in the natural world. That is not very informative so far, but even without specifying it more precisely it already seems to exclude some things that many people have apparently believed in. Naturalism on any reading is opposed to supernaturalism. Here we have what looks like a substantive issue, or at any rate something controversial. Not everyone regards exclusive naturalism as beyond question or as an unqualified good thing.

This is the first of the two exceptions I mentioned. By "supernaturalism" I mean the invocation of an agent or force that somehow stands outside the familiar natural world and whose doings cannot be understood as part of it. Most metaphysical systems of the past included some such agent. A naturalistic conception of the world would be opposed to all of them. Supernaturalism as a doctrine about what is so can have consequences for the study of human beings—in particular, how they believe and come to know things. In epistemology there have been many supernaturalists. Descartes thought that human knowledge cannot be accounted for without a benevolent, omniscient, and omnipotent God who guarantees the truth of what human beings clearly and distinctly perceive to be true. For Berkeley, God's agency is the only active force there is in the world of things we perceive and know about. Without him there would be nothing for us to know. Even Locke relied on a benevolent agent as the ultimate source of those cognitive faculties that are all that human beings need to get along in the world they find themselves in. These are not fully naturalistic accounts of human knowledge. They appeal to something beyond the natural world. In going against this supernatural consensus, Hume is almost alone among the greats. His credentials as a fully naturalized—or at least as a nonsupernaturalized—metaphysician and epistemologist are impeccable. The same is probably true of John Stuart Mill, if he counts as one of the greats. But there have not been many.

In the sense in which naturalism is opposed to supernaturalism, there has been no recent naturalistic turn in philosophy. Most philosophers for at least one hundred years have been naturalists in the nonsupernaturalist sense. They have taken it for granted that any satisfactory account of how human belief and knowledge in general are possible will involve only processes and events of the intelligible natural world, without the intervention or reassurance of any supernatural agent. Many people regard that as, on the whole, a good thing. But it is nothing new.

In fact, the long-standing naturalistic consensus is being challenged more directly now, when the virtues of naturalism are being so loudly proclaimed, than it was during the long period when they went more or

less without saying. Alvin Plantinga, for example, argues that no satisfactory general explanation of human knowledge can be given on a naturalistic basis. He thinks that justification or warrant, which is essential
to knowledge, can be understood only in terms of the proper function
of human cognitive capacities. And that in turn, he thinks, requires a
divine designer of those capacities. Successful epistemology therefore
"requires supernaturalism,"[3] in particular what he calls "theism."[4] He is
apparently not alone in that belief. If Plantinga and his friends convince
others, there will be a general turn *away* from naturalism. That shows
that it is naturalism that is now old hat. It is not something toward which
there has been a recent, glorious turning.

Even supernaturalists like Plantinga, Descartes, Locke, Berkeley, and
others would still count as "naturalized epistemologists" in at least one
current sense that has been given to that phrase. Epistemology has been
said to be "naturalized or naturalistic" as long as it tries to explain only
how human beings do in fact arrive at their beliefs rather than how they
ought to arrive at them.[5] If that is enough to make an epistemology
naturalistic, then virtually every philosopher in history has been a naturalized epistemologist. They have all been concerned to describe and
understand the human condition as it is, to see and to explain how we
actually get all the knowledge we've obviously got. If God plays a role
in human beings' coming to know things, that will be part of the answer
to the purely "descriptive" question of how human beings in fact arrive
at their knowledge. Even supernaturalism as a view of what is so is not
incompatible with naturalized epistemology in this curiously weak, so-
called purely "descriptive" sense.

This shows that the first aspect of naturalism dominates over the second. If you do not start out with any restrictions at all on what the world
you are studying contains, studying things only as part of the natural
world does not amount to anything very definite. Some determinate conception of what the natural world is like is needed to give substance to
the claim that one's epistemology, or one's study of any other aspect of
the world, is naturalistic.

The second exception to the idea that there is no real dispute about
naturalism is perhaps best illustrated (at least in epistemology) by Quine,
who after all, as far as I know, is the person who coined the phrase
"epistemology naturalized." He was responding to Carnap, with whom
he had a real dispute. Carnap sought a reduction of all talk of external
bodies to talk only about possible sense experiences. It was intended as
what came to be called a "rational reconstruction" of our science or
knowledge. It would have shown how our conception of the world could

be supported solely by materials to be found in immediate sense expe- rience. But no satisfactory translation or reduction was found. The idea of "rational reconstruction" does not in itself require that statements about the external world must be *translatable* into statements about im- mediate sense experiences. It requires only that it be shown how our beliefs about the world *could be* justified by information that we *could* get through experience or observation. That general task of what might be called "hypothetical (or reconstructed) justification" was pretty much *the* task of analytic epistemology through the middle fifty years or so of the twentieth century. One form it took, and perhaps still takes, is confir- mation theory.

Quine's so-called "naturalistic" turn was to say, "Why all this creative reconstruction, all this make believe?"[6] Why ask how statements of the kinds human beings believe could be confirmed by sense experiences they could conceivably have? As Quine put it: "Better to discover how science is in fact developed and learned than to fabricate a fictitious structure to a similar effect."[7] The question is how science is "developed and learned." It is not just a question of the logical relations among the propositions human beings believe.

Something is at stake here between Quine and Carnap, but it is not the merits of naturalism. It is really a dispute about what *philosophy* is or ought to be doing. Quine obviously has no quarrel with the idea of reducing one domain of discourse to another, if you can do it. Carnap and the positivists obviously have no quarrel with the idea of natural scientific studies of human belief and knowledge, or even of institutions like science. Naturalism as a way of investigating the world is thought by all to be nothing but a good thing. But for logical positivism no such studies could be part of philosophy. Philosophy could be only *a priori*. Its only subject matter could therefore be the "concepts," or the logical relations among the "principles," employed in the sciences. Its only task could be "analysis." It could not pronounce professionally on the actual acquisition and development of science, but only on what it called its "logic."

Quine's rejection of the very notion of the *a priori* left him with no such constraints. Study human knowledge in the same way you would study anything else in nature, he says, and don't worry much about what label you attach to what you are doing. That meant that a task continuous with what epistemologists had attempted in the past could now proceed scientifically. Epistemology would in that sense be part of natural science, and it would study the acquisition, transmission, and growth of natural science. The idea is, in Quine's words, "that knowledge, mind, and meaning are part of the same world that they have to do with, and that they are to be studied in the same empirical spirit that animates natural science. There is no place for a prior philosophy."[8]

That same empirical spirit is present in the study of the history of science, which could also be described as a form of naturalism in the investigation of human knowledge. The history of science has, of course, been with us almost as long as science has, but its flourishing in the 1960s was in part also a reaction against the abstractions of logical positivism. The positivists focused on *what* is known, or on the form of what is known, rather than on the knowing of it, or on the processes of finding it out. They did not study science as a human enterprise that develops in different ways at different times as a result of different sorts of forces. That could not be a part of philosophy for them. The growth of the history of science in the last thirty years has changed and enormously enriched the picture. And it certainly has been a very good thing.

Quine himself at one time seemed not so sure. He thought the historically oriented work of people like Kuhn, Polanyi, and Hanson had "loosed a wave . . . of epistemological nihilism" (as he put it) and tended to "discredit the idea of observation," to "belittle the role of evidence and to accentuate cultural relativism."[9] These are curious complaints for a fully naturalized epistemologist to make. Scientific epistemology must be prepared to accept whatever the empirical study of human beings actually reveals. If it turns out that human knowledge is acquired without there being a firm, fixed line between so-called "observational" and "non-observational" terms, or if what a philosophical "theory of evidence" calls "evidence" is never actually appealed to in the acceptance and rejection of scientific hypotheses, then so be it. That will have to be accepted as the way knowledge is in fact acquired. If cultural relativism turns out to be the best way to account for what happens in human life, the committed naturalist has to accept cultural relativism. (What he should do first of all, of course, is try to figure out what the term "cultural relativism" actually means. But that is another story.)

The point is that conclusions of naturalized epistemology can be drawn only from the study of what actually goes on with human beings. If it turns out that women's knowledge differs in certain ways from men's, for instance, or poor southern blacks' knowledge from that of affluent urban whites, that is something that a naturalized epistemologist should welcome, or at any rate should not resist. Studies in the sociology, economics, and politics of knowledge could also be called "naturalistic epistemology" too. The lively interest in such matters these days is certainly on the whole a good thing. Not because naturalism is a good thing, but because coming to see more and more differences among things in the world—if they are actually there—is almost always a good thing.

I want to draw attention to a conflict or tension that I think is present in a commitment to naturalism. It arises most clearly when we move beyond questions about this or that culture or this or that institution within a culture to that more general level at which philosophers typically ask about apparently universal features of human life. Now I mean naturalism in every area of philosophy, not just epistemology.

Naturalism as a view of what is so, or what the world is like, must be given some determinate and restricted content. That means that anything that human beings think about, believe in, care about, or value that lies outside that restricted conception cannot really be seen as part of the natural world in which they live. But since it cannot be denied that people do have the very thoughts, beliefs, values, and concerns in question, the contents of those attitudes will have to be understood and accounted for in terms of something less than their possible truth. What human beings think, feel, and care about must be fully expressible somehow within the restricted resources available in the naturalist's world. And that can lead to distortion. If, to accommodate psychological phenomena and their contents in all their complexity, the restrictions are lifted, naturalism to that extent loses its bite. This is the basic dilemma I want to bring out.

I can illustrate it by starting with an extreme naturalist view. I would say that it is a ridiculously extreme position, were it not for the fact that many philosophers I respect appear to hold it. It says that the natural world is exhausted by all the physical facts. That is all and only what the natural world amounts to on this view; there is nothing else in nature. First of all, this view is probably not itself reached by purely naturalistic means. It not only states all the physical facts, which presumably *can* be determined by broadly naturalistic means, but it goes on to say that those are all the facts there are—that they are the *whole* truth about the world. And that claim is more than the conjunction of all the physical facts. It excludes everything else from being true, as they alone do not. Is the exhaustiveness that is essential to physicalism something that is naturalistically or physicalistically arrived at? That is one question.

Second, a natural world conceived of only as the totality of all the physical facts obviously does not contain any psychological facts. There are no truths to the effect that someone believes, knows, feels, wants, prefers, or values anything. Of course, anyone who holds that the physical is all there is might hold that everything we think along those lines is really just physical facts in disguise. In any case, that would leave no psychological facts for a naturalistic theory of the world to explain. The study of human beings on such a restricted physicalist conception would be just a study of physical goings-on, including some that happen to go on in human organisms.

The case is extreme because it does not include very much for a study of human beings to explain. Without at least biological facts in your naturalistic conception of the world, you will not have much to investigate that is distinctively or interestingly human. But if the physicalist conception is expanded to include biological facts as well, what exactly are such facts thought to add? Do biological facts include the "intentional" facts of human beings believing, knowing, feeling, wanting, preferring, and valuing certain things? Some would say not, since these are just "folk" ways of speaking. Organisms inhabiting the natural world are not to be thought of as having any such attitudes, or as acting from them, on that view. That would mean that naturalism could never be faced with the problem of explaining how and why human beings come to believe and feel and want the things they do. There would be no such facts. Naturalism as to what is so would be so restrictive as to leave naturalism as a method of investigation with much less to do.

There is an embarrassing absurdity in this position that is revealed as soon as the naturalist reflects and acknowledges that he believes his naturalistic theory of the world. If persons with attitudes like belief and knowledge are not really part of nature, he cannot consistently say that about himself. I mean he cannot say it and consistently regard what he is saying as true. In fact he cannot say anything and regard it as true, or think of himself as saying it, if he holds such a restricted naturalistic conception.

It looks as if any sensible naturalism will have to acknowledge that human beings do in fact have a complex set of attitudes, feelings, evaluations, institutions, and so on. If it is going to explain what is so, it will have to explain how and why human beings think and feel and act in all the ways they do. It will offer those explanations by appealing not only to the ways human beings are, but also to facts of the natural world surrounding and affecting those human beings. To explain why people believe that there are such things as rectangular tables, for example, or red apples, it will trace the connections between human beings who perceive things and a world that contains rectangular tables and red apples. It is because things are as they are in the natural world and because humans are as they are, and interact as they do with their surroundings, that they get the beliefs they do and are, on the whole, right about the natural world.

Even this simple general picture leaves room for human attitudes directed toward objects or states of affairs that restrictive forms of naturalism can find no room for within their conception of the world. For example, many philosophers now hold that things as they are in the world of nature are not really colored. There are rectangular tables in the natural world, perhaps, and there are apples in the natural world, but no red apples (and no yellow or green ones either). This view appears to be held largely on the grounds that colors are not part of "the causal order of the world" or do not figure essentially in any purely scientific account of what is so. Scientific naturalism accordingly excludes them.

But even on this view those false beliefs and illusory perceptions of the colors of things must themselves be acknowledged as part of nature. A naturalistic investigator must somehow make sense of them as the psychological phenomena they are. Since he holds that there is no such fact as an object's being colored, he cannot specify the contents of those perceptions and beliefs in terms of any conditions that he believes actually hold in the world. If he could, that would amount to believing that there are colored things in the world after all. Scientific naturalism denies that. But still, the beliefs and perceptions with those particular contents must be accounted for.

An easy way around this difficulty has suggested itself to many philosophers, at least in this case. They take the apparently more sensible scientific naturalist view that there really is no systematic error in our beliefs about the colors of things. The beliefs are not in general false, since there is something in the restricted naturalist's world to give content to them after all. Beliefs about the colors of objects, it is said, are really beliefs about certain dispositions that those objects have to produce perceptions of certain kinds in certain kinds of perceivers in certain kinds of circumstances. Objects in nature really do have those dispositions. So the beliefs are preserved as largely true. The color of an object depends on what kinds of perceptions it is disposed to produce.

A dispositionalist theory of this kind can succeed only if it can specify the contents of the perceptions of color, which it says physical objects have dispositions to produce. They cannot be identified as perceptions of an object's having some quality that objects actually have in that restricted naturalist's world. They cannot be identified simply as perceptions of an object's having a disposition to produce just *these* perceptions under certain circumstances. The question is: Which perceptions? There must be some way of identifying the perceptions independently of the object's disposition to produce them. So it looks as if they must be identified only in terms of some so-called "intrinsic" quality that they have. Not a quality that the perception is a perception *of*, but simply a quality of the perception itself.

I doubt that we can make the right kind of sense of perceptions of color in this way. So I doubt that any dispositional theory can give a correct account of the contents of our beliefs about the colors of things. The way we do it in real life, I believe, is to identify the contents of perceptions of color by means of the colors of objects they are typically perceptions of. It is only because we can make intelligible nondispositional ascriptions of colors to objects that we can acknowledge and identify perceptions as perceptions of this or that color. But if that is so, it requires our accepting the fact that objects in the world are colored, and that is what the restrictive naturalist who denies the reality or the objectivity of color cannot do.

None of this is something I can hope to establish here. The point is only to draw attention to what I see as a general problem of restrictive naturalism. Exclude colored objects in general from the world, and you are in danger of losing the capacity to recognize perceptions of and beliefs about the colors of things. Include colored objects, and the contents of those perceptions and beliefs no longer go beyond what is so in the natural world.

I have found in my experience that this tension is not widely felt or acknowledged. Most philosophers regard it as so obvious and uncontroversial that colors are not real, or are in some way only "subjective," that they simply do not recognize what I think is the distortion or incoherence they are committed to. That is something I continue to ponder and try to get to the bottom of. But a problem of this same form is at least sometimes recognized elsewhere.

Two large areas of philosophy are problem areas precisely because some form of restrictive naturalism looks like the only possibility in those cases. I have in mind the areas of mathematics and morality, or evaluation generally. Human beings have evaluative beliefs and attitudes, they regard some things as better than others, they think that a certain thing is the thing to do on a certain occasion, and so on. To understand and acknowledge the presence of these human attitudes in the world, the naturalist must understand their contents—what those human beings actually think or believe. Naturalism is widely understood to imply that no evaluative states of affair or properties are part of the world of nature. On that assumption, either evaluative thoughts and beliefs take as their "objects" something that is not to be found in the natural world at all, or their contents are equivalent to something that *is* true in that world, so they are not really evaluative.

One way to embrace the first option would be to say with G. E. Moore that evaluative statements are assertions about a "nonnatural" world, or that they ascribe "nonnatural" properties to objects in the natural world. We might then wonder what that "nonnatural" domain is like, and how it is related to what goes on before our eyes. And whatever it is, we might wonder why we should ever take any interest in it. Values might then be otherworldly, and have nothing to do with us. If all that is just too mysterious, we could keep to this first option by saying instead that evaluative attitudes do not have contents that are true or false at all. In evaluating something we are prescribing, recommending, approving, or encouraging something, but not ascribing any properties to it or saying anything true of it beyond the "natural" properties we think it has.

This last idea, I believe, distorts our actual thought and practice. It cannot give the right kind of sense to the evaluative thoughts we have or the inferences we regard as valid when combining evaluative and non-evaluative propositions. Again, that is not something I am going to try to prove here. I simply draw attention to the source of the pressure toward some such emotivist or expressivist theory. It comes from a re-stricted naturalistic conception of what the world contains. Nature itself, it is said, is value-free. So evaluations cannot be, strictly speaking, either true or false. That is one alternative. It is not an inevitable consequence of a restricted naturalistic view of the world. The same restrictive view of nature is what leads a nonexpressivist like Moore to the idea of values as "nonnatural" or, in some sense, "otherworldly."

Dissatisfaction with both nonnaturalism and expressivism leads the re-strictive naturalist to the second option, and so to some form of reduc-tionism. Human attitudes that appear to be evaluative are to be seen as attitudes with contents that can and do hold in the restricted natural world after all. They can be true or false, but the conditions of their truth are purely natural and so nonevaluative.

If such a reduction is expressed in terms of the dispositions natural objects or states of affairs have to produce certain reactions in human beings, it faces the same kind of problem as the dispositionalist view of colors. Those reactions themselves must somehow be identified, and if they are left as reactions with evaluative contents, no naturalistic progress will have been made. Reductionism threatens to take away the evaluative aspect of the attitudes, feelings, and reactions that objects are said to produce, just as I think it cannot make the appropriate identifications in the case of perceptions of color. It cannot get the contents of our beliefs or attitudes right. To insist that evaluative attitudes simply must be so reducible, and to restrict oneself to reduced or nonevaluative terms alone, would be, in effect, to eliminate the evaluative vocabulary altogether. Everything we say or think that is intelligible and either true or false would have to be said or thought without it. Here again, it is the restric-tive naturalism that produces the pressure.

The same pattern is present in the philosophy of mathematics, where the quandary is perhaps most obvious, and has certainly been widely acknowledged. There is no question that we have mathematical and logical knowledge. Could there be an explanation exclusively in restricted naturalistic terms of how we come to have that knowledge? It would have to make sense of *what* we believe in mathematics and logic, and could it do so by giving an account of the conditions under which such things are true or false? If so, would that mean that mathematical and logical facts are to be understood as part of nature? Many would insist that even if, in some sense or other, it is true that seven plus five is twelve, it is not a natural fact, not a fact of the natural world. But we do all believe it, even know it to be true. A restrictive naturalist who holds that what mathematical statements assert is not part of the natural world he believes in would have to explain our knowledge of logic and mathematics without himself appealing to any mathematical or logical facts at all.

This has been tried, or at least proposed. But when we look at what has been the most widely canvassed strategy for carrying it out, I think everyone has to confess to a certain dissatisfaction. The main idea has been to locate the source of mathematical and logical truth somehow "in us," and not in the world independent of us. All such truths have been said to be "analytic" or "true solely in virtue of the meanings of their constituent terms," something that "we" are, in some sense, solely responsible for. Since words mean only what we determine or "decide" they are to mean, logical and mathematical truths are said to be true, if at all, only "by convention." These are all attempts to make sense of mathematical and logical knowledge on the assumption that all of it is "empty" or, in the positivists' phrase, "devoid of factual content," and says nothing about the way the world is. Anyone who holds such a view would have to account for human beings' believing certain things that he himself does not acknowledge to be states of affairs that hold in the world as he conceives of it.

There is good reason to think that no such theorist would be equipped even to identify, let alone explain, the mathematical knowledge he admits we all have. For one thing, no naturalistic reduction looks even remotely plausible in this case. Facts about what human beings do, how they think or speak, even how they decide to think and speak, or what conventions or rules they have adopted—all this seems, in principle, insufficient to express the contents of the things we believe when we believe that seven plus five equals twelve, or that everything that is both red and round is red. All of human beings' doing or deciding or intending whatever they do is contingent and is something that could have been otherwise. But it could not have been otherwise than that seven plus five is twelve or that everything that is both red and round is red. No contingent truths, however important, could be adequate to express such necessities.

What is more, any naturalism that takes a specifically scientific form, and says that the natural world is the world described exclusively in the terms of the natural sciences, would seem forced to accept truths of logic and mathematics anyway. They are needed in the formulation of physical, chemical, and biological theories. And in any case, it is completely un- realistic to expect a naturalistic theorist of any persuasion to get along without any mathematical and logical beliefs of his own. The acceptance of some such truths might even be essential to coherent thought; we could not think without them. If that is so, is that a natural fact, a fact of the natural world? If that meant that it had to be contingent, it is hard to see how it could be. But if for whatever reason we grant the indis- pensability of logical truths for the possibility of thinking at all, then we have to face the consequences of our really accepting it. That is, we must acknowledge that we do in fact think in those ways, that we do believe that everything that is both red and round is red, that seven plus five equals twelve, and so on. We thereby acknowledge that those and other such demonstrable or undeniable propositions are true.

If the naturalist does or must accept logical and mathematical truths in order to have a determinate conception of the world at all, what be- comes of the idea that those propositions do not state anything that holds in the natural world? What is the conception of nature that is said to exclude them? It can no longer be identified as simply the world that a scientific naturalist believes in, since if he now accepts logical and math- ematical propositions, they are not excluded from what he believes. If this still counts as naturalism, it will be a more open-minded or more expansive naturalism. It does not insist on, or limit itself to, a boundary fixed in advance. It will have expanded to include whatever has been found to be needed in order to make sense of everything that is so in the natural world. What cannot be avoided is to be accepted. To say that not everything that is accepted is accepted as a part of nature raises the question of how the naturalist distinguishes what he thinks of as the natural world from all the rest of what he takes to be the case. And more importantly, what, if anything, now turns on making that distinction?

The same question arises in the case of evaluation. If the goodness or other evaluative aspect of something is not a "natural" quality of it, what exactly is a natural quality? After years of effort G. E. Moore admitted that the best he could come up with was that a natural property is a property "with which it is the business of the natural sciences or of psychology to deal."[10] But if that is what a natural property is, then the famous "naturalistic fallacy"—the mistake of giving a "naturalistic" definition of "good"—would be simply the attempt to replace ethics by one of the natural sciences. "Nonnaturalism" in ethics would then be nothing more than the view that ethics is not one of the natural sciences. There would be nothing otherworldly or mysterious about that kind of nonnaturalism. Who would not want to be an ethical nonnaturalist on that definition?

To agree that ethics is not one of the natural sciences, or that goodness or badness is not a scientific matter, is not to concede that nothing is better than anything else, or that no evaluations are true or false. Not everything that is so is the subject matter of some natural science. If it is true that evaluations cannot be reduced in general to nonevaluative propositions, then our understanding of evaluations cannot be seen as built up out of nonevaluative ingredients alone. Anyone who could identify the presence of evaluative attitudes in the human beings he observes must understand what evaluative attitudes are, even if he does not agree with those he discerns in others. That suggests that he must have some evaluative attitudes of his own, on pain of his not being able to recognize them in others. If he acknowledges those attitudes of his, his total view of what is so will contain evaluative states of affairs. He will hold that certain things are better than others, that a certain thing is the thing to do on a certain occasion, and so on. His conception of what is so will have been forced to expand, just as I think it must expand in order to recognize beliefs in logical and mathematical truths, and perceptions and beliefs concerning the colors of things. It expands in each case into a more open-minded or less restricted naturalism.

What I am calling more open-minded or expansive naturalism says we must accept everything we find ourselves committed to in accounting for everything that we agree is so and want to explain. We want to explain the thoughts, beliefs, knowledge, and evaluative attitudes that we think people have got. If mathematical and logical truths have to be accepted in order to make sense of those attitudes, then they must be accepted, however in some sense "non-natural" they might seem. If some evaluative propositions must be endorsed in order even to recognize the evaluative attitudes of others, then evaluative states of affairs must be included too, however difficult it might be to decide which particular evaluations are correct. If we have to hold that objects are colored in order to specify and acknowledge all the perceptions and beliefs that we know people have, then the colors of things must be allowed into the picture, and not in reductionist form.

Those who remain committed to a determinate and restricted conception of the natural world will have to locate the contents of all those attitudes somehow within that restricted world. If that leads to a distorted conception of the attitudes that people on earth have actually got, as I think it does, the determinate and restricted naturalism is what is responsible for the distortion. A more open-minded or expansive naturalism will admit states of affairs and psychological phenomena that are found problematic from a more restricted naturalistic point of view. With no restrictive commitment in advance, a more open-minded naturalism will feel no pressure to exclude from the picture anything that is needed.

By now it should begin to look as if this expandable or more open-minded form of naturalism does not amount to anything very substantive or controversial. It is "open" because it is not committed in advance to any determinate and therefore potentially restrictive conception of what is so. Rather than calling it open-minded naturalism, we could just as well drop the term "naturalism" and call it open-mindedness. It says that we must accept as true everything we find we have to accept in order to make sense of everything that we think is part of the world. If that is still called "naturalism," the term by now is little more than a slogan on a banner raised to attract the admiration of those who agree that no supernatural agents are at work in the world.

∾ 2

The Miracle of Monism

JOHN DUPRÉ

$\mathcal{A}$s BARRY STROUD nicely displays in his APA Presidential Address "The Charm of Naturalism," naturalism is far from an unequivocal idea.[1] Versions of it are as old as philosophy, and many ideas frequently associated with naturalism are either too vague to make much sense or too banal to have much interest. As Stroud notes, one substantive naturalist theme is antisupernaturalism. This has been philosophical orthodoxy for at least a century, if never without its dissenters, so it fails to capture the reasons why many philosophers appear to think that naturalism is a fairly recent philosophical movement. But perhaps antisupernaturalism may nevertheless provide a good way into some of the ideas associated with contemporary naturalism. One thing I want to suggest in this paper is that among the many philosophical defects of monism is the fact that it involves more than a whiff of supernaturalism. So by my title I mean not merely that it is miraculous that so many otherwise sensible philosophers subscribe to the doctrine of monism, but also that the doctrine to which they subscribe is itself a doctrine with a miraculous dimension.

By antisupernaturalism I mean something like the denial that there are entities that lie outside of the normal course of nature. It is easier to point to some of the things that are agreed to lie outside the normal course of nature than it is to characterize the normal course of nature. Central cases of such outliers are immaterial minds or souls, vital fluids,

36

angels, and deities. My aim in this paper is to investigate some of the reasons that contemporary naturalism has often come to be associated with a doctrine that seems to me wholly incredible: monism. One part of the answer, I suggest, is that monism is a gross exaggeration of what is indeed plausible about antisupernaturalism. The grounds for the denial of the existence of souls and vital fluids have been taken as grounds for the denial of minds and, in a sense, even bodies. But in fact the argument should go exactly the opposite way. The arguments against souls and suchlike are really the kinds of arguments that should lead us to reject monism. Or so I shall claim.

What is wrong, according to most philosophers, with souls and vital fluids? One of their central defects is their being immaterial. There are of course perfectly respectably immaterial entities—concepts, numbers, or hypotheses, for example—but souls and suchlike are not the right kinds of things to be immaterial. Part of the reason for this is that they are taken to be subjects of causal agency, and immaterial causes are seen as contravening naturalism. This is not an entirely straightforward matter. One might well claim that the concept of evolution, or of class struggle, had changed the world. But I think it is fairly clear that we don't want to treat this as the exercise of a causal power by an entity, or at any rate we don't if we are any kind of naturalists. I'm not exactly sure why we feel this way. Perhaps the answer is that knowledge of causality does, as a number of influential philosophers have argued, derive ultimately from our material transactions with things. Even for material things that are much too small for us to interact with, there is considerable force in Ian Hacking's much-cited remark about electrons *(Representing and Intervening)*: If you can spray them they are real.[2] Perhaps there is a cruder picture here, that Nature is ultimately composed of material things pushing and pulling at one another. Pushes and pulls from outside this material universe are just the sorts of supernatural interventions that naturalists rule out. At any rate, I propose to take for granted that there is something importantly fundamental to our ontology about material things, material here merely in the Cartesian sense of things that occupy space, albeit sometimes, like electrons, not very much, or, like gases, not very fully. Being in the same space as we are is, of course, a minimal condition of being in a position to engage with us in pushings, pullings, and sprayings.

Important threats to this ontological primacy of space occupiers have come from physics. Physics tells us about fields that, while they have particular strengths at particular locations, don't appear to occupy the locations where they occur. And worse, quantum mechanics tells us that what might have seemed like the most fundamental space occupiers, physical particles, are actually not, from some perspectives, particles at all, but waves, which are apparently not space occupiers at all. These claims are particularly important to the contemporary naturalistic philosophy that I am here considering, because most contemporary naturalists include among the central commitments of naturalism not materialism, but physicalism. The move from materialism to physicalism, in large part motivated by such developments in physics, aimed to avoid being committed to a long-superseded, broadly Newtonian physics. Physicalists instead committed themselves to take whatever physicists ended up saying about the nature of reality as an ultimate ontological criterion for reality. If the ultimate constituents of reality couldn't make up their minds whether to be particles or waves, or turned out instead to be ten-dimensional bits of string, so be it.

I have, of course, no objection to allowing physicists whatever authority there is to be had about the ultimate structure of matter. What might be a worry, however, is whether physicalism, as just described, is in the same line of business as the materialism it has replaced. Materialism, as I introduced it, was part of the expression of antisupernaturalism. If you can't kick it, or at least spray it, you should treat it with some suspicion. We can kick things or spray them because they live in the same space as we do, and there is nothing and nowhere else. Materialism is, of course, also contrasted with dualism, a specific form of supernaturalism, and a doctrine that explicitly insists on the existence of things that are not in the space of electrons, stones, and ourselves, and in most versions insists on the causal efficacy of such things.

Materialism, as just described, has no obvious connection to any particular scientific doctrine, though no doubt it was substantially motivated by the success of certain scientific projects. More specifically, and here is a central naturalistic argument, science has proved increasingly successful at solving all kinds of explanatory projects in basically materialistic ways. To subscribe to anything supernatural, an explanatory *deus ex machina*, is mere pessimism, and profoundly unwarranted pessimism in the light of the successes of science. It is in connection with this sort of argument that monism insinuates itself into the naturalistic viewpoint. Reflection on "the successes of science" may well motivate an interest in what exactly science is, and an answer to that question will potentially limit severely what kinds of entities are amenable to the investigation through science that naturalism mandates. And the deliberately vague phrase "in basically materialistic ways" that I used to qualify scientific explanatory projects may invite much sharper specification in terms of the actual conceptual resources of the physical sciences. Very summarily, naturalism is explained in terms of antisupernaturalism, which is in turn cashed out in terms of materialism; the developments of radically new conceptions of matter by the physical sciences leads from materialism to physicalism; and physicalism is often understood as entailing monism.

I don't propose to explore in great detail these routes from naturalism to monism. Rather, I want to emphasize a quite different philosophical commitment often associated with naturalism: empiricism. And what I want to claim is that the move to monism violates this commitment. Monism, far from being a view of reality answering to experience, is a myth. And myths are just the sort of thing that naturalism, in its core commitment to antisupernaturalism, should reject.

The Myth of the Unity of Science

While my ultimate target in this essay is monism as a metaphysical thesis, as I have just indicated, a main bridge from naturalism to monism is through a commitment to the explanatory reach of science. If this is combined with the idea that science is a largely continuous and homogeneous activity, and even more specifically that its explanatory resources depend on its sole concern with the material structure of things, then we are well on the way to naturalistic monism. But monism, I claim, is a myth. And it is a myth that derives what credibility it has from its connection to another myth, the unity of science. So I shall now explain in some detail why this latter doctrine, the unity of science, is indeed a myth.

There are at least two minimal implications of calling something a myth, and in so referring to the unity of science I intend both of them. First, myths are literally false. No doubt there are some complications here. Perhaps it is some kind of a solecism to refer to a myth as either true or false, since the conveying of factual information is not what they are for. Still, myths do include statements with literal meanings, even if these are not the relevant meanings for sympathetic understanding of a myth. As philosophers are wont to say, "Athene emerged fully armed from the head of Zeus" is true if and only if Athene emerged fully armed from the head of Zeus. Most of us, doubting even the historical existence of Athene or Zeus, and even more skeptical of this medical marvel, are confident that nobody emerged fully armed from anyone's head, and hence that the statement "Athene emerged fullarmed from the head of Zeus" is false.

I pretend to be no authority as to what segment of the population of ancient Greece believed in the literal truth of Greek mythology. Certainly many contemporary myths are widely believed. I have heard that more Americans currently believe in alien abductions than believe in the theory of evolution; and myth or fact, I know that quite a few Americans believe in evolution. And very many people now believe in the virgin birth or the resurrection from the dead of Jesus Christ. From a contemporary perspective one person's fact is another's myth. This brings me to the second implication of calling something a myth. Those of us who think that virgin births, resurrections, or alien abductions are myths generally hold that they are nevertheless something more than merely unsuccessful attempts at stating the facts. Religious myths, it is often said, provide wider meanings to people's lives, or offer consolation for the unavoidable tragedies of disease and death. Even those who believe in the literal truth of religious claims will often acknowledge such functions; and they will almost certainly acknowledge the significance of such functions to the epistemically benighted adherents of other, false religions. So myths are, minimally, false stories that serve often central and important functions in the lives of their adherents distinct from stating how things are. This is the sense in which the Unity of Science, I hold, is a myth. So I want now to say why I take the doctrine of the Unity of Science to be false, and to say something about the non-truth-dependent functions I think it serves.

An obvious prerequisite for thinking seriously about whether science is unified is an account of the extent of this subject of unification. There is a threat of vacuity in the offing. Would the discovery that, say, microeconomics failed, on some account of unity, to be unified with the rest of science, refute the account of unity in question, or show that microeconomics was not a science? But recalling that the object of the present inquiry is to explore the consequences of the idea that science should provide the right tools for investigating whatever is real, it is clear that the relevant brand of unified science must potentially provide us with an account of the world that is complete and exhaustive. There are some obvious worries about this idea—where does it leave common sense or history, for example?—and I shall develop some of these concerns later in this paper. For now I note only that unless unified science is, if not the only way of finding out about the world, at least unequivocally the best, then it will be of no relevance to any argument for establishing the truth of monism.

In view of this point, it seems that science must be taken to include any projects of inquiry that have in fact produced worthwhile empirical results. And the discovery that some empirical inquiry has produced valuable results, but cannot be unified with the rest of science, should be taken as a refutation of the conception of scientific unity in question. But this presents some immediate difficulties. Many practical activities, for example violin-making, have achieved considerable success and empirical knowledge. To be sure, the goal of violin-making is not to discover how to make the best violins, but just to make the best violins. But to exclude from science projects that are practically directed would remove a great deal of what we take as clearly scientific (most of medical research, or the investigation of nuclear fusion, for instance). "Applied science" is surely not an oxymoron. And then consider history, sometimes classed with the social sciences, sometimes with the humanities, and surely a repository of more empirical knowledge than many prima facie sciences. We would like some more principled ground for its classification.

This raises more generally the question of the social sciences. Should the word "sciences" here be taken seriously? This is a point at which the issues surrounding the unity of science really make a difference. Much work done in the social sciences, especially work that is quantitative or based on some kind of mathematical modeling, quite explicitly aims to be scientific. On the other hand, other social scientists, or at any rate other people with the same departmental and disciplinary allegiances as the first group, oppose these methods as inappropriate to the study of humans. They claim, for various reasons, that such quantitative approaches are inadequate to the subtleties of a human culture and insist on the necessity of something like semantic interpretation. These disputes are often bitter. Anthropology departments can sometimes only resolve their disputes over such questions by separating into distinct disciplines of cultural anthropology and (aptly named) physical anthropology.

It is not my intention here to adjudicate this dispute. My point is rather that the thesis of the Unity of Science threatens to resolve it from outside. If science is the one and the true path to knowledge of the world, then we should certainly back those projects that meet the basic conditions for integration into science. Such an appeal is clearly part of the rhetoric of advocates of "hard" social sciences—mathematical economics, and neo-sociobiologists, for instance, deriding the fuzziness of cultural anthropologists or interpretative sociologists.

So we cannot assume at the outset which disciplines are to be joined together in unified science. The natural strategy is to start with a minimal conception of science. I take it that a unified science that didn't include at least physics, chemistry, and biology would be of a little interest. Should we establish a unified account of at least these sciences, we could then ask what other disciplines could be included in this conception and decide whether the excluded disciplines should be seen as something less than scientific, or as counterexamples to the conception in question. If, on the other hand, an account of unified science cannot be sustained even for this minimal extension, we should have no difficulty in rejecting the unifying project.

Several features might be held to provide science with unity. The most important division among such factors is that between those that propose a unity of content to science and those that provide for a unity of method. Paradoxically, while unity of scientific method is intuitively a far more plausible thesis than is unity of content, contemporary philosophical defenders of science generally defend the latter rather than the former. So let me begin by mentioning some reasons why the idea of unity of scientific method has gone into decline.

I suggested that the idea of a unique scientific method has some plausibility. At least, there is still a good deal of talk, not all of it ignorant, about the "Scientific Method." A little reflection, on the other hand, soon suggests that the idea of a single scientific method is problematic. If one thinks of the daily practice of a theoretical physicist, a field taxonomist, a biochemist, or a neurophysiologist, it is hard to believe that there is anything fundamentally common to their activities that constitutes them all as practitioners of the Scientific Method, though all are engaged in activities that fall within the minimal extension of science just proposed.

Note that an account of the Scientific Method must also serve as a criterion of demarcation, a criterion, that is, that can answer the question of whether any practice should count as scientific. If there is just one Scientific Method, then a practice is scientific if and only if it follows that method. It would, of course, be very nice to have a criterion of demarcation, but considerations that have already begun to emerge suggest that there may not be one to be had. My own view, to which I shall return at the conclusion of the paper, is that the best we can do is to draw up a list of epistemic virtues and apportion our enthusiasm for knowledge-claiming practices to the extent that they meet as many as possible of such criteria. Such epistemic virtues will include certainly coherence with empirical data and with other things we take ourselves to know, and these virtues will of course be subject to detailed elaboration. They will surely include other things: perhaps aesthetic virtues such as elegance and simplicity; perhaps even moral virtues. There will no doubt be an unavoidable element of boot-strapping in this project. To some extent our enthusiasm for epistemic virtues will derive from their conspicuous role in providing us with what we take to be outstanding examples of scientific knowledge. This is not viciously circular to the extent that, in the end, we can ground this enthusiasm in genuinely empirical support.

Returning to more ambitious theses, probably the last account of a unique scientific method to be widely accepted was Karl Popper's theory of falsificationism. According to this well-known view, an investigation was scientific to the extent that it attempted to falsify hypotheses within its domain. And Popper also deployed this with some gusto as a criterion of demarcation against some practices, notably marxism and psychoanalysis, that he considered pseudoscientific. Popper's ideas had a great deal of influence with scientists and surely had a significant effect on the kind of scientific work that was carried out. It is my impression that many scientists still consider Popper's the last word on scientific method; and no doubt this is especially true among those scientists employing quantitative or experimental methods in fields also explored by more qualitative and discursive approaches. But although there are still a few able defenders, among philosophers of science Popper's view of science has been very largely rejected.[3] There are some serious conceptual problems that have contributed to this, most centrally a persisting worry about the great difficulty of falsifying hypotheses: given a recalcitrant observation, how does one decide whether the observation was inaccurate, some unknown factor has interfered, some unquestioned background assumption is erroneous, or finally, that a hypothesis under test is false? It seems that this variety of options always leaves it open to a scientist to rescue a hypothesis. And the work of Kuhn and others has even made it plausible that this is almost always the right thing for a scientist to do.

But I don't want to pursue this kind of objection in detail here. For present purposes I would rather point simply to the prima facie inadequacy of Popper's thesis to the huge variety of activities that form parts of the practice of science. Consideration of this diversity should, moreover, make us suspicious of any unitary account of scientific method. So although the official target of this discussion is falsificationism, I hope it will also indicate the enormous difficulty that would be faced by any alternative attempt to provide a uniform account of scientific method. I shall briefly compare four admittedly schematic examples of relatively indisputably scientific work, and consider how useful falsificationism is in understanding what is happening:

1. *The attempt by physicists to detect a new particle.* This activity has been quite widely described by historians and other students of science (Galison, *How Experiments End* [Chicago: Chicago Univer-

sity Press, 1987]; S. Traweek, *Beamtimes and Lifetimes: The World of High Energy Physicists* [Cambridge: Harvard University Press, 1988]). Particle physicists divide themselves into theoreticians and experimentalists. The former, unsurprisingly, devise theories that the latter attempt to test. These theories have often involved predictions that under certain conditions, for example high-energy collisions in an accelerator, specific particles should be produced. The experimentalists then try to create the relevant conditions and observe the particles. For a moment this might look like good Popperian methodology. We have hypotheses, and even a specialized caste of hypothesis generators, predictions, and experiments. The problem, however, is that no one would imagine for a moment that the failure to observe the sought-after particle would refute the theory under test. In accord with the line of argument sketched above, there are far too many alternative explanations of the failure of the experiment for it to make sense to reject the hypothesis at any particular stage of the experimental process. Whether or not one has observed a subatomic particle is hardly a trivial matter to decide. And in fact historical accounts of this kind of work make it clear that it is typically a long and difficult process to make such experiments work and convince the community of physicists that they have worked.

2. *The attempt by molecular biologists to find the genetic basis of cancer.* First, a vast amount of background to this project is not a candidate for falsification. I suppose that a persistent enough failure to progress with the project might eventually contribute to the rejection of the view that there is a genetic basis to cancer, but testing this view is not part of the work of contemporary molecular geneticists. One might suppose that the real science here involved testing hypotheses, such as gene X is implicated in the development of pancreatic cancer; and no doubt something like this could be said to happen in this kind of research. The trouble is that of at least equal, and perhaps much greater, significance are the processes by which such hypotheses are produced. A fundamentalist Popperian, I suppose, would have the geneticist randomly select sequences of DNA and test the hypotheses that these sequences constituted genes involved in the development of a particular cancer. This would be a slow-moving science. What predominantly determines progress in this area is the search procedure by which likely candidates for relevantly interesting genes are selected. These search procedures will include synthetic elab-

oration of current theoretical ideas about the matters in question. Why should the development of such procedures be somehow less fundamentally scientific than the subsequent empirical testing of hypothesized effects on the organism?

3. *The classification of the beetles of a hitherto unexplored terrain.* The background the coleopterist brings to this project is an extensive knowledge of the classificatory scheme applied to the already discovered beetles. (Not, of course, a detailed knowledge of every recognized species, for there are hundreds of thousands of these, but a knowledge of the outlines of the hierarchy into which they are to be arranged.) The task will then be to collect as many specimen beetles as possible, and try to assign them either to a particular already-known species, or to a new species suitably related to the existing hierarchy. The scientist might recognize that a novel specimen belonged to the family Silphidae or the particular genus *Necrophorus,* and invent an appropriate name for it. Perhaps these attributions could be conceived as hypotheses. If the coleopterist is a cladist, she might claim, for example, that this is a sister species to *Necrophorus vestigator,* and this would be a fairly precisely defined thesis. But there is no process of testing this hypothesis that routinely follows its formulation. It is really better seen as a judgment based on the accumulated knowledge and expertise of the investigator. It may subsequently be challenged on a variety of grounds by other scientists, but more commonly it is not challenged, but simply accepted as a part of our overall taxonomic system put in place by a competent contributor. In this case as in the last, it is the method by which the piece of scientific knowledge is acquired, in this case through the judgment of a properly trained practitioner, that matters more than any subsequent testing to which the hypothesis may be subjected.

4. *The statistical investigation of a sociological hypothesis.* Here, I think, is where we see the most superficially Popperian domains of scientific practice. Indeed, when investigating a hypothesis such as, for instance, being female causes one to be paid less, it is natural to start with an investigation of the extent to which pay is correlated with gender. The fact that women are, on average, paid less than men provides prima facie, though of course not conclusive, evidence for the hypothesis. Unfortunately, just the reasons that prevent this from being conclusive evidence for the hypothesis are equally reasons why the lack of such a correlation could not re-

fute the hypothesis. Women could be paid less because they are
qualified for less-skilled and hence less-well-paying jobs, or they
could be paid no more than men despite being better qualified
and hence doing generally better-paid jobs. So we cannot see the
statistical investigation as a Popperian attempt to falsify the hypothesis. We can strengthen the evidence for or against the hypothesis by considering more and more potential causal factors.
But the hypothesis cannot thereby be irrevocably proved or dis-
proved. Now in fact it is common to express results of this kind
in an extremely Popperian-looking way, specifically by noting that
the Null hypothesis, the hypothesis that the correlation between
being a woman and being poorly paid comes about by chance,
can be rejected. (Or, more accurately, that the probability of this
correlation having come about by chance is very low.) The origins of this kind of talk are complicated, and I don't claim to
know how much, if anything, their popularity has to do with
Popper. It does, at least, illustrate nicely the way in which negative results provide limited information. All the falsification of the
Null hypothesis accomplishes is the demonstration that there is
some kind of causal chain relating the factors under investigation.
No amount of falsification can replace the hard work of building
up a positive case for a specific causal claim by a suitable sophisticated and varied set of empirical investigations.

I have focused on the inadequacy of Popper's falsificationism to illuminate the ways that various kinds of scientific work contribute to the
growth of scientific knowledge. However my point is not simply or even
mainly to criticize Popper,[4] but rather to reinforce the suggestion that
the variety of scientific practices makes any uniform account of scientific
method unlikely. Methodologies have developed in wholly different ways
in response to different kinds of problems, and the methodologies we
have accumulated are as diverse as those questions. I therefore turn to
what is currently a more popular conception of scientific unity: unity of
content.

How could the sciences be, in any sense, all about the same thing?
The simple answer, and one that is still quite widely accepted, is that the
only science, ultimately, is physics, so that all the sciences are really about
whatever physics is about. The classical version of this doctrine is the
doctrine of physicalistic reductionism. According to this theory, the sciences should be thought of as arranged in a hierarchy, with particle physics at the base, then (perhaps) chemistry, molecular biology, and organ-

ismic biology, and at the top ecology and the social sciences. All sciences other than elementary particle physics were to be reduced to the next lowest level in the hierarchy by characterizing the entities with which they dealt in terms of their structural makeup, and deriving the behavior of those entities from the laws governing the structural parts of which they were made. Ultimately, therefore, everything was to be understood as an arrangement of elementary particles and the behavior of everything was to be derived from the laws governing the behavior of such particles.

As an account of the real workings of science, this picture has been widely, though by no means universally, abandoned. But its spirit has by no means been abandoned, and indeed continues to govern thinking in central areas of philosophy. It also, and no doubt more importantly, continues to have a profound effect on the way many scientific problems are approached. I shall next point to some of the reasons for the abandonment of the classical version of reductionism, and then discuss the somewhat weaker doctrines in which its spirit continues to live on.

A pivotal arena in which conceptions of reductionism have been tested has been genetics. Detailed studies of the inheritance of the characteristics of organisms had occurred for half a century before the famous chemical analysis of DNA in 1953. A good deal of information was collected in this period about patterns of inheritance, and it was natural to suppose that this information could subsequently be translated into the successor language of molecular genetics. This appears not to have been possible, however. The simplest explanation of this failure is in terms of the impossibility of correlating organismic traits, of the kind the inheritance of which was the subject matter of earlier transmission genetics, with anything describable in the terminology of molecular genetics. This, in turn, is because typically many genes are involved in the production of any trait, and any gene is involved in the production of many traits. This suggests a more general perspective on the problem: attempts to understand phenomena at a particular organizational level determine schemes of classification at that level. Such schemes of classification need not, and typically will not, correlate in any manageable way with schemes of classification at lower levels. The force of this point is still controversial, and there are other kinds of objections to reductionism. There has, however, been extensive discussion of the failures of reductionism as a practical project, including my own book-length treatment (*The Disorder of Things: Metaphysical Foundations of the Disunity of Science* [Cambridge: Harvard University Press, 1993]), which includes a variety of arguments against the possibility of various putative reductions. So in this paper I shall take this failure for granted and look at some of the main reactions to it. The most widespread reactions attempt to maintain the basic metaphysical assumptions underlying scientific unity. I want to argue that such responses are not the most plausible, and certainly not the responses that should appeal to a committed empiricist.

The first such move is suggested immediately by my brief remarks about genetics. If classical genetics cannot be correlated with contemporary molecular genetics, so much the worse for classical genetics. Ultimately it is genes that determine the transmission of traits, and so we must aim to produce a theory of trait transmission based directly on the real molecular causes of the phenomena. The concepts and theories of traditional transmission genetics will very probably not appear at all in this successor science. A little reflection on the hopelessness of this reductionist project will also indicate the kinds of difficulties typical of many or most such enterprises.

Doubts about the present case start with worries about the assumption that "genes determine the transmission of traits." This, I think, has become a commonplace, and the fact that it has become a commonplace reflects the grip of this kind of reductionist thinking. Nevertheless it is a highly problematic assumption. What does it mean? Certainly not that any aspect of the genome is by itself capable of guaranteeing that, say, I will have brown eyes. Clearly a vast array of causal conditions throughout a good part of my early development are also necessary conditions for the development of this trait. More promising might be the idea that the factors that differentiate me and others with brown eyes from those with eyes of a different color are genetic. But this is still by no means obviously true. We should note in passing that even in the case of eye color a genetic characterization of the class of people with a particular eye color will be much more complicated than is often supposed, and will involve several or even many genes. But for most traits no such characterization is possible in principle. Many complex constellations of genetic and environmental factors can lead to someone being six feet tall, say. And when we move to standbys of present investigations of inheritance such as intelligence, the variety and complexity of the possible causal backgrounds would be hard to exaggerate. The temptation to say that only the genetic parts of these constellations are inheritable should quickly be resisted. Wealth, education, and so on, themselves of course diverse and complex factors, are certainly transmitted from one generation to another, and certainly affect the inheritance of height, intelligence, and so on. Once we have given up the idea that genes determine the inheritance of traits, we can see that the replacement of classical genetics by molecular genetics can only be an abandonment of the subject matter. There is no translation between the language of transmission genetics and the language of molecular genetics. And quite typically there is much more to the causal basis of the phenomena to be reduced (in this case trait transmission) than merely the subject matter of the putative reducing science (in this case genes).[5]

To mention one more very prominent example, consider the prima facie absurd proposal of a number of contemporary philosophers that we should replace talk of the mind with talk of bits of the brain. This remains absurd on more careful reflection. The problem is simply that to replace mind talk with brain talk requires that the latter can serve the purposes of the former. But it is exceedingly unlikely that this is so. Even if, in some sense, we are talking about the brain when we refer to features of our mental lives, there is not the slightest reason to believe that, say, my belief that the U.S. stock market will crash soon can be identified with some well-defined part of my brain; still less that the same part of my brain will consistently correspond to just this belief; and least of all that everyone has a structurally identical part of their brain if, and only if, they believe that the U.S. stock market will crash soon. And it seems that it is this last that would be needed if there were to be some piece of brain talk with which, in principle, one could replace this bit of belief talk. (I suggest, indeed, that this is a place where the supernatural qualities of monism appear clearly. Magical powers are being attributed to brain cells on the basis of no empirical evidence, merely from metaphysical commitment.)

Finally, even if one or other of these reductionist projects could somehow go through, it should not encourage us to see the strategy of replacement as generally applicable. The kinds of obstacles to reduction I have mentioned seem likely to occur in most or all cases, forcing us to resort at every stage in the hierarchy to some kind of replacement. Thus we will not have reached physicalistically impeccable categories until we have gone all the way down to fundamental physics. But the suggestion that we could replace talk about beetles, people, or ecosystems with talk about physical particles seems to have lost all contact with the realities of scientific work.

Despite the absurdity of taking this replacement talk seriously, it is clear what is the intuition underlying it, and this is an intuition that seems far from absurd to most philosophers. This is the idea that whatever we may say about beliefs, intentions, and the like explaining or even causing our behavior, there is also a set of physical causes that must simultaneously fully explain our physical movements. This brings us, finally, to the doctrine of the completeness of physics. A remarkable amount of contemporary work in the philosophy of mind, in the philosophy of biology, and in the philosophy of the social sciences is concerned with the attempt to reconcile the assumed completeness of physics with the perceived failure of attempts to reduce higher-level science in the direction of physics. One solution is the eliminativism I have just been discussing, the view that the march of science will eventually sweep away the vocabularies of biology, folk psychology, or sociology. A more modest solution is the instrumentalism defended by those who admit that we cannot, perhaps for reasons of principle, get by without biology, psychology, or the social sciences, but add that since the entities of which these sciences speak are incommensurable with those of physics, the former cannot be recognized as ultimately real.[6]

A much better solution, it seems to me, is to abandon the dogma of the completeness of physics, together with the doctrine of the unity of science that it underpins. Let me mention a few reasons why we should be happy to abandon this dogma. Foremost among these is the commitment to empiricism insisted on earlier in this essay, and the observation that there is essentially no evidence for the completeness of physics. We can begin to see this by noting the extent to which the failure of reductionism in various crucial areas of science undercuts the plausibility of the completeness of physics. There are, of course, no actual accounts of the behavior of mice or men, or even bacteria, as flowing from the physical properties of their smallest physical parts; and no such accounts appear to be in the offing as reductionist science develops. The belief that such an account must exist in principle, or in the mind of God, is at best an inference from what we do know about the behavior of systems simpler by many orders of magnitude, and hence an inference that goes beyond any decent empiricist strictures. It is, in short, a supernaturalist belief.

Of course, it will be said that these simpler systems give us knowledge of laws of nature, and these laws can then (in principle) be applied to far more complex systems. But what could possibly license this extension in the admitted absence of any direct evidence for the applicability of the laws to these more complex systems? As Nancy Cartwright pointed out many years ago, even as apparently simple and robust a law as the law of universal gravitation only applies to situations in which no other forces (electromagnetic, for example) are acting.[7] Of course we have good procedures for dealing with some situations in which there are forces of different kinds acting. But it is still the case that the principles by which we combine different forces are principles distinct from and additional to those laws describing the sources of specific forces. When we move from systems of a few particles under the influence of one or two fully understood forces to systems involving trillions of complexly organized particles subject to many, perhaps very many, different kinds of forces, we are embracing a rather more ambitious augmentation of the basic physical laws.

These objections to the completeness of physics are strongly reinforced by even the most cursory consideration of the actual methods by which physical laws are discovered and confirmed. Accounts of work in high-energy physics laboratories, the central testing ground for contemporary work in fundamental physics, show that conducting experiments in this arena is a very difficult matter. A great deal of time and energy is required to get such experiments to work.[8] The point is not that this should cast doubt on the results of these experiments, but only that we should reflect on what makes this work so difficult. And the answer, plainly enough, is that it is the process of separating an effect of interest from all the interferences, unwanted effects of the apparatus, and so on, that is required before any meaningful result can be attained. Hence the results we do finally attain are results that apply to quite simple, effectively isolated systems. Their extrapolation even to interactions with other simple factors is not guaranteed. Their extrapolation to every system in the universe, however complex, is easily resistible. Some people seem to be very impressed by the very high precision of predictions from quantum mechanisms that are sometimes experimentally confirmed. This seems to me a red herring. Precise confirmation of predictions of course adds to the impressiveness with which the application of laws to the systems in which they are being tested is supported. It is also a testament to the skill with which the experimenters have succeeded in isolating the effect from unwanted interferences. But it has little or no effect on the plausibility of extrapolating to the applicability of those laws to quite different kinds of systems.

My conclusion is that there is at least very little reason to believe in any kind of unity of science. The idea of a unity grounded in method fails to survive a cursory scrutiny of the variety of methods employed in science. The idea of a unity of content, grounded in the completeness of physics, seems to lack any convincing rationale and, most importantly, any empirical support. And since it is a powerful and, I think, counterintuitive view, I am inclined to think its hold on us is best explained either in terms of a degenerating historical tradition or, more interestingly, in terms of nonepistemic functions it serves. It is to this possibility I now turn.

The Functions of the Myth

The foregoing arguments have, it seems to me, been thoroughly naturalistic in spirit. They assume that our knowledge of the world should be derived from our experience of it and our interactions with it. First and foremost among these will be the projects—often remarkably successful, explicitly aimed at gaining knowledge about the world—that comprise the sciences. Naturalism suggests, however, that we not think about these in terms of Procrustean a priori epistemology, but rather as natural objects apt for empirical scrutiny. Such scrutiny reveals a diverse set of practices using methods some of which are common to a variety of investigations but others of which are peculiar to particular areas. Though it certainly reveals local attempts at reductions, it reveals few if any fully elaborated reductions of one level of phenomena to a lower level of structural complexity or replacements of accounts of one domain by a lower-level domain. I think one may go one step further. The universe-wide microphysical machine, the integrated realm of microscopic particles that forms the substance of reductionist fantasies, is not a product of naturalistic inquiry, but a supernatural construct of the scientific dreamer. Naturalists should reject the image not just because it lacks proper naturalistic credentials, but because it violates the most basic naturalistic commitment to the rejection of the supernatural. In this concluding section I offer some speculations about the appeal of reductionism and unity to many who see themselves as card-carrying naturalists. This should also suggest some of the likely and desirable consequences of abandoning this relic of supernatural thinking.

The first function that unity of science theses serve is as a ground of demarcation. Science carries an epistemic authority that generally greatly exceeds that of nonscientific practices of knowledge production. And I do not wish to question the assumption that our most compelling examples of epistemic excellence come from the sciences. It would presumably be a threat to the credentials of more dubious areas of science if scientific practices were evaluated piecemeal for epistemic worth. The impression that macroeconomic theory, say, or evolutionary psychology, has serious empirical credentials surely owes much to the idea that they are part of science, and that science, surely, has significant empirical warrant.[9] Unity provides solidarity and protects the weaker brethren. This would obviously be the case if science had a unity of method as then, presumably, we could suppose that that method was generally a reliable one. But a similar conclusion would at least be suggested by any kind of unity.

Unity, in short, distributes epistemic warrant. The claim to be scientific is not an important one for solid-state physicists or organic chemists; it is one they take for granted. But on the more controversial margins of science such claims are all-important. Economists claim to be scientific in ways that their more interpretative rivals among the social sciences cannot aspire to, and evolutionary psychologists claim to be uniting the study of humanity with science in ways that must spell the end for more traditional exceptionalist accounts of our species. The importance of such rhetorical moves, it seems to me, depends on some version of the thesis of the Unity of Science.[10] If science is no more than an overlapping collection of practices for investigating the world, with diverse assumptions and methods, and often incommensurable results, then it is unclear why anything much hangs on the claim to scientificity. The status of "science" might, on such a view, much better be used as an honorific to be bestowed on investigative practices when they have provided convincing evidence of success in their investigations. (Of course it is also possible that it is just such an honorific that economists and others intend to bestow upon themselves.) On the other hand, if there is just one system of interconnected truths that constitutes science, a science moreover that ultimately, at least in principle, exhausts the truth about the world, then everything depends on establishing the claim of one's practice to belong to this totality. And if such could be done on general grounds that do not require the demonstration of actual empirical successes, the relevance of such claims will obviously be greater still. Here I suggest we see Science as a whole in its supernatural guise. Just as membership of the True Church guarantees redemption, so membership of the One True Science guarantees credibility. In both cases the details of how this trick are pulled off remain obscure. And neither strategy should appeal to a naturalist.

The consequences of the ideology of scientific unity are not limited to matters merely theoretical. Reductionist models of scientific unity have a particularly and potentially damaging effect on the practice of science. The ultimate goal of articulating unified science in its full glory leads naturally to a preference for seeing phenomena as depending on the internal structure of the entities that produce them rather than emphasizing the influences of the environment. Probably the most serious practical consequences of this tendency are in the human sciences, and most especially in the medical sciences. Consider, for instance, the several million American children (mostly boys) recently discovered to be suffering from Attention Deficit Disorder Syndrome but, happily, being treated with apparent success with the drug ritalin. It is somewhat surprising that such a widespread disorder should have been unknown a few decades ago. But of course this doesn't mean that there were not numerous sufferers. Albert Einstein is sometimes mentioned as a prominent victim.

No doubt among these millions are some seriously sick children. But I do not find it a bit surprising that many children now, and in the past, have had difficulty paying attention in schools. I do doubt whether this proves that there is something wrong with these children's heads that is appropriately treated with psychotropic (and, apparently, addictive) drugs. Schools are, after all, often boring. The fact that powerful drugs can alleviate the manifestations of the syndrome shows very little. Threats of violence may be equally effective at concentrating the minds of recalcitrant students, but this would not prove that they were suffering from corporal punishment deficiency syndrome. There are many ways of influencing behavior. It is evident that there is some kind of mismatch between the dispositions of the problem child and the social context in which that individual is placed. Such a mismatch could, on the face of it, be addressed by changes to the child, to the environment, or both. I do not deny that changes to the child brought about by the ingestion of psychotropic substances may, in the end, be the best solution in many cases, though it is disturbing that anyone distributing such substances at the school gate rather than in the doctor's office would be risking decades of incarceration. My worry is that the reductionist perspective on science makes this sort of response look natural, if not inevitable. Millions of drugged children—or, to take a different case, slashed, burned, and poisoned patients in unrelievedly carcinogenic environments—are, arguably, the price we pay for action on the basis of this myth. The suggestion that this sort of thing is explicitly part of the function of the myth is perhaps uncomfortably close to conspiracy theory or even serious paranoia. It is of course true that drug companies make many billions of dollars from their expertise in adjusting people's minds to the demands of the environment, and it is surely also true that it is much easier and generally cheaper for governments to point to the defects of individuals than attempt to make positive changes in the environments to which people appear maladapted. Whether there are connections between the prevalence of reductionist thinking and its obvious advantages for some of the most rich and powerful is not, at any rate, something about which I pretend to have any evidence.

Conclusion

The main point of this paper has been to emphasize that monism, and the unity of science doctrine on which contemporary monism rests, far from being inevitable concomitants of a properly naturalized philosophical perspective, are elements of a new mythology. Monism is surely not grounded on empiricism. For one thing, if it were, there would be no need of the vast amounts of work expended in the elaboration of eliminativist, instrumentalist, and supervenientist theses designed to explain the empirical failures of monism. More simply, our empirical experience of nature is, on its face, an experience of a huge diversity of kinds of things with an even huger diversity of properties and causal capacities. Some of these properties are open to casual inspection; others require careful, even inspired, scientific investigation. Neither casual experience nor detailed investigation suggest that all these properties are best understood through attention to the physical stuff of which things are made. The advance of science does indeed lend credence to the view that we do not need to appeal to supernatural things in explaining phenomena. One variety of supernatural things are those that are made out of nonphysical stuff, like angels or Cartesian minds. So we may allow that naturalism commits us to the monism that insists that all stuff is material, even physical, stuff. The corollary that insight into the properties of stuff holds the key to understanding the properties and behavior of all those diverse things that are made of that stuff is another matter altogether. And this indeed is the kind of doctrine that suggests the attribution of supernatural powers to physical stuff in a way wholly inimical to naturalism.

Casual and not so casual inspection of the world suggests that it contains a great diversity of kinds of things. Similarly, inspection of science, our best ways of finding out about the world, suggests that there is a great diversity of projects that can be directed toward the investigation of the natural world. Does this leave us without resources for distinguishing the credible (scientific) projects from the worthless (unscientific) projects? Not quite. There is no a priori criterion for distinguishing successful projects of inquiry, but that, I think, is what we should expect as naturalists. A posteriori we can distinguish success well enough in terms of familiar epistemic virtues such as understanding, explanation, prediction, and control. Many parts of the physical and biological sciences are unmistakable successes on the basis of their production of such goods. A more abstract level of reflection allows us to see particular methodological virtues that have contributed to the success of these projects. Many

investigative projects that have been championed at different times lack
both the products of success and the virtues that have been seen to lead
to success. It is of course a difficult matter of judgment when we should
conclude that such a project is irredeemably flawed, but it is surely a
judgment we must sometimes be willing to make. However, Science as
a unified reification and as a fig leaf behind which broken-backed investigations can hide is nothing but an obstacle to the process of deciding
which projects belong to science, in the merely honorific sense.

There are further benefits to be gained from a pluralistic naturalism.
C. P. Snow's famous jeremiad about the Two Cultures, the opposed forces
of science and humanism, is outdated in one sense.[11] No cabal of Ox-
bridge dons now effectively opposes the application of science to such
problems as world hunger for which science has essential contributions
to make. Even in Britain, science has gained the upper hand over its
humanist enemies. On the other hand the opposition between the two
camps sometimes seems as strong as ever. In the contemporary Science
Wars, in which angry scientists rail against the humanists alleged to have
discussed science with insufficient respect and expertise, it is still clear
that science is assumed to form a hegemonic unity, and there is a strong
tendency for the opposition to be constructed as an equally unified Lud-
dite whole. Enemies, real or imagined, are of course a classic device for
reinforcing solidarity or unity.

In the hope that this may tend to reduce these hostilities, I suggest
that the rejection of the unity of science is the path to what there is of
value in a genuine unity of knowledge. The sciences offer us a diverse
group of practices with a diverse set of partially overlapping virtues.
Some encompass large ranges of empirical facts; others enable us to predict or control natural events; others again provide theoretical equipment
for thinking more clearly about complex phenomena; and so on. But
some of these virtues also characterize the traditional nonsciences. History is an essential repository and organizer of empirical fact; studies of
the Arts provide us with insight into aspects of human life that are still
far removed from the more mechanical approaches of psychology or the
social sciences; even philosophy provides us tools for thinking about the
natural world; and so on again. What is most valuable about this picture
of diverse and overlapping projects of inquiry is that it makes unsurprising what seems empirically to be the case, that complex phenomena are
far more likely to be understood if a variety of distinct but complemen-
tary approaches are brought to bear on them.[12]

But having insisted on a variety of practices of knowledge production
with diverse and overlapping epistemic virtues, I can now allow that there

are characteristics that distinguish much of science from much academic work outside of science. For example, science tends to aim at the expansion of empirical knowledge, whereas humanistic disciplines are often more theoretical and more critical. And this leads to perhaps the most essential form of interaction between the two. One of the contributions that has made Kuhn's *The Structure of Scientific Revolutions* so fundamental to current understanding of science is the insight that science does not, on the whole, promote criticism.[13] Of course, scientists have very heated disputes about the details of their empirical or theoretical claims, but these take place within a context that is not, on the whole, called into question. The contemporary studies by sociologists of the details of how scientific work is really done; by historians of how it has been done in the past and how the doing of it has led to the consensuses that exist in various contemporary scientific fields; the attempts by philosophers to expose and analyze those assumptions that are not called into question in the doing of science; and much else that goes under the very general rubric of science studies, not least in the philosophy of science, has surely improved our understanding of science and even, in the end, may encourage the doing of better science. The division between C. P. Snow's Two Cultures can only be deepened by those who, for whatever reasons, insist that there are indeed two, and that those on one side have no right to say anything about what goes on on the other side. But there are not two grand cultures, but many small and overlapping subcultures. And knowledge will advance to the extent that the members of different subcultures make whatever efforts they can, even if sometimes critical efforts, to inform the work of those in others.

And this leads finally to a point at which pluralistic naturalism does really diverge from more standard recent versions of naturalism. Quine, famously, held that philosophy was continuous with science. Given that science is perceived as a unity, and as a unity that will contain all the genuine insight into the nature of the world that we manage to acquire, the only possible positions for philosophy appear to be as part of science or in the dustbin of history. In light of that choice, Quine's decision is understandable. No such predicament faces a pluralist. Indeed, for a pluralist the thesis that philosophy is continuous with science faces the obvious question, Which science? Philosophy, on the contrary, emphasizes rather different epistemic virtues from most sciences and has typically different goals. Its characteristic epistemic virtues are, perhaps, analytic rigor and clarity of argument, though certainly it is subject to others, such as sensitivity to empirical fact, that are central to most sciences. Its goals are typically more abstract, theoretical, and critical. There are, surely, fundamentally important classes of questions for which the methods of philosophy are particularly suited and even essential, though I certainly do not propose here to make any claims on the controversial matter of what those questions are. However, the view of philosophers as a kind of laboratorially challenged scientist seems to me to have been a total failure. Pluralistic naturalism offers a way out of this backwater, but one that does not consign the philosopher to even more unpromising undertakings in the noumenal world or Plato's heaven.

3

The Content and Appeal
of "Naturalism"

HILARY PUTNAM

$\mathcal{A}$ s my title suggests, there are just two questions about "naturalism" that I mean to address: what it *means* to say that one is a "naturalist" (or, more precisely, what it means if a certain popular definition of the term is accepted); and why, in spite of (what we shall find to be) the extreme unclarity of the position and the host of problems it faces, this sort of "naturalism" seems to be so appealing.

The Content of "Naturalism"

Today the most common use[1] of the term "naturalism" might be described as follows: philosophers—perhaps even a majority of all the philosophers writing about issues in metaphysics, epistemology, philosophy of mind, and philosophy of language—announce in one or another conspicuous place in their essays and books that they are "naturalists" or that the view or account being defended is a "naturalist" one; this announcement, in its placing and emphasis, resembles the placing of the announcement in articles written in Stalin's Soviet Union that a view was in agreement with Comrade Stalin's; as in the case of the latter announcement, it is supposed to be clear that any view that is not "naturalist" (not in agreement with Comrade Stalin's) is anathema, and could not possibly be correct. A further very common feature is that, as a rule, "naturalism" is not *defined*.

59

One happy exception to this rule is that in the glossary to Boyd, Gasper, and Trout's *The Philosophy of Science*, naturalism is actually defined, namely as "[t]he view that all phenomena are subject to natural laws, and/or that the methods of the natural sciences are applicable in every area of inquiry."[2] However, the definition is a *disjunctive* one, and the two disjuncts are actually very different. In effect, we are being offered *two* definitions of "naturalism" rather than one. Let us consider them in turn.

According to the first definition (or the first disjunct) a naturalist is a philosopher who believes that "all phenomena are subject to natural laws." But what exactly is this supposed to mean? Consider the following "phenomenon": someone whose prose is usually very clear writes a paragraph that is quite difficult to interpret. A naturalist (in the sense of this first definition) must believe that this phenomenon is subject to natural laws. Is it clear what this means? Certainly, the writer didn't *violate* any natural laws when he wrote the difficult paragraph. If all that is involved in being a naturalist is thinking that there aren't phenomena that actually *violate* natural laws, then who *isn't* a "naturalist"? Or is it required to be a naturalist that one believe that there are "natural laws" containing the concept *difficult to interpret?* (And every other concept used to describe a "phenomenon"?) Or would it be enough (to count as a "naturalist") to think that the token event of writing the unclear paragraph is identical with some token physical event (à la Davidson)? (Would thinking that "token identity" has no clear definition at all make one a "nonnaturalist"?)

According to the second definition (the second disjunct), on the other hand, a naturalist is a philosopher who believes that "the methods of the natural sciences are applicable in every area of inquiry." Well, what would it mean to say that the methods of the natural sciences apply to *the interpretation of texts?* Or is the interpretation of texts not an "area of inquiry"? If what is involved is believing that there is a science that resembles physics (complete with laws, theories, experiments, and so on) of every single thing (for example, that history is a science, as the logical positivists used to claim), then why wouldn't it be perfectly respectable *not* to hold such an implausible view?

At first blush, the fact that so many philosophers are proud of calling themselves "naturalists," without spelling out what the term means, might suggest "naturalism" has no definite content at all.[3] But this would be a mistake; there *is* a content to "naturalism" (in the scientific understanding of the term that I am criticizing), but the unfortunate term "naturalism" conceals it instead of making it clear. To find what that content is, we have to consider what the *opponents* of (scientistic) naturalism really defend. What they defend is, of course, not "supernatural" or "occult" explanations (although the term "naturalism" is intended to suggest that that is what they defend). What they defend is, rather, *conceptual pluralism*. But what is "conceptual pluralism"?

Pluralism

Conceptual pluralism might be briefly defined as the denial that any one language game is adequate for all our cognitive purposes, but this description is not yet very helpful. "Naturalists" too can easily concede that this is the case—but with qualifications. The most common qualification is represented by Quine's distinction between a first-class conceptual system (science, or rather science properly formalized) and what he called "our second-grade conceptual system."[4] Quine, as everyone knows, simply ruled that only our first-grade conceptual system represents an account of what the world contains that we have to take seriously. Since nothing in the conceptual scheme of physics, for example, corresponds to a *meaning fact*, the closest we can come to such facts is bare behaviorist psychology in the style of Skinner. (Today many "naturalists" would say, "neurophysiology.") And if Skinnerian psychology cannot provide an account of meaning or reference, so much the worse for meaning and reference! While other "naturalists" would draw the line between the first-grade and the second-grade elsewhere (no two "naturalists" seem to draw it in the *same* place), what is common to most versions of "naturalism" is that those conceptual resources and conceptual activities that do not fit into the narrowly scientific first-grade system are regarded as something less than *bona fide* rational discourse.

The heart of my own conceptual pluralism is the insistence that the various sorts of statements that are regarded as less than fully rational discourse, as somehow of merely "heuristic" significance, by one or another of the "naturalists" (whether these statements be ethical statements or statements about meaning and reference, or counterfactuals and statements about causality,[5] or mathematical statements, or whatever) are *bona fide* statements, "as fully governed by norms of truth and validity as any other statements," as James Conant has put it.[6]

The Instability of "Naturalism"

While Quine (and today, Simon Blackburn and—as it seems at times—Bernard Williams)[7] represent what might be called "minimalism" with respect to what can be included in the first-grade conceptual system, the system that alone can be taken seriously when our interest is (in a famous phrase of Quine's) "limning of the most general traits of reality,"[8] many naturalists are understandably uncomfortable with the idea of dismissing *so much* of our discourse to the murky reaches of our "second-grade conceptual system." This discomfort pushes some "naturalists" to try to show that large parts of what Quine, Blackburn, Williams, and others would push out of the realm of the first-grade system (what Williams calls "the absolute conception of the world") can actually be *reduced to* first-grade properties and thus shown to be first-grade after all. In short, one wing of the "naturalist" camp gets pushed in the direction of (physicalist) *ontological reductionism*. At their most ambitious, ontological reductionists seek to rehabilitate even the property of being ethically *good* (Richard Boyd and, perhaps, Peter Railton),[9] but philosophers who are willing to go this far are comparatively rare. Others—Jerry Fodor is a famous example—try to give physicalist accounts of *meaning*.[10] Still others have tried to give physicalist accounts of the content of mathematics (Hartry Field, Penelope Maddy, albeit in very different ways). The trouble is that none of these ontological reductions gets *believed* by anyone except the proponent of the account and one or two of his friends and/or students. So—as always in philosophy—a "recoil" sets in. But whither is a "naturalist" to recoil?

The area of discourse that has been recognized by "naturalists" themselves as most resistant to reductive explanation, and hence as problematic from their own point of view, is "intentional" discourse (talk of reference, meaning, belief, desire, and the like), although mathematics is also frequently regarded as a problem because of the fact that, as it is often put, "we don't causally interact with mathematical entities."[11] Already in the nineteenth century Brentano had taken the irreducibility of intentionality to refute naturalist and physicalist accounts of mind. Quine was willing to agree with Brentano that intentionality is irreducible, but concluded that it was no genuine phenomenon at all:

> One may accept the Brentano thesis either as showing the indispensability of intentional idioms and the importance of an autonomous science of intention, or as showing the baselessness of intentional idioms and the emptiness of a science of intention. My attitude, unlike Brentano's, is the second.[12]

Moreover, it is not only the "nonextensional" intentional idioms that Quine viewed as "baseless." The fundamental notion of extensional semantics is *reference;* and reference, Quine famously held, is "indeterminate." One of his routes to this conclusion is via his doctrine of "onto-logical relativity." Here is an example: Suppose we define "X *complement-drinks* Y" to mean that whatever object (counting regions of space as "objects") is left when we take away X from the entire physical universe (the "cosmos") drinks whatever is left over when we take away Y from the entire cosmos. Quine once had a cat named "Tabitha." A moment's reflection suffices to convince oneself that Tabitha drinks milk when and only when the cosmos-minus-Tabitha *complement-drinks* the cosmos-minus-the-milk. Quine contended that it is objectively indeter-minate *whether, in the sentence "Tabitha is drinking the milk," the name "Tabitha" refers to Tabitha and "is drinking" to the act of drinking and "the milk" to the milk, or "Tabitha" refers to the cosmos minus Tabitha, "is drink-ing" to complement-drinking, and "the milk" to the cosmos minus the milk.*[13]

Here Quine was characteristically up-front about the counterintuitive consequences of his philosophical theories. A number of present-day "naturalists" either seem to be unaware of them, or believe that they can accept much the same account of reference without "going as far" as Quine. An example is Stephen Leeds's account in a fascinating paper in the *Pacific Philosophical Quarterly* some years ago.[14] The most common view of reference—and one that I agree with, as long as it is not confused with the quite different position that reference can be *defined* in terms of causal connection—is that reference to empirical particulars and prop-erties *presupposes* information-carrying causal interaction with those par-ticulars and properties, or at least with particulars and properties in terms of which identifying descriptions of those particulars and properties can be constructed. Leeds rejects this idea entirely. Instead he simply posits that the familiar "disquotational" formulas such as " 'Caesar' refers to Caesar" define the relation of reference. But Quine's "Tabitha" example already showed the error in this claim. If there is no determinate cor-respondence between any of our terms and nonlinguistic objects—if there is neither a context-sensitive correspondence nor a context-insensitive one—then I can utter (or inscribe in the mythical "belief box" in my brain that some "naturalists" like to posit) the sentence

"Tabitha" refers to Tabitha

and as many other instances of the "disquotation" scheme

"T" refers to Ts

as I want, and no relation between the term "Tabitha" and any particular object external to my words is thereby defined. Even saying: "I specify that the extension of the two-place predicate 'refers' is the set of ordered pairs {<'Tabitha', Tabitha>, <'Taj Mahal', the Taj Mahal>, <'cat', the set of all cats>}, and so on" still leaves totally undetermined what I am talking about when I say "Tabitha" or "Taj Mahal" or "cat" or whatever.

To put the same point in model-theoretic terms: a model[15] according to which the word "Tabitha" names the cosmos minus Tabitha immediately extends to a model for the meta-language of the relevant portion of my language in which " 'Tabitha' refers to Tabitha" is *true* (not false, as one might expect)—true because the second occurrence of the proper name "Tabitha" in this sentence (the occurrence without quotation marks around it, the one that is 'used' and not 'mentioned') corresponds to *the cosmos minus Tabitha* in that model of the meta-language, as well as in the submodel, which is the model of the object-language. (As Quine might have put it, in all the different models corresponding to the various "proxy-functions" it is true that "Tabitha" refers to Tabitha—whatever *Tabitha* is.) Leeds's account simply abandons the idea that there is even a partly determinate correspondence between terms and objects without acknowledging that this is what it does.

Sometimes philosophers who hold views like Quine's or Leeds's have replied as follows when I have raised the foregoing objection: "Yes, we give up the idea that reference is a words-world correspondence," they say, "but that doesn't mean that language *isn't* connected to objects. It is connected to objects *causally*, not referentially." It is remarkable that this response happens to be the central thesis of a philosopher whom the "naturalists" I am discussing regard as an opponent: Richard Rorty. (To be sure, Rorty might also call himself a "naturalist," but not in the scientistic sense that the definition in Boyd, Gasper, and Trout's glossary attempted to capture.) The "naturalists" that Boyd, Gasper, and Trout were thinking of, and whose views I have been criticizing, typically say that they are "scientific realists." (Quine called himself a "robust realist.") For them, science is first philosophy. For Rorty, however, "realist" is a dirty word.[16] And rejecting the idea that we possess "discrete component capacities to get in touch with discrete hunks of reality"[17] (in other words, that there is a semantical connection between a given utterance of the word "Tabitha" and a given discrete furry hunk of reality) seems to Rorty (but evidently not to Quine, Leeds, Field, and others) virtually to *require* that we abandon realism. And he is not being unreasonable, for once one loses the thought that there is a determinate relation between one's words and scientific or other objects, what does calling oneself a "realist" actually come to?

Well, it is clear what it came to for Quine: a positivist insistence that all our language is (cognitively speaking) a machine for anticipating and controlling the stimulations of one's nerve endings. And it is true that to choose this as one's criterion for what one will take "seriously" is very different from accepting Rorty's more elastic criterion of whatever helps us to "cope." But if neither criterion has any pretension to providing a sense in which our propositions are capable of mapping the behavior of specific hunks of reality (and how can there be *mapping* without any *mapping relation?*), then valorizing prediction of nerve-stimulations over "coping" broadly construed is (as Rorty tirelessly points out) utterly arbitrary. Quine, it seems to me, gave up realism without noticing that he did, because he thought that as long as he valorized scientific discourse above all other discourse, this *made* him a "realist." And I suspect that Leeds, Hartry Field, Paul Horwich, and the other "deflationists" follow him in this. "Naturalism" is unstable indeed if it slides so easily into Rortian antirealism.

(My aim in this essay is simply to examine the content and appeal of "naturalism," not to offer an alternative picture. But if I were to offer an alternative account, I would begin by pointing out that while Frege was right to say that only in the context of a statement [or a question, or a command, and so on] does a word have reference or meaning at all, it is only in the context of such a practice as *talking about cats* that such a sentence as "Tabitha won't drink milk" constitutes a *statement*. And not only is there no reason to think that the practice of talking about cats [or about cabbages or kings or sealing wax and so on] can be defined in physicalistic terms, but there is not even a way to begin to talk about that practice without talking about the various things we do with cats [with cabbages, with kings, with sealing wax], starting with *perceiving* them—that is, *talking about things* is a vast and ever-expanding motley of *world-involving practices.* Just uttering marks and noises that are "causally connected" to things is not yet *engaging in a practice*—not under the description "uttering marks and noises that are causally connected to things," anyway.)[18]

However, not all "naturalists" recoil from the problem of "naturalizing semantics" in a deflationist direction. David Lewis famously insisted that certain properties (or rather, *certain classes*) are "objective similarities," where the property of being an objective similarity is not to be understood as in any way relative to our interests. Reference, for Lewis, is largely fixed by the requirement that typical predicates in the language denote objects that are objectively similar.[19] But for Lewis's idea to work, *one* similarity that has to be recognized as "objective" is *being designed for the function of being sat upon.* (Think of the predicate "chair.") But to be

designed for a function presupposes being *thought of* as capable of fulfilling that function, and this is an intentional condition. Only a being
that can *think about things as fulfilling a function* can design things to fulfill
it. So the primitive notion (for that is what it was in Lewis's metaphysics)
"objective similarity" mustn't just refer to similarities in, say, color or
shape; it must refer to similarities in "form," in the old Aristotelian sense.
If one sort of contemporary naturalist is a Rortian antirealist in disguise,
another sort—Lewis being the most brilliant recent example—is a high
medieval Aristotelian metaphysician in disguise! The laudable aim of a
modest nonmetaphysical realism squarely in touch with the results of
science is lost in both cases.

The Appeal of "Naturalism"

Considering the failures and instabilities of the various forms of "naturalism" we have briefly canvassed, one can be sure that there wouldn't
be so many philosophers still proudly announcing "I am a naturalist" or
"this is a naturalist view" if the view didn't have strong appeal. In some
cases the appeal may be genuinely "appealing"; that is, the vision of a
state of knowledge in which everything—everything that we have to take
seriously when we are "limning the most general traits of reality"—is
made clear in the manner in which physics is imagined to make things
clear[20] may correspond to a deep scientistic or positivistic outlook on the
part of a few philosophers. Positivists,[21] in this loose sense, are always
with us. In the great majority of cases, I believe, the "appeal" is more
likely the "appeal" of a medicine that tastes awful (and even has some
unpleasant side effects) but that one takes to avert or cure a serious
illness. "Naturalism," I believe, is often driven by fear, fear that accepting
conceptual pluralism will let in the "occult," the "supernatural." But before I say a word or two more about the nature of this fear, let us first
look at the arguments for naturalism that seem to convince more philosophers (more students, at any rate) than any others. In my experience
there are two:

1. *The argument from evolution/composition.* There was a time when
   the world contained nothing but fields and particles, and everything we find in the world now came into being as a result of
   physical processes (including Darwinian evolution, at a relatively
   recent stage in the history of the cosmos). Hence things *are* nothing but mereological sums of physical objects (counting space-
   time regions as physical objects). Hence all explanations in terms

of intentional notions, propositional attitudes, all value-judgments, all counterfactuals (some, but decidedly not all, "naturalists" would add "mathematical statements") must either be shown to be reducible to the nonintentional noncounterfactual level of something like Quine's "canonical notation," or else shown to be cognitively spurious, part of the heuristic "second-grade conceptual system" at best.

2. *The "you're leaving something unexplained" argument.* It is contended that in some cases (the case of semantics, but usually not the case of the so-called "special sciences" like geology),[22] failure to give a reductive explanation of something—say of what it is to *refer* to something, or how there can be such things as *true counterfactual conditionals* or *true mathematical sentences*—is to leave it "unexplained," and hence to admit a "mystery" (in the sense of something occult) into the (fundamentally unmysterious) "physical world."

Let us look at these arguments in turn.

Re the first argument: it is simply not the case that "things are nothing but mereological sums of physical objects." To be sure, the Quinian conception of philosophy that influenced so much subsequent "naturalism," the conception of philosophy as *theory that tells us what we can and what we cannot quantify over in that part of our language that alone we can take with metaphysical seriousness, namely the properly formalized scientific part of our language,* fits very well with the idea of taking a concrete (nonabstract) thing to be simply a mereological sum of particles, or in more recent physics, a mereological sum of fields and particles, even if this was not Quine's own preference.[23] Here, in the mereological sums of particles (or fields and particles) we are supposed to have a nice set of physical objects, describable in what is supposedly a precise language (if we pass over the fictitious physics involved),[24] the language of symbolic logic, counting mereology as a part of symbolic logic. The remaining tasks of philosophy then become, first, to decide how many abstract entities (if any) we need to quantify over in order to do first-class science and which ones are avoidable (for example, Quine thought that *intentional* entities, meanings and attributes, are avoidable, but sets are not), and second, to show how other things that we apparently have to quantify over can be reduced to the privileged scientific objects, or to dismiss them to our "second-grade conceptual system."

But there is a deep problem with this whole line of thought, one pointed out by Kripke when he introduced the idea of "rigid designation."[25] Although I owe the point to Kripke, I shall develop it in a somewhat different way. I suggest that one way of seeing the inadequacy of the whole idea of seeing a (concrete) object as a mereological sum of molecules or atoms or elementary particles (or anything of that kind) is to note a certain ambiguity in the very claim that something "is" a mereological sum. Am I (or is my body) the mereological sum of the atoms in my body? In one sense, yes. Those atoms are parts of my body, and there is no part of my body that is wholly disjoint from every one of those atoms. In that sense, likewise, Massachusetts is the mereological sum of the counties that make it up. Those counties are parts of Massachusetts, and no part of Massachusetts is wholly disjoint (that is, fails to touch) at least one of those counties. But typically the statement that I am the mereological sum of the atoms in my body, or that Massachusetts is the mereological sum of the various counties, is understood to mean more than this; it is understood as a statement of "logical identity," the identity (symbolized by the sign "=" in symbolic logic) that satisfies Leibniz's Law, the principle that if x = y (x is identical with y) then every property of x is a property of y and vice versa. The statement that I am (or my body is) the mereological sum of the atoms in my body is easily seen to be false if understood as a statement of identity in this logical sense.

Let us suppose (this is certainly a physical possibility) that the atoms in my body all existed a thousand years ago. Of course, they were not in my body at that time; some were in the earth, some in the air, and so forth. The mereological sum of the atoms in my body exists whenever those atoms exist, and this means that the mereological sum of the atoms in my body existed a thousand years ago. By Leibniz's Law, if I am that mereological sum, it follows that I existed a thousand years ago, which is clearly false. Moreover, if—and here we come closer to Kripke's own version of the argument—I had simply eaten different food for dinner last night, I would now consist of different atoms, and hence I would not be identical with the particular mereological sum with which I *am* identical, on the supposition that the sense in which "I am" the mereological sum of those atoms is logical identity.[26] (But why should I care about what would happen if a *different person* had a different diet than I do? As Kripke emphasizes, our use of counterfactuals depends on the supposition that the proper names in them designate *rigidly*, that is, that they designate *identical* individuals in the various possible worlds we contemplate. And it doesn't help [to meet this] to say that I am identical with a mereological sum of *time-slices* of atoms [where a "time-slice" is supposed to be a temporal "part" of an atom, say the atom between time t_1 and time t_2], for if I had had a different dinner I would now consist not just of different atoms but of different time-slices of atoms.)

David Lewis, whose views Kripke discusses in *Naming and Necessity*, would "bite the bullet" here and say that if I had had something else for dinner last night, then I would not exist now but a *counterpart* of me would exist now, but very few philosophers are willing to follow Lewis here. In short, if we accept an ontology in which the world consists only of atoms and mereological sums of atoms (let us pretend for simplicity that all objects consist of atoms, and that atoms are indivisible), it will not be the case that that ontology contains all the *familiar* physical objects, and the only price one has had to pay for adopting the basic postulate of mereology (to the effect that, for any x and y, there is a mereological sum of x and y) is a certain counterintuitive *extravagance*; that is, it is not the case that one now has all the familiar objects (without having had to worry about principles of unity and persistence), and what one has done is to *add* certain unfamiliar objects to them, such as the mereological sum of my nose and the Eiffel Tower (an addition that might be thought justified on the grounds that it does *at least* provide us with a "clean," "simple" ontology that *includes* everything [physical] that we want to include). *Just* the familiar objects, the "ships and shoes and sealing-wax and cabbages and kings," are completely *missing* in this ontology. This ontology is, in fact, the ontology of *physics* (and only of an oversimplified physics, at that).

What alternatives are there, however, to "an ontology of time-slices of atoms (or of particles, or of fields and particles) and mereological sums thereof"? Kripke would say that I am not *identical* with the mereological sum of the atoms that are parts of me (or with the mereological sum of time-slices of atoms). I am a different thing from my matter, although I *consist* of my matter. I am a thing with different persistence conditions from my matter, and different identity conditions across possible worlds. I consist of certain matter, as things actually are, but had things been different, had I had pot roast for dinner last night, I would consist of different matter but I would be the very same person.[27]

Accept Kripke's point, however, and the idea that the ontology of basic physical entities and mereological sums includes all the familiar objects that we want to include has to be given up. Mereology is an elegant mathematical theory, but no mathematical theory can overcome the fact that there is no closed set of scientific objects that includes all the things that we quantify over—and find it indispensable to quantify over—in our actual life with our language.

Re the second argument: to say—as I, for one, do say—that no clear meaning at all has been given to the idea of "reducing" our ability to refer to something (for example, our ability to talk about cats and dogs) to the "nonsemantical," and that further, "deflationism" provides no account at all of this ability, is not at all to say that something "occult" is going on when we talk about cats and dogs. There are all sorts of nonreductive studies of various aspects of language acquisition and use in existence, none of them a *definition* of "talking about" in "nonsemantical" terms, but none of them an account of something "occult" either.

The very fact that no "naturalist" philosopher thinks that *geology* is "occult," even though the predicates used in geology cannot be reductively defined in the language of fundamental physics, gives the show away. What is really behind the invidious distinction between the "semantical" and the, so to speak, merely "geological" is that describing language use involves *normative* concepts: things we say are variously *true* and *false*, *justified* and *unjustified*, succeed in *referring* and fail to *refer*, *appropriate* and *inappropriate*, and so on. The fact is that naturalists regularly assume that if the normative cannot be eliminated or reduced to the nonnormative, then some "occult" realm of Values must be postulated. The possibility that goes missing here, as I remarked at the outset, is that an indicative sentence can be a *bona fide* statement without being a "description of reality." Developing this theme has to be the subject of a different set of essays.[28] But I cannot close without mentioning that the same missing possibility accounts for 1) the widespread failure of most philosophers to notice the inadequacy of Quinian definitions of logical validity[29]; and 2) the weird oscillation between nominalism and "Platonism" that we find in the philosophy of mathematics.

In sum, to the extent that the appeal of "naturalism" is based on *fear*, the fear in question seems to be a horror of the normative. In the case of logical positivism, there was a not-dissimilar horror, the horror that the slightest trace of realism about scientific objects was tantamount to the acceptance of "metaphysics." We got over that horror when we realized that talk of unobserved entities did not need either metaphysical interpretation or positivist reinterpretation. We need to learn that the same is true of normative language.

4

Naturalism Without Representationalism[1]

HUW PRICE

1. The Relevance of Science to Philosophy

What is philosophical naturalism? Most fundamentally, presumably, it is the view that natural science constrains philosophy, in the following sense. The concerns of the two disciplines are not simply disjoint, and science takes the lead where the two overlap. At the very least, then, to be a philosophical naturalist is to believe that philosophy is not simply a different enterprise from science, and that philosophy properly defers to science, where the concerns of the two disciplines coincide.

Naturalism as spare as this is by no means platitudinous. However, most opposition to naturalism in contemporary philosophy is not opposition to naturalism in this basic sense, but to a more specific view of the relevance of science to philosophy. Similarly on the pronaturalistic side. What most self-styled naturalists have in mind is the more specific view. As a result, I think, both sides of the contemporary debate pay insufficient attention to a different kind of philosophical naturalism—a different view of the impact of science on philosophy. This different view is certainly not new—it has been with us at least since Hume—but nor is it prominent in many contemporary debates.

In this paper I try to do something to remedy this deficit. I begin by making good the claim that the position commonly called naturalism is not a necessary corollary of naturalism in the basic sense outlined above.

71

There are two very different ways of taking science to be relevant to philosophy. And contrary, perhaps, to first appearances, the major implications of these two views for philosophy arise from a common starting point. There is a single kind of core problem, to which the two kinds of naturalism recommend very different sorts of answers.

I'll argue that the less well-known view is more fundamental than its rival, in a sense to be explained; and that in calling attention to the difference between the two, we call attention to a deep structural difficulty for the latter. I'll thus be defending philosophical naturalism in what I take to be its more fundamental form, while criticizing its popular contemporary manifestation.

Both the difficulty for the popular view and the conceptual priority of its unpopular rival turn on the foundational role of certain "semantic" or "representationalist" presuppositions in naturalism of the popular sort. This role is not well understood, in my view, but of considerable interest in its own right. (It deserves a more detailed examination than I can give it in this paper.) For present purposes, its importance lies in four facts. First, the presuppositions concerned are noncompulsory, and represent a crucial choice point for naturalism—reject them, and one thereby rejects naturalism of the popular variety. Second, the standpoint from which the choice is properly made is that of naturalism of the unpopular variety—this is the sense in which this kind of naturalism is conceptually prior to its more popular cousin. Third, the possibility of rejection of these suppositions is no mere idle threat; it is a corollary of some mainstream views in contemporary philosophy. And fourth, and potentially worst of all, the presuppositions concerned turn out to be doubtfully acceptable, by the standards of the kind of naturalism they themselves are supposed to underpin.

Concerning naturalism itself, then, my argument is something like this. To assess the prospects for philosophical naturalism, we need a clear sense of the task of philosophy, in the areas in which science might conceivably be relevant. Clarity about this matter reveals not only that the approach commonly called naturalism is not the only science-sensitive option for philosophy in these areas, but also that a different approach is the preeminent approach, in the various senses just outlined. As bad news for contemporary naturalists of the orthodox sort, this may sound like good news for contemporary nonnaturalists. But I hope it will be clear that my intentions are much more evenhanded. Many nonnaturalists share the representationalist presuppositions of their naturalist opponents, and in questioning those presuppositions, we question both sides of the debate they underpin. So I oppose both naturalism and non-naturalism as popularly understood, and favor a different kind of naturalism—a naturalism without representationalism.

2. Two Kinds of Naturalism

The popular kind of naturalism—the view often called simply "naturalism"—exists in both ontological and epistemological keys. As an ontological doctrine, it is the view that in some important sense, all there *is* is the world studied by science. As an epistemological doctrine, it is the view that all genuine knowledge is scientific knowledge.[2]

I'll call this view *object naturalism*. Though it is widely endorsed in contemporary philosophy, many of its supporters agree with some of its critics in thinking that it leads to some profound difficulties. The view implies that insofar as philosophy is concerned with the nature of objects and properties of various kinds, its concern is with something in the natural world, or with nothing at all. For there simply is nothing else. Perhaps there are very different ways of talking about the world-as-studied-by-science—different "modes of presentation" of aspects of the same natural reality. But the object of each kind of talk is an aspect of the world-as-studied-by-science, or else nothing at all. The difficulties stem from the fact that in many interesting cases it is hard to see what natural facts we could be talking about. Different people will offer different lists of these "hard problems"—common candidates include meaning, value, mathematical truth, causation and physical modality, and various aspects of mentality, for example—but it is almost an orthodoxy of contemporary philosophy, on both sides of the issue between naturalists and their opponents, that the list is nonempty.

More in a moment on these issues—*placement problems*, as I'll call them. Before we turn to such issues, I want to distinguish object naturalism from a second view of the relevance of science to philosophy. According to this second view, philosophy needs to begin with what science tells us *about ourselves.* Science tells us that we humans are natural creatures, and if the claims and ambitions of philosophy conflict with this view, then philosophy needs to give way. This is naturalism in the sense of Hume, then, and arguably Nietzsche.[3] I'll call it *subject naturalism.*

What is the relationship between object naturalism and subject naturalism? At first sight, the latter may seem no more than an obvious corollary of the former. Contemporary "naturalists"—object naturalists, in my terms—would surely insist that they are also subject naturalists. After

all, if all real entities are natural entities, we humans are surely natural
entities. But in my view, the relationship between the two approaches is
much more interesting than this. Subject naturalism comes first, in a very
important sense.

I want to defend the following claim:

Priority Thesis: Subject naturalism is theoretically prior to object naturalism, because the latter depends on validation from a subject naturalist perspective.

What do "priority" and "validation" mean in this context? As I noted
earlier, subject naturalism directs our attention to the issue of the scientific "respectability" of the claims and presuppositions of philosophy—
in particular, their compatibility with the recognition that we humans
are natural creatures. If the presuppositions of object naturalism turn out
to be suspect, from this self-reflective scientific standpoint, then subject
naturalism gives us reason to reject object naturalism. Subject naturalism
thus comes first, and could conceivably "invalidate" object naturalism.

In my view, this threat to object naturalism is very real. I'll also defend
this claim:

Invalidity Thesis: There are strong reasons for doubting whether object naturalism deserves to be "validated"—whether its presuppositions do survive subject naturalist scrutiny.

As advertised, my case for this claim will depend on the role of certain
"semantic" or "representationalist" presuppositions in the foundations of
object naturalism. The crucial role of such presuppositions is far from
obvious, however. To make it visible, we need to examine the structure
of the well-recognized hard cases for object naturalism, the cases I've
termed placement problems.

3. The Placement Issue

If all reality is ultimately natural reality, how are we to "place" moral
facts, mathematical facts, meaning facts, and so on? How are we to locate
topics of these kinds within a naturalistic framework, thus conceived? In
cases of this kind, we seem to be faced with a choice between forcing
the topic concerned into a category that for one reason or another seems
ill-shaped to contain it, or regarding it as at best second-rate—not a
genuine area of fact or knowledge.

One way to escape this dilemma is to reject the naturalism that produces it. If genuine knowledge need not be scientific knowledge, genuine facts not scientific facts, there is no need to try to squeeze the problem cases into naturalistic clothing. Thus placement problems provide the motivation for much contemporary opposition to naturalism in philosophy. However, there are two very different ways to reject the kind of naturalism that gives rise to these problems. One way is to be nonnaturalistic in the same ontological or epistemic keys—to be an object nonnaturalist, so to speak. The other way is to be naturalistic in a different key—to reject *object* naturalism in favor of a subject naturalist approach to the same theoretical problems.

At first sight, there seems to be no conceptual space for the latter view, at least in general, and at least if we want to avoid a universal subjectivism about all the hard cases. For subject naturalism rests on the fact that we humans are natural creatures, whereas the placement problems arise for topics that are at least not obviously human in nature. This is too quick, however. The possibility of a distinctive subject naturalist approach to the placement issues turns on the fact that, at least arguably, these problems *originate* as problems about human linguistic usage.

In fact, it turns out that there are two possible conceptions of the origins of placement problems—two conceptions of the "raw data" with which philosophy begins in such cases. On one conception, the problem begins with linguistic (or perhaps psychological) data; on the other, it begins with the objects themselves. These two conceptions are not often clearly distinguished, but the distinction turns out to be very important. As I'll explain, the priority of subject naturalism, and hence the vulnerability of object naturalism, rests on the thesis that the linguistic conception is the right one.

4. Where Do Placement Problems Begin?

On the face of it, a typical placement problem seeks to understand how some object, property, or fact can be a *natural* object, property, or fact. Ignoring for present purposes the distinction between objects, properties, and facts, the issue is thus how some thing, X, can be a *natural* thing— the sort of thing revealed by science (at least in principle).

How do such issues arise in philosophy? On one possible view, the starting point is the object itself. We are simply acquainted with X, and hence—in the light of a commitment to object naturalism—come to wonder how this thing-with-which-we-are-acquainted could be the kind of thing studied by science. On the other possible view, the starting point lies in human linguistic practices, broadly construed. Roughly, we note that humans (ourselves or others) employ the term "X" in language, or the concept X, in thought. In the light of a commitment to object naturalism, again, we come to wonder how what these speakers are thereby talking or thinking *about* could be the kind of thing studied by science.

Let us call these two views of the origin of the placement problem the *material conception* and the *linguistic conception*, respectively. In favor of the material conception, it might be argued that the placement problem for X is a problem about the *thing* X, not a problem about the *term* "X." In other words, it is the problem as to how to locate X itself in the natural world, not the problem about how to locate the term "X."

In favor of the linguistic conception, on the other hand, note that some familiar moves in the philosophical debates to which placement problems give rise simply don't make sense if we assume a material construal of the problem. Consider noncognitivism, which tries to avoid the placement problem by arguing that *talk* of Xs—that is, standard *use* of the term "X"—does not have a referential or descriptive function. Here, the claim is that in the light of a correct understanding of the *language* concerned, there is no *material* problem. Of course, noncognitivism might be mistaken in any particular case, but if the material view of the placement problem is right, it is not so much wrong as completely wrongheaded—a view that simply starts in the wrong place. Perhaps noncognitivism is wrongheaded in this way. But the fact that this is not a common view reveals widespread implicit acceptance of a linguistic conception of the placement issue.

This appeal to philosophical practice isn't meant to be conclusive, of course. Instead, I'm going to proceed as follows. For the moment, I'll simply assume that the linguistic conception is correct, and explore its consequences for object naturalism. (I'll remind readers at several points that my conclusions depend on this assumption.) At the end of the paper I'll come back to the question whether the assumption is compulsory—whether object naturalism can evade my critical conclusions by adopting the material conception. I'll argue, albeit somewhat tentatively, that this is not a live option, and hence that my earlier conclusions cannot be sidestepped in this way.

5. The Semantic Ladder

If the linguistic conception is correct, then placement problems are initially problems about human linguistic behavior (or perhaps about human thought). What turns such a concern into an issue about something else—about value, mathematical reality, causation, or whatever? The answer to this question was implicit above, when our attention shifted from the *term* to what it is *about*. The shift relies on what we may call the *representationalist* assumption. Roughly, this is the assumption that the *linguistic* items in question "stand for" or "represent" something *nonlinguistic* (at least in general—let's leave aside for present purposes the special case in which the subject matter is also linguistic). This assumption grounds our shift in focus from the *term* "X" or *concept* X to its assumed *object*, X.

At first sight, however, the required assumption may seem trivial. Isn't it a truism that "X" refers to X? Isn't this merely the referential analogue of the fact that "Snow is white" is true if and only if snow is white? The familiarity of these principles masks a serious confusion, in my view. True, the move in question is in one sense a familiar semantic descent. A semantic relation—reference, if we are dealing with terms, or truth, if we are dealing with sentences—is providing the "ladder" that leads us from an issue about language to an issue about nonlinguistic reality. But it is vital to see that in the present case, the move involves a real shift of theoretical focus, a real change of subject matter. So this is a *genuine* logical descent, then, and not a mere reversal of Quine's deflationary "semantic ascent." Quine's semantic ascent never really leaves the ground. Quine himself puts it like this: "By calling the sentence ["Snow is white"] true, we call snow white. The truth predicate is a device of disquotation."[4] So Quine's deflationary semantic ladder never really takes us "up," whereas the present semantic ladder does need to take us "down."

If we begin with Quine's deflationary semantic notions, in other words, then talking about the *referent* of the term "X," or the *truth* of the sentence "X is F," is just another way of talking about the *object*, X. So if our original question was really about language, and we rephrase the issue in these semantic terms, we've simply changed the subject. We haven't traversed the semantic ladder, but simply taken up *a different issue*, talking in what Carnap called the formal mode about objects, rather than talking about language. On this deflationary view, then, object naturalism commits a fallacy of equivocation, a kind of mention—use fallacy, in fact[5]—on the way to its formulation of what it takes to be the central issue.

This point is easy to overlook, because we run up and down these semantic ladders so easily. But if Quine is right, the reason the climbs are so effortless is that the ladders lead us nowhere. In the present case, we do need to get somewhere. If we begin with a linguistic conception of the origins of the placement issues—if we see these issues as initially questions about linguistic usage—then it takes a genuine shift of theoretical focus to get us to an issue about the nature of nonlinguistic objects. If the shift is to be mediated by semantic properties or relations of some kind, they must be substantial properties, in the following sense. They must be such that in ascribing such properties to a term or sentence we are making some theoretical claim about the linguistic items concerned, rather than simply using those items to make a claim about something else.

True, these properties must also be such as to allow us to make the transition to an issue about objects. Our theoretical focus must be led from the issue about the terms and sentences to an issue about their assumed semantic objects or values. For the object naturalist's conception of the resulting program, moreover, it is vital that this transition track the disquotational schema. (How else could a concern with the use of the term "X" lead us to an interest in X itself?) My point is that unless there is more to the semantic notions than simply disquotation, the starting point is not genuinely linguistic, and so there is no transition at all. (One might argue that this is good news, because the placement issue begins at the material level in any case. But for the moment we are assuming the linguistic conception of the origin of the problem, and this response is therefore excluded.)

Given a linguistic view of the placement issue, then, substantial, non-deflationary semantic notions turn out to play a critical theoretical role in the foundations of object naturalism. Without such notions, there can be no subsequent issue about the natural "place" of entities such as meanings, causes, values, and the like. Object naturalism thus rests on substantial theoretical assumptions about what we humans do with language—roughly, the assumption that substantial "word–world" semantic relations are a part of the best scientific account of our use of the relevant terms.

However, these assumptions lie in the domain of subject naturalism. Moreover, as the conceptual possibility of deflationism already illustrates, they are noncompulsory; more on this in a moment. Hence my Priority Thesis: given a linguistic conception of the origin of placement problems, subject naturalism is theoretically prior to object naturalism, and object naturalism depends on validation from a subject naturalist perspective.

6. Should Object Naturalism Be Validated? Three Reasons for Pessimism

It is one thing to establish a need, another to show that there are serious grounds for doubting whether that need can be met. However, it seems to me that there are actually strong grounds for doubting whether object naturalism can be satisfactorily validated, in the above sense. These grounds are of three kinds.

A. The Threat of Semantic Deflationism

I have already noted that deflationism about truth and reference blocks an object naturalist's access to the kind of semantic ladder needed to transform a theoretical question about terms into a question about their assumed objects. Given the attractions of deflationism, this is clearly grounds for concern, from an object naturalist's point of view.

It is worth emphasizing two further points. First, deflationism itself is clearly of a subject naturalist character. It offers a broadly scientific hypothesis about what linguistic creatures like us "do" with terms such as "true" and "refers"—what role these terms play in our linguistic lives. Of course, the use of these terms itself comprises the basis of one particularly interesting placement problem. So semantic deflationism *exemplifies* a subject naturalist approach to a particular placement problem— an approach that seeks to explain the *use* of the semantic terms in question—as well as providing a general obstacle to an object naturalist construal of placement problems at large.

Second, it is worth noting in passing how the distinctions in play at this point enable semantic deflationism, to avoid Paul Boghossian's charge that any such view is inconsistent.[6] Boghossian argues that irrealism about semantic notions is incoherent, because irrealism involves, precisely, a *denial* that the term or sentence in question has semantic properties (a referent, or truth-conditions). If this characterization of irrealism is indeed mandatory, then Boghossian seems right. Irrealism *presupposes* semantic notions, and hence the denial in question is incoherent in the case of the semantic terms themselves.

However, the point turns on the fact that so construed, irrealism relies on the kind of theoretical framework provided by the representational view of language. So long as a semantic deflationist simply *rejects* this theoretical framework, her position is not incoherent. Of course, one might insist that the resulting position no longer deserves to be called irrealism, but this is merely a terminological issue. The important point is that it is indisputably deflationary. A deflationist can consistently offer a use-explanatory account of semantic terms, while saying nothing of theoretical weight about whether these terms "refer," or "have truth-conditions."

The answer to Boghossian's challenge to deflationism thus depends on a distinction between *denying in one's theoretical voice* that these terms refer or have truth-conditions (which Boghossian is right to point out that a deflationist cannot do); and *being silent in one's theoretical voice* about whether these terms refer or have truth-conditions. A deflationist can, indeed must, do the latter, having couched her theoretical claims about the terms concerned in other terms entirely—and having insisted, *qua* deflationist, that the semantic notions do no interesting causal-explanatory work.

I'll return to Boghossian's argument in a moment, for in my view it does comprise a problem for my object naturalist opponents. For the moment, what matters is that it does not provide an obstacle to a well-formulated deflationism.

B. Stich's Problem

We have seen that in the light of a linguistic conception of the origins of the placement problem, semantic deflationism is incompatible with object naturalism. Insofar as deflationism is an attractive view, in other words, the "validation" of object naturalism must remain in doubt. But rejecting deflationism does not necessarily solve the object naturalist's problems. One way to appreciate this is to adapt the considerations discussed by Stephen Stich in Chapter 1 of *Deconstructing the Mind* (New York: Oxford University Press, 1996). In effect, Stich argues that even a nondeflationary scientific account of reference is unlikely to be determinate enough to do the work that object naturalism requires. Stich's own immediate concern is with eliminativism, and thus (in linguistic mode) with issues as to whether terms such as "belief" refer at all. He argues that so long as we retain a linguistic conception of our starting point in metaphysics, these questions inevitably become hostage to indeterminacies in our theory of reference. Evidently, if Stich is right, then the problem is not confined to eliminativism. It affects the issue "What is belief?" for example, as much as it affects the issue "Are there any beliefs?" So realist as well as antirealist responses to the placement problem are equally afflicted.

Stich himself responds by disavowing the linguistic conception of the *explanandum*. We'll return to the question as to whether this is really an option. For the moment, I simply help myself to Stich's useful discussion of these issues, in support of the following tentative conclusion. Even setting aside the threat of deflationism, it is very far from clear that a "scientific" account of semantic relations is going to provide what we need, in order to turn an interesting theoretical issue about *terms* ("causation," "belief," "good," and so on) into an interesting issue about *objects*.

C. Is Object Naturalism Coherent?

We have seen that if placement problems originate at the linguistic level, substantial semantic notions are needed to transform a question about linguistic usage into a question about nonlinguistic objects. Object naturalism thus presupposes substantial semantic properties or relations of some kind. The two previous reasons for doubting whether object naturalism is entitled to this presupposition turned first on the possibility of deflationism, which denies that semantic properties are load-bearing in the appropriate sense; and second on the possibility that even a nondeflationary scientific account of reference might be too loosely constrained to be useful as the required semantic ladder.

Now to an even more serious difficulty. In view of the fact that object naturalism presupposes the semantic notions in this way, it is doubtful whether these notions themselves can consistently be investigated in an object naturalist spirit. Naturalism of this kind seems committed to the empirical contingency of semantic relations. For any given term or sentence, it must be to some extent an empirical matter whether, and if so to what, that term refers; whether, and if so where, it has a truthmaker. However, it seems impossible to make sense of this empirical attitude with respect to the semantic terms themselves.

Part of the difficulty turns on Boghossian's objection to semantic irrealism. In that context, the problem was that if semantic notions are presupposed in the issue between realists and irrealists—for example, if the realist/irrealist issue is taken to *be* that as to whether the terms and sentences of some domain refer, or have truth-conditions—then irrealism about these notions themselves is incoherent. Here, the problem is as follows. The object naturalist's project requires in general that irrealism be treated as live empirical possibility; but Boghossian's point shows that the object naturalist cannot adopt this attitude to the semantic terms themselves.

Boghossian takes the point to amount to a transcendental argument for a nonnaturalist realism about semantic content. In my view, however, it is better seen as a pronaturalist—pro*subject* naturalist—point, in that it exposes what is inevitably a nonnaturalistic presupposition in the leading contemporary conception of what is involved in taking science seriously in philosophy. Of course, the possibility of this interpretation depends on the fact that there is a consistent alternative naturalism, which walks away from the usual semantically grounded conception of the issue. (In a different way, it also depends on a linguistic conception of the starting point, a conception we are assuming at this point, and a conception to which Boghossian himself is obviously committed.)

It might seem implausible that there could be a problem here that is specific to object naturalism. After all, I have suggested that it is an empirical possibility that the subject naturalist standpoint might not yield the kind of substantial semantic relations required for object naturalism. Isn't this same possibility all that object naturalism needs to make sense of the possibility of irrealism about semantics, in its sense?

No. The empirical possibility we have discussed is not that subject naturalism will discover that there are no semantic properties of the right sort, but simply that it will find no reason to say that there are. This is the distinction I appealed to above, in explaining how deflationism escapes Boghossian's trap. The subject naturalist's basic task is to account for the use of various terms—among them, the semantic terms themselves—in the lives of natural creatures in a natural environment. The distinction just mentioned turns on the possibility that in completing this task, the subject naturalist might simply find no need for an explanatory category of semantic properties and relations. (At no point would she need to say that the term "refer" does or does not refer to anything, for example, except in the deflationary, nontheoretical sense.) Of course, from the object naturalist's perspective this looks like an investigation as to whether there are semantic properties, but the subject naturalist has no reason to construe it that way. Indeed, she has a very good reason *not* to construe it that way, if, as Boghossian has argued, that construal is simply incoherent.

The issue of the coherence of the object naturalist approach to the semantic terms is subtle and difficult, and I don't pretend to have made a case that the difficulty is conclusive. What I hope to have established is something weaker. A naturalist has neither need nor automatic entitlement to a substantial account of semantic relations between words or thoughts and the rest of the natural world—no automatic entitlement, because by naturalism's own lights, it is at best an empirical matter; and no need, because there are ways of being naturalist that don't depend on any such assumption. Nevertheless, the stronger thesis, the incoherency thesis, seems to me both fascinating and plausible, and I want briefly to mention another way of fleshing out the difficulty.

If there is a coherent object naturalist account of the semantic relations, then as we noted earlier, the object naturalist will want to say that the right account is not *a priori*—there is more than one coherent possibility, and the issue is in part an empirical matter. Let's consider just two of the coherent possibilities—two rival accounts of what reference is, for example. Account one says that reference is the natural relation R^*, account two that it is the natural relation R^{**}. Thus, apparently, we have two incompatible views as to what reference actually is.

But do we? Let's think a little more closely about what each of these views claims. The first account claims that the ordinary term "Reference" picks out, or refers to, the relation R^*—in other words, by its own lights, that

"Reference" stands in the relation R^* to the relation R^*.

The second account claims that the ordinary term "Reference" picks out, or refers to, the relation R^{**}—in other words, by its own lights, that

"Reference" stands in the relation R^{**} to the relation R^{**}.

Are these claims incompatible? Not at all. The term "Reference" might very well stand in these two different relations to two different things, even if we allow (as proponents of both views will want to insist) that, in the case of each relation singly, no term could stand in that relation to both.

Again, the problem stems from the fact that the object naturalist is trying to ask a question that renders its own presuppositions fluid. There is no fixed question, with a range of answers, but, so to speak, a different question for each answer. I leave as an exercise another puzzle of this kind. It is multiple choice:

The option selected below is:
A. Option A [ ]
B. Option B [ ]
C. Option C [ ]
D. None of the above [ ]

The problem is not that there is no right answer, but that there are too many right answers.[7] Again, the upshot seems to be that in the light of the role of semantic notions in the object naturalist's conception of the task of philosophy, that task does not make sense with respect to the semantic terms themselves.

7. Does the Problem Lie with the Linguistic Conception of the *Explanandum?*

As I have emphasized, the above discussion has assumed a linguistic conception of the origins of the placement problem. Is this an optional assumption? Can a material conception get object naturalism off the hook? I close with two reasons for skepticism on this point.

A. The Cat Is Out of the Bag

It is clear that the linguistic conception of the placement issue is already in play. I noted earlier that to treat noncognitivism as an option in these debates is to commit oneself to a linguistic conception of the origin of the problem. The threat to object naturalism takes off from this point, noting that the representationalist assumption is noncompulsory—that there are other possible theoretical approaches to language in which semantic notions play no significant role. We have thus been offered the prospect of a (subject) naturalistic account of the relevant aspects of human talk and thought, from the perspective of which the material question ("What are Xs?") simply doesn't arise.[8] At this stage, the only way for object naturalists to regain control of the ball is to *defend* the representationalist assumption (a project fraught with difficulty, for the reasons noted above).

Couldn't an object naturalism challenge the current conception of the starting point? What is wrong with Stich's proposal, that we simply begin at the material level and do metaphysics without semantic crutches? What is wrong with it, I think, is that it amounts to the proposal that we should simply *ignore* the possibility that philosophy might have something to learn from naturalistic—*subject* naturalistic—reflection on the things that we humans do with language. (If this seems controversial, note that it would be to ignore the possibility of noncognitivism.) So it is a radically antinaturalistic move. For someone who takes science seriously, the only route to object naturalism is the hard one: to concede that the problem begins at the linguistic level, and to defend the representationalist view.

B. Semantic Notions Are Part of the Toolkit of Modern Metaphysics

The second consideration deserves a much more detailed discussion than I can give it here. Briefly, however, it seems that semantic notions such as reference and truth have become instruments in the investigative program of contemporary metaphysics. It has become common practice to identify one's objects of interest in semantic ways—as truthmakers or referents, say, or more generally as "realizers" of semantic roles.

However, the relevance of this observation about philosophical practice is far from straightforward. One of the difficulties is to decide which of the many uses of such semantic notions are "substantial" theoretical uses, and which can be regarded in a merely Quinean fashion—convenient but theoretically uncommitted uses of deflationary semantic terms. For the reasons discussed earlier, the use of deflationary semantic notions in metaphysics is not incompatible with a material conception of the origins of the placement issue. But if more substantial notions are in play, then the linguistic domain seems to play a correspondingly more significant role. Claims about language come to play a role analogous to that of observational data in science, with the semantic relations supporting inferences to an unobserved reality. The enterprise thus becomes committed to a linguistic conception of its starting point.

There are many strands in this linguistic retooling of contemporary metaphysics—the "Linguistic Return," as we might call it. One significant strand runs as follows, I think. In David Lewis's influential conception of theoretical identification in science,[9] objects of interest are identified as occupiers of causal roles. If the theoretical term "X" is defined in this way, we know what to do to answer the question "What is X?" We experiment in the laboratory of the world, adjusting this, twiddling that, until we discover just what it is that does the causal job our theory assigns to X.

In the view of many, however, Lewis's program is fit not just for science but metaphysics as well.[10] Indeed, some who think this would reject the suggestion, implicit in my formulation, that metaphysics is something different from science. But there is one difference at least. In metaphysics, there is no guarantee that our objects of interest will be the kinds of things that have *causal* roles. We might be interested in numbers, or values, or indeed in causation itself, and for all of these things it is at least controversial whether they can be identified as the cause of this, the effect of that.[11]

So in the global program, the place of causation must be taken by something else. What else could it be? It seems to me that there are two possibilities. One is that causal roles get replaced by semantic roles. In this case, the procedure for answering a question of the form "What is X?" is analogous to the one described above, except that the aim of our fiddling and twiddling—conceptual, now, rather than experimental—is to discover, say, to what the term "X" *refers*, or what *makes true* the claim that X is F.

That's the first possibility—that semantic relations play the same substantial role in the general program as causal relations played in the original program. If so, then the upshot is as we have seen. Language has become the starting point for metaphysics, and the resulting position is vulnerable in the ways described above.

The second possibility is that *nothing* specific replaces causation. It simply depends on the particular case, on what the Ramsey-Lewis method turns out to tell us about the X in question. Semantic terms may figure in the description of the task, but on this view they are no more than deflationary. We say, "X is the thing that makes this Ramsey-sentence true," but this is just a convenient way of doing what we could do by saying "X is the thing such that . . ." and then going on to *use* the Ramsey-sentence in question.

I think that this second version does avoid essential use of nondeflationary semantic notions, and is hence compatible with a material conception of our starting point in metaphysics. The problem is that it thereby cuts itself off from any general argument for (object) naturalism, of a kind that would parallel Lewis's argument for physicalism about the mental.[12] Lewis's argument relies on a premise to the effect that all causation is physical causation—the assumption of "the explanatory adequacy of physics," as Lewis puts it. Without such a premise, clearly, there is nothing to take us from the conclusion that a mental state M has a particular causal role to the conclusion that M is a physical state. The problem for the second of the two versions of the generalized Lewisean program is that without any single thing to play the role that causation plays in the restricted program, there can be no analogue of this crucial premise in support of a generalized argument for physicalism.

Thus it seems to me that object naturalists face a dilemma. If they appeal to substantial semantic relations, they have some prospect of an argument for naturalism, couched in terms of those relations—for example, an argument that all truths have natural truthmakers. In this case, however, they are implicitly committed to a linguistic conception of the "raw data" for these investigations, and face the problems identified earlier. If they don't appeal to substantial semantic relations, they avoid these difficulties, but lose the theoretical resources with which to formulate a general argument for naturalism, conceived on the object naturalist model.

Without the protection of such an argument, the difficult opponent is not someone who agrees to play the game in material mode but bats for nonnaturalism, defending a primitive plurality of ontological realms. The difficult opponent is the naturalist who takes advantage of a nonrepresentationalist theoretical perspective to avoid the material mode altogether. If such an opponent can explain why natural creatures in a natural environment come to *talk* in these plural ways—of "truth," "value," "meaning," "causation," and all the rest—what puzzle remains? What debt does philosophy now owe to science?

Summing up, it is doubtful whether an object naturalist can avoid a linguistic conception of the placement issue, and thereby escape the difficulties identified earlier. Some versions of object naturalism help themselves to the linguistic conception in any case, in order to put semantic relations to work in the service of metaphysics. In other cases, the inescapability of the linguistic conception turns on the fact that it is always available to the object naturalist's subject naturalist opponent, as the basis of an alternative view of the task of philosophy in these cases. The object naturalist's instinct is always to appeal to the representational character of language to bring the issue back to the material level; but this, as we have seen, is a recipe for grave discomfort.

8. Natural Plurality

Linguistically construed, the placement problem stems from a striking multiplicity in ordinary language, a puzzling plurality of topics of talk. Given a naturalistic conception of speakers, the addition of a representationalist conception of speech makes the object naturalist's ontological interpretation of the placement problem almost irresistible. Term by term, sentence by sentence, topic by topic, the representationalist's semantic ladder leads us from language to the world, from words to their worldly objects. Somehow, the resulting multiplicity of kinds of entities— values, modalities, meanings, and the rest—needs to be accommodated within the natural realm. To what else, after all, could natural speakers be related by natural semantic relations?

Without a representationalist conception of the talk, however, the puzzle takes a very different form. It remains in the linguistic realm, a puzzle about a plurality of *ways of talking*, of forms of human linguistic behavior. The challenge is now simply to explain in naturalistic terms how creatures like us come to talk in these various ways. This is a matter of explaining what role the different language games play in our lives— what differences there are between the functions of talk of value and the functions of talk of electrons, for example.[13] This certainly requires plurality in the world, but of a familiar kind, in a familiar place. Nobody expects human behavior to be anything other than highly complex. Without representationalism, the joints between topics remain joints between kinds of behavior, and don't need to be mirrored in ontology of any other kind.

For present purposes, what matters is, on the one hand, that this is a recognizably naturalistic project; and on the other, that it is a very different project from that of most contemporary philosophical naturalists. I have argued that the popular view (object naturalism) is in trouble by its own lights, in virtue of its semantic presuppositions. The availability of the subject naturalist alternative makes clear that the problems of object naturalism are not problems for naturalism *per se*—not a challenge to the view that in some areas, philosophy properly defers to science.

We began with the relevance of science to philosophy. Let's finish with the relevance of science to science itself. Object naturalism gives science not just center stage but the whole stage, taking scientific knowledge to be the only knowledge there is (at least in some sense). Subject naturalism suggests that science might properly take a more modest view of its own importance. It imagines a scientific discovery that science is not all there is—that science is just one thing among many[14] that we do with "representational" discourse. If so, then the semantic presuppositions of object naturalism are bad science, a legacy of an insufficiently naturalistic philosophy. The story then has the following satisfying moral. If we do science better in philosophy, we'll be less inclined to think that science is all there is to do.

∼ II
MIND

5

Naturalism in the Philosophy of Mind

JOHN MCDOWELL

1) Modern epistemology is beset by distinctive anxieties. We can base an understanding of them on a remark of Wilfrid Sellars: "In characterizing an episode or a state as that of *knowing*, we are not giving an empirical description of that episode or state; we are placing it in the logical space of reasons, of justifying and being able to justify what one says."[1] Sellars implies that to say how an episode or state is placed in the space of reasons is not to give an empirical description of it, and I think that is infelicitous. A better way to put the thought might be to say, as Sellars almost does elsewhere, that epistemology is vulnerable to a naturalistic fallacy.[2] On a familiar modern understanding of nature, a contrast opens between saying how something is placed in the space of reasons—a logical space that is organized by justificatory relations between its inhabitants—and saying how something is placed in nature. The contrast is such as to suggest that the content of concepts that belong in the space of reasons, such as the concept of knowledge, cannot be captured in terms of concepts that belong in the contrasting logical space, the space of placement in nature.

The conception of nature that yields this contrast is one whose origins lie in the development of modern science. The contrast Sellars implicitly appeals to was not available before modern times. This can help us understand why modernity brings with it a new tone, distinctively panicky and obsessive, for philosophical reflection about knowledge.

91

Consider how Aristotle or a medieval Aristotelian would have conceived the relation between the idea of knowledge and the idea of the natural. For such a thinker, the capacities that equip human beings to acquire knowledge could be, as such, natural powers, and the results of their exercise could be natural states of affairs. Not that those premodern thinkers were innocent of the connection Sellars insists on, between the idea of knowing and ideas of justification—as if premodern people could not entertain the thought that becomes so pregnant in modern epistemology, that knowledge is a normative status. But they did not feel a tension between the idea that knowledge is a normative status and the idea of an exercise of natural powers. Before the modern era, it would not have been intelligible to fear a naturalistic fallacy in epistemology.

But the rise of modern science has made available a conception of nature that makes the warning intelligible. The natural sciences, as we now conceive them, do not look for an organization for their subject matter in which one item is displayed as, say, justified in the light of another item. (This is one interpretation of the slogan that natural science is value-free.) It is tempting to identify nature with the subject matter of the natural sciences so conceived. And now the contrast Sellars draws can set an agenda for philosophy.

Some followers of Sellars, notably Richard Rorty, put the contrast as one between the space of reasons and the space of *causes*.[3] But I think it is better to set the space of reasons not against the space of causes but against the space of subsumption under, as we say, natural law. Unlike Rorty's construal of the contrast, this version does not preempt the possibility that reasons might *be* causes. We need not see the idea of causal linkages as the exclusive property of natural-scientific thinking.[4]

If we conceive nature in such a way that delineating something's natural character contrasts with placing something in the space of reasons, we can no longer take in stride the idea that powers to acquire knowledge are part of our natural endowment. Knowing, as a case of occupying a normative status, can no longer be seen as a natural phenomenon. And now it is easy for knowing to seem mysterious. It is no use expanding our conception of what is real beyond what is natural, if the effect is to make it seem that acquiring knowledge must be a supernatural feat. So with the new conception of nature, the knowing subject threatens to withdraw from the natural world. That is one way in which it comes to look as if philosophical epistemology needs to reconnect the knowing subject with the rest of reality.

2) I began with epistemology, but parallel considerations extend into the philosophy of mind in general. It is not just knowing that threatens to

be extruded from nature on the basis of the contrast between nature and the space of reasons. Sellars says that characterizing something as a case of *knowledge* is placing it in the logical space of reasons. Compare Donald Davidson's claim that our talk of *propositional attitudes* is intelligible only in the context of "the constitutive ideal of rationality."[5] We could reformulate Davidson's thesis in Sellarsian terms: the concepts of believing, desiring, and so forth, are understood only in the framework of the space of reasons.

And Davidson's thesis is not idiosyncratic. It has, for instance, an obvious affinity with Daniel Dennett's claim that intentionality is in view only from the intentional stance, which organizes its subject matter within a framework put in place by a postulate of rationality.[6] We could reformulate Dennett's position using Sellars's phrase "the logical space of reasons" or Davidson's phrase "the constitutive ideal of rationality."[7] There is an evident resonance with the tradition in which *Verstehen* is distinguished from *Erklären*.

So Sellars's thought about knowledge generalizes into a thought about propositional attitudes. In that case, we can expect the epistemological implications of Sellars's contrast between nature and the space of reasons to be mirrored in implications for our thinking about all of sapient mental life, not just knowledge.[8] Modern epistemology sees itself as under an obligation to reconnect the knowing subject with a natural world from which it seems to have withdrawn. Much modern philosophy of mind sees itself as under a parallel obligation to reintegrate the thinking subject into a natural world from which it has come to seem alien.

Rorty famously urges that the supposed gulf-bridging obligation of epistemology is an illusion. Anyone sympathetic to this conviction of Rorty's should have a similar suspicion of much modern philosophy of mind.

3) I have suggested that knowledge and intentionality can be in view only in the framework of the space of reasons.[9] When Sellars warns of a naturalistic fallacy, he is implying that the structure of the space of reasons is *sui generis*, by comparison with the kind of structure that the natural sciences find in nature. It is intelligible that the resulting sense that knowledge and thought are *sui generis*, by comparison with what can present itself as a compelling conception of the natural, should generate metaphysical anxieties about them, which crystallize in a felt threat of supernaturalism.

Now we can avoid those anxieties if we can entitle ourselves to count thinking and knowing as natural phenomena after all, even though Sellars's suggestion raises a question about how they can be. I want to distinguish two ways of undertaking such a project. The first accepts the equation of nature with the realm of law. The idea is that the organization of the space of reasons is not, as Sellars suggests, alien to the kind of structure natural science discovers in the world. No doubt relations of warrant or justification are not visibly present, as such, in nature as the paradigmatic natural sciences depict it. But according to this approach, we can display the concepts of warrant or justification as not, after all, foreign to the natural on that conception. So thinking and knowing can after all be revealed as natural phenomena, even on that conception of what it is for a phenomenon to be natural.

On one version of this approach, the idea is that the structure of the space of reasons can be *reduced* to something else, which is already unproblematically natural on the modern conception. On another version, one might aim to reveal concepts that work in the space of reasons as themselves, after all, directly serving to place things in the realm of law. The details do not matter. The essential point is that this approach, whether reductively undertaken or not, takes Sellars's starting point to be a mistake. Sellars contrasts the logical space of subsumption under law with the logical space within which the concept of knowledge operates. This is a contrast between the realm of law and the realm of freedom, to put it in a way that makes Sellars's Kantian roots explicit. Against that, this first kind of naturalism holds that we can continue to equate nature with the realm of law but reject the Sellarsian suggestion that nature so conceived cannot be a home for knowing and thinking subjects.

This kind of naturalism would be well motivated if it were the only way to avoid supernaturalism about knowing and thinking. But there is an alternative, still within the project of representing knowing and thinking as natural phenomena. In a Kantian spirit, we can refuse to accept that the structure of the realm of freedom can be naturalized in the sense of the first approach—that is, insist that Sellars's contrast is well-taken—but disown a commitment to supernaturalism by holding that what the modern scientific revolution yielded was clarity about the realm of law, and that is not the same as clarity *about nature*. Sellars's contrast is between the space of reasons and the realm of law, and it need not imply that the space of reasons is alien to the natural.

To avoid conceiving thinking and knowing as supernatural, we should stress that thinking and knowing are aspects of our lives. The concept of a life is the concept of the career of a living thing, and hence obviously the concept of something natural. But there are aspects of our lives whose description requires concepts that function in the space of reasons. We are rational animals. Our lives are patterned in ways that are recognizable only in an inquiry framed within the space of reasons. On these lines, we can see thinking and knowing as belonging to our mode of living, even though we conceive them as phenomena that can come into view only within a *sui generis* space of reasons. Thinking and knowing are part of our way of being animals. Thus the fact that we are knowers and thinkers does not reveal us as strangely bifurcated, with a foothold in the animal kingdom—surely part of nature—and a mysterious separate involvement in an extranatural realm of rational connections.

The first approach—a restrictive naturalism—aims to naturalize the concepts of thinking and knowing by forcing the conceptual structure in which they belong into the framework of the realm of law. This second approach—a liberal naturalism—does not accept that to reveal thinking and knowing as natural, we need to integrate into the realm of law the frame within which the concepts of thinking and knowing function. All we need is to stress that they are concepts of occurrences and states in our lives.

This liberal naturalism enables us, like medieval Aristotelians, to take in stride the idea that our capacities to acquire knowledge are natural powers. But unlike medieval Aristotelians, we can combine that idea with a clear appreciation of the *sui generis* character of the conceptual framework within which the concept of a capacity to acquire knowledge operates. Similarly, when we generalize Sellars's point, for the concepts of propositional attitudes, we can acknowledge a genuine achievement of the modern scientific revolution, in firmly separating natural-scientific understanding from the sort of understanding achieved by situating what is understood in the space of reasons. We can accept that concepts that subserve the latter kind of understanding, such as the concepts of knowledge and the propositional attitudes, cannot be captured in terms that belong in the logical space of natural-scientific understanding. So Sellars is right that there is a risk of fallacy. But when he suggests that what we risk is a *naturalistic* fallacy, he implies that the logical space of natural-scientific understanding can be equated with the logical space of nature. And we can avert the threat of supernaturalism by rejecting that equation.

For liberal naturalism, the significance of getting the idea of the realm of law into clear focus is simply to isolate the associated mode of intelligibility. There is no implication that concepts of the natural are restricted to concepts that subserve that mode of intelligibility. Rejecting that implication enables us to see the philosophical anxieties I have been considering as groundless, somewhat as Rorty urges. But this exorcism of philosophy is combined with acknowledging the *sui generis* character of the concepts of thinking and knowing. If we see how easy it is to suppose that getting the idea of the realm of law into clear focus is getting the idea of nature into clear focus, we can have a lively appreciation of how those philosophical anxieties arise, even combined with an immunity to them.

4) Both restrictive and liberal naturalism aim to avoid supernaturalism by finding a way to see knowing and thinking as natural phenomena. That sets them apart from a different style of response to Sellars's contrast, exemplified by Rorty's attitude to epistemology. Rorty's reading of traditional epistemology pivots on Sellars's contrast. The concept of knowledge works only in the space of reasons, and the space of reasons is *sui generis* in comparison with nature on the restrictive conception. So a restrictive naturalism about knowledge is ruled out. But for Rorty the natural is what figures on the other side of Sellars's contrast, and that obliterates, for him, the very possibility of a liberal naturalism about knowledge.[10]

With both types of naturalism unavailable, Rorty has no option but to deny that knowing is a natural phenomenon. As Rorty sees it, trying to cast knowing as a natural phenomenon is, precisely, the pervasive defect of traditional epistemology. The result of the attempt is that philosophers try to make the quite different sorts of relations that organize the subject matter of natural-scientific investigation do duty for the relations of justification or warrant that alone provide the proper context for talk of knowledge. Traditional epistemology thus commits exactly the fallacy Sellars warns against. It conceives knowing as a syndrome in "the physiology of the understanding."[11] To avoid this, Rorty suggests that we should not conceive knowledge as a natural phenomenon. Of course that is not to say we should conceive it as a supernatural phenomenon. Instead, Rorty urges that we stop thinking of knowledge as a phenomenon—a feature of actuality—at all, and shift to talking about the social role of attributions of knowledge.

I have urged a parallel between Sellars's thought about knowledge and a thought about intentionality expressed in different ways by Davidson and Dennett. So there is room for a view about intentionality like Rorty's view about knowledge—a denial that talk of intentionality deals with natural phenomena. Curiously enough, Rorty himself does not occupy this position. For Rorty, thoughts and even meanings are, if anything, posits in a naturalistic psychology, where "naturalistic" marks a contrast with the normativity imported by talk of the space of reasons.[12] I hesitate to identify an occupant of the position that mirrors Rorty's view of knowledge with a denial that there are natural phenomena of intention-ality.[13] Perhaps there is a whiff of it in the aspect of Dennett's thinking that attracts the accusation of instrumentalism.[14]

I think Rorty's reading of traditional epistemology has much to be said for it. Rorty is very convincing on how useless it is to try to make re-lations of the sort that organize the realm of law do duty for relations of warrant. Given that, he makes it look compulsory not to think of knowl-edge as a natural phenomenon. But this merely reflects the fact that he does not consider a liberal naturalism. Liberal naturalism is immune to Rorty's attack on the confusions of traditional epistemology. And the same failure of compulsoriness would infect a structural analogue of Rorty's line of thought, if anyone wanted to produce one, yielding the analogous conclusion that intentionality is not a natural phenomenon.

5) I have stressed that a clear conception of the realm of law was a modern achievement. What underlies a familiar philosophical anxiety about knowing and thinking is the ease with which this conception can be equated with a conception of the natural. That threatens to extrude knowing and thinking from nature, given that the concepts of knowing and thinking belong in a logical space that contrasts with the space of subsumption under law.

Consider now an early stage in the development of modern science. Imagine a dawning sense that the concepts of knowing and thinking are special, by comparison with the concepts that figure in the emerging natural sciences. Such a sense will have begun to influence reflection about the mental before there was a clear appreciation of what it is about the concepts of the mental that makes them special—before there was a clear appreciation of what comes into focus in Sellars as the contrast between the space of reasons and the space of natural-scientific under-standing.

This intuition of specialness reflects a conception, putatively of the natural, that, when fully in focus, works to exclude the mental. But the intuition will have been operative before that fact was clear. And before that fact was clear, it would be intelligible that one might try to respond by conceiving the mental as a specially marked out part of nature, with nature understood according to a rudimentary form of the very concep-tion that in fact excludes the mental.

This yields a way of understanding Cartesian philosophy of mind, at least on the Rylean reading that figures in a common contemporary pic-ture of how modern philosophy of mind developed.[15] On this reading, Descartes wanted the relations that organize the mental to be special cases of the sorts of relations that organize the subject matter of the natural sciences. But the specialness of the mental, to which on this reading Descartes was responding without a proper comprehension of its basis, requires these relations, supposedly suitable for natural-scientific treatment, to do duty for the relations that constitute the space of reasons. That is why Cartesian thinking takes a form to which Ryle's term of criticism "para-mechanical" is appropriate. Cartesian immaterialism is intelligible within the framework I am describing; no part of material nature could be special enough to serve the essentially confused purposes of this way of thinking. If one tries to make connections of the sort that figure in descriptions of law-governed processes do duty for relations of justification or warrant, one will inevitably lapse into an appeal to magic, masquerading as the science of a peculiar subject matter; what one intends to postulate as mechanisms of a special kind will degenerate into what Ryle lampoons as para-mechanisms. On this reading, Cartesian philosophy of mind is a confused version of the first of the two kinds of naturalism I distinguished, an attempt to integrate thinking and knowing into nature on the modern conception that the second kind of naturalism rejects.

What I have said about para-mechanisms coincides with an element in Rorty's reading of modern epistemology. But Rorty depicts a train of thought that starts from an obsession with the fragility of certainty, and lapses into para-mechanism because of a wish to disclaim the burden of responsibility for one's putative knowledge, which shows up as a wish to represent one's putative knowledge as the result of the world forcing itself on one. I find this reading less satisfactory than the one I have sketched for at least two reasons. First, the onset of the obsession with certainty—which surely does come to characterize epistemology with Descartes—still seems to need explanation. In my reading, the obsession with certainty can fall into place, not as a starting point for a train of thought that issues in the characteristically Cartesian conception of the mental, but as manifesting an explicable anxiety over the felt threat that the knowing subject withdraws from the rest of the world. Second, the peculiarities of the Cartesian subject are not restricted to its role as knower; this is the point about the generalizability of Sellars's contrast, which I have already noted that Rorty misses.[16]

6) In the perspective I am urging, the fundamental mistake of Cartesian philosophy of mind is its failure to take the point of Sellars's contrast. What is special about concepts of the mental is that they make sense

only in the framework of the space of reasons. Cartesian thinking intuits a specialness about concepts of the mental, but misunderstands it, taking it to reflect a peculiar mode of belonging to nature, with nature understood according to a conception that, when it comes into clear focus, actually stands opposed to the logical space within which alone concepts of the mental are intelligible.

The idea of para-mechanisms, realized in an immaterial substance, figures in this reading as a mere result of trying to force the specialness of the mental into that unsuitable mold. The fundamental mistake is not the notion of a ghostly mechanism, but the idea that the mental can be in view from a standpoint that organizes its subject matter in the manner of the natural sciences. But this idea is still widespread in contemporary philosophy of mind. In a common view, at least part of the truth about the mental is the truth about a demarcated region of nature, conceived as the realm of law: specifically, the truth about the internal machinery that controls behavior in response to impacts from the environment. This is not the whole of the truth about the mental, according to this style of thinking, because on its own this body of truth cannot incorporate the bearing of mental states on objective reality. But it is the whole of part of the truth about the mental.[17]

I want to suggest that this conception of the mind as internal machinery is, in one respect, no advance over the Cartesian conception. Of course this style of thinking has shed the familiar ontological embarrassments of Cartesianism. It does not envisage immaterial substances, and it has no need for the role Descartes attributes to the pineal gland, as the site of a mysterious interaction between an immaterial substance and the rest of nature. But this style of thinking still makes what I have suggested is the fundamental mistake of Cartesianism. It supposes that truth about the mental can be in view when the subject matter of the inquiry is conceived as framed in the realm of law, and not as framed in a *sui generis* space of reasons. On this score, which is separable from the benefit of discarding those ontological embarrassments, looking for regular mechanisms is no better than postulating para-mechanisms.

Indeed in one way the change is for the worse. At least the old Cartesian thinking registers, in its confused way, the intuition that thought and talk about the mental are special. The modern version avoids immaterialism and the pineal-gland mystery by taking as its subject matter something that is not special at all, but just a more or less ordinary part of nature. Of course there is nothing wrong with having the internal machinery that controls behavior as one's subject matter. The warmed-

over Cartesianism I am describing consists not just in taking an interest
in that bit of nature, but in thinking that the truth about it is truth about
the mental.

7) I want to illustrate this in connection with a common contemporary
attitude to a Fregean conception of intentionality. The idea is that "ex-
ternalistic" considerations have demolished Frege's apparatus of sense
and reference. Versions of this view have been expressed by many people.[18] But I am going to consider a particularly clear expression by Ruth
Garrett Millikan, in directing against Frege her campaign against what
she calls "meaning rationalism."[19] I want to suggest that Millikan's argument is vitiated by adherence to the residual Cartesianism I have identified, and that reflecting on her thinking is a good way to see how small
an advance is constituted by discarding Cartesian immaterialism.

The fundamental thesis of the "meaning rationalism" Millikan attacks
is that samenesses and differences in elements of thought-content are
transparently available to a rational subject.[20] A stronger version adds that
it is transparently available to a rational subject whether or not a putative
content-element really is a content-element, so we cannot make sense of
the idea that a thinking subject might take herself to be entertaining a
thought when there is no thought there to be entertained.

Now Frege's notion of sense is fixed by the principle that we must
distinguish senses whenever the price of not doing so would be to leave
a possibility that a rational subject could, at the same time, take rationally
conflicting attitudes—for instance, belief and disbelief—to a single
thought (where thoughts are the senses expressible, perhaps in suitable
contexts, by utterances of whole sentences). This is indeed a form of
"meaning rationalism." Frege's requirement is that senses must be sufficiently fine-grained to secure that we need not describe rational subjects
as, say, believing and disbelieving the same thing. And if the difference
between the same sense twice over and two different senses is to correspond with the closing or opening, to a rational mind, of possibilities for
combining attitudes, the difference must be available to the rational mind
in question.

This "meaning rationalism" is weaker than Millikan's fundamental thesis, with its general transparency of sameness and difference in content-
elements. (Let alone the further thesis that excludes illusions of existence
for content-elements.) Frege's principle forces a difference of sense only
if rationally conflicting attitudes to what would otherwise have to be
conceived as the same thought are present in a rational mind *at the same
time*. Frege says nothing to exclude a subject's losing track of a thought

over time, which would make room for holding conflicting attitudes to the same thought at different times without the subject's rationality being impugned.[21] Nor does Frege's principle rule out a subject's taking what is in fact a different thought to be the same as one she entertained earlier, so that she wrongly supposes she is already committed to an attitude to it.[22] But I can ignore this; Millikan's argument against Frege does not depend on crediting him with a stronger "rationalism" than he accepts.[23]

Millikan's argument goes like this: Grasping a sense would need to be an achievement characteristic of the intact mind. But Frege wants grasping a sense of the relevant kind to be having an object—the associated *Bedeutung*—in mind. For this to be so, the rationality that figures in Frege's attempt to place the notion of sense would have to be semantic rationality, a matter of, for instance, what can and cannot be true together. Frege's picture of sense and reference requires "the assumption that the intact mind is, as such, semantically rational."[24] Millikan argues that this assumption is substantive, and indefensible.

She sees the assumption as substantive because she takes it that for one's mind to be intact is for one to have one's "head . . . intact, in good mechanical order, not diseased, not broken."[25] Her thought is that the only sort of "rationality" (so called) that is legitimately available for Frege to appeal to, as a context for his talk of sense, is "mechanical rationality"—the head being in good mechanical order. So the substantive assumption is that internal machinery could be so arranged that its states and changes of state track the requirements of semantic rationality.

And Millikan seems right that this assumption is indefensible. We cannot engage in the kind of assessment of semantic rationality that Frege wants to exploit in his account of sense, say in connection with possible and impossible combinations of singular predicative thoughts, until we have secured that the items that are allowed or not allowed to be combined are directed at determinate objects. And there are modes of directedness at determinate objects—for instance, those expressible by perceptually based demonstratives—that we cannot get into our picture without appealing to environmental circumstances—circumstances external to the intraorganismic machinery that Millikan thinks would have to be meant by "the intact mind."[26]

8) Millikan's argument, then, is this: "the assumption that the intact mind is, as such, semantically rational" is substantive, and indefensible; therefore sense and reference cannot hang together as Frege supposes. Now the inferential step here is fine. But surely Frege's line is to contrapose. Sense and reference do hang together as he takes them to; so

much the worse for the thesis that intactness in a mind is independent of semantic rationality. The assumption is not substantive. Millikan makes it look as if it is by insisting that "the intact mind" must be healthy machinery in the head; so much the worse for that interpretation of mental intactness. Rather, to have an intact mind just *is* to be semantically rational.[27]

Frege is famous for railing against psychologism in logic. His point is that the concept of, say, deductive inference is available only within a normative framework, and an inquiry that restricts itself to transitions minds regularly make, without the normative framework of logic, properly conceived, does not get as far as bringing deductive inference into view. But the thought is not limited to logic. Frege's attack on psychologism is a way of expressing the generalized version of Sellars's point that I have been working with in this paper. (The correspondence is unsurprising in view of how important Kant is for both.) Already in the logical case, it is not just the idea of deductive inference that is available only within a normatively framed inquiry; the very idea of what deductive inferences start from and issue in—beliefs—makes sense only within the normative context that psychologistic logicians deny themselves.

Now Millikan's conception of "the intact mind" is psychologistic in the generalized sense; it purports to have the mind's states and operations as its topic even though the topic is not conceived as framed within a *sui generis* space of reasons. We should not be misled here by her phrase "mechanical rationality." When the machinery in the head is in good working order, that is not to say that its states and changes of state are related by the sorts of relation that constitute the space of reasons, any more than are the states and changes of state in, say, a healthy kidney. This is just a way of putting Millikan's own point. "Mechanical rationality" (so called) cannot ensure semantic rationality, but it is semantic rationality that structures the space of reasons.[28]

A psychologistic conception of the mental is not a promising context in which to look for what Frege, of all people, might have wanted from the notion of sense. No wonder his thinking comes out looking so unsatisfactory. For Frege, grasping a (singular) sense should simply *be* having a *Bedeutung* in mind (under a mode of presentation)—a notion that works only in the framework of semantic rationality. Millikan takes the introduction of sense to be a tool for characterizing the internal mechanics of having one's mind on objects.[29] She rightly concludes that grasping a sense, so construed, cannot be what Frege wants it to be, but she does not see that this might tell against the construal.

This is a blind spot. I think it amounts to not seeing the possibility of a liberal naturalism. The proper home of the idea of "grasping senses" is in describing patterns in our lives—our mental lives in this case—that are intelligible only in terms of the relations that structure the space of reasons. This patterning involves genuine rationality, not just "mechanical rationality" (so called). Liberal naturalism needs no more, to make the idea of "grasping senses" unproblematic, than a perfectly reasonable insistence that such patterns shape our lives.

If someone refuses to take the notion of sense as a tool for characterizing the internal mechanisms that underlie having one's mind on objects,[30] Millikan detects a commitment to a spooky idea that, as she puts it, "meanings move the mind directly."[31] The spookiness is that of Cartesian para-mechanisms. She recoils into a neo-Cartesian search for regular mechanisms, and supposes Frege must have been after that too, though she finds his attempt inept—rightly, given her construal of Frege's thinking. But Frege's thinking is quite different. It involves, if you like, the thought that "meanings move the mind directly," but in a form that is not spooky at all. The idea of a mind's being moved by meanings involves a metaphor from the logical space of mechanical understanding, but the way the idea functions must be understood in the contrasting space of reasons. Trying to take the metaphor literally is a form of the basic Cartesian mistake.

9) What ground is there for accepting that it is a mistake? Millikan's position is quite suggestive here. Like ordinary Cartesianism, it poses a threat to a commonsense conception of thinking things.

What is it that thinks? One might suppose it should be what Millikan calls "the intact mind." But the activities of "the intact mind" as Millikan conceives it do not amount to thinking. That is just to affirm her own point that its activities exemplify only "mechanical rationality," and not semantic rationality.

What is it that exercises semantic rationality? Millikan's answer to this question shifts the relevant boundary out from the one around "the intact mind," past the boundary around the animal whose behavior it controls, to encompass a system that combines "the intact mind" with conditions in the animal's environment. "Rationality is . . . a biological norm effected in an integrated head-world system under biologically ideal conditions."[32] But "externalism" is grotesque if it implies that exercising semantic rationality is an activity of a "head-world system"—as if the environment of what we ordinarily conceive as thinkers is partly responsible for doing the thinking that gets done. The environment is partly responsible for there being a possibility of doing that thinking. But the thinking is done by something that lives in the environment, which includes thinking about it. This piece of mere sanity is obscured by Millikan's concern with the mechanics of thinking (with how rationality is "effected"). If we conceive the animal as a complex mechanism, what we have in view is not a realization of semantic rationality any more than its internal control machinery is, and now it looks as if nothing less than a "head-world system" will do.[33] If the only respectable intellectual orientation toward rationality is inquiry into how it is "effected" in a mechanism, we lose our grip on rationality as something exercised in the activities of an animal.

Millikan's "intact mind" is a counterpart to the Cartesian *res cogitans*. There is a difference; Millikan realizes that her counterpart cannot actually be a *res cogitans*, although she still calls it "the mind"—perversely, one might think, since it does not do what minds are supposed to do, namely think (exercise semantic rationality). This is the result of a familiar trade-off; the price of discarding Cartesian immaterialism, while staying within restrictive naturalism, is that one's singled-out part of nature is no longer special enough to be credited with powers of thought.[34] But Millikan's conception, for all its freedom from immaterialism, is like the original Cartesian conception in threatening the sane belief that a *res cogitans* is also a *res dormiens*, a *res ambulans*, and so forth. Millikan's "intact mind" does not exercise rationality, and the "head-world system," which does exercise rationality, is not the thing that sleeps and walks. The rational animal finds no place in the picture.

Properly understood, the claim that the activities of the intact mind include directing itself at objects, which Millikan cannot make room for, is perfectly acceptable; it is a way to say it is the rational animal that thinks. We do not in any way denigrate the reality of the mental if we say the word "mind" labels a collection of capacities and propensities possessed by a minded being. It is a recipe for intellectual disaster to assume that what we mean by "the mind" must be something more substantial than that, but less than the rational animal itself: an organ in which the thinking we credit to the animal, loosely or derivatively on this view, takes place.[35] That is the original sin of Cartesian philosophy, and it is no redemption to replace the para-organ postulated by Descartes himself with a regular organ, something a more sophisticated contemporary biology can countenance.[36] Of course there is a relevant organ, the brain, and none of what I have said casts doubt on investigating how it works. But on pain of losing our grip on ourselves as thinking things, we must distinguish inquiring into the mechanics of, say, having one's mind on an object from inquiring into what having one's mind on an object is.

10) My topic in this paper has been a cultural effect of the maturation of modern science. The associated clarification of the relevant mode of intelligibility, which separated it from the mode of intelligibility revealed by placing things in the space of reasons, was in itself an unqualified intellectual advance. But I have been urging that there is a strand in the philosophy of mind, exemplified alike in Descartes and in the writings of contemporaries who think they are fully emancipated from Cartesian confusions, which should be seen as a toxic by-product of a frame of mind—scientism—made possible only by that intellectual advance.

❧ 6

Naturalism and Skepticism[1]

DAVID MACARTHUR

𝒯HE PROBLEM OF the external world can be understood, broadly, as the problem of how we can know, or justifiably believe, that there is an external world on the basis of sense experience. In the *Critique of Pure Reason* (1787) Kant famously wrote:

> it remains a scandal to philosophy and to human reason in general that the existence of things outside us . . . must be accepted merely on faith, and that if anyone thinks good to doubt their existence, we are unable to counter his doubts by any satisfactory proof.[2]

Modern philosophy has, from its beginning in Descartes's *Meditations*,[3] been haunted by the threat posed by skepticism and the demand to find a "satisfactory proof" of the external world. Presumably such a proof would argue from premises to which the skeptic is, or must be, committed, to the conclusion that there is an external world having many of the features that we pretheoretically believe that it has. Call this the project of refuting the skeptic.[4]

Repeated efforts have been made to refute skepticism by appeal to God (Descartes),[5] necessary conditions of sense experience (Kant),[6] common sense (Moore),[7] inference to the best explanation (Harman),[8] a contextualist account of knowledge (Cohen),[9] and an argument based on self-knowledge and content-externalism (Warfield).[10] Despite their interest

106

and ingenuity these attempts have been uniformly disappointing. Either they, implicitly or explicitly, beg the skeptic's question without explaining why they are entitled to do so. Or, in their efforts to rationally reconstruct human knowledge on a basis of certainties or necessary conditions or explanatory posits, they tend to put a false cast on the very justification and knowledge they are trying to defend.

Against the background of the many failures of the enterprise of refuting the skeptic, one might have expected that what Kant called a "scandal to philosophy" would be even more acutely felt. Surprisingly, quite the reverse is the case, so much so that those who take skepticism seriously can complain of philosophy's unearned insouciance in the face of the undiminished challenge of skepticism.[11] What accounts for this philosophical indifference and relative lack of concern about an issue that was of central importance for almost all the major early modern philosophers?

A large part of the answer can be found in the rise of *scientific naturalism* (henceforth, simply "naturalism") and its status nowadays as a philosophical orthodoxy. Naturalism, understood broadly as the view that the account of nature provided by the natural sciences is our only guide as to what genuinely, or unproblematically, exists and/or to what is genuinely, or unproblematically, known, is widely popular within contemporary analytic philosophy.[12] The attraction of this doctrine is due in no small part to a conception of naturalism as providing a quite distinctive way of responding to the skeptic. As Richard Fumerton has put it,

> the naturalist epistemology seems moved, in large part, by the conviction that it is only by taking a naturalistic turn that the epistemologist can avoid massive skepticism.[13]

Inspired by Hume, who said that "nature breaks the force of all skeptical arguments in time,"[14] and more recently by Quine, who remarked that "sceptical doubts are scientific doubts,"[15] the naturalist has become supremely confident that naturalism, even if it cannot refute skepticism, at least provides a distinctive response that undermines the threat that it poses.

Naturalism is widely supposed to provide what I shall call a *quietist* response to the skeptic.[16] The aim of quietism is not to refute the skeptic but to entitle oneself not to need to.[17] This is a laudable ambition and, in contrast to the project of refutation, seems to stand a real chance of success. What is required in order to earn the right not to answer the skeptic is, presumably, a demonstration that there is something defective about the skeptical problem. Different versions of quietism are distinguished by their different accounts about where the defect lies, whether it is a matter of the sensicality of the skeptic's premises, their motivation, or their theoretical presuppositions. In all cases, if quietism is to be convincing it must explain why, in spite of the defect in the way the skeptic raises his question, it could have seemed to have been a legitimate problem that we had no option but to answer.

The main aim of the present paper is to argue that naturalism does not have the resources to expound a satisfactory quietist response to the skeptic. Consequently, the naturalists' confidence in being able to engage in postskeptical epistemology is misplaced. Moreover, I hope to show that far from providing a satisfactory response to skepticism, naturalism in fact plays right into the skeptic's hands. Naturalism is, as I shall put it, *inherently skeptical*. This is not to say that naturalism inevitably leads to skepticism. The claim is, rather, that naturalism can only resist skepticism dogmatically, by begging the question against skepticism.

The paper is divided into two sections. In Section 1, I discuss Hume's extension of naturalist explanation to the workings of the human mind and the central role given within this account to efficient causal explanations. The relevance of this discussion to contemporary concerns is this: it shows how naturalist reflection upon sense experience (henceforth, simply experience) naturally gives rise to the threat of external world skepticism. We might call this *Hume's Insight*, since Hume was acutely aware that the results of his natural science of man led naturally (and, he thought, unanswerably) to skepticism with regard to the external world, causation and the self, among other things. In the present paper I shall only be concerned with the first of these and the term "skepticism" will refer to external world skepticism throughout.

In Section 2, I consider three representative and influential contemporary naturalist responses to skepticism, two associated with the work of Quine and the third with that of Strawson. I argue that these attempts to fashion a naturalistic quietism all fail. Assuming that the prospects of a refutation of skepticism are dim, the naturalist can neither answer nor undermine the skeptical challenge that the naturalistic worldview naturally invites. The common conception of the relation between naturalism and skepticism is the reverse of the truth. Naturalism is not the cure, but one cause, of skepticism.

Section 1: Hume and the Origin of Naturalism

Hume is one of the first and most representative of modern naturalists.[18] In this section I should like to consider a line of Hume's thought leading from naturalism to skepticism. I want to show that this argument retains its force even if we give up certain of Hume's questionable assumptions, in particular his residual commitment to dualism and an empiricist conception of experience.

In the introduction to the *Treatise* (1740) Hume proposes a radically new alternative to the old method of "metaphysical reasonings" (p. xiv) according to which the traditional metaphysician would presume to establish a priori and once for all the presuppositions, extent, and limits of what exists and what is known. The alternative, which Hume calls "experimental philosophy" (p. xvi), is the view that in considering philosophical questions about such things as existence and knowledge, philosophy ought to employ scientific, or broadly empirical, methods of inquiry. The touchstone of the naturalist is the claim that philosophy ought to employ the methods of "experience and observation" (p. xvi) and "careful and exact experiments" (p. xvii). A representative contemporary naturalist, Quine inherits this conception, arguing that naturalism is "the recognition that it is within science itself, and not in some prior philosophy, that reality is to be identified and described."[19] It follows that, for the naturalist, all dualisms and realities posited and supported on purely a priori grounds are rejected as supernatural.

The Science of Man

An important motivation for naturalism is the idea that human beings are not distinct from nature but are in fact part of it. Naturalism holds that we are natural creatures and, like other natural things, susceptible to properly scientific forms of understanding by way of scientific methods of investigation. Hume regards the new "science of Man" (p. xv) as "the only solid foundation for the other sciences" (p. xvi), one that it is the central concern of the *Treatise* to articulate. According to this new science, the method of studying the human mind is explicitly modeled on the scientific study of nature:

'Tis no astonishing reflection to consider, that the application of experimental philosophy to moral subjects should come after that to natural (p. xvi).

Just as the aim of the science of nature is to limn the causal structure of the universe and discover its principles, so too the aim of the science of human nature is to discover universal causal principles or laws of the mind, and, in particular, to "explain the nature of the ideas we employ, and of the operations we perform in our reasonings" (p. xv).

Naturalists can be divided into two groups depending upon whether or not they hold that efficient causation is the sole criterion of ontological commitment. For some naturalists such as David Armstrong, entities are posited solely on the basis of playing a causal role, either being a cause or being caused.[20] The relevant notion of cause is efficient causation, something that brings about a change or difference in a lawlike way.[21] For this sort of naturalist, causation, as it were, carves nature at the joints, and it is the job of science to describe the elements of nature and the causal laws that relate them.[22] Of course, such a naturalist need not be committed to Hume's particular theory of causation as a species of constant conjunction. For instance, there are prominent naturalists who regard causation as a relation of necessitation in the world.[23]

Alternatively there are naturalists such as W. V. Quine who recognize noncausal abstract entities like numbers and sets on the grounds that they are an indispensable part of the language of the natural sciences. For Quine, since terms referring to such abstract objects figure in a properly regimented account of scientific knowledge, they exist on the grounds that the existential quantifier ranges over them. For present purposes, I shall leave the debate between these two versions of naturalistic ontology aside.[24]

What is important for our purposes is that the naturalist, on either view, is committed to *a causal account of the mind*. The mind is thought of as nothing but a realm of efficient causal states, events, and processes. And, giving up Hume's residual commitment to dualism—not Cartesian substance dualism but Hume's bundle dualism[25]—most contemporary naturalists would say that these causal states, events, and processes are realized in the brain or body.

Hume's Insight

In Hume's thought, the empiricist conception of experience as a direct awareness of mind-dependent "impressions" is treated as a consequence of the application of, and so a part of, his naturalism. Hume has traditionally been thought of as drawing a skeptical conclusion from the empiricist tradition, demonstrating that if we are directly aware of impressions in the mind, as British Empiricists such as Locke and Berkeley believed, then there is no plausible non-question-begging argument to show that the external world exists or, if it does, that it "resembles" our impressions.[26] If we accept that empiricism is a part of naturalism, then we cannot avoid concluding that reflection upon naturalism naturally (or reasonably or intuitively) leads to skepticism.

But contemporary naturalists block this inference. In contrast to Hume, they distinguish commitment to an empiricist account of experience from commitment to naturalism. Since the vast majority of contemporary naturalists do not follow Hume in thinking of experience as a matter of being confronted by mind-dependent "impressions," they can acknowledge the connection between empiricism and skepticism without thinking that this has any skeptical implications for a naturalism freed from Hume's mistakes.

On the standard reading, then, Hume demonstrated the bankruptcy of the British Empiricist tradition by showing how the consistent development of classical empiricism leads, inevitably and unanswerably, to a radical skepticism about the external world.[27] Naturalism can then be thought of as Hume's response to an empiricist-generated skepticism.[28] However, there is reason to think that the standard reading is seriously flawed. Apart from misinterpreting Hume's conception of the relation of naturalism and skepticism, this reading overlooks the fact that Hume discerned more than one route to skepticism from reflection upon a naturalist conception of experience.

Naturalists, in the broadly Humean tradition of thinking about the mind, are committed to what I shall call *the causal model of experience*. This is the view that sense experience can be decomposed into two components: 1) an inner component that carries no existential commitment to the existence of any external object (call this subjective experience);[29] and 2) an efficient cause (for example, an external object) that produces subjective experience. According to the causal model, the mind, thought of as an inner realm, and the world, thought of as an external realm, are separated by an efficient causal gap. As we shall see, it is this feature of the model that invites skeptical challenge.

It is well known that Hume interpreted this model along empiricist lines, treating the inner component as mind-dependent "impressions," and following Berkeley in rejecting Locke's account of the "resemblance" of impressions and external objects. However, it is important to see that the causal model, as I have characterized it, is independent of any empiricist assumptions about how we are to understand subjective experience. The naturalist need not think in terms of the impressions or sense-data of the empiricist tradition. He may prefer treating subjective experience as bearing an externally directed intentional content given by a that-clause. Or he may think of subjective experience along adverbialist lines, in which experiencing a red square is treated as experiencing red-ly and square-ly.[30] And there are no doubt other options.

For present purposes, we can think of the causal model in abstraction from these various theoretical differences about the nature of subjective experience. Understood in this theoretically neutral way, the causal model of experience is a minimal consequence of the naturalists' commitment to the causal account of the mind, one that is compatible with both direct realism and representative realism in the philosophy of perception.

I now want to argue that, quite apart from any allegiance to classical empiricism, the naturalists' causal model of experience is inherently skeptical, by which I mean that there is an *intuitive* route from naturalist premises to a skeptical conclusion. Consequently, it is a mistake to think that in moving beyond a classical empiricist conception of experience, naturalism insulates itself from the threat of skepticism. As we shall see, Hume comes very close to demonstrating that reflection upon the causal model naturally leads to skepticism, which bears out *Hume's Insight* that naturalism is inherently skeptical.

The Skeptical Implications of the Causal Model of Experience

Consider this passage:

> By what argument can it be proved, that the perceptions of the mind must be caused by external objects, entirely different from them, though resembling them (if that be possible) and could not arise either from the energy of the mind itself, or from the suggestion of some invisible and unknown spirit, or from some other cause still more unknown to us? It is acknowledged, that, in fact, many of these perceptions arise not from anything external, as in dreams, madness, and other diseases . . . The mind has never anything present to it but the perceptions, and cannot possibly reach any experience of their connexion with objects. The supposition of such a connexion is, therefore, without any foundation in reasoning.[31]

If we replace Hume's reference to "perceptions" by theoretically neutral "subjective experiences," then we can reconstruct the main line of thought here as follows. It is part of our understanding of efficient causation that *the very same effect can have indefinitely many causes.* In accordance with the causal model of experience, we can think of our subjective experiences from the first-person perspective as a temporally extended stream of inner effects. If one asks, "What is the cause of these experiential effects?" from this internal perspective, then the mere existence of a causal relation to some cause or other provides no clue. The fact that a particular effect, say, fire, occurs tells us nothing about what actually caused it to occur; whether it was a match, a cigarette, lightning, a chemical reaction, or something else. Similarly, what we pretheoretically assume is the cause of our subjective experiences may be quite different from what actually causes them. The existence of a causal law is no help either if our only basis for its existence presupposes that some of our appearances are caused by the objects that they are apparently about. For what is in question is precisely what justifies such a presupposition.

We might conclude that from a consideration of the mere fact that we are sensuously confronted by such and such inner effects in consciousness, the looseness or indefiniteness of the causal relation does allow us to say what caused them. The cause could be a familiar external object but it could also be, as Hume puts it, "the mind itself," or some "unknown spirit," or "some other cause still more unknown to us."[32]

In this way the naturalist can make perfectly good sense of the skeptical possibilities. On the naturalists' own reckoning, skeptical possibilities are alternative causal hypotheses capable, in principle, of accounting for the entire history of one's inner experiences. Illusions, dreams, and hallucinations can serve to help illustrate this point but they are inessential. All we require is a scenario in which we are caused to have the very same subjective experiences by some peculiar power of our own minds or by some "world" quite unlike the world we believe in: for example, the brain-in-a-vat scenario.

The idea that there is an efficient causal gap between the mind and world plays a large part in explaining the motivation for skepticism, and especially in helping to provide a plausible explanation of how we could have the very same thoughts and experiences even if the external world had few of the features we believe it to have, or even if it did not exist.[33] The idea that the very same experiential states, when considered from the first-person perspective, could have been produced by one of an indefinitely large number of sets of causal antecedents, strongly supports the view that the content of such states does not depend upon any conditions external to one's mind. These causal considerations lead us to think that we could understand and individuate our subjective experiences, understood as inner effects, in complete independence of the external world that, we presume, causes them.[34]

This is a perceptual form of what has come to be known as *individualism:* the view that one's mental states and processes (including those that are intentional or representational) can, in principle, be individuated in complete independence of the existence or nature of the external world (including, of course, the social world).[35] Supposing we can acquire basic sensory concepts on the basis of subjective experiences independently of the external world, then it seems possible to acquire other concepts by virtue of reference-fixing descriptions that employ these basic concepts. In other words, local individualism with regard to experience can provide a plausible basis for the global individualism that is presupposed by the intelligibility of the skeptical problem.

The naturalist will, no doubt, resist the claim that we do not know the causes of our subjective experiences by saying that we ordinarily assume that perception is a *reliable* source of beliefs about our environment. That is, we assume that our inner experiences are generally, and for the most part, caused by the external objects that they are, apparently, experiences of; or at least we assume this in *core* cases of perception, those regarding medium-sized objects under normal conditions of observation.

Of course, it is precisely the naturalists' assumption of the epistemic reliability of perception that the skeptic questions. He asks, "What reason do we have for believing that perception is a reliable (that is, mostly true) source of beliefs?" Once perception is thought of as an awareness of a subjective experience whose cause may be any one of indefinitely many causes, then the claim that the cause is the external world rather than whatever it is according to one or other of the skeptical hypotheses seems dogmatic and ad hoc.

Especially so when we consider that the naturalist is committed to the view that the scientific image of the world, as Sellars famously called it, is the last word as to what, properly speaking, exists and what, properly speaking, is known.[36] In considering how we are to conceive the world that is manifest to the senses and common sense, we face a stark choice. Insofar as the manifest image diverges from the scientific image, we must either translate or reduce its features to those of the more austere scientific image, or else convict the manifest image of error and illusion— perhaps with the qualification that it is instrumentally useful.[37] According to the majority of naturalists, natural science tells us that ordinary folk are in error in thinking that sensory qualities (for example, colors) are objective features of the world. Rather, such features of the manifest image of the world are considered to be a "projection" of the mind onto the world.

This projective metaphysics implies that there is a systematic causal mismatch between mind and world, between the contents of subjective experience and the actual nature of the world that is causally responsible for them. That thought can only strengthen the skeptical case for questioning our assumption of perceptual reliability. The requirement for a rational justification of so important an epistemic assumption seems, especially in this context, entirely appropriate. Yet, as the history of modern philosophy attests, we seem unable to satisfy it.

What I take the foregoing argument to show is that there is a natural (intuitive, reasonable) route from naturalistic premises to a skeptical conclusion. I have not claimed that this is a valid deductive argument, so a naturalist is not inevitably a skeptic. I do not deny that a naturalist can block the argument I have offered in a number of different ways. The point of the argument is to make plausible the claim that naturalism can only avoid skepticism dogmatically. So long as the naturalist must at some point in his reasoning presuppose that appearances do, at least sometimes, provide us access to external reality, then he simply begs the skeptic's question.

I shall not now attempt to show that this is true of every naturalistic attempt to answer the skeptic—although I think it is strongly suggested by the naturalist denial of empirically indefeasible a priori truths and the assumption of at least some a posteriori scientific knowledge.[38] But supposing that it is true, then the situation is as follows. From a naturalist perspective, antiskepticism is no more or less reasonable than skepticism.[39] Reason does not favor either side in this debate. Is such a result acceptable to a naturalist? It is not, since, as ancient skepticism has taught us, the skeptic wins the standoff in which reason counts no more in favor of a given conclusion than in its denial. In such a situation neither side can properly claim to be rationally justified. For the skeptic who sees himself as uncommitted to any substantial doctrine—one who works dialectically from within the naturalistic worldview[40]—this is a perfectly acceptable conclusion. But surely the naturalist cannot similarly admit that his position cannot finally claim to be rationally justified.

Section 2: Naturalist Responses to Skepticism

The main aim of the present paper is to explore the feasibility of a naturalistic quietism, but before I do that, there is one version of refutation that I must briefly discuss, namely inference to the best explanation—if only because it has been described as "perhaps the best skepticism-rebutting argument in favour of the existence of body."[41] What is at issue here is an inference to the existence of the external world as the best explanation of the coherence, order, or regularity of our subjective experiences. There is, of course, nothing wrong with inference to the best explanation as a form of inference. The problem is with its application in the special context of skepticism. Specifically, I deny that subjective experience *has* the coherence, order, or regularity that is thought to stand in need of explanation.[42] Of course, what our experiences are of is orderly events in the external world. But we cannot infer from that that the experiences that report such events are *themselves* orderly. Think of visual experience and the way it is interrupted by blinking, quick side glances, and so on. And note that we are not to appeal to such facts as that we are experiencing things from a certain location and orientation. This would, of course, beg the very question at issue.

In the context of the skeptical challenge, we have to abstract away any assumptions about the environment, the body, and the normal course of nature in considering our experiences themselves rather than the world they apparently present. I think once this is done it is clear that the hypothesis of an external world, far from explaining some intrinsic order in our experiences themselves, is itself required in order to make our experiences orderly. If one is inclined to say that the intentional content of one's experiences is orderly, I suspect one is really referring to the orderliness of the ordinary objects of perception.

For example, if we make no prior assumptions about an external world, then when we are inclined to say that we seem to see a table, that could equally well be reported in this way: we seem to see a series of exactly similar tables that are replacing one another so quickly that one fails to notice. And, of course, we could think of further descriptions.

I have argued that one cannot refute the skeptic by appealing to inference to the best explanation. And other strategies have proven equally ineffectual. Suppose, then, that we come to admit that there is no way of refuting the skeptic.[43] Quietists, at least, see no calamity in acknowledging this. It seems a virtue of quietism that it concedes, at the outset, that we cannot provide the reasons that the skeptic demands of us. The quietists' aim is to show that there is no such requirement as we had thought because the skeptical problem is misconceived. As a way of progressing beyond what one might think of as the inevitably hopeless task of refuting the skeptic, quietism is a modest, but respectable, way of defusing the power of skepticism.

Different versions of quietism find fault with the skeptical problem in different places. The Rortian quietist attempts to show that the skeptical problem depends upon a false representationalist picture of the mind.[44] The Wittgensteinian quietist attempts to show that the skeptical problem is subtly incoherent.[45] But I want to focus on a third version of quietism associated with naturalism.

Central to the appeal of naturalism is the claim that, in spite of our inability to answer the skeptic, naturalism can defuse the skeptical threat by showing that the skeptical problem is not well motivated. I shall now consider three influential responses that answer to this general description: those of Quine, the reliabilist tradition, and Strawson.

1) Quine's Response

It is possible to read Quine as simply turning his back on the traditional problem of the external world.[46] In particular, if we consistently replace any reference to conscious experience by reference to a physicalistic correlate such as neural stimulation, then there is no way of even formulating the traditional problem, since there is no longer a contrast between the inner realm of experience and the outer world that it is apparently about.[47] But it seems ridiculous to deny or avoid the very existence of perceptual consciousness;[48] and there is ample evidence that, at least sometimes, Quine *does* mean to engage the traditional problem and that he does recognize the obvious truism that we enjoy subjective experience as of various objects. So, even if what follows does not represent the fully physicalized third-personal perspective that Quine sometimes adopts, it does represent an important aspect of his thinking, one that has been very influential beyond the confines of his philosophy.

Quine's naturalistic response to the skeptic is summed up in the phrase "scepticism is the offshoot of science."[49] In this expression we can find both his diagnosis and his cure. Quine regards the skeptic as one who assumes the truth of science in order to refute science. The skeptic's doubts are, we are told, really scientific doubts that rest on accepting a number of facts, observations, and memories regarding such things as bent sticks in water, towers in the distance, mirages, afterimages, and dreams. The cure is to realize that circularity is, in spite of a long tradition of resistance to it, no problem at all. In the justification of science the naturalist, like the skeptic, relies on science, if necessary reshaping it as he sees fit.

I think it is clear that we should not read Quine as saying that a naturalist is entitled to argue in a circle, for that presupposes that the naturalist aims to answer the skeptic. He is better read as saying that the skeptic cannot rightly ask his question about the rational justification of empirical knowledge in general without relying on some empirical knowledge. In short, there is no general question, of the sort that the skeptic imagines, to answer. Once we see that the skeptic's formulation of his problem is at fault, it simply lapses.

Unfortunately this response is inadequate for several reasons. In the first place, it trades on an ambiguity about the scope of skeptical doubt. Quine's position is that we cannot question all of our knowledge all at once. Afloat in Neurath's boat we can only question our knowledge piece-meal, the very act of questioning depending upon a provisional accep-tance of some background knowledge. But the skeptic is perfectly happy to accept all of that. What the skeptic challenges is not all knowledge *überhaupt* but only knowledge of the world external to his mind. For instance, he does not doubt that he has knowledge of his own inner experience or of the meanings of the concepts that he employs in de-scribing it. While it may be self-defeating to doubt all knowledge all at once, we can and do raise general skeptical questions about our cognitive grasp of the external world.

Furthermore, in asking his general questions Quine says that the skep-tic is "overreacting" to our vulnerability to illusion.[50] He argues that "Illusions are illusions only relative to the acceptance of genuine bodies with which to contrast them."[51] It is not clear what this means. Quine might mean that in order for there to be illusions we must count some-thing as an instance of veridical perception. Perhaps it is true that we can only discover an illusion relative to taking something else as veridi-cally perceived, but that does not imply that there could not be unde-tectable illusions. Furthermore, while it might be true that the concept of illusion depends upon the concept of veridical perception, that is not to say that the concept of a veridical perception has any genuine appli-cation.

In any case, Quine apparently overlooks the point that the skeptic need not appeal to the traditional argument from illusion. As we have seen, a more powerful argument for skepticism is based upon the naturalists' causal model of experience and the character of the causal gap between the mind and the world. This argument does not require any question-able inference from being wrong on occasion to the possibility of global error. So, in spite of Quine's claim to the contrary, the naturalist does not seem entitled to deny that the skeptic's questions of rational justifi-cation are legitimate and well motivated.

2) *The Reliabilist Response*

Philosophers in the so-called Reliabilist tradition, such as Alvin Goldman and David Armstrong, have found the resources for another antiskeptical response in Quine's famous remark that

> Epistemology, or something like it, simply falls into place as a chap-ter of psychology and hence of natural science.[52]

In Quine's view, traditional epistemology—roughly, the theory of how beliefs are rationally justified and what kind of rational justification constitutes knowledge—is to be superseded by a causal account of belief formation. The reliabilist can be thought of as replacing the skeptic's assumption that a rational justification for our beliefs must be internally available by the view that justification is a matter of whether a belief has been produced by a reliable process, say, by being caused by the fact that it purports to represent.[53] A belief might be appropriately caused without its being the case that we know or believe that it is. On this account, there can be external justification for one's beliefs via a reliable procedure without any requirement that such justification be internally available.

This response certainly provides a way of defending the claim that knowledge or justified belief is *possible* without our having, or being aware of, the kind of rational justification that the skeptic seeks. If the satisfaction of our cognitive aims depends upon the holding of some external condition that we need not be aware of, then, for all that the skeptic shows, it remains possible that we have indeed achieved our cognitive aims. But skepticism ought not to be thought of as primarily concerned with, or exhausted by, its challenge to the *possibility* of knowledge or justified belief.[54] As the ancient skeptics recognized, skepticism owes its devastating force to the way it challenges whether we have any good reason to think that we *actually* have knowledge or justified belief, as a matter of fact.[55] Attacking the possibility of knowledge is only one way of attacking the actuality of knowledge. And securing the possibility of knowledge still leaves open the question of its actuality. And the same goes for justified belief. Unless the naturalist can provide adequate reason for believing that his beliefs are produced by a reliable process (and citing his own reliability will be one such reason), then he is not entitled to regard them as knowledge, or as externally justified, even by his own lights.[56]

The naturalist thus finds himself facing a dilemma: either 1) he quixotically assumes, without reason, that perception is a source of mostly reliable beliefs; or 2) he (externally) justifies that perception is a reliable process by appealing to that very same process, the reliability of perception—a move that is iterable at higher and higher levels of belief. But neither position can provide a satisfying response to a skeptic who questions the underlying assumption of reliability. The naturalist cannot avoid the skeptical challenge by dogmatically assuming, at some point in his reasoning, that perception is a reliable belief-forming process.

3) Strawson's Neo-Humean Response

I shall finally turn to consider Strawson's naturalistic response to skepticism as developed in his *Skepticism and Naturalism: Some Varieties* (1985). The naturalist strategy, as Strawson explains it, is to earn the right to refuse to answer the skeptic by coming to appreciate the special character of the belief in the external world. There are two strands in Strawson's exposition. In the first place, Strawson appeals to Hume in claiming that we are naturally and inescapably committed to this belief in such a way that reasoning is powerless to alter. Given our natural constitution we have no choice but to believe that the external world exists. Additionally, Strawson appeals to Wittgenstein in claiming that the belief in the external world is not open to doubt or question but forms an (almost) immutable part of the framework of our conceptual scheme—something he calls a "natural limit"[57]—within which, and only within which, our rational capacities, including those of doubting and questioning, are exercised.

In articulating his position, Strawson quotes from Hume's with approval:

> Nature, by an absolute and uncontroulable necessity has determin'd us to judge as well as to breathe and feel . . . Whoever has taken pains to refute the cavils of this total skepticism, has really disputed without an antagonist, and endeavour'd by arguments to establish a faculty, which nature has antecendently implanted in the mind, and render'd unavoidable.[58]

As Strawson reads it, this passage suggests that since the belief in the existence of the external world is naturally "implanted" in the mind, its position in our cognitive life is fixed irrespective of how rationally persuasive the skeptical argument against it is. Skepticism is a sham because there is quite simply no possibility of arguing oneself out of the belief in the external world.

Yet it is important to see that this is not because the skeptical conclusion is logically illegitimate. According to Strawson there is no reason to deny that the skeptical argument is fully intelligible, and so, that its conclusion is, in some sense, genuinely possible.[59] The impossibility of accepting the skeptical conclusion is a natural psychological fact about us. The human mind is so constituted that we cannot fail to believe in the external world. Since it is an "inescapable natural commitment" (p. 13), there is no point in arguing against the skeptic. It is, Strawson explains,

[a] natural commitment . . . so profound that [it] stands fast, and may be counted on to stand fast, through all revolutions in scientific thought or social development. (p. 27)

Since we owe the belief in an external world to human nature, not reason, the skeptic is misguided in thinking that any serious consequences follow from a demonstration that this belief lacks rational justification. It cannot lead us to suspend or deny this belief for it belongs to a framework that we have no option but to presuppose in all the operations of reason. On this ground Strawson enjoins us to see that skepticism "is idle, unreal, a pretence" (p. 19). There is quite simply no point in engaging in skeptical arguments or in the attempt to refute them.[60]

An initial problem with this position is the positing of unrevisable framework beliefs. All Strawson offers in defense of this claim is Wittgenstein's so-called "theory of hinge propositions" in *On Certainty*.[61] I shall leave aside discussion of the flaws in Strawson's exegesis of Wittgenstein except to remark that Wittgenstein repeatedly warns against reading him as holding any philosophical thesis.[62] In any case, one might wonder how Strawson can appeal to a meta-level claim about the character of specific beliefs, since such claims will, on the naturalists' account, presumably be established empirically. Why are they not also undermined by the skeptical hypotheses? It is a weakness in Strawson's presentation not to provide any account of his entitlement to these theoretical claims about the character of natural belief.

Moreover, there is an internal conflict between unrevisability and the commitment to naturalism. In Quine's famous image of knowledge as a field of force, even central elements in the field, such as mathematical statements and statements of logical laws, are not immune from revision.[63] Even those who do not follow Quine in entirely rejecting the notion of the a priori have tended to accept that the tradition was mistaken in conceiving of the a priori as unrevisable.[64] So this is a shaky basis for securing the immunity of natural belief from skeptical challenge.

Belief and Reason

More significantly, naturalists generally tend to overlook the internal relation that exists between belief and reason. For example, reliabilists replace the traditional concern with internalist rational justification with externalist nonrational justification. I shall first explain the connection between belief and reason-giving in some detail and then discuss how it bears upon Strawson's conception of natural belief.

To believe that P is, at a minimum, to be committed to the truth of P. It is to take P to be true. But we also know from past mistakes in judgment and the ever-present fact of disagreement with others that it is possible to believe what is, in fact, not true. So we are aware that taking-true is distinguishable from truth even though in the first-person present there is no such distinction to be drawn.

Belief is not simply an attitude of taking-true, however. If belief were merely taking-true then it could not be distinguished from other attitudes of taking-true such as assuming or hypothesizing or entertaining. Belief is distinguished from these attitudes by being governed by the norm of truth rather than, say, pragmatic norms. As David Velleman puts it: "An attitude's identity as a belief depends on its being regulated in a way designed to make it track the truth."[65] To believe involves a commitment to its being the case that one's truth-taking is regulated by what is in fact true. What performs this regulative function is the answerability of belief to rational criticism.[66] Of course, we sometimes accept something on faith, without any evidence or reasons. But our entitlement to think of any given belief as true, including a belief accepted on faith, depends on its being answerable to rational criticism should we acquire sufficient reason or evidence to suggest it may be false.

That helps explain why beliefs are states for which we are responsible in the sense that we can properly be criticized for the beliefs we hold. Doxastic responsibility depends upon the fact that, if occasion arises, we are obliged to engage in rational reflection of our beliefs in order to determine whether we are entitled to continue to endorse them. Rational criticism plays a regulative role that we have some control over, helping to ensure that what we think is true is not mere guesswork or accident but genuinely tracks the truth. Our entitlement to regard our beliefs as true thus depends upon their openness to criticism and the way such criticism is conducted.

Let us consider how these considerations bear upon Strawson's account of natural belief. A natural belief is "implanted" and sustained by nature independently of reason or reasoning. No doubt we did not acquire all, or even most, of our beliefs on the basis of reasoning. For example, many beliefs are acquired noninferentially on the basis of perception. The trouble with a natural belief is not its origin but the claim that we would continue to hold it irrespective of the results of any actual or possible rational criticism, even in the event of there being overwhelming evidence or reasons against it. The most compelling reasons to reject such a belief could not dislodge it. Yet, as a belief, it *must* be answerable to rational criticism. The skeptic trades upon this feature of belief by apparently demonstrating that we have a fundamental belief that we ought not to accept. Far from showing that skepticism is pointless, then, Strawson's position plays right into the skeptic's hands by picturing us as holding an apparently unreasonable but psychologically irresistible belief.[67]

Strawson admits that the skeptical question is perfectly intelligible and that the skeptical hypotheses are indeed relevant to the question of justification, but instead of answering the skeptic he reminds us that the skeptical conclusion has no lasting impact upon our beliefs. But, as Hume saw, this psychological observation leaves the skeptic's question as pressing as it ever was whenever we are moved to reflect upon it. The sense that the skeptic is fully within his rights to raise his question of rational justification is left intact and this cannot but create a strange sense that our ordinary commitments involve us in unanswerable difficulties whenever we reflect upon their epistemic credentials. Rather than defusing skeptical anxieties, the naturalists' psychological observations point to a paradoxical clash of everyday life and naturalistic reflection upon it.[68]

Conclusion

For those who are pessimistic about the possibility of refuting skepticism, the naturalist attempt to provide a quietist response seems admirable. The general aim of the quietist is not to refute the skeptic but to undermine the skeptical problem itself. The present paper has argued that such quietism cannot properly be developed from within a naturalist perspective.

In order to show this I have rehearsed a slightly modified version of one of Hume's arguments in which a skeptical conclusion is derived from reflection upon the (efficient) causal model of experience to which naturalism is committed. This required us to abstract from certain of Hume's own assumptions, notably his empiricist conception of experience. In this way I hope to have shown that *Hume's Insight* is vindicated: naturalism is, indeed, inherently skeptical. Naturalism naturally gives rise to skepticism and the naturalists' only way of answering such skepticism is to beg the skeptic's question. Radical skepticism is not, as naturalists tend to think, a dispensable feature of the new scientific account of man but its natural corollary.

The deep connection that exists between belief and reason-giving helps to account for the power of the skeptical problem. The skeptic demands a rational justification just where our reasons have given out: in the present case, for the assumption that perception is a source of mostly true beliefs. Both the reliabilist, who posits external justification by way of reliable processes, and Strawson, who trades on (questionable) psychological facts about our belief in the external world, fail to undermine the apparent legitimacy of the skeptical concern with rational justification.

I have been imagining a skeptic who, for the sake of argument, takes on board the naturalist position and who, from within that position, finds good reason for denying its basic epistemic assumptions. Such a skeptic can happily accept that a dogmatic naturalist can resist skepticism. What he wants to show is simply that there is a persuasive argument for a skeptical conclusion from within the naturalist position, and that there is no way the naturalist can regard his own position as rationally justified without begging the skeptic's question. This dogmatic stance is surely an unsatisfactory position and at the very least shows that naturalism has not earned the right to refuse to answer skepticism.

If naturalism naturally gives rise to skepticism, then the claim that naturalism provides a satisfactory quietist response to the skeptic can be laid to rest. Its inherently skeptical character provides a strong incentive to reexamine the adequacy of naturalism and its pretension to provide a complete and satisfying account of the human mind.

Intentionality and Norms[1]

AKEEL BILGRAMI

I

A good place to begin a discussion of naturalism and the normative nature of intentionality is with the suggestion that intentional states are distinct from dispositions. For those convinced of the deep relevance of norms to intentionality, the distinction aspires to be a clean one, but there is a question as to how clean it can be. This paper confronts that question.

Perhaps the first suggestion of the clean version of this distinction is to be found in Wittgenstein. Though one could go straight to Wittgenstein for an exposition, it is more efficient to turn to the less masked and less contrived formulation it gets in Kripke's commentary on Wittgenstein.[2] In strikingly straightforward terms, Kripke points out repeatedly in this work that

> the important problem for Wittgenstein is that my present mental state does not determine what I *ought* to do in the future . . . The fundamental problem is . . . whether my actual dispositions are "right" or not, is there anything that mandates what they *ought* to be. [pp 56–57, his emphasis] . . . The dispositionalist gives a *descriptive* account . . . But this is not the proper account . . . which is *normative*, not *descriptive*. [p. 37, his emphases]

Kripke is talking here (and throughout his book) indifferently about meaning and intentionality. I have argued elsewhere that one has to be very careful about the different ways in which the question of normativity affects meaning and intentionality, despite the obviously close relation between meaning and intentionality.[3] The present paper is restricted in its theme entirely to the normative nature of thought or intentionality. Kripke's general point is that intentionality is a normative notion and thoughts, therefore, cannot get a dispositional account. He is explicit in his criticisms of functionalism and other such accounts of our intentional states of mind, which stress their dispositional character and their causal roles, for completely overlooking and in fact flouting their irreducibly normative character.[4]

Even before Kripke, some philosophers had pointed out that there is a normative, and even an irreducibly normative, character that is possessed by intentional states. But (and this is a point of real importance that will be stressed throughout the paper) Kripke's remarks suggest something much more clean and clear than what is often acknowledged by those who think that intentional states are affected by normativity. To illustrate this, a recurring interlocutory contrast with Kripke will be drawn by reference to Davidson's view of the matter.

Davidson was one of the early proponents of an explicitly normative element in intentionality. This element was essential to the argument of his celebrated paper "Mental Events,"[5] to the effect that intentional states are not reducible to physical states, that they are not type-identical with physical states. (He actually makes his argument, citing events and not states, but it should be obvious that the argument can be made to apply to states as well.) However, Davidson never took the view that intentional states, if they are normative, cannot be dispositions. That is simply not a conclusion he ever drew from their normative character. In fact he has always claimed that intentional states are dispositions, and he described the relevance of normativity to them in the following further claim: intentional states are mental dispositions that unlike other dispositions are "constrained" or "governed" by normative principles of rationality.

Various questions arise. What exactly is this notion of "constraining" and "governing" that is done by normative principles of rationality? How can states themselves thought of as states defined by their causal roles, as second-order properties of the brain, as tendencies in nature, how can—as Kripke puts it—states that are essentially characterized in descriptive terms as dispositions are, be thought of as being governed or constrained by normative principles? Of course we may say that a disposition is rational or irrational, but that does not make it constituted by rationality. It does not make it a normative state. It merely says that it either is in accord or fails to be in accord with rationality. So, on this picture, intentional states, being dispositions, are therefore not themselves normative, but they are assessable for whether they are in accord with the normative principles of rationality. I will return to this picture of intentionality a little later.

Now, the fact that Davidson says that intentional states are dispositions does not immediately make it impossible for them also to be irreducibly normative, since one can characterize dispositions in a way that makes that possible. But even if one did so, one cannot avoid the point that Kripke has stressed: that dispositions are, at least prima facie, just the kinds of states that are thought of in naturalistic terms. So prima facie there is an issue here to be addressed, work to be done, before one can reconcile intentional states—so conceived as dispositions—with their irreducibly normative status. I will return to this question later as well.

Davidson himself does not pause to explicitly address these fundamental questions, despite his insightful insistence on the relevance of normativity to intentional states. His position, therefore, even if not wrong, at the very least is somewhat underdescribed. What makes Kripke's remarks much clearer and more explicit is that he does make a clean distinction between dispositions and intentional states, on grounds of the latter's normativity.

In doing so, he is—implicitly—bringing back to center stage the hallowed wisdom of the "open question" argument of G. E. Moore. I want to take that as my point of departure.[6]

II

Despite their similarities, much to be exploited in the next few pages, two basic differences between Moore's and Kripke's interests are obvious and elementary. First, Moore's theme was not something as general as intentionality, but rather moral values in particular. It was Kripke's innovation (pursuing some remarks in Wittgenstein) to introduce the strategy of Moore's open question argument to our understanding of the normative element of the much more general question of intentionality.

Second, Moore's targets of attack were certain naturalistic reductions of normative terms such as "good" and "ought" to external natural properties. He particularly targeted properties such as social aggregate utility in its Benthamite naturalist versions, though it is a question how external these are in the end. But the argument, as Kripke and Wittgenstein are—implicitly—deploying it, applies equally to reduction of norms or normative properties (such as intentional properties or states) to internal natural properties such as (mental) dispositional properties.

With these differences registered, one can present the Moorean structure of argument on behalf of the broadly Kripkean claim, roughly as follows. It is always a nontrivial or open question (always a question that is unlike asking, say, "This is a bachelor, but is he unmarried?) to ask, "I have this disposition to f, but ought I to f?" If this is a genuinely nontrivial question, then that is some indication that an affirmative answer to it, "Yes I ought to f," expresses a mental state of ours that is not a disposition to f; it is something over and above a disposition to f. The state that is being expressed by this answer may have various relations to that disposition but, given the fact that it is an answer to a nontrivial question, we cannot identify what it expresses with the disposition to f. And the point is that intentional states are states such as this. They are internal "oughts" (or, I suppose one must add, "ought-nots").

Beliefs are oughts of this kind. So are desires. In order to say this, there is no need to deny that we often use the word "desire" to describe dispositions such as, say, an urge to smoke a cigarette, which I may have even if I think I ought not to smoke. But all that shows is that we need to disambiguate the term "desire" between the term used to describe such urges and the term used to describe intentional states proper that are, as Kripke insists, normative states. (Throughout this paper, I will be using the term "desire" in this latter sense.)

In this latter usage, to desire something, to believe something, is to think that one ought to do or think various things, those things that are entailed by those desires and beliefs by the light of certain normative principles (whether those codifying deductive or inductive[7] or decision-theoretic rationality).[8] It is not to be disposed to do or think those things, it is to think one ought to do and think them.

A good word that is often used to describe such internal oughts that are not defined in terms of the corresponding dispositions is that they are "commitments,"[9] commitments to think various things and to do various things. If I believe something, say, that there is a table in front of me, then I am committed to believing various other things, such as (to take just one of them) that there is something in front of me. Those commitments characterize the belief. Similarly with desire. If I desire something, say, that I should help the poor, then I am committed to doing various things, such as, say, giving money to charity or joining a communist party. What exactly intentional states commit us to depends (familiarly) both on other intentional states or commitments we have, and on various norms of logic, decision theory, and so on. Those, like Davidson and a host of others, who think intentional states are dispositions also insist on both this holistic and this logical element, but they do not see those elements as forcing a characterization of beliefs and desires as themselves being commitments. On my reading of Kripke's remarks, he, unlike Davidson, is insisting on this latter claim.

This claim that intentional states are commitments does not mean that dispositions do not have a lot to do with intentional states. In fact, as we shall see, it does not even really mean that dispositions are not involved in the characterization of intentional states. But what the Moore- and Kripke-style arguments establish is that a certain simple identification of intentional states and dispositions is not possible. What they establish is that one may have a certain first-order intentional state (say again, a desire that one help the poor), which is a certain sort of commitment, even if one has no corresponding first-order disposition to do anything at all that would count as fulfilling the commitment to help the poor. That is the very least they establish, and it is very important to have done that, for it makes it possible to argue, as I will try and do, that even if there is a more complex relevance of dispositions to the characterization of intentional states, its complexity is precisely of the sort that rules out a naturalism about intentional states. The importance of the Moore- and Kripke-style arguments is that it provides the first step toward this antinaturalism.

So in a sense what this paper is pursuing is a completion of the argument that Kripke's Moorean remarks, cited earlier, get us started on. If the argument is effective, it should give us the conclusion that Kripke vigorously asserted, namely that it is not possible to entertain the highly prevalent view in philosophy that we may concede that intentional states lack a behavioral or a neurophysiological reduction, but nevertheless claim that they have a naturalistic reduction to states characterized in terms of their causal roles.

III

I have said that it is Moore's open question argument that underlies Kripke's remarks against a dispositional view of intentionality. But it is a striking feature of Moore's argument and perhaps, from our more recent perspective, we can portray it as a striking limitation of Moore's argument, that it is only effective (and is only intended to be effective) against

naturalisms that are definitional. It is effective, that is, against reductions
of moral properties that proceed via (presumably nonarbitrary) stipulations regarding the meaning or connotation or sense of evaluative terms
such as "good."

If so, it is a perfectly fair objection that those are not the most interesting forms of naturalism about value, and they are certainly not how
the most current naturalisms present themselves. In keeping with more
current thinking, we might think of naturalistic treatments of value as
proceeding via discoverable identities between evaluative properties or
states and natural properties or states, and not proceeding via definitional
claims about the meaning of evaluative terms such as "good."

Against this, the open question argument will be quite ineffective. That
is to say: one might think that there is a naturalistic reduction of good
to some natural property via some a posteriori identity claims such as
those we have for natural kinds, identities such as, for example, "water
= H₂O." This is a reduction that takes good to be a natural kind, and
"good" to be a natural kind term that is to be understood in terms of a
causal theory of reference of a familiar sort.[10] Such a reduction, which is
not dependent on senses or connotation or meaning, is not vulnerable
to the open question argument, which only targets definitional reductions. So someone may grant that Moore's argument is fine as far as it
goes, but object that it does not go far enough to overturn these other
more current forms of naturalism about value.[11]

It is important to note that raising this difficulty is not intended to say
that there is any fault in Moore's argument itself. It is rather to point
out that the argument is only effective against particular kinds of naturalistic reduction, those that depend on definition, meaning, connotation,
and senses. It is not effective against reductions based on causal theories
of reference yielding only contingent or a posteriori rather than definitional identities.

So far I have raised the question of this limitation for Moore. But
exactly this sort of difficulty can be raised about Kripke's Moorean argument against a dispositional view of intentional properties. In this context, as I said earlier, the open question targets not the identification of
good with social aggregate utility, but the identification of intentional
states qua commitments with certain sorts of dispositions. It is only if
this identification was made via meaning or definitional stipulations that
the open question argument works. But here too, there is no reason to
think that those are the best ways to make the identifications. After all,
many reductive views of the mind today are based on empirical claims,
so here again one might insist that the identification of intentional states

(commitments) with dispositions is not definitional but based on a posteriori identities dependent in the familiar way on causal accounts of reference. Against this, the Moorean strategy will be ineffective.

Let us pursue this a little further. For the sake of convenience and abbreviation only, one can restrict oneself to the case of Moore's original argument, which pertains to moral rather than intentional properties. But since intentional properties or states, on the normative picture owing to Kripke, are evaluative properties or states, anything one says about the former will carry over to the latter because the structure of the argument is exactly the same, and applies to value in general.

Is this difficulty raised for Moore decisive? I shall be arguing it is not, and the argument will be based on raising Fregean considerations to supplement the Moorean considerations raised so far. Familiar Fregean considerations[12] raise an issue for these more recent forms of naturalistic reduction of value, even as they seem to have escaped the net of Moore's argument.

Keeping things quite general, suppose such a reduction appealed to some a posteriori identity of the form good = x, where x was some natural property. Now, it is surely possible that someone may without irrationality deny that good = x, just as someone may deny without irrationality that Hesperus is Phosphorus, or deny that London is Londres, or that water is H_2O. Mere lack of information about astronomy or geography or chemistry (or morals) cannot make one irrational. But if someone can coherently and meaningfully say, "It is not the case that good is x," then we must ask what the term "good" in this coherent, meaningful false statement means. Let the term denote whatever it is supposed to, given the a posteriori identity; the point is that we need to posit a sense, we need to say what it connotes, in order to find the statement coherent and rational, even if it is false. That shows that even in the identity statement "good = x," the term "good" has a sense, over and above a reference.[13]

And now the question is, what is this sense or what are these senses expressing? Here we have a choice. We can either say that these modes of presentation, which are presumably often specified in descriptions, are expressing further naturalistic properties, once again. Or we can say that they are expressing moral and evaluative properties. Either choice leads to serious trouble for the naturalistic reduction.

If we opt for the former, if we say that they express further naturalistic properties, then we are back once again to being vulnerable to Moore's open question argument. For recall that Moore's argument was never said to be at fault in itself. That was not the point of the difficulty we raised. It was only supposed to be limited in what it was effective against. It was only effective against definitional reductions that are based on meaning or connotation or senses. But if we grant, under pressure from the Fregean considerations just raised, that our morally badly informed but rational protagonist is rational only because his term "good" is being given a sense or meaning, then we cannot go on to say that that sense expresses a naturalistic property. That is just the idea that Moore's argument had devastated.

What if we opt for the other choice? What if we say that they, the relevant descriptions specifying the modes of presentation, do not express a naturalistic property? Well then, there is no fully effective naturalistic reduction in the first place. To choose this option is to give up on the naturalism.

The point is that if the difficulty was that the Moorean argument was fine as far as it went but it did not go far enough to overturn this sort of naturalism, the reply is that with a little help from a familiar Fregean argument, the Moorean argument can be made to go exactly that far. And as I said, exactly the same structure of argumentation can be made to defend the naturalistic irreducibility of intentional states, under their normative reading, to dispositional states.

It looks, then, as if there is something like a pincer effect that disallows any naturalistic reduction of normative notions, whether moral ones or those involved in intentionality. These reductions are either vulnerable to 1) Moore-style arguments or 2) Frege-style arguments. If naturalists think they are not vulnerable to 1), it is only because they are in thrall to a naturalism that is susceptible to 2), and if they think that they can forestall 2) by appealing to the sort of thing (meanings, sense) that 2) demands while retaining their naturalism, then they are once again susceptible to 1). In short, naturalism cannot escape the crushing grip of Moore's hand because it is pushed right back there by the other, Fregean hand. "Pincer" is a good word to describe this effect.

IV

Various objections can be raised against the pincer argument, just given, to undermine these naturalisms regarding value in general and intentionality in particular.

A) Some may resist the pincer dialectic by digging their heels in and saying that there simply are no senses involved at all in our understanding of natural kind terms, and so the Fregean considerations of the pincer need not be taken seriously at all. They were taken seriously at the point where we said that merely being misinformed does not make one irrational, it does not make one's statements denying the relevant a posteriori identities incoherent and meaningless. It is at that point that one appealed to senses or descriptions to account for their meaningfulness and rationality. But this is all illegitimate, it might be said. At most, descriptions come into originary reference-fixing events, but after that these descriptions completely drop out and in no way amount to modes of presentation or sense. They play no role at all in our understanding of terms like "water," "gold," or for that matter, "good," once the reference-fixing event is over and done with. This is sometimes the view taken by the strict forms of the causal theory of reference.[14] If we thought of "good" along these strict causal-theoretic lines, then there are no senses that hold of "good," no stereotypes, no descriptions, no modes of presentation, nothing of that sort to which we may tie our term "good" in a way that has philosophical significance. If so, there is nothing for the other hand of the pincer to come down on. There is no definitional element, no element of Fregean sense to which the Moorean argument can apply.

But if that is really so, it is possible that we could be and always have been completely wrong about what good is; if that is really so there would be nothing in itself incoherent about imagining that every judgment about good we have ever made might be completely off the mark. We would simply have been fooled into thinking on all occasions of judgment that "fool's good" is good. On such a strict causal theory of reference, how we conceive of good (or gold or water) can altogether come apart from what good is, what it refers to, what the relevant a posteriori identities reveal it to be identical with. If the strict causal theories of reference allow for such consequence, one would have thought that the consequence is quite enough to show that we have here a reductio ad absurdum of the idea that good is a natural kind. It would be bad enough if this was a consequence for gold or water, namely that it is possible that we are and always have been systematically deceived about them. But about good, it seems utterly unacceptable to think that it is possible that we have never got it right. It is unacceptable in the sense that in the face of such a consequence, we would be perfectly within our rights to say that the interesting normative notion is "fool's good" and not good.

However, precisely because such a consequence threatens to produce a reductio ad absurdum of the very idea of natural kinds, it is not clear that too many people really do hold to such a strict version of a causal theory. Most people now think of causal accounts of reference as really only falling back on some idea such as "whatever it is that underlies and explains the stereotypical properties p, q, r, to which we tie our terms 'water,' 'gold,' and so forth."[15] This is, then, perhaps how they will also think of "good." But then that move brings us right back to the idea of senses or definitions. The stereotypes, descriptions, senses, and so on, are part of the characterization of reference. There is no characterizing the reference, as these nonstrict causal accounts make clear, unless we build into it these defining and sense-giving stereotypes that the stricter causal accounts of reference left out once the originary reference-fixing baptisms were over. And if the claim is that a naturalistic reduction of good relies on treating "good" as a natural kind term with such a non-strict causal account of its reference, then the question must arise: Are these senses or stereotypes that are built into our characterization of its reference expressing natural properties or not? If they are, then they are vulnerable to Moore's open question argument. If not, there is no nat-uralistic reduction, in any case. The pincer is effective again.

B) Philosophers will undoubtedly worry that this entire appeal to Frege and to senses in one hand of the pincer (in order to set things up for the other, Moorean hand of the pincer) is assuming that senses always express properties, and they will question the assumption. If the sense or senses of "good" were not seen as expressing genuine properties, then the Moorean arm of the pincer (which is intended to undermine a re-duction of good to a certain kind of property—a natural property—via an appeal to meaning, definition, sense) would have nothing to work on. No nonnatural or any other kind of property is being expressed by the sense of "good."

The objection, then, will be that we are never required to say that a sense always expresses a property. They often do not, so perhaps they do not in the case of evaluative terms such as "good" (or "commit-ments"). So unless I am taking the quite implausible view that senses always express properties, the pincer is not effective.

Now, of course one needn't deny that some very idiosyncratic senses could be dismissed as not having any corresponding properties or facts that they express. Nor need one deny that there are senses that seem to us to be obviously depicting something false. Those too are similarly dismissable. An example: someone's sense for "water" might be "what the Hindu gods drank after their sport." The claim that this sense and others like it express facts and genuine properties may of course be legitimately dismissed. So in my argument, I am talking about senses that are not only communitywide and nonidiosyncratic, but also senses that are not dismissable in this way as not describing facts and properties. If for any relevant natural kind term ("good" included, if that is indeed what "good" is) there is always a cluster of senses, some of which were and some of which are not dismissable as idiosyncratic and obviously false, then a certain amount of disentangling would have to be done before the force of the Frege-Moore argument I am presenting can be seen. The Moorean open question applies to the undismissable senses or descriptions remaining after the disentangling has been done. If these express natural properties, then they will be susceptible to Moore's open question, and if they do not express natural properties, there is no naturalistic reduction of good in the first place.

C) It might be said that in saying this I have still not addressed the most principled critical response to this Frege-Moore strategy with which I am confronting the contemporary naturalist. The Fregean part of the strategy has the effect of necessarily throwing up senses, often a cluster of senses, and I have talked of disentangling the dismissable from the undismissable among these senses in order to set things up for the application of the Moorean part of the pincer strategy. The principled objection to all this is to say, "Let the Fregean part of the strategy throw up senses. It still may be the case that the senses involved in the case of 'good' by their nature are never undismissable ones and therefore they never express any properties at all, that they are merely concepts and conceptions but there are no corresponding real things, facts, or properties." So one just cannot create the setup for the application of the Moorean part of the pincer strategy.

This echoes what we had said earlier about fool's good, but with a difference. We had said earlier that if senses played no role at all in our understanding of natural kind terms (as claimed by the strict causal theories), then all our judgments regarding what is good could, in principle, be and always have been off the mark, an illusory pursuit of fool's good. Now we are being told that even if we countenance nonstrict causal theories where senses do play an intrinsic role in natural kind terms, the senses for "good" in particular could all be dismissable as never describing real properties. This scenario would really be simply coextensive with the fool's good scenario that I was protesting earlier, when senses were not allowed in as relevant at all. The only difference is that it might be thought that being only coextensive but not cointensive with that scenario, it is not possible to reject this naturalism for being based on a too strict and too implausible causal theory of reference that admits of no senses.

But here a very basic question arises. What could possibly justify this claim that the senses of "good" are all dismissable out of hand as not really describing properties and facts and real things? We certainly do not say any such thing about senses such as "the first visible object in the sky in the evening" or "the city that contains Big Ben" or "the substance that fills oceans." If one does not say it of the senses of "Hesperus" or "London" or "water," why does one say it of the sense of "good"? Nothing else but a scientistic prejudice about the criteria for property existence could lead one to say it. If a sense or description is not purporting to express properties that will play a role (or if it is not expressing properties that are eventually reducible to properties that will play a role)[16] in our basic scientific understanding of the world, if it is not purporting to describe anything that figures in the causal-explanatory scheme of a natural science, then it has nothing but a mere conceptual status. It expresses no real properties. This would be a scientistic prejudice[17] and a question-begging claim on the part of the naturalist. The naturalist was supposed to give an argument for a reduction of value to natural properties and facts by appeal to causal theories of reference and a posteriori identities. Against that argument a Frege-Moore counterargument had been presented. If it turns out that in one's response to this counterargument one is assuming a criterion for property existence that takes for granted the truth of naturalism, the naturalist has begged the question against the counterargument. I conclude, then, that the pincer argument, despite these objections, remains effective and there is no non-question-begging way out for the naturalist, once one sees its force.

There is a great deal more to be said by way of elaboration of these antinaturalist strategies I am deploying, more to be said about how they apply to these naturalistic efforts I have already discussed, and more to be said about how they have to be applied to other sorts of naturalistic efforts regarding value than the ones I have discussed.[18] But I cannot elaborate any of this in a short paper. I just wanted to put it into the air that even for those who think that there are more current reductions of intentionality (mimicking cases of reduction within science via discoverable identities) than those that are vulnerable to Kripke and Moore's simpler arguments with which we began—there are reasons to think that these too are vulnerable to a different style of argument (owing to Frege) whose effect is to force the naturalist to make an appeal to the very sorts of thing that brings him right back via a very tight pincer movement to being vulnerable to the Moorean arguments.

I have restricted the presentation of the pincer argument to talk of evaluative notions such as "good" because that was Moore's target, but the structure of the pincer argument is a perfectly general one and applies to all evaluative notions, and so it holds of intentional concepts, if these are indeed normative and not dispositional.[19]

V

The last two sections took up Kripke's dialectic of presenting the naturalistically irreducible normativity of intentional states via their contrast with the notion of mental dispositions. They have tried to fortify his conclusion with the pincer argument. With that antinaturalistic argument in place, let me take up the question about how to positively characterize the nature of intentional states if they are not to be defined (or otherwise characterized) naturalistically in terms of dispositions.

As I said earlier, their relations to dispositions needs to be explored once we give up on the rather straightforward naturalistic appeal of the relevance of dispositions to intentionality, which Kripke criticizes. In a characterization of intentional states, it may well turn out that dispositions are relevant, but in ways that are more complex and indirect than in naturalistic characterizations of them. I have, following some others, called intentional states "commitments." What are these?

Take belief. It is sometimes said that when we say that a belief is a commitment, we are saying that we are prepared to defend it against those who deny or challenge it. I should like to disassociate myself from such a conception of commitments. Even if there is something to it, it seems to me to be a superficial feature of commitments. It stresses a social aspect of commitments that does not have to be seen as defining of them, even if it is often true of them. When I think the challenge from another is not worth taking seriously, I would certainly not be prepared to defend my belief. And I may in general not be prepared to listen to others' views. Such indifference to denials of my beliefs cannot possibly threaten the idea of belief as commitment. They do not threaten the claim that I have the beliefs and commitments in question, so it cannot be that being prepared to defend them is a defining feature of commitments. By pointing to the possibility of indifference to denials and challenges to one's beliefs, I don't mean that we could give up on testimony as a source of information and belief-acquisition; I mean rather that I would not think of my fellows as essential interlocutors, in the sense of questioners and watchdogs of my belief. In general, despite what Rorty and some others say, there is no reason to think that persuading others or justifying oneself to others is an essential aspect of epistemology, even if it is essential to sociability, to intellectual propagation, to self-advancement, and the like. And if one sheds the social aspect of this conception of commitment, if one sheds the idea that one justifies and defends one's beliefs against challenges from others, then all that is left of the conception is that one would defend a belief against evidence to the contrary, and that would in fact be a foolish way to hold a belief qua commitment. Presumably a commitment should be questioned, not defended, if evidence to the contrary comes in. This conception of commitments starts off in the wrong direction. Let's try another tack.

A belief or desire, I said earlier, was a commitment to believe other things or to do certain things, respectively. And I have denied that we have to be disposed to believe or do those things that one is committed to believing and doing, by one's beliefs and desires. (One may be disposed to thinking or doing them, but there is no requirement that one be so disposed in order to have the belief or desire, qua commitments.) The claim here is quite strong. It says not only that one need not have had to live up to a commitment in order to possess it, but that one need not even be disposed to do whatever it takes to live up to it.

If that is really so, a question arises as to how one can tell the difference between someone who has a certain intentional state and someone who lacks it. After all, if one does not have to live up to a commitment in order to have one, and if one does not even have to have the disposition to act so as to live up to it, then it is a real question how one may distinguish the having of the commitment from lacking it.

Simply placing the demand that we can verbalize the commitment, with the words "I believe that p" or "I desire that p," will be insufficient, since the words may be phony, and the further demand that the words be sincere does not get us much beyond the initial question. That is to say, asking when someone has a commitment is not all that far from asking when someone's avowal of a commitment is sincere. To put it as Polonius might have, "actions speak louder than words," and it is precisely the actions, even potential actions, that go missing if there need be no disposition to act on a commitment in order to have one. So, evidently some further demand must be placed on the idea of an intentional state than its avowability before one can plausibly be said to think of it as a commitment.

Here is one. We can put it down as a necessary and defining condition of having a commitment. To have a commitment, one must be prepared to have certain reactive attitudes, minimally to be self-critical or to be accepting of criticism from another, if one fails to live up to the commitment or if one lacks the disposition to do what it takes to live up to it; and one must be prepared to do better by way of trying to live up to it or cultivating the disposition to live up to it.

This defining condition brings out some part of the normative element of intentional states by stressing the idea of criticism of failures. More important, while it brings out the close links between intentional states and dispositions, it does so without abandoning the more crucial normative element, that is, without actually saying that they are dispositions, or even saying that they are to be defined directly in terms of having the dispositions to do those things that are cases of living up to the commitment.

I say "directly" because clearly I have indirectly invoked dispositions in the characterization of a commitment when I said that in order to be said to have a commitment, one must be prepared to accept criticism for not having the disposition to do things that live up to one's commitment or be prepared to cultivate the disposition to do those things if one fails to live up to it or if one fails to have the disposition to do something that is a living up to it. These are all occurrences of the idea of dispositions in the very characterization of commitments. However, what one is not saying is required in order to have a commitment is that one has the disposition to do things that are cases of living up to it. So no first-order disposition has to be present in order for there to be a first-order commitment. In fact it has to be absent for the indirect appeal to dispositions above to come into play, since it is the cultivation of absent dispositions that the indirect appeal mentions. To require that those dispositions actually be present would be to invoke dispositions in the "direct" fashion in the way that I, following Kripke, deny.

But there is an obvious problem here. I have been determined to keep out the presence of dispositions in the characterizing of the minimal conditions for having a commitment, but have I not in fact at one level required that dispositions of a certain sort be present? How is one to understand the requirement that one be prepared to accept criticism for not having lived up to a commitment, when one has failed to live up to it, that one be prepared to do better by way of living up to it, and so forth? Is this idea of "preparedness" not just to be thought of as second-order dispositions to accept criticism? And if so, have I not ushered in at the second order precisely what I was keen to keep out at the first, that is, the presence of dispositions?

I am not particularly invested in keeping out the presence of dispositions at the second order. So I am not invested in resisting this understanding of the idea of "preparedness" in the minimal conditions characterizing commitments, namely that the preparedness is just second-order dispositions to accept criticism and to cultivate the necessary first-order dispositions that are absent sometimes[20] when one fails to live up to commitments. Why is that? Doesn't requiring the presence of dispositions at the second order make one vulnerable to the charge that one has in the end conceded everything to the naturalist, who wants to give a dispositionalist analysis of intentional states? I don't think so at all. No interesting naturalistic and dispositional analysis of intentional states follows just because one has introduced dispositions into the analysis of intentional states qua commitments in this way. The reason for this is quite straightforward.

If the preparednesses in question were to be understood as the presence of certain sorts of dispositions, dispositions have entered into my characterization of intentional states qua commitments in a way that is entirely parasitic on first-order commitments. They have no independent standing, no independent way of being spelled out. They are generated by the simplest and crudest of algorithms that presuppose that something normative like a commitment is inescapably present at the first order.

So, suppose with me that intentional states are internal oughts or commitments. And suppose that I have the desires (or beliefs) that p, that q, that r, all of which are to be thought of as commitments. And suppose that I fail to live up to these commitments and I am not disposed to do anything that lives up to them. I have said that if and when that happens, I must have the "preparedness" to, among other things, accept criticism for my failure to live up to these commitments. I am worrying now that the preparedness, if it is seen as a second-order disposition, is going to amount to a capitulation to a dispositional analysis of intentional states. And I am soothing my worry with the following thought. The second-order dispositions that each of my preparednesses amounts to can get no characterization but the following: the disposition to accept criticism for not having lived up to the commitment that p, the disposition to accept criticism for not having lived up to the commitment that q, the disposition to accept criticism for not having lived up to the commitment that r.[21] Any effort to characterize the second-order disposition (the preparedness to accept criticism) that leaves out the commitments at the first-order from its formulation is going to fall afoul of all the considerations that led one to see intentional states as internal oughts or commitments in the first place, namely the Kripkean and Moorean open question argument, the Frege-style arguments, and so on, all of which I mentioned earlier. But if the commitments at the first order always have to be in place in order to characterize the second-order dispositions, then these second-order dispositions (the preparednesses to accept criticism for not having lived up to the first-order commitments, the preparedness to cultivate the first-order dispositions to do or think things that will live up to the first-order commitments, and so forth) are simply reeled off algorithmically and parasitically in the manner mentioned above. There is an ineliminable reference to commitments in the analysis of intentional states, even if the analysis requires that dispositions be present at the second order. That is enough to resist the claim that such a dispositional reading of the idea of preparedness in our characterization of commitments capitulates to any interesting naturalistic dispositional analysis of intentional states.[22]

Someone might resist this by insisting that the description of the second-order dispositions that go into the idea of the relevant sorts of preparedness need not ineliminably mention the first-order commitments. The minimal defining conditions for commitments at the first order, on this view, would (in deference to the Moore-Kripke arguments) not require any first-order dispositions, but they would require second-order dispositions of various kinds such as the disposition to accept criticism for not having the first-order dispositions to do the actions that the content of the first-order commitments would count as living-up to the commitments. Or they would require second-order dispositions to cultivate first-order dispositions to do actions of those kinds. Though I have mentioned the first-order commitments in the description of these second-order dispositions, that mention is eliminable, it will be said. Take my desire (commitment) that I help the poor. The minimal requirement for having this commitment, on this view, would first make clear which actions or sorts of actions satisfy the predicate ("helping the poor") used to specify the content of the commitment. It would then state the requirement that in order to have that commitment I must minimally have a disposition to accept criticism for not having done each of those actions or to accept criticism for not having the disposition to do those actions, and I must have a disposition to cultivate the disposition to do those actions. (And normative talk of accepting "criticism" would itself have to be redescribed in terms of complex dispositions of various sorts.) In this statement of the minimal defining conditions of a commitment, there will inevitably be a very complicated set of nested and disjunctive dispositions that will have to mentioned, but if they are complicated enough no mention at all of the commitment being defined need be made. There might be a problem as to whether what is common to all these dispositions can be made out without mention of the commitment they are trying to define. But that may not seem to the dispositionalist to be an insuperable problem, in principle. We therefore have a naturalistic dispositional analysis of commitments, he will claim. But we don't have anything of the kind, because even if he can overcome the problem just raised, which he has dismissed as not being insuperable in principle (something that is not obvious at all), the Moore-Kripke argument raises its head again.

Suppose that I have these complicated second-order dispositions purporting to give a naturalistic definitional analysis of commitments. I can still ask nontrivially, "I have these second-order dispositions, but ought I to help the poor?" If that is a genuinely nontrivial question, then one cannot define the first-order commitment in terms of (or we cannot identify the first-order commitment with) these complicated second-order dispositions. If I answer "yes" to this nontrivial question, I have announced something over and above the complicated second-order dispositions I see myself as having. I have made or announced a commitment. The dispositionalist in order to make his case would have to say that this is a trivial question, akin to asking, "Here is an unmarried man, but is he a bachelor?" and therefore if the answer is affirmative, nothing over and above the possession of the second-order dispositions is announced. But to say that is to misdescribe things.

That is the whole point of the Moorean open question argument. It follows that there is no avoiding mention of the first-order commitments in characterizing the second-order dispositions that constitute the relevant sorts of preparedness that define what commitments are. The only way in which Moore's argument lapses, the only way in which the question Moore raises ceases to be an open or nontrivial question in this context, the only way in which it can be akin to raising the question about bachelors, is if the specification of the second-order dispositions do mention the first-order commitments.

But in that case there is no problem to begin with, since it in effect thwarts the naturalistic and reductive aspirations of the appeal to dispositions. The lesson is that we can and should, without anxiety, allow a nonnaturalistic defining second-order dispositional element in the characterization of intentional states qua commitments.

So the dialectic is really this. In this section I have not tried to give an argument for why intentional states, which are normative states, that is, commitments, cannot be reduced naturalistically to dispositions. That argument was presented over the last two sections, and I have just repeated a fragment of it in the last paragraph. In this section I am only trying to give a characterization of intentional states as commitments, a characterization that if it appeals to dispositions (at the second order) does so without any naturalistic intent. If someone (the interlocutor I have just addressed) says that it is quite possible to appeal to them at the second order with naturalistic intent, nothing that I have said in this section gives one an argument against that. All I am doing in this section is to say that it is perfectly possible to appeal to second-order dispositions in characterizing intentional states without that appeal being naturalistic.

If my interlocutor insists on the appeal to second-order dispositions being naturalistic, what I need to do (in fact what I have just done in the last paragraph) is to appeal to (part of) the argument I have already given in the last two sections to show that this appeal must fail.

At the outset of the paper I had said that I would be probing, on behalf of the antinaturalist convinced of the deep normativity of intentional states, how clean a break intentional states can make from dispositions. It is turning out that the break need not be complete. A less than complete break can still leave the naturalistic irreducibility and normative status of intentional states quite intact. It may seem odd that one is making appeal to a notion of disposition that is not naturalistic, since paradigmatically the notion of dispositions are central to naturalistic philosophical treatments of the mind. But that oddity can be amicably resolved by disambiguation.

Dispositions on all accounts of them have a counterfactual component. They are states that in certain circumstances—not necessarily actual, but when actual—will be triggered and manifested. But dispositions are also widely thought of as states with a causal component, which makes them part of the causal nexus of nature, in a familiar naturalistic understanding of "nature." These are two quite different components in our understanding of dispositions, and it is not compulsory that the former component must be understood in terms of the latter, or as requiring or entailing the latter. When philosophers say that the counterfactual component has underlying it a causal mechanism or a scientific-realist causal basis, we are adding a further and substantive component to what we mean by dispositions. So we may, if we wish, speak sometimes of dispositions in very minimal terms, in terms only of the first component, without the second.[23] When we do so, there is no reason to think that dispositions are to be naturalistically understood.

I have made central to one's understanding of intentional states qua normative states or commitments, a second-order disposition. And the challenge to me was: How can I characterize this disposition, and therefore the commitment itself that is defined in terms of it, in non-naturalistic terms, when the usual understanding of the notion of dispositions in the philosophical study of the mind assumes that mental dispositions are naturalistic states? My answering thought has been that the only sense of dispositions that commitments require in their characterization is one that is minimally characterized in terms of the first, counterfactual component only.

No doubt, and with some right, it will be asked that I say more than I have about what is meant by a notion of disposition that is not natu-

ralistic, and that I do so by saying more about what underlies this counterfactual component, if it is not the standard causal and psychologistic
picture familiar from naturalistic conceptions of dispositions. I will take
this question up at the end of the next section. I actually have no objection even to the use of the term "cause" in expounding this notion of
disposition, so long as it is not developed along naturalistic lines. But for
now, we may tentatively rest with the conclusion that intentional states,
shown by the argument given in Sections III and IV to be naturalistically
irreducible because evaluative, can be characterized as I have in this Section V, in terms that appeal to dispositions without spoiling their naturalistically irreducible status.

VI

Let me close by distinguishing what I think are real advances brought
by Kripke's way of stressing the normative nature of intentionality, which
I have tried to develop in this paper, from other ways that are present in
the philosophical literature. I have introduced the distinction between
genuinely normative states and dispositions as ordinarily understood,
with a view to claiming that intentional states are the former sorts of
states. In saying this, I have been resisting those like Davidson who have
no truck with the idea that intentional states are commitments and would
like to retain the idea that intentional states are dispositions, and account
for the normativity of intentional states in other ways, ways that I have
claimed are, in the light of Moore and Kripke's arguments, misleadingly
underdescribed. It is not a very clear or explicit way of keeping faith with
what is established by Moore and Kripke to account for the normativity
of intentional states by saying—as Davidson does—that they are dispositions "governed" by principles of normativity. The clearer and more
explicit way of doing so rather is to say that intentional states are themselves normative states. Having recognized this, calling them internal
oughts or "commitments" is natural and proper.

It is tempting to resist the claim that beliefs and desires are themselves
commitments by saying that we have no other commitments but commitments to think (believe, desire, etc.) in accord with the principles of
rationality that govern thought. If we have any commitments they are to
these principles. There are no commitments other than to think logically
and rationally, and these minimal commitments do not make the
thoughts (which we are committed to being rational) themselves commitments.

But this is most unsatisfactory. If thoughts themselves were not commitments, and the only commitments we had were to the principles of logic and of rationality generally, then in the following scenario we would get quite the wrong instruction. Suppose I believed that p, and in a fit of distraction, I also went on to assent to something inconsistent with "p" (to put it at its crudest for the sake of convenience, say, "not-p"). Then the only thing that the commitments to the principles of rationality would oblige me to do would be to get rid of the inconsistency. The only instruction coming from them would be: "Get rid of either the belief that p or withdraw assent from not-p." But it is obvious that in this scenario, the fully right instruction is not that; rather it is much more specific. It is: "Withdraw assent from 'not-p.' " Just by the way the scenario has been set up, it is obvious that the instruction "Clean up your act" or "Get rid of the inconsistency" is not a specific enough instruction. But it is the only instruction that the commitment to the basic principles of rationality gives us. If we want the more specific instruction we should be getting in this scenario, we have to acknowledge that beliefs themselves are commitments. That is to say, we have to acknowledge that all that I believe in this scenario is p, which is therefore my only commitment, and that "not-p" is just a distracted assertion that does not genuinely express a belief, hence a commitment.

This gives a compelling reason to think of intentional states as themselves normative states or commitments, and once we do so, the great and striking relevance of the Moorean and Fregean arguments of Sections III and IV comes right into focus. If they are themselves values, and Moore's argument (with some help from Frege) is designed to show that values are not natural properties, intentional states are thereby immediately demonstrated to be irreducible to naturalistic dispositional properties.

However, Davidson may still insist that he too has come to the conclusion that intentional states are not naturalistically reducible; and he may deny that he needs to say that they are themselves commitments in order to do so. The argument he provides for this conclusion in fact assumes that intentional states are dispositions, not commitments, and goes on to say that being mental dispositions they are constrained by rationality principles that have no echo in the natural sciences, and as a result these mental dispositions, will not be integrated in any serious way with the dispositional or categorical states posited by the natural sciences. This is his thesis of the "anomalousness of the mental." Quite independently of considering this argument of his, I have tried to give reasons (in the paragraph before the last one) for why he is wrong to deny that mental states are commitments. But now what should we make of this argument from "the anomalousness of the mental" for the naturalistic irreducibility of intentional states? How does it compare with the argument we have given in Sections III and IV for the same conclusion?

It does not compare favorably because it is susceptible to Ockham's razor. Let me explain. We have concluded, via an argument of Moore (with some supplementation by Frege), that value in general is irreducible to natural properties. Davidson no doubt agrees with that general conclusion. He wants to conclude on the basis of his argument from the "anomalous" nature of the mental that there is another irreducibility, that of intentional properties to natural properties. However, if we take intentional states to be commitments themselves, we do not need to conclude that there are two irreducibilities here. The first one is enough. If intentional states are commitments, they are oughts or values, and the first argument shows that values are naturalistically irreducible. Parsimony therefore suggests that Kripke is not merely more clear and explicit, but he is simpler and neater, about what really is at stake in thinking of intentional states as irreducible. And when we add to the considerations from parsimony, the added advantage of being given the right instruction for what to do when we assent distractedly to things that are inconsistent with our beliefs, the idea that intentional states are themselves commitments begins to look much the more plausible philosophical view of them.

To pursue the contrast between Kripke's and Davidson's picture of the normativity of intentional states a little further, notice that there is a very important and far-going implication of intentional states being viewed as commitments. Seeing desires and beliefs as commitments requires us to radically distinguish between two different questions: 1) "Why did someone do what she did?" and 2) "Did what she did live up to her commitments?" To say that the distinction is a radical one is to say that there is no way to make these questions coincide nor to see them as in any deep or interesting way integrated. This point is not made by Kripke but is surely implied by some of the quotations from Kripke I cited above. The first question can be answered by citing such things as dispositions (and motives). The second question is answered by looking to whether actions are in accord with one's intentional states.

Davidson has never been too eager to distinguish between these two questions as distinct in the radical way being insisted on here, and that is of a piece with him not making a clean distinction between dispositions and intentional states. Why does he not distinguish sharply between these two questions? Because of a firm conviction on his part—a conviction that has pervaded his philosophy of mind and language—that we are by and large disposed to do what is in accord with our commitments.

This idea, which he sometimes presents as a necessary form of charity (something that is not an option in interpreting others' words, thoughts, and actions),[24] convinces him that the two questions cannot diverge in any radical sense. And because he thinks the two questions are not really radically divergent, he sees no compulsion to think that beliefs and desires are commitments in the first place.

By contrast, in the picture in which the two questions are radically separated, things are not like that. One does what one does because of one's dispositions, motives, and so on. The relations between one's doings and these states we cite in answering the first question are causal. Whether these doings are in accord with our commitments or not is not a question about causality, but another question about another relation altogether. However, if one is convinced, as Davidson is, that we do by and large do what we are "committed" to, then one would find it an unnecessary scruple to keep apart the relations between one's doings and their psychological causes from the relations between one's doings and the "commitments" with which they are (as he sees it) by and large in accord. Given that conviction in the idea of "charity," we could simply identify the "commitments" with the states that we cite when we answer the question "Why did someone do what she did?" In other words, one need not feel any particular theoretical pressure to see why "commitments" and dispositions should be distinguished in the first place. (Thus my placing of "commitment" in courtesy quotes throughout while expounding his position.) This is the thinking that underlies his identification of intentional states with dispositions, despite recognizing the normative element in intentional states, despite recognizing that there is a normative question about actions being in accord with one's intentional states.[25]

There is a subtle qualification that is necessary at this point. It is not that I want to deny Davidson's basic point here, which he erects into a principle, "a principle of charity." (We really should call it the principle of "necessary" charity, since he is very clear that it is not an option, which charity presumably is.) If we formulate the principle of necessary charity as follows, it does not deserve the notoriety it has fetched: we cannot be creatures who are massively irrational without ceasing to be thought of as creatures with a sophisticated level of intentionality. If this principle were not true, one would be hard put to say why the maple tree in front of my window does not have all the sophisticated form of intentionality that I have, hard put to say why it does not have all of this intentionality but simply sits stationary in the park outside because it is massively irrational, massively weak-willed, say. Being weak-willed, it lacks all the dispositions that would allow it to live up to all these commitments that comprise its intentionality. We could not rule out this absurd hypothesis that the tree is an intentional creature without admitting to the minimal claim of his principle. The impossibility of massive irrationality that the principle of necessary charity demands is what allows us to rule out the hypothesis we find absurd. The principle, therefore, has a point.

If this much is right in what he says, where then does Davidson go wrong? He goes wrong in drawing quite the wrong conclusion from this principle; he goes wrong in identifying what exactly it is that this principle defines. What I have just admitted to being right in the principle suggests that all it defines is what it is to be a subject with a sophisticated level of intentionality. To be such a subject, one cannot be massively irrational in just the way that the principle claims. However, Davidson explicitly uses the principle not just to define a subject who can be properly said to possess intentional states of a certain level of sophistication, but to define the very idea of an intentional state. He has repeatedly said that what it shows is that our very idea of an intentional state is the idea of a state where the dispositional element and the normative element tend to converge. In other words, the principle of necessary charity has the effect of showing that it is built into the nature of a belief or of a desire that its possessor will by and large do and be disposed to do what it's normative element requires her to do. (When charity takes in not just rationality but truth, Davidson also says things such as, "a belief, by its nature, tends to be true.") And convinced that it has this effect, he sees no reason to distinguish between the two questions "Why did somebody do what he did?" which is answered by citing his dispositional states, motives, and so on, as radically separate from the question, "Did what he did live up to his commitments?" The idea of an intentional state itself being an internal ought or commitment, as distinct from a disposition, therefore never so much as occurs to him.

But the principle of charity does not and cannot define what an intentional state is, it can only define what it is to be a creature with intentional states (of a certain level of complexity). Minimal rationality requirements (even generously understood) can only rule out the absurd hypothesis that certain sorts of subjects such as trees be counted as sophisticated intentional subjects; they cannot rule out the distinction between the very idea of commitments and dispositions. Despite his principle that shows what is required to be a subject of sophisticated intentionality, there is in fact always enough failure on the part of such a subject to live up to his commitments, to see the distinction between disposition and commitment as having a deep theoretical point and place.

If there was no failure (or hardly any) then one could perhaps avoid making the distinction and say that intentional states are dispositions, though even that is doubtful.[26] But things are manifestly not like that. So nothing in his principle, therefore, allows it to be used in the way that Davidson does; and it is only his illicit extrapolation from using the principle to define a subject possessing intentional states to using it to define the very nature of intentional states that screens him off from seeing the importance of radically separating the two questions mentioned above and from making the clean distinction between intentional states and dispositions that Kripke is insisting on.

If these criticisms of Davidson are right, the question arises as to what remains of his idea that intentional states cause and are part of the causal explanation of our behavior. Quite apart from Davidson, there is a closely related question that we had left hanging at the end of the last section. There, having admitted that a certain sort of disposition is part of the characterization of commitments, it was also made clear that the relevant notion of disposition was not a naturalistic one in that, if it appealed to a notion of causality, it was not in any standardly understood sense of causality. At that point, I had said that there was a minimally counter-factual component in the defining of dispositions, to which one need or need not add a further substantive claim that it was underpinned by a naturalistic causal element. In particular, I went on to say that the sort of dispositions that were involved in the characterization of commitments do not have such an underpinning. It is a fair demand to ask: What then is the counterfactual component underpinned by if not that sort of causal element?

It has been argued that there are two radically separable questions: 1) "Why did someone do what she did?" and 2) "Did her doing it live up to her commitment?" And now the question is, if these are so radically separate, if the former is only a descriptive question as Kripke says and not a normative one like the latter, if commitments are really irrelevant to the former and if only nonnormative states such as dispositions and motives are relevant to it, then is there no causal point and efficacy that normative states, which we are insisting beliefs and desires are, have? Though I will not be able to present in an already too long paper the full answer such a fundamental question deserves, I will close by stating the core of an answer that is worth developing in detail.

Whatever we say about the question of the causal relation between commitments and our doings better keep faith with what we have characterized commitments to be: that they involve the presence of no first-order dispositions, but at most require a preparedness to accept criticism for not having lived up to them and the preparedness to do better by way of living up to them. On the basis of this characterization, we can say only this much about the causal power of commitments and no more: our commitments cause us to try and live up to them. To make this sort of causal claim is quite different from saying that they cause us to do what we do, where these doings are specified in terms quite independent of the uninformative description of them as attempts to live up to the commitments in question. It is to say something far more trivial, far more akin to saying something that is properly vulnerable to charges of "virtus dormitiva." It says nothing more than what is already built into the very characterization of a commitment. It implies no subsumption under any laws; in fact, it says nothing informative even short of that. Once we understand what a commitment is, it adds no extra information to say it.

This should not be surprising. Since, as we saw, commitments are minimally defined in terms of second-order dispositions that we specify in a way that necessarily mentions those very commitments, the causal power that such commitments get from these dispositions is not going to be such that there is any description of those causal powers that can leave out the mention of the commitments themselves. They will have to take the form of saying not that someone's commitment that—or to— x caused him to do y, not even that his commitment to x caused him to do x, but that his commitment to x caused him to try to live up to the commitment to do x. The second-order dispositions (as we have specified them above) that go into characterizing commitments are after all spec-ifications of forms of preparedness to do what is needed by way of living up to them.

Once we see that intentional states involve dispositions only in a sense that the causal element underlying them is so explanatorily powerless, we have a diagnosis for why attempts at explanations citing intentional states are familiarly and routinely found by many to be so unhelpful, compared to other forms of explanation. The triviality and uninforma-tiveness of the causal idiom when it attaches to intentional states viewed as commitments is just a reflection of the fact that if there is any causal point to commitments, it is perhaps more teleological than anything else. All it does is define an area of the mind that is goal directed (though of course, there is no extrapolation to any generalized teleology in which minds are not in play). Davidson spent a lot of remarkable philosophical effort and ingenuity in seminal and influential papers arguing that a series of "little red books," as he called them, were completely off the mark in denying that reasons can be causes, which can be invoked in illuminating causal explanations.[27] Well, if the criticisms of Davidson in this paper, coming from a broadly Kripkean perspective, are at all on the mark, those little red books (whatever their other shortcomings, and there were some rather serious ones) had it more right on this score than he did. How to develop what they had right is of course a matter about which a great deal needs to be said, and it is quite apparent that it is not said in those books. But the books contained enough hints to allow us the thought we are claiming here, namely, "Why did someone do what she did?" and "Is what she did in accord with her commitments" are two questions that cannot be yoked together except by doing violence to something basic about the normative element in intentionality.

If that normative element of intentionality involves dispositions, thought of in minimal counterfactual terms, it is a fair question, as I said, to ask what underpins that minimal counterfactual element. The idea that something causal must underlie it need not be denied. But the causal powers that underlie intentional states when they are themselves thought to be commitments do not reveal much more than this: in specifying intentional states we are specifying elements of a sort of goal directedness that is quite peculiar to human beings. That notion of causal power gives no succor to the naturalist.

~ 8

Could There Be a Science
of Rationality?

DONALD DAVIDSON

$\mathcal{M}$ANY PHILOSOPHERS HAVE doubted whether psychology can be made a serious science. Wittgenstein writes:

> The confusion and barrenness of psychology is not to be explained by calling it a "young science"; its state is not comparable with that of physics, for instance, in its beginnings . . . For in psychology there are experimental methods and *conceptual confusion* . . . The existence of experimental methods makes us think we have the means of solving the problems which trouble us; though problem and methods pass one another by.[1]

I take this to apply not just to psychology as it existed when Wittgenstein wrote, but to be a judgment *sub specie aeternitatis*. Gilbert Ryle seems to have been of the same mind. When it comes to explaining human behavior, it is pretentious, he thinks, to hope to do better than common sense:

> [W]hen we hear the promise of a new scientific explanation of what we say and do, we expect to hear of some counterparts to those impacts [like those of which physics treats], some forces or agencies of which we should never have dreamed and which we shall certainly never witness at their subterranean work. But when we are in a less

152

impressionable frame of mind, we find something implausible in the promise of discoveries yet to be made of the hidden causes of our own actions and reactions. We know quite well what caused the farmer to return from the market with his pigs unsold. He found that the prices were lower than he had expected. We know quite well why John Doe scowled and slammed the door. He had been insulted.[2]

Where Wittgenstein and Ryle are contemptuous of the idea of a serious science that aims to explain human behavior, Quine is ambivalent. Does Quine think the concepts of meaning, communication, interpretation, belief, and so on, can be worked into a serious science of behavior? Given the attention Quine has paid to the understanding of language, and his view that philosophy is continuous with science, you might think Quine would say yes. And as I shall show in a minute, there is some reason to think this is Quine's answer. But there is also reason to think it is not.

J. B. Watson, the originator of modern behaviorism, thought that concepts like those of belief and desire were "heritages of a timid savage past," "medieval conceptions," of a piece with "magic and voodoo." B. F. Skinner, a longtime friend of Quine's, put it more mildly: "The objection [he says of such concepts as those of intention, belief and desire] is not that these things are mental but that they offer no real explanation and stand in the way of a more effective analysis." He speaks repeatedly of "an alternative to mentalistic formulations," and adds, "I would not be involved in this if I did not think that mentalistic ways of thinking about human behavior stand in the way of much more effective ways."

Quine seems to agree with Skinner and Watson, as his open endorsement of behaviorism suggests he would. "All in all, [he writes] the propositional attitudes are in a bad way. These are the idioms most stubbornly at variance with scientific patterns."[3] Much of the chapter of *Word and Object* titled "Flight from Intension" is directed against those who think we can talk freely of propositions and the propositional attitudes without asking for a basis in behavior. This is consistent with providing such a basis, that is, legitimatizing these very concepts. But further remarks put such a possibility in doubt. After accepting Brentano's claim that intentional idioms (those we use to report propositional attitudes) are not reducible to nonintentional concepts, Quine remarks, "One may accept the Brentano thesis either as showing the indispensability of intentional idioms and the importance of an autonomous science of intention, or as showing the baselessness of intentional idioms and the emptiness of a science of intention. My attitude, unlike Brentano's, is the second."[4]

Perhaps that should settle the matter, but I'm not sure it does. For what, after all, is the status of Quine's attempt to give a behavioristic account of what is sound in translation? Quine does not attempt to reconstruct the concepts of meaning, analyticity, and the rest as philosophers have thought of them. But what he does provide is intended to make sense not only of speakers, but of what they say. It does this by telling when a translation of the speaker's words is acceptable on behavioristic grounds. My question remains: Is this enterprise merely the best we can do, but not even the beginning of a science, or is it the direction we must take if we want to be scientific about verbal behavior? In particular, are even the behaviorally sound substitutes for meaning and analyticity (for example, stimulus meaning and stimulus analyticity) still irreducible to physiological or physical matters, or may they give way, in the fullness of time and the increase of knowledge, to the more precise sciences? Quine often speaks as if they may.

In "Mind and Verbal Dispositions" Quine distinguishes three levels of "purported explanation" of linguistic phenomena: the mental, the behavioral, and the physiological. The mental he dismisses as "scarcely deserving the name explanation." But does this mean that transposing to the behavioral level must change the subject? Not at all: "let us recognize that the semantical study of language is worth pursuing with all the scruples of the natural scientist. We must study language as a system of dispositions to verbal behavior." Earlier in the same essay he remarks on the "conspicuous fact that language is a social enterprise which is keyed to intersubjectively observable objects in the external world," and suggests that this opens the door to getting "on with a properly physicalistic account of language."[5]

The first step, then, from the mental to dispositions to behavior, does not change the subject, which is the semantic analysis of language; it just puts it in the way of being more scientific. Dispositions for Quine are physical states—physiological states when the disposition is what we would usually call mental, like gullibility; physical in the case of the dispositions of physical objects, like solubility. And while Quine does not think anyone now knows how to give a physiological account of any behavioral disposition, he seems sure there must be one. (Since for present purposes there is no point in distinguishing physiology from a special domain of physics, I'll talk from here on as if physics were the whole of natural science.) On this point, Quine writes:

A disposition is in my view simply a physical trait, a configuration or mechanism . . . Dispositions to behavior, then, are physiological states or traits or mechanisms. In citing them dispositionally we are singling them out by behavioral symptoms, behavioral tests. Usually we are in no position to detail them in physiological terms. [However] [t]he deepest explanation, the physiological, would analyze these dispositions in explicit terms of nerve impulses and other anatomically and chemically identified organic processes.[6]

The reasoning seems to be this; if an object has a disposition, this fact must depend on the physical properties of the object. So whatever can be explained by appeal to the disposition must be explicable in physical terms, whether or not we know how to give the relevant physical description. Solubility illustrates the point: at one time we knew there was some unknown physical property of an object that made it soluble; now we know what that property is. Quine also seems to hold that a fair account of the concept of evidence can ultimately be given in physical terms. In *Word and Object* he says, "Any realistic theory of evidence must be inseparable from the psychology of stimulus and response, applied to sentences,"[7] and in *Roots of Reference* he adds, "Our liberated epistemologist ends up as an empirical psychologist." The learning process, he thinks, is accessible to empirical science. "By exploring it, science can in effect explore the evidential relation." Since "[t]he attribution of a behavioral disposition, learned or unlearned, is a physiological hypothesis, however fragmentary," we may conclude that "mental entities are unobjectionable if conceived as hypothetical physical mechanisms and posited with a view strictly to the systematizing of physical phenomena."[8]

Several ideas emerge in these passages. The theme of the irreducibility of the mentalistic vocabulary, when combined with the thesis that there could be a serious—that is, physiological or physical—account of the evidential relation and other mental concepts, is consistent only with giving up our present talk of propositional attitudes in favor of a vocabulary limited to that of physiology or physics. The claim that "dispositions to verbal behavior" are physical configurations suggests that far from being irreducible to the physical vocabulary, a sensible reduction is in the offing.

It may be that at one time Quine was uncertain about the relation between the mental and the physical vocabularies, but in more recent writings he has settled for the view that talk of beliefs, desires, actions, and meanings is not reducible to something more scientific, but that its usefulness for everyday descriptions and explanations cannot be denied. The relation between the mental and the physical that Quine now seems to accept is what I have called "anomalous monism," the position that says there are no strictly lawlike correlations between phenomena classified as mental and phenomena classified as physical, though mental entities are identical, taken one at a time, with physical entities.[9] In other words, there is a single ontology, but more than one way of describing and explaining the items in the ontology.

There are several reasons for the irreducibility of the mental to the physical. One reason, appreciated by Quine, is the normative element in interpretation introduced by the necessity of appealing to charity in matching the sentences of others to our own. Such matching forces us to weigh the relative plausibilities of different deviations from coherence and truth (by our own lights). Nothing in physics corresponds to the way in which this feature of the mental shapes its categories.

Another reason, perhaps easier to grasp, lies in the irreducibly causal character of mental concepts. Let me give a nonmental example first. The state of being sunburned is necessarily a state caused by the action of the sun. No completed physics would make use of the concept of sunburn, not only because part of the explanation is already built into the characterization of the state, but also because two states of the skin could be in every intrinsic way identical, and yet one be a case of sunburn and the other not.

The propositional attitudes, the semantics of spoken words, and behavior as we normally understand it, are all like this. The reason, both in the case of the attitudes and in the case of semantics, is the same: what our words mean, and what our thoughts are about, is partly determined by the history of their acquisition. The truth conditions of my sentence "The moon is gibbous," or of my belief that the moon is gibbous, depend in part on the causal history of my relations to the moon. But it could happen that two people were in relevantly similar physical states (defined just in terms of what is within the skin), and yet one could be speaking or thinking of our moon, and the other not.

When it comes to explaining behavior, as normally conceived, this feature of the propositional attitudes is an asset, for behavior, thought of as actions, is also an irreducibly causal concept. This is because actions are typically described not merely as motions but as motions that can be explained by the reasons an agent has—his or her beliefs and desires. Thus if I pay my bill by writing a check, it is necessarily the case that I wrote the check because I wanted to pay my bill and believed that by writing a check I would be paying my bill. Actions are individuated along the same lines as propositional attitudes; this is why the attitudes do as good a job as they do in explaining actions. But this way of individuating and of picking out actions is not going to help create a science of behavior that might in principle become an identifiable province of physiology or physics.

There have been numerous attempts to extract from the propositional attitudes a purely subjective (or "narrow") content not subject to the difficulties for science introduced by externalism. If this could be done, it would remove a major obstacle to making psychology a science, leaving only the normative aspect of the mental to make trouble. The reason thinkers like Jerry Fodor and Noam Chomsky want to find a purely internal element or aspect of the propositional attitudes is obvious: it is only if mental properties are supervenient on the physical properties of the agent that there can be any hope of identifying the mental properties with physical properties, or of finding lawlike connections between the two. If mental properties are supervenient not only on the physical properties of the agent but in addition on the physical properties of the world outside the agent, there can be no hope of discovering laws that predict and explain behavior solely on the basis of intrinsic features of agents. Both Fodor and Chomsky have made clear that they think an internal variety of the intentional is essential to making psychology a serious study. For related reasons, Fodor has also rejected most forms of holism, at least so far as language is concerned. He gives a number of reasons, but what seems to motivate the rejection is the conviction that unless the meanings of expressions can be tied in lawlike ways to specific neural configurations, there is no hope for a serious account of linguistic phenomena. Such ties would, of course, rule out externalism.

What I think is certain is that holism, externalism, and the normative feature of the mental stand or fall together: if these are features of the mental, and they stand in the way of a serious science of psychology, then Ryle, Wittgenstein, and Quine in his more pessimistic mood are right. There can be no serious science or sciences of the mental. I believe the normative, holistic, and externalist elements in psychological concepts cannot be eliminated without radically changing the subject. I do not want to argue these points in this paper, having done so at length elsewhere.[10] My interest here is rather to ask what follows if I am right. Pretty clearly, it does not follow without argument that there cannot be a scientific psychology: whether this follows depends on what you mean by "science," and whether the features that I maintain characterize the mental stand in its way. What does follow is that psychology cannot be *reduced* to physics, nor to any other of the natural sciences. But unless we simply legislate science to be what can be reduced to a natural science, the failure of reduction should not in itself be taken to show that what cannot be so reduced does not deserve to be called science.

Since my own approach to the description, analysis (in a rough sense), and explanation of thought, language, and action has, on the one hand, what I take to be some of the characteristics of a science, and has, on the other hand, come under attack by both Fodor and Chomsky as being radically "unscientific," I plan to examine my theory, if that is the word, to see how or whether it can be defended as science. I should remark at the start that I think the outcome is mixed.

One way to think of the moment when psychology came of age as an empirical science is with the work of Gustav Theodor Fechner, whose life spanned most of the nineteenth century (1801–1887). Fechner began as a physicist, but then drifted through chemistry, physiology, and medicine to metaphysics (and beyond, to mysticism). Fechner was interested in the relation between mind and body, or matter and spirit, and he approached this problem by seeking quantitative laws that connect the mental and the physical. Weber had already suggested that the smallest change in the intensity of a physical magnitude required to produce a perceivable difference in sensation is not a fixed physical difference, but is proportional to the magnitude of the stimulus. Fechner generalized the law: the experienced intensity of a physical stimulus is equal to some constant times the log of the physical stimulus. Roughly: as a physical stimulus increases (say intensity of loudness or pitch in sound), equal increases in the magnitude of the physical stimulus will result in smaller and smaller increases in the felt sensation. The constant varies with the sense involved. This law can, of course, be tested, and it is approximately correct. The decibel scale of loudness is an informal example: equal intervals on the decibel scale are (more or less) equal subjectively, but the ratio of two amounts of acoustical power is equal to ten times the common logarithm of the power ratio.

Fechner had the right idea. If scientific methods can be applied to the mental, it is by proposing a solid theory and asking how it can be tested and interpreted empirically. Theories describe abstract structures; their empirical interpretations ask whether these structures can be discovered in the real world. Fechner's theory is relatively easy to interpret in some cases, which is perhaps not surprising, given the neurological basis of sensory discrimination. What we now know about neurons, neural nets, and the processing of information (so called) that takes place in the sense organs and the brain, suggests that we should expect to find quantitative laws relating sensory discrimination and the physical magnitudes of stimuli. But there are closely related scalings of perceived sensations that are definitely surprising, at least to me. A good example is the perception of the relations among intervals in the pitch of sounds. The Greeks knew that if you divide a vibrating string in half, each half sounds an octave above the full string, and two-thirds of the string produce the fifth above the full string. (Pythagoras is credited with discovering this.) But what is surprising is that if you sound two notes some arbitrary distance apart and ask a subject to tune a third note to the perceived midpoint, not only do different hearers arrive at approximately the same pitch, but pitches so determined are related in such a way as to produce an interval scale, that is, numbers can be assigned to various pitches in a way that keeps track of the relations between intervals, not on the basis of a physical magnitude, like string length or vibrations per second, but entirely on the basis of what is subjectively perceived. The theory that describes this fact has every right to be called a psychological theory, for it deals with nothing but the relations among psychological phenomena.

In a way, I have already given good examples of scientific theory in the field of psychology, one in the form of a general law relating the perceived intensity of sensory stimuli to physically measured aspects of the stimuli, the other in the form of the fundamental measurement of perceived intervals of pitch. But of course these examples do not speak to the concerns of those who ask whether, or in what way, psychology can be scientific. What they are interested in is the description, prediction, and explanation of intentional actions, and of associated attitudes such as intention, belief, desire, and linguistic meaning. Here I will consider a particular theory that I have proposed; I shall describe it in outline, and then ask in what respects it has the features of a scientific theory.

The theory I have in mind relates the concepts of belief, desire, and linguistic meaning. Since the theory treats belief in a quantified form, sometimes called subjective probability, and desire as measured on an interval scale (like Fahrenheit temperature or the subjective pitch scale I just mentioned), it includes a version of what is sometimes called decision theory; thus it is suited to the explanation of intentions and intentional actions. Unlike traditional decision theory in the form first given it explicitly by Frank Ramsey, or the somewhat different version invented by Richard Jeffrey,[11] the theory I have in mind integrally includes a theory of meaning. It may therefore be called a unified theory of speech and action, or the Unified Theory for short.

The Unified Theory describes or defines an abstract structure. This structure has certain interesting and desirable properties that it is possible to prove. Thus one can prove, with respect to the part borrowed from decision theory, both a representation theorem and a uniqueness theorem. The first says in effect that numbers can be assigned to beliefs and desires that preserve the qualitative constraints imposed by the theory;

the second says the numbers assigned to measure probabilities constitute a ratio scale and the numbers that track desires constitute an interval scale.[12] This is adequate to yield (as least "in theory") predictions of intentional actions. The part of the theory that copes with linguistic meaning is in effect a modification of a Tarski-type theory of truth, and so is provably capable of supplying the truth conditions of all utterances of sentences in a language of which it treats. The final part of the theory joins decision theory and truth theory by a formal device that I shall not attempt to describe here.[13] The possibility of marrying the two theories depends on two things. The first is that decision theory shows how to extract both cardinal utilities and subjective probabilities from simple preferences. The second is that subjective probabilities, when taken as applied to sentences, are enough to yield a theory of meaning. There is thus a route, technically rather byzantine, but intuitively clear in each of its steps, from simple choices to a detailed interpretation of words, desires, and beliefs.

The possibility of such a theory rests on structures dictated by our concept of rationality. Both decision theory as I have used it, in the version developed by Richard Jeffrey, and theories of truth, for example, depend in part on logic. Jeffrey's decision theory and Tarski's truth definitions take an underlying logic for granted: these theories would be true only of perfect logicians. Beyond this, there is the assumption of a rational distribution of probabilities over propositions, and of a proportioning of degrees of belief in accord with the conditional probabilities: in other words, propositions are held true to the degree made rational by their evidential support. Thus the entire structure of the theory depends on the standards and norms of rationality.

These considerations cast considerable doubt on the scientific pretensions of the Unified Theory. But before I entertain doubts, let me dwell a bit more on the overall pattern. Like any scientific theory, the Unified Theory presents a clear and precise formal structure with demonstrable merits. There are only a few undefined concepts, and these are extensional. The basic primitive concept is the three-place relation between an agent and two sentences that holds when the agent would weakly prefer one sentence true rather than the other. This relation is extensional in the technical sense that a statement that this relation holds of three appropriate objects (an agent and two of that agent's sentences) retains its truth value (true or false) regardless of how those three objects are described. Yet if the observed pattern of such relations fits the terms of the theory, it is possible to infer the degrees of belief the agent accords his or her sentences, how much the agent would like those sentences to be true, and what the truth conditions (or meanings) of those sentences are. In other words, the theory, if true of an agent, would serve to interpret the beliefs, values, and words of that agent.

This claim, even guarded as it is by the "if true" clause, needs plenty of defense. It is a question, for example, whether belief, evaluation, and meaning are enough to support such broad-based interpretation without adding, say, intention or perception as further related but independent variables, not to mention the emotions. It is also uncertain whether a theory of truth is adequate to the interpretation of speech, even assuming that a theory of truth could be made to cover all the idioms of a natural language. But important as these matters are, I plan to leave them aside for now so that I can get on with the question whether a theory more or less like the Unified Theory can be thought of as scientific. My conclusion so far is: from a purely formal point of view, it is a powerful theory, and insofar as it corresponds to many of our intuitions concerning the nature of rationality, it is an attractive theory.

It is when we attend to the empirical interpretation of the theory that the basic questions and problems arise. Here I want to distinguish between the official story about how the theory can be interpreted, and an unofficial account. Officially, it is essential to be able to show how the theory can be interpreted without appeal to evidence that assumes the individuation of the contents of any propositional attitude. One such form of evidence is, as I mentioned, protocols that specify an agent's preference that one sentence rather than another be true. Given enough such evidence, a picture can be built of the agent's beliefs, desires, and meanings (that is, the truth conditions of his or her utterances). A finite amount of such evidence can only confirm the theory, of course; it cannot verify it. That is what we would expect.

In brief outline, the official story takes the following route. Jeffrey's version of decision theory, applied to sentences, tells us that a rational agent cannot prefer both a sentence and its negation to a tautology, nor a tautology to both a sentence and its negation. This fact makes it possible for an interpreter to identify, with no knowledge of the meanings of the agent's sentences, all of the pure sentential connectives, such as negation, conjunction, and the biconditional. This minimal knowledge suffices to determine the subjective probabilities of all of the agent's sentences—how likely the agent thinks those sentences are to be true—and then, in turn, to fix the relative values of the truth of those sentences (from the agent's point of view, of course). The subjective probabilities can then be used to interpret the sentences. For what Quine calls observation sentences, the changes in probabilities provide the obvious clues to first-order interpretation when geared to events and objects easily perceived simultaneously by interpreter and the person being interpreted. Conditional probabilities and entailments between sentences, by registering what the speaker takes to be evidence for his beliefs, provides the interpreter with what is needed to interpret more theoretical terms and sentences. This is the official story. Its merit lies not in its plausibility as an account of how we actually set about understanding others, but in the fact that it amounts to an informal proof of the adequacy of the theory to yield what is needed to support the interpretation of the basic propositional attitudes. (One should compare the official story of how Ramsey's decision theory yields sufficiently unique results to explain choice behavior on the basis of simple preferences.)

Unofficially, one can admit that as living, working interpreters, we never have enough of the sort of evidence needed to follow the official route, and we always have a great deal of other sorts of evidence. We make endless assumptions about the people we meet, about what they want, what they are apt to mean by what they say, what they believe about the environment we share with them, and why they act as they do. Our skills as interpreters come into play mainly when one or another of these assumptions turns out to be false, and by then we have much more than the poverty-stricken evidence the Unified Theory depends on. But this is as it should be. The point of the theory was not to describe how we actually interpret, but to speculate on what it is about thought and language that makes them interpretable. If we can tell a story like the official story about how it is possible, we can conclude that the constraints the theory places on the attitudes may articulate some of their philosophically significant features.

I have described in its most transparent form the art of applying the formal theory to an actual individual, with both interpreter and speaker outfitted with a mature set of concepts and the linguistic aptitudes for expressing them. All that is lacking at the start is a shared language and prior knowledge of each other's attitudes. Since the theory and the official story of how it can be applied are already remote from actual practice, we must expect that the theory will throw only the most oblique light on the acquisition of a first language, and less still on the origins of speech. The most that can be said is that if we agree that the pattern of attitudes is as the theory depicts it, one can perhaps see that a creature properly endowed by nature could acquire it in the company of others already possessed of thought and speech. The theory may also prompt an interesting hypothesis about the origins of language; I shall mention this at the end.

I should emphasize how much belongs to the province of interpretation, of trying to give an empirical application to the formal theory. The intended application is to individuals, strictly speaking at a given time, since we can expect many of the values and beliefs of anyone to change swiftly as the world changes. The apparently quantitative ingredients, the measures of degree of desire and degree of belief, do not belong to the theory itself; like any theory of fundamental measurement, the numbers simply make use of the theory without being part of it. We could, if we pleased, use the theory simply as a device for recording the relations among the attitudes and the relations of the attitudes to the world, their semantics. But in the case of beliefs and the evaluative attitudes, it is convenient to represent these relations in the numbers, as the representation theorems for decision theories prove that we can.

Here a special feature of the Unified Theory emerges, one that may well excite suspicion. For what plays the role of the numbers when it comes to assigning *contents* to the words and attitudes of an agent? What is required is some potentially infinite supply of entities with a pattern or structure complex enough to provide a model for the attitudes. Given such a supply, we can then keep track of the roles of the attitudes and the truth conditions of sentences. Everyone who has a language has available such a set of entities, namely the (infinite) set of his or her own sentences; and these are all we have available for interpreting other people. It is obvious that we employ our own sentences whenever we attribute a particular belief or desire, intention or meaning, to someone else. This is not to say that my sentences are the *objects* of your attitudes; I merely use my sentences to keep track of what you think and mean, or to say, to myself or another, what you think and mean. The attitudes don't have objects in any psychological or epistemic sense. The attitudes are simply states, and no more require objects before the mind than sticks require numbers in order to have a certain length.

Now to return to the question with which I began: To what extent, or in what ways, is a theory like the Unified Theory scientific? Such a theory is not, I think it is clear, reducible to a science like physics or neurobiology: its basic concepts cannot be defined in the vocabulary of any physical science, and there are no precise bridging laws that firmly and reliably relate events or states described in the psychological vocabulary with events and states described in the vocabulary of a physical science. But it would be uninteresting to define science to be what can be reduced to physics. Are there other difficulties? Three features of the Unified Theory (and other theories like it) that have been thought to remove it from the domain of serious science are its assumptions of holism and of externalism, and its normative properties.

The entire theory is built on the norms of rationality; it is these norms that suggested the theory and give it the structure it has. But this much is built into the formal, axiomatizable, parts of decision theory and truth theory, and they are as precise and clear as any formal theory of physics. However, norms or considerations of rationality also enter with the application of the theory to actual agents, at the stage where an interpreter assigns his own sentences to capture the contents of another's thoughts and utterances. The process necessarily involves deciding which pattern of assignments makes the other intelligible (not *intelligent*, of course!), and this is a matter of using one's own standards of rationality to calibrate the thoughts of the other. In some ways, this is like fitting a curve to a set of points, which is done in the best of sciences. But there is an additional element in the psychological case: in physics there is a mind at work making as much sense as possible of a subject matter that is being treated as brainless; in the psychological case, there is a brain at each end. Norms are being employed as the standard of norms.

The Unified Theory is holistic through and through. It is designed to assign contents to beliefs, utterances, and values simultaneously because these basic attitudes are so interdependent that it would not be possible to determine them one at a time, or even two at a time. Its treatment of each of these domains is also holistic: sentences are interpreted in terms of their relations to other sentences, beliefs in terms of their relations to other beliefs, and so on. Such holism is characteristic of any scheme of measurement: items owe their measure to their relations to other items. A meaning could no more be assigned to a single isolated sentence than a weight or location could be assigned to a single isolated object. The holism of the mental cannot, then, in itself be a obstacle to the scientific claims of a theory of the mental. Quite the reverse: the possibility of theory rests on holism.

The truth conditions of a speaker's utterances determine, and so depend in part, on the logical relations of the sentence uttered to other sentences. In the case of observation sentences, the truth conditions can also depend on the causal history of the situations in which the sentence was learned and used; this is one form externalism takes. Since perceptual externalism of this sort introduces an irreducibly causal element into the interpretation of the theory, the theory cannot hope to emulate physics, which has striven successfully to extrude all causal concepts from its laws. Externalism sets limits to how complete psychological explanation can be, since it introduces into the heart of the subject elements that no psychological theory can pretend to explain. On the other hand, this feature in itself makes psychological theory no less scientific than volcanology, biology, meteorology, or the theory of evolution.

Both Fodor and Chomsky have criticized the Unified Theory and the proposed method of its interpretation, which I have called *radical* interpretation (radical because it assumes no prior knowledge of the agent's propositional attitudes). Some of their criticisms seem to me to miss their mark.[14] Both Fodor and Chomsky observe that radical interpretation gives a completely wrong account both of how linguists study new languages and of how children acquire a first language. Here they have understandably been misled by the age-old tendency of philosophers to discuss the theoretical question how a linguist or a child *could* learn an unknown or first language as if it were a practical question about how they actually do it. I have often explained that radical interpretation does not attempt to provide useful hints to real linguists, or to criticize their methods. Much less does it pretend to yield an insight into the mysterious (to me, at any rate) business of first-language acquisition.

Fodor and Chomsky criticize the fact that radical interpretation makes use of so much less information than is available to the informed and methodologically sophisticated linguist. This irritation is fed by their conviction that I hold that the evidence on which I say radical interpretation could be based is all the evidence that is legitimately available. Chomsky in particular thinks I ignore his discoveries about how much of the syntax of natural languages seems to be genetically programmed. I have argued, as I mentioned above, that it is one condition on the correctness of a theory of meaning that it be such that if an interpreter knew it to be true of a speaker, the interpreter could understand what the speaker said. Of course I denied that interpreters generally have, or at least know they have, such a theory; the theory is, rather, what the philosopher wants if he is to describe certain aspects of the interpreter's interpretive abilities. I then added, in an essay that particularly provoked Chomsky, "It does not add anything to this thesis to say that if a theory does correctly describe the competence of an interpreter, some mechanism in the interpreter must correspond to the theory."[15] Chomsky quotes this remark, and comments that "from the standpoint of the natural sciences, [this] comment is utterly wrongheaded." His subsequent discussion makes clear that what annoys him is that he thinks I am denying that there would be any interest in knowing what the mechanism is. But of course this is not my view, nor is this what I said. What I said was, and was intended as, a tautology: if a pill puts you to sleep, it adds nothing to say something about the pill had the power to put you to sleep. It would be vastly interesting to know more about the nature of our linguistic abilities, and the mechanisms underlying them. Who would deny it? If I have any doubts, they concern only the philosophical conclusions Chomsky and some of his followers have drawn from their results in this area.

Chomsky has accused me, and particularly Quine, of supposing that all we know about language must be based on behavioristic evidence. Quine has spoken for himself on this matter, but I would certainly deny the accusation; if we want to know everything about language, its acquisition and uses, there are no a priori limits on what evidence may be relevant. But I do share with Quine the conviction that our understanding of what speakers mean by what they say is partly based, directly or indirectly, on what we can learn or pick up from perceiving what they do. No matter how much grammar we come equipped with from the cradle, we must learn what the words of any particular language mean—we are not born speaking English or Hebrew or Mandarin; we must pick up our first language from those who already speak it. (The behaviorism I speak of is not, incidentally, reductive in nature: I do not expect any basic intentional predicates to be defined in terms of nonintentional terms. The point simply concerns evidence.)

The criticisms Fodor and Chomsky have leveled at certain philosophers seem to me largely (though not entirely) based on their having read into those philosophers views they do not hold: I have tried to point out some instances. But there is also a failure to appreciate a difference in fundamental aims and interests. Chomsky apparently sees me as trying to understand and explain the same phenomena he is, and therefore as proposing competing hypotheses. This seems altogether wrong. I want to know what it is about propositional thought—our beliefs, desires, intentions, and speech—that makes them intelligible to others. This is a question about the nature of thought and meaning that cannot be answered by discovering neural mechanisms, studying the evolution of the brain, or finding evidence that explains the incredible ease and rapidity with which we come to have a first language. Even if we were all born speaking English or Polish, it would be a question how we understand others, and what determines the cognitive contents of our sentences. It doesn't matter whether we call some of these projects "scientific" and withhold the term from others.

It does matter, however, in what ways the study of the attitudes I have been discussing is limited just as, in another context, it matters in what ways Chomsky's or Fodor's work is limited. (The limitations are, of course, different.) What are the most obvious shortcomings of the Unified Theory of thought and speech? Well, first and perhaps most striking is the fact that the formal theory (as opposed to features of its empirical application) says nothing at all about inconsistencies. It not only postulates perfect logic and a consistent and rational pattern of beliefs and desires, but it assumes rationality in the treatment of what we take to be evidence. Inconsistencies and failures of reasoning power must be accommodated by injecting large doses of what has been called charity in the fitting of the theory to actual agents.

Perhaps all straightforward irrationality shows up as inconsistency, but clearly not all inconsistency is what we normally call irrationality. The formal theory leaves no room for irrationality, and therefore is powerless to explain it. Any explanations of irrationality we care to proffer must work against the Unified Theory, not with it.

The Unified Theory, as I have described it, is static; it says nothing about the forms of rationality that deal with the incorporation of new information into a going system of thought. However, this is an area in which there is hope. Much work has been done, by Richard Jeffrey and Isaac Levi, for example, on making decision theory dynamic.

Finally, and perhaps most significantly, the interpretation of the formal theory does not rest entirely on ordinary intersubjective evidence. In measuring physical magnitudes, we can use the numbers to keep track of the properties of events and objects as publicly observed. The relevant properties of the numbers can also be agreed to by all concerned. But things are different when one mind tries to understand another. People are as publicly observable as anything else in nature, but the entities we use to construct a picture of someone else's thoughts must be our own sentences, as understood by us, or other entities with the same provenance and structure. The meanings of our sentences are indeed dependent on our relations to the world that those sentences are about and our linguistic interactions with others. But there is no escape from the fact that we cannot check up on the objective credentials of the measure we are using as we can check up on our understanding of the numbers; we cannot check up on the objective correctness of our own norms by checking with others, since to do this would be to make basic use of our own norms once more.

Whether the features of a psychological theory I have been rehearsing, especially the last one, show that a psychological theory is so different from a theory in the natural sciences as not to deserve to be called a science I do not know, nor much care. What I am sure of is that such a theory, though it may be as genuine a theory as any, is not in competition with any natural science.

Afterword (2001)

Naturalism often includes the claim that the study of human thought can emulate or be absorbed into what are called the natural sciences. Emulation suggests that the study should be empirical, descriptive, and methodologically precise. Absorption implies reduction, in one sense or another, to the natural sciences. In "Could There Be a Science of Rationality?" Reprinted in this volume, I examine how far these two aspects of naturalism can be separated in the cases of elementary logic, decision theory, and formal semantics. I argue that the theories I discuss cannot be reduced nomologically or definitionally to the natural sciences, though I endorse ontological reduction. The theories scrutinized are, I claim, methodologically precise and may be treated as descriptive. Empirically, they are indispensable as the largely unacknowledged underpinning of our everyday attempts to understand human thought and action, but the issues that arise in the attempt to regularize the empirical application of such theories raises the question of how "scientific" they are.

I am in sympathy with Quine's proposal that philosophy should attempt to describe how we defend our theories about the world rather than itself take on the defensive task, and that philosophy should not balk at availing itself of the methods of science in giving the description. This project is compatible with the conviction that the cognitive task of justification cannot be fully described using the vocabularies of the natural sciences alone. It is also compatible with the view that it is fruitless to try to give an exhaustive account of how empirical knowledge depends on nonconceptualized evidence or causes. Thought is tied to the world in basic and essential ways, but the description of these ways cannot depend on positing epistemic way stations between the world and our concept of the world.

Serious science demands that what is treated as evidence should be publically observable. How well do the theories described here fare in this respect? We think of Fechner's psychophysical laws as relating sensations and physical magnitudes, but in fact the sensations are only indirectly inferred from judgments of the character or strength of sensations. In most tests of the rationality of reasoning, whether of logical reasoning or of decision making in the face of uncertainty, the evidence consists in conscious judgments. Since we cannot reduce the subject matter of cognitive psychology to behavior nonintentionally described, or to neurology, the experimental testing or application of these theories of rationality is, it seems, compromised from the start by the inherent normativity and subjectivity of the evidence. But this exaggerates the threat. It is the judgment that is subjective and private; its manifestations are not. This is particularly true in the case of verbal utterances, which by their nature are directed at others. The observing public (or scientist bent on testing a theory of rationality) cannot, however, make direct use of utterances unless the utterances are understood. Here we are confronted by circularity: the theories are expressions of our understanding of essential aspects of rationality, but we cannot test the theories unless the utterances are those of a more or less rational mind. In other words, if the utterances can be treated as evidence of rationality, they have already been interpreted as confirming the presence of rationality.

The circle is virtuous. It is to be expected that a theory that makes explicit aspects of our usual ways of understanding human thought and intentional behavior will find that what it takes as evidence tends to confirm the theory. The scientifically minded can treat the theory as a hypothesis, and ask how well it captures our intuitions. We can distinguish two issues. One is whether the formal theory is adequate or can be improved. The other is whether the empirical interpretation, what to count as evidence, can be sharpened. In practice the issues merge when we ask what it is, more exactly, that we want to understand. Though the study of rationality poses special problems it is, in its apparent circularity, much like many other sciences.

~ III
AGENCY

~ 9

Agency and Alienation

JENNIFER HORNSBY

1) David Velleman's "problem of agency," in his paper "What Happens When Someone Acts?"[1] is the problem "of finding an agent at work amid the workings of the mind." This problem arises when "a naturalistic conception of explanation," implicit in the "standard causal story" of action as belief-and-desire-caused behavior, is adopted.[2] In my opinion, the standard story, as it is standardly naturalistically understood, should be rejected. Rather than seeking an agent amid the workings of the mind, we need to recognize an agent's place in the world she inhabits. In order to do so we have to resist the naturalistic assumptions of the standard causal story.

I use "naturalism" and cognates here in Velleman's sense, which is the sense of my opponents. (Thus "naturalism" stands for a doctrine rejected by many authors in the present anthology, albeit that we may subscribe to a different doctrine at least as deserving of the name naturalism.) I single out Velleman's "What Happens When Someone Acts?" for criticism because Velleman is very explicit there about his naturalistic prejudices, so that it provides a clear example of a certain style of thinking.[3]

2) There are various phenomena of human agency that we are apt to describe using the language of alienation, or of estrangement, or of non-participation. In Velleman's account, the agents who are alienated are those who lack self-control, or self-understanding, or who undertake pro-

173

jects halfheartedly. There is the addict who injects heroin in spite of knowing that it would be better if she could resist doing so. There is the person who lacks motivation because of depression or fatigue. And there is the agent who finds herself accounting for her behavior by saying, "It was my resentment speaking, not I." In all of these cases, Velleman thinks that we have belief-and-desire-caused behavior, and that the standard causal story applies. But the standard story is adequate to these cases, Velleman thinks, only because in these cases the relation between a human being and her action falls short of what is needed for a case of genuine agency. That is why Velleman tells us that we have to embellish the standard story to characterize what he calls agency *par excellence:* that we can only characterize the relation that obtains between a human being and her action in cases of *nonalienated* agency if we add something extra to the standard story's states and events. But my idea is that Velleman's problem of agency vanishes when the standard story is discarded.

I want to discuss different kinds of alienated agency in what follows, in order to try to corroborate my opinion that the standard story should be rejected, not embellished. Besides the real phenomena that are describable using the language of alienation, there is alienation of a kind that I shall call "unthinkable." We know that we are not alienated agents of the unthinkable kind, so that we can also know that we must resist whatever assumptions lead to our feeling that we might be so alienated, and that we must not assimilate the real phenomena of alienation to the unthinkable kind. I shall use a discussion of unthinkable alienation (§§ 3, 4) to elicit the errors of the standard causal story of action (§ 6) and to show that Velleman's problem is misconceived (§ 7). That will put me in a position to say how we might think about phenomena that interest Velleman and that we describe using the language of alienation (§ 8).

3) When he endorsed the conception of explanation that gives rise to his problem of agency, Velleman cited Thomas Nagel. Nagel invited us to adopt a picture of the world in which all events and states of affairs are seen as caused either by other events and states or by nothing at all. If you try to imagine your actions as part of the flux of events in this picture, then you will find yourself alienated from them. As Nagel put it:

> Everything I do or that anyone else does is part of a larger course of events that no one "does" but that happens.[4]

It seems that in order to adopt the picture that Nagel invites us to, we have to view actions as set apart from the agents whose actions they are.

But if actions are events—as Nagel assumed in presenting the picture, and as my naturalist opponents here all assume—then they are surely not events from which agents are set apart. The phenomenon of human agency can be caught in the first instance with the idea of *someone's doing something intentionally*. When that idea is put together with acceptance of an event ontology, there is a way to define "an action." Thus, one might say: there are human beings who do things; when someone's doing something is her doing something or other *intentionally*, human agency is exemplified, and an event that is *her doing the thing* is an action. It is no wonder then that we should feel alienated if we are meant to think of our actions among the course of events and proceed to speculate about how we might fit in. For where an action has been picked out, an agent has been: the action is *her* doing something. (It isn't true quite in general that an agent has been picked out whenever an action has been picked out. One might for instance know that some human being had caused something without knowing who had caused it. Such examples, however, do nothing to suggest that one ought to look for a human being within the flux of events present in the picture from Nagel's external perspective.)

Nagel encourages a sense of alienation by speaking as if you stood to an event that is your action in a relation expressible using the word "do." This makes it seem as if you could participate as agent only by being related to something that might be present in a scene in which you yourself were not involved. It can then be tempting to think that in order to make a difference, you would have to butt in as a cause at the point at which your action is found. Hence, perhaps, some of the attractions of the claim that agents cause actions. But even if the idea of agents' butting in might somehow help to give sense to the thought that agents contribute to what happens, there would still be a difficulty about supposing that the world to which agents make a difference is occupied only by events and states that are part of a flux in which agents themselves might never have been involved. For we take ourselves to be influenced by, not only to act upon, the world to which our actions make a difference. In order to escape from a general threat that we are alienated from the world we inhabit as agents, we have to avoid thinking of ourselves as standing in a relation either of *doing* or of *causing* to the events that are our actions.

(It should be acknowledged that it is only in a semi-technical, philosophical usage that "action" stands for events, and that it is not ordinarily so used. But it is only in this sense that actions are particulars and thus candidates to be "part of a larger course of events." It adds to the general confusion in this area that "event," as well as "action," has uses in which it doesn't stand for particulars. My policy here is to use both "action" and "event" as I think naturalists mean to—only for things in an ontology of particulars.)

When the relation between agents and the events that are their actions is understood, it will not seem possible to locate actions among a causal flux in which agents might play no role. Human agents are not merely things within which things happen, and they clearly do play a role in the arena within which their actions are found. For an event of someone's doing something is typically an event of her bringing something about; and the event that is her action (her doing the thing) brings about that which she brings about. A driver slams on her brakes and brings it about that the car comes to a sudden stop; the event that is her slamming on the brakes brings it about that the car comes to a sudden stop.

Nagel was surely right, then, to say that the very idea of agency is threatened when we try to accommodate actions in an "external perspective." The role of agents in a world of events is evident only when it is appreciated that agents cause things—things that ensue from their actions. It seems unthinkable that agency should be manifest from any point of view from which it is impossible to locate agents.

4) Nagel asked us to imagine looking at things from far away in order to pose his question about actions' place in the natural world. One can produce the mystery also by looking at human beings close up and looking inward—as Hume did. Hume expressed great bafflement about our role in the explanatory order when he looked at agents' insides:

> We learn from anatomy that the immediate object of power in voluntary motion is not the member itself which is moved, but certain muscles and nerves and animal spirits, and, perhaps, something still more minute and more unknown, through which the motion is successively propagated ere it reach the member itself whose motion is the immediate object of volition.... [T]he power by which this whole operation is performed, so far from being directly and fully known to an inward sentiment or consciousness, is to the last degree mysterious and unintelligible. How indeed can we be conscious of a power to move our limbs when *we have no such power*, but *only* that to move certain animal spirits which, though they produce at last the motion of our limbs, yet operate in such a manner as is wholly beyond our comprehension?[5]

There are two things to notice about this passage. (Hume's own agenda here is not to the present point.)[6] First, Hume's proffered reason for denying that we are conscious of a power to move our limbs is that we do not have such a power. Second, Hume's denial that we have a power to move our limbs does not (at least at this juncture) spring from any general mistrust of the idea of power; for he tells us straightaway that there *is* a power we have—a power to move certain animal spirits, whose excitations eventually produce motions of limbs. Hume's is then a view of ourselves as agents from which we are bound to feel estranged. The only power we have is a power to produce effects, which are, as Hume says, "totally different from" the ones that we intend. Such effects— events in brains—not only fail to be within the scope of our intentions, but seem not to belong to the world that we inhabit as agents. Agents, in a word, are alienated.

One might want to blame Hume's strange view on his ignorance of science, and one might want to blame it on his dualistic thinking. But I suggest that it has another source. If one looks inside someone's skull, expecting to see the makings of intentional bodily movements there, one is sure to encounter a mystery about them.

To see this, imagine someone called Jane who is given a very detailed account of electrochemical impulses, neural transmission, and so on, but an account that doesn't mention any organism inside which this all takes place. Jane is told that, by knowing the scientific story, she knows *every-thing* that happens when someone moves his arm at will. She might reasonably be puzzled. Certainly knowledge of relevant portions of electro-chemistry and understanding of the operation of neural transmission make her better placed than Hume was to know what goes on when someone moves: she can understand how a limb comes to move. But science doesn't make her better placed than Hume was to say what some-one's intentionally moving his arm *consists* in. Hume's mystery does not go away by providing a neuroscientific account of what goes on inside.

Philosophers who are used to thinking that accounts at the subpersonal level record all the personal-level truths won't allow that Jane's predic-ament is anything like the one that Hume puts us in. They may say that Hume follows Descartes in separating mind from brain, and they may attribute his strange claims to this. But notice that there is actually no mention of a mind in Hume. Hume is hostile to substances, whether mental or physical; and he is happy to assume that volitions set the animal spirits in motion. His expressions of mystery and unintelligibility relate not to the operation of mind but to the production of motion by events in the brain and nervous system. Hume's reason for thinking that our only power is to do things that we do not intend to do is that volitions, being at a distance from the limbs, are in no position to move the limbs directly. When causation is pictured, as it is by Hume, as proceeding always from event to event by relations of contiguity, the depths of the brain are the only place for the operation of a causal power antecedent to a limb movement. With that picture in place, the only question one can raise about causal history concerns how the limb gets to move. One loses sight of questions about the agent, and why she did what she did.

If this diagnosis is correct, then the thing that explains Hume's strange view is the absence of a human being from his account. There is nothing inside the skull—where causality, as Hume conceives it, is to be observed—which is in a position to move anything that it might have a reason to move: there is nothing for a predicate such as "moves the arm" to apply to. Jane's difficulties about locating actions in the scientific story have a similar source, then. Among the flux of internal events, she cannot find any event to identify with x's doing something, where x is a human being. Presumably if Jane sought the advice of a present-day naturalist, she would be told that some tract of cerebral events adds up to an event of someone's intentionally doing something. (Compare Velleman, who writes: "One is surely entitled to assume that there are mental states and events within an agent whose causal interactions constitute his being influenced by a reason.")[7] But we should wonder now whether Jane is not being asked to find an agent amid the workings of the brain by fabricating out of naturalistic elements something that can do duty for a Cartesian mind. Hume felt forced to deny that we have the power to move our arms. And so it seems should Jane—unless she is allowed to take a different view in order to find human beings making movements of bits of their bodies. Until she does so, agents will seem to be alienated even from the bits of their bodies that they can move. It is unthinkable that this should be our situation.

5) What is it for someone intentionally to raise her arm, if it is not, as Hume says, the operation of a power of hers to affect minute things inside her? Well, when someone raises her arm intentionally, there is (arguably)[8] an event of her trying to raise it, and an event of its rising. For some causal theorists of action, this will seem to be the beginning of an analysis. If it is agreed that both a trying-to condition and an arm-rising condition are necessary, the next idea will be that a causal condition—saying that x's arm's rising depends causally on x's trying to raise it—supplies a third necessary condition of x's raising her arm intention-

ally. And it might be suggested that these three conditions are jointly sufficient. But anyone who knows the history of this idea will be ready with counterexamples. Perhaps a neuroscientist intervenes between *x*'s trying to raise his arm and his arm's going up, so that even though there is causal dependence of the latter on the former, it was the scientist rather than *x* who raised *x*'s arm (if anyone did). An analysis of "*x* raised his arm" would need to include a condition that specified what it would be for a causal connection to be of the right kind. (It would need to find an informative way of excluding "internal deviant causal chains.")[9]

But if we resist the kind of alienation bred by Humean thinking, we shall be satisfied with something less than an analysis. The right kind of causal connection here, we can say, is the kind there is when someone's arm going up is an exercise of her capacity to raise her arm at will. (The neuroscientist's role in the counterexample is to preempt the exercise of such a capacity.) So we could say that someone raises her arm intentionally if and only if i) she tries to raise it, and ii) she therein exercises her capacity to raise it so that iii) her arm rises because she tries to raise it. Possession of the relevant capacity is presupposed to an agent's *trying* to raise her arm. The capacity is not exercised by someone whose arm makes movements against her will—as in anarchic hand syndrome;[10] it is thwarted when someone is impeded in raising her arm; and it is destroyed if an arm is paralyzed. We can only latch onto the facts about someone who intentionally raises her arm when we allow her to be capable of raising it.

For all its circularity, this nonreductive account may be instructive. Of course its lack of analytical ambitions ensures that it cannot be of any help to anyone who had hoped to find naturalistically approved terms for describing the events that occur on an occasion when someone raises her arm intentionally. But it is genuinely a causal account, which reveals bodily agency as involving psychophysical capacities that depend on human beings' causal complexity. It acknowledges, as Hume could not, that we have the power to move our arms. And it shows immediately that there is something wrong with the standard causal story of an action—as a belief-and-desire-caused piece of behavior.

6) The standard story has no dispute with my characterization of an action as an event of someone's doing something intentionally.[11] And it can be agreed on all hands that a causal explanation of a certain sort can be given of why someone did something that she intentionally did. An explanation of the relevant sort shows that, in the circumstances the agent found herself or took herself to be, doing the thing was warranted or

seemed to her to be. Those who are prepared to stretch the idea of "having a reason" somewhat put this by saying that the agent had a reason to do the thing. And those who have a simplistic conception of a reason will then think of x's having a reason for __-ing is then thought of as x's having a desire that x thinks will be satisfied if she __-s.

So far, there need be nothing wrong with this story, beyond its over-generalization of the role of *reasons* and of *desires*. But it is from this story that naturalists reach "the standard causal story." They do so by converting the claim that x's __-ing is explained by her having a desire that she thinks will be satisfied if she __-s into the claim that belief-desire pairs cause bodily movements. The conversion takes place by way of three transitions. First, x's desiring something and believing something is translated into talk of items with causal potential, so that x's having a reason is taken to be a matter of the existence of a pair of states.[12] Second, the fact that these states are cited in a causal explanation of why x did what she did is taken to be equivalent to their being causes of an action. And third, an action is thought of as something on the physical side of a supposed mental/physical divide and called a bodily movement. The central claim of the standard story of action, then, in its most familiar version, is that belief-desire pairs cause bodily movements. When "try to" is introduced, the claim may be that a "belief-desire pair" causes "a trying," which causes a movement in its turn.[13]

There is no need to look at further details to see that the story creates the problem that Velleman called the problem of agency. In relying on the idea of items linked in a causal chain, the standard story treats causation as Hume did, and takes it to be possible to find an action without locating any bodily being who can move. We cannot then see any agent making any difference to anything: we have the problem "of finding an agent at work amid the workings of the mind."

7) Velleman saw no difficulties about *bodily* agency when he posed his problem of agency. That problem is supposed to arise specifically in cases where the agent does not suffer from being or feeling alienated, whereas there is bodily agency—of which Hume gives such a strange account—whether or not the agent is alienated. The standard causal story is fine with Velleman so long as it is told about agents who are depressed or fatigued, or who lack control, or who would prefer to be motivated differently from how they actually are.

Inasmuch as Velleman's own problem of agency is restricted to what he calls agency *par excellence*, Velleman must think that the picture got from Nagel's external perspective, from which human beings are absent, succeeds in containing the truth about agency at least some of the time. But one wonders then how Velleman can think that Nagel's external perspective reveals "the obstacle to reconciling our conception of agency with the possible realities [given our] scientific view of the world."[14] For as Nagel saw things, there appears to be no room at all for agents in the naturalistic explanatory order.

Well, part of the explanation of Velleman's belief that the standard story sometimes has application is his thinking that there is agent participation of a sort wherever there is human action. He says that "every action must be . . . such than an agent participates in it, in the sense that he does it."[15] Here he relies upon assuming that we encounter a trouble-free kind of agency as soon as we can say, "He does it." But in making this assumption, Velleman refuses to face up to the threat of unthinkable alienation. Nagel said that his external perspective presented a *general* threat to "he does it" being true in any sense; and we saw that this seems exactly right if we construe "he did it" as expressing a relation between a person and an event in the naturalistic explanatory order.[16] It is true that we also saw that "he did it" is not actually understood in this way, and that Nagel's threat is engendered by a misunderstanding about how people relate to the events that are actions. But the present point is that Velleman cannot consistently hold both that Nagel's external perspective poses some genuine threat to our agency, and that someone's action is unproblematically accommodated in the naturalistic explanatory order by virtue of his having "done it."

In fact Velleman appears to acknowledge that there is a more general problem than the one he labels the "problem of agency." For he tells us that the *mind-body problem* is that of "finding a mind at work amid the workings of the body."[17] And if we are to think of "a mind" as something that may move the body, then the phenomenon of bodily agency presents us with the mind-body problem as Velleman thinks of it and as we encounter it so vividly in Hume. (Notice that given this account of the mind-body problem, the problem Velleman labels the problem of agency is a problem about locating something amid the workings of something that has a problematic location amid the workings of the body.)

However exactly Velleman arrives at his view of the extent of the problem that he labels the "problem of agency," he proposes to solve it by introducing a particular mental state, not usually admitted by the standard story's advocates, among actions' causal antecedents. The state in question is one that "plays the functional role of an agent," and Velleman postulates that such a state is operative when there is "agency *par excellence*." But we can see now that this proposal is not addressed to the standard story's real difficulties. If human actions cannot be located among states and events viewed as part of "the flux of events in nature," then introducing another state into that same flux could never be a recipe for bringing them in. A state supposedly playing the functional role of an agent brings too little too late. Such a state is literally too little, because full-sized human beings, not merely the putative inhabitants of their minds, are agents. Such a state arrives on the scene too late, because, as we shall see, human beings are thoroughly involved not only in their actions but also in their actions' causal pasts.

8) Velleman thinks that an agent's feeling or being alienated from what she does is a matter of the relation between her and her action falling short of what is required for a case of real agency, or of "agency *par excellence.*" But if, as I have argued, the agent-action relation is simply that between *a* and *a*'s doing something, then it is impossible to make literal sense of this. And if, as I have argued, human beings are actually ineliminable from an account of their agency, then someone who fails to exhibit agency *par excellence* cannot be treated as someone in whom some functional role state fails to do its bit. Evidently we need to think differently from Velleman in order to draw distinctions between alienated, non-full-blooded agency and agency *par excellence.* But we shall discover that we naturally think differently: it is only to those in the grip of the naturalistic conception of what happens when someone acts that it could seem that differences between actions had always to be recorded as differences between causally efficacious items that produced them.

The agents for whom Velleman thinks the standard story is adequate are (as we saw) people who lack self-control, or self-understanding, or who fail to act wholeheartedly. In these cases explanations may appeal (respectively) to the strength of the agent's desires, to the impotence of her reasons, and to the force of an emotional reaction that she herself has not fully acknowledged. But in none of these cases should we succumb to thinking of states and events that are items inside her and that cause her body's movements. When someone's springs of action are ones she would prefer to be rid of, it is understandable that we should liken them to constraints, and it is true that the language of forces and inertia then comes very naturally. But a person who appreciates that her conduct is out of accord with what she values, or is swayed by factors whose influence she regrets, admits her own motivations even if she does not approve of them. The desires and emotional states that explain what she does are after all states of *hers*—of the human being whose capacities to make movements are exercised—and, even where she feels alienated from them, they are not adventitious forces in her brain. (To think of adventitious forces in the brain seems more appropriate in understanding, say, the involuntary movements of sufferers from anarchic hand syndrome, which lack any personal psychological explanation.)

Of course we must allow that an agent can be, or feel, more or less alienated. To allow for this, we might think of agency as coming in degrees. There is a range of properties possessed by agents that they may exhibit more or fewer of on occasion, and to a greater or lesser extent. Our conception of an agent-in-the-highest-degree might be a conception of someone who is fully self-reflective and has complete self-control, who has values and makes valuational judgments upon which she acts, who uses reason and argument effectively, who is sensitive to her circumstances, who puts her heart into what she does, and who, as we say, *identifies* with her motivations and with what she does.[18] To the extent to which a person's doing something on an occasion shows her as deficient compared to an agent-in-the-highest-degree, we could think of her as failing to participate in Velleman's agency *par excellence*. This is now to think of her as falling short of some ideal or other, and not as lacking some causally potent brain state.

A particular division among agents' properties will be important in considering what might be demanded of an agent in the highest degree. For we want to distinguish between the agency of mere animals, the regulation of whose lives follow biological patterns, and the agency of self-determined, human beings. In the animal case, drives, instincts, and desires of certain sorts loom large in the etiology of behavior. In the human case, the influence of reason is characteristic. Yet even where the agent is a human being, what is done sometimes fails to be caught up with the appropriate functioning of a reasonable being and is then explicable in a more or less animal mode. Acting out of an addiction would be a case in point. We can understand why someone who has the capacities of a human agent may feel distanced from what is thus explicable, and why one should think that her agency then is less than full-blooded agency. But this is not to follow Velleman in thinking that the standard story can be told. For we still have an agent, something she does, and a psychological account of that.

Velleman sometimes writes as if his problem of agency were a problem about setting human action apart from the rest of animal behavior. "What makes *us* agents," he says, "—in our conception of ourselves, at least, if not in reality—is our perceived capacity to interpose ourselves into the course of events in such a way that the behavioural outcome is traceable directly to us."[19] Provided that "interposing ourselves" is understood here as a matter of exercising our distinctively human capacities, and standing as we do to the events that are our actions, this seems exactly right (cf. end of § 3). But in that case Velleman's qualification "if not in reality" is surely needless. And there can be no need to deny that animals too can exercise their (animal) capacities (although the events of their exercising them are evidently not human actions).[20]

Philosophers are interested in human beings. And they are interested inevitably in defects of agency—whether lack of self-control, weakness of will, failures of self-understanding, or features that impugn responsibility. This interest encourages one to forget about the mundane and habitual. When someone, say, puts on her coat, leaves the office, and buys the evening newspaper before getting on the bus that will take her home, she does not express any deeply held values, or deliberate very much, or display particular self-knowledge or self-control. But nor is her agency defective: there are straightforward explanations of what she does, and even if these allude only to mental states of kinds recognized in the standard story, we feel no pressure to add an extra ingredient in order to reveal her as a more or less reasonable, conscious being. Velleman leaves out the relatively mundane when he contrasts various kinds of defective, alienated agency with agency *par excellence*. The omission presumably stems from his thinking that the standard causal story needs some special supplementation if it is to contain a genuine agent. But when human beings themselves are an acknowledged part of the subject matter in explanations of things they do, there ought to be no pressure to add special states of mind, beyond those that are ordinarily recognized, to ordinary explanations. We can then understand why, in unremarkable cases, a person does not have to exhibit *any* of the properties that one might associate with "agency *par excellence.*" And we shall find no reason to think, as Velleman does, that there has to be some single line to be drawn between defective agency and the real thing—some one state that makes human beings the sorts of agents that they are. It would actually be very remarkable if someone could exhibit *all* of the properties of an agent-in-the-highest-degree (all at once, as it were)—which is what a case of agency *par excellence* seems to demand.

One can understand Velleman's special interest in agency *par excellence.* For we certainly don't wish everything we do to be the product of desires we share with nonhuman animals, or to be a matter of habit or routine. But inasmuch as we do aspire to participate in agency *par excellence*, that need not be because we hope that some particular mental state should be operative in us as often as possible, but because we hope that we have all those standing capacities that we associate with agency in the highest degree. The extent to which we should wish actually to exercise such capacities obviously depends upon the kind of conduct that might be called for from us on occasion. An account of agency *par excellence*, then, can be focused on what should be contained in a description of a human being ideally equipped for life's contingencies. There is no need to think of it as an account of a particular sort of psychological machinery at work on each and every occasion of action when the agent is not alienated.

9) There are faults in the standard causal story (as I sketched it in § 6) of a sort that I have not spoken to here. Nearly everyone would agree that an adequate account of human motivation would include mental states of many more kinds than the standard story recognizes, and that it is the product of overgeneralization. It is widely accepted, for instance, that people's having intentions and plans cannot be reduced to their having reasons.[21] And not only (as I suggested above) does the notion of "a reason" have to be stretched if human agency is always to conform to the standard story, but it is also true and widely acknowledged (and it leads to an opposite sort of distortion) that with its casting of *desire* as a ubiquitous motivational ingredient in the genesis of action, the standard story obliterates distinctively rational and deliberational influences on an agent's conduct. Sticking with the standard story's conceptual resources then has the consequence that someone who acts always out of nonreasoned desires can be a paradigm of a human agent. This could provide another part of the explanation why Velleman takes the story to be adequate to telling us what happens when someone acts in some defective way, but to have peculiar difficulties when it comes to agency that is distinctively human or especially full-blooded.

But once it is allowed that full-blooded human beings are the topic of an account of human agency, the project of providing an account will not seem to be that of adding further pieces of psychological machinery to states of belief and desire. An account of human agency that is allowed to be a part of an account of human beings can speak of states of mind from a broad range—virtuous or vicious traits of character, dispositions of evaluation, patterns of emotional reaction, personal loyalties, and commitments that derive from people's various individual projects.[22] It is ways to avoid the distortions that the standard story introduces with its supposition that everything we can know about our nature as practical beings is to be incorporated in a psychological theory that speaks of our inner workings.

10) Let me try to sum up, and reach the main conclusions. I have claimed that there is alienation of an unthinkable sort when an agent is portrayed as if she were merely an arena for events. And I have also claimed that

the project of looking for an agent amid the workings of a mind could never assist in getting rid of such alienation. No one ever does anything in Nagel's picture, and it could hardly make any difference to this which particular kinds of states and events are supposed to be present from the external perspective. From that perspective, the events that are actions are missing, and they cannot be introduced by postulating a special kind of cause for them.

I suggested that there is something peculiar about thinking that the standard story of agency encounters a particular problem in cases of nondefective agency. How could it be that the story is fine so long as it is told about agents who are depressed or fatigued, or who lack control or self-determination, or who would prefer to be motivated differently from how they actually are? Our understanding of such agents relies upon our knowing that they lack some capacity, or are unable to, or fail to, exercise some capacity. But then we understand them as beings who might have possessed, or have exercised, the relevant capacities; and their status as human agents is presupposed in their conduct's being explicable as it is. Someone who falls short of displaying the properties of the paragon agent on some occasion is not treated as if they were then simply the locus of series of mere happenings.

If one ignores the gross physical facts of bodily agency, then it will be relatively easy to suppose that an agent's participation requires nothing that is obviously missing from the standard story of states and events as causes. But it becomes clear that Velleman's problem of agency would be a general problem (if it were a genuine problem at all) when one considers bodily agency, and encounters the species of unthinkable alienation introduced by Hume.

Velleman himself puts his problem of agency in a quite general way at one point: he says that it is difficult to know "how the existence and relations of . . . mental states and events, . . . connected to one another and to external behaviour by robust causal relations, . . . can amount to a person's causing something rather than merely to something's happening in him." To this the answer now is simple: "They cannot." No compounding of states and events in the naturalistic picture from which human beings are absent could constitute someone's doing something that she intentionally does.[23]

Velleman assumes that only *mental* states feature in the causation of actions, and he treats *states* as things to be lumped together with events in a single ontological category of "items" or "occurrences."[24] The assumption might seem to be recommended and the treatment necessary if the causal dependencies recognized when people do things had to be discernible among the causal chains that constitute the world's naturalistic workings. But the real causal dependencies are not discernible there. Nor can they be introduced by superadding a surrogate for a human being on top of—or (more literally, as Velleman sees things) in the middle of—the standard causal story.[25]

Is Freedom Really a Mystery?

MARIO DE CARO

> ... LIBERTY, NECESSITY, and so forth, upon whose desperate and
> unconquerable theories so many fine heads have been turned
> and cracked.
> ~ *L. Sterne, Tristram Shandy*

I. A Philosophical Scandal

In the early decades of the twentieth century, the community of analytic philosophers substantially neglected the problem of free will.[1] Few wrote extensively on the subject, and most of them simply held, with few minor changes, the classic Humean view on the matter, later called "compatibilism."[2] According to this view, the problem could be easily solved by correctly defining freedom as the lack of compulsion or impediment in action. If freedom was such a thing—the compatibilists affirmed—how could it be threatened by the possible causal determination of our actions?[3] From this point of view, it was common to conclude that the whole freewill debate simply idled around a pseudoproblem. Moritz Schlick, for example, famously wrote:

> [I]t is really one of the greatest scandals of philosophy that again and again so much paper and printer's ink is devoted to this matter, to say nothing of the expenditure of thought, which could have been applied to more important problems.[4]

Four decades later, Donald Davidson echoed this point, with reference to the arguments that would supposedly prove the incompatibility of freedom and causal determination:

I will not be directly concerned with such arguments, since I know of none that is more than superficially plausible. Hobbes, Locke, Hume, Moore, Schlick, Ayer, Stevenson, and a host of others have done what can be done, or ought ever to have been needed, to remove the confusions that can make determinism seem to frustrate freedom.[5]

Even Quine—the maestro of analytic philosophy in the second half of the last century—made it clear that in his opinion the "problem of free will" had an obvious solution (which probably explains why he never wrote on this subject at length):

Like Spinoza, Hume, and so many others, I count an act as free insofar as the agent's motives or drives are a link in its causal chain. Those motives or drives may themselves be as rigidly determined as you please. . . . It is for me an ideal of pure reason to subscribe to determinism as fully as the quantum physicists will let me.[6]

Thus, for many years compatibilism represented the orthodoxy on the issue of free will, at least among analytic philosophers. And it was also common to agree with Schlick in thinking that only the persistent influence of an obsolete way of doing philosophy could make it possible to believe that human freedom represented a philosophical problem worthy of serious discussion.

Today, however, the situation is very different, since the problem of free will has regained the prestigious position it traditionally held in the philosophical discussions of the past. Undoubtedly, Moritz Schlick would not be happy to see how many books, articles, and conferences have been dedicated to the issue of free will in the last few years:[7] "the scandal"— he would probably growl—"has arisen again." Nor would he like the indisputable fact that nowadays compatibilism has lost much of its appeal, whereas no other conception has gained large credit. Finally, Schlick would probably be quite incredulous about a striking feature of the contemporary debate on free will: the increasing fortune of skepticism. A relevant number of philosophers currently claim that the problem of free will is, and will always remain—*pace* Schlick—utterly mysterious; and many others state, even more radically, that the idea that freedom is possible—much less that it is real—should be simply given up.

In the present essay I shall argue that this wave of skepticism is the most important consequence of a very common strategy of facing this problem—and the most evident sign of this strategy's inadequacy. In fact, such a strategy crucially depends on some (often tacit and dogmatic) metaphysical premises that are consequences of a "restricted" or "scientific" naturalism.[8] In the last part of the essay, I shall claim that once these metaphysical premises are given up, as it would seem reasonable to do, the rationale to be skeptical about the problem of free will appears much less compelling.

II. Mystery and Illusion

If one compares the current discussion on free will with the debates regarding other crucial philosophical issues, one could easily realize that the former proceeds in a very peculiar way. With regard to the debates concerning, say, personal identity, the mind-body problem, or the nature of ethical concepts, alternative conceptions face each other, none of which is perhaps entirely convincing, but none (or almost none) is completely implausible either. However, when one comes to the question of free will, the situation is much more intricate and unsatisfactory. To describe it, it is helpful to appeal to Thomas Kuhn's accounts of the periods of "extraordinary science."[9] According to Kuhn, it happens sometimes that a scientific theory, which used to represent the dominant "paradigm" in a certain field, goes through a deep crisis, and loses much of its appeal, whereas none of the alternative conceptions is able to gain any significant consensus. The result is a serious theoretical conflict, which may lead to the restoration of the old paradigm, to the emergence of a new paradigm, or to the recognition that "the problem resists even apparently radical new approaches." And in the latter case the scientific community may "conclude that no solution will be forthcoming in the present state of the field."[10]

This account applies well, I believe, to the present discussion of free will. Compatibilism—which, as we have seen, until recently was the majority view—is currently undergoing vehement attacks. As a result, its credibility is weakened to the point that, according to an authority in the field, compatibilism is "nowadays widely regarded as implausible."[11] However, certainly all the alternative conceptions—and particularly the main of them, *libertarianism*—are in no better shape. The reason is easy to tell: convincing arguments have been offered *against* all the major views, as we will see shortly, but no truly persuasive arguments have been conceived in support of any of them. In describing this situation, Thomas Nagel writes:

> [M]y present opinion is that nothing that might be a solution has yet been described. This is not a case where there are several pos-

sible candidate solutions and we don't know which is correct. It is a case where nothing believable has (to my knowledge) been proposed by anyone in the extensive public discussion of the subject.[12]

Indeed, Nagel concludes pessimistically, "at the end of the path that seems to lead to freedom and knowledge lie skepticism and helplessness."[13]

Similarly, for a long time Peter van Inwagen has been arguing that none of the alleged solutions of this problem is even slightly convincing. Moreover, in the last years van Inwagen's skepticism has become even more radical. In several sharp essays, including the eloquently titled "The Mystery of Metaphysical Freedom" and "Free Will Remains a Mystery,"[14] he has argued that probably no human being will *ever* be able to solve the problem of free will. This problem is, according to van Inwagen,

> so evidently impossible of solution that I find very attractive a suggestion that has been made by Noam Chomsky (and which was developed by Colin McGinn in his recent book *The Problems of Philosophy*) that there is something about our biology, something about the ways of thinking that are "hardwired" into our brains, that renders it impossible for us human beings to dispel the mystery of metaphysical freedom. However this may be, I am certain that I cannot dispel the mystery, and I am certain no one else has in fact done so.[15]

Finally, as van Inwagen says, also Colin McGinn defends a similar position ("Free will is a mystery, and therein lies its possibilities").[16] Nonetheless, Nagel's, van Inwagen's, and McGinn's views, however radical, are far from being the most extreme in the contemporary debate on free will. In spite of their pessimism, these authors think (even though for different reasons) that the idea that we enjoy free will plays a relevant and unavoidable role in our lives, and that it would be wrong, and even absurd, to try to dismiss it.[17] They are skeptical only about the possibility of *explaining* how freedom can be reconciled with a world that seems entirely ruled by the objective, inescapable laws of nature. It is because such an explanation looks unattainable that, according to Nagel, van Inwagen, and McGinn, the whole issue of free will is a *mystery*.

In the last years, however, many philosophers have been far more skeptical in arguing that the idea of freedom is a mere *illusion*—a useful one, perhaps, but nothing more than an illusion. A mere listing of titles of some recent books dedicated to this topic will make the point apparent: *The Non-Reality of Free Will, Free Will and Illusion, Living Without Free Will, The Illusion of Conscious Will.*[18] These works, and many others,[19] aim at dissolving, from different points of view, the same idea of free will, as it has been conceived by modern Western philosophy. In this perspective, the point is not that we do not, and perhaps cannot, know how to reconcile freedom and nature, but that the idea of freedom is hopelessly delusive.

Furthermore, this radically skeptical attitude has been frequently extended to another fundamental philosophical notion, that of moral responsibility. The usual rationale for this is that, in spite of some remarkable attempts to prove the opposite,[20] moral responsibility is still thought to require some substantial form of free will.[21] In this perspective, numerous philosophers who think that the kind of freedom that is morally relevant is either unreal or impossible have consequently drawn the same conclusion with regard to moral responsibility. Richard Double, for example, has put the point in these terms: "The most-likely-to-be-true picture of what exists contains neither free choices nor moral responsibility, irrespective of whether human choices are determined."[22]

To sum up, two different forms of skepticism are nowadays common with regard to the freewill problem (and to its implications for moral responsibility). According to the first, expressed by Nagel, van Inwagen, and McGinn, this problem, even if genuine, is a mystery because of its *insolubility.* This view is a form of epistemic skepticism; let us call it the *mystery view.* According to the second form of skepticism, on the contrary, there is no genuine problem of freedom—and of course no real mystery either—since the same idea that we have, or even that we *could* have, free will is *illusory,* and can be shown to be so. This is a form of *antirealistic* skepticism; let us call it the *illusion view.*

I will argue below that in most cases, and notwithstanding their differences, the mystery view and the illusion view have a common origin—and one that it is instructive to analyze. But before discussing this point, two preliminary considerations are necessary. First, I am not claiming that skepticism—in either of the two particular forms mentioned above—has become the dominant view in the contemporary discussion on free will. On the contrary, it is evident that many philosophers still support compatibilism and libertarianism.[23] Even so, in the last couple of decades, the number of authors who have assumed a skeptical stance on this matter has become remarkably high, and it seems to keep increasing. This is a new relevant fact in the history of the debate on free will, and one that should be explained. (Of course, it is not that skepticism about free will was unknown in the past;[24] nowadays, however, it is much more commonly held, and arguably much better justified.)

Second, it should be noticed that the above-mentioned skeptic views about free will, far from being at odds with our best epistemic practices, in fact *spring* from them—or rather, as I will argue, from a very common way of interpreting them. As we will see shortly, the mystery view and the illusion view share the assumption that what science finds out about the ontology, the laws, and the kind of causation of the natural world is radically at odds with the conceptual requirements of freedom; then, from this assumption the mystery view infers that freedom cannot be proven, whereas the illusion view infers that freedom is impossible altogether. However, in both cases *positive* reasons are adduced for a skeptical thesis, reasons that derive from a scientific view of the world—or, more precisely, from what many contemporary naturalist philosophers consider *the* scientific view of the world.[25] It is time, now, to consider these positive reasons further in detail.

III. Springs of Skepticism

Commonsense definitions tell us that agents are free when they *control* what they do, or when their decisions and actions are *up to them*, or are *in their power*. Generally, these vague notions are interpreted as expressing two conditions: the *self-determination* (or autonomy, or self-direction) of the free agent, and the *possibility of doing otherwise* (that is, the availability of alternative possibilities to the agent). It seems very reasonable to think that, in order to be satisfactory, any theory of freedom should account for both conditions.[26] The crux of the freewill problem is that both *compatibilism* (for which freedom is compatible with causal determinism) and *libertarian incompatibilism* (for which freedom is compatible only with causal indeterminism) have difficulties in accommodating these conditions—or perhaps they are just unable to do so. Therefore, since it seems that causal determinism and causal indeterminism are logically exhaustive, we are in a serious predicament. Let's consider this line of argument in more detail.

Traditionally, the main difficulty faced by compatibilism is to show how the "possibility-to-do-otherwise" condition can be reconciled with causal determinism. The long debate on this issue is, in truth, a little tedious: the compatibilists keep on proposing increasingly sophisticated ways out (in particular, conditional readings of this condition), and their adversaries continue in labeling those moves as entirely *ad hoc*.[27] However, the main reason why, in the last decades, many people have started doubting the alleged virtues of compatibilism is a new, important argument: the so-called "Consequence Argument," different versions of which have been offered by van Inwagen, David Wiggins, Carl Ginet, Thomas McKay and David Johnson, Alicia Finch and Ted Warfield.[28]

Here is an informal version of the argument. In order to act freely with respect to any particular action, an agent has to *control* that action; however, to be able to do this, the agent should control either the events in the remote past or the laws of nature on which—if causal determinism is true—that action depends. Alas, both factors are beyond one's control, since the past is *inalterable* (nothing, or nobody, can control it), and the laws of nature are *inescapable* (no human being can affect them). Thus, since every action is beyond the control of the agents, nobody can ever act freely.

This argument has been, and still is, widely discussed, especially because its formal versions depend on a controversial rule of inference in which the lack of control is transmitted over time.[29] Even so, in my opinion this argument is convincing, and so think many philosophers who, because of it, oppose compatibilism. Yet not a few of these philosophers are also unconvinced by the opposite view of libertarianism, especially because of a critical argument that, in different versions, has bothered such a view since it was presented by Hobbes and Hume. According to the basic version of this antilibertarian argument, indeterminism cannot allow any space for freedom, as the libertarians would like to think, since it can only produce lack of causation, that is, randomness—something on which, of course, nobody can exercise any control.[30] However, now most authors think that this version of the argument is effective only against *some* libertarian views, the ones that equate indeterminism with lack of causation.[31] Actually beyond deterministic causation, there can also be indeterministic, or probabilistic, forms of causation that do not seem to make the attributions of power and responsibility impossible.[32] (Assuming, for the sake of the argument, that the effect of throwing dice is not determined, it does not follow that the number that comes out is uncaused too.) Therefore, stated in the traditional way, the antilibertarian argument only works against one kind of libertarian view.

Nevertheless, this argument can be reformulated in a more general way. If an action A is indeterministically caused, then in the causal chain of events that ends with that action there has to be a moment, t, in which more than one future course of action is possible; yet it is not *determined* which of these courses of action will become actual. (If, after the action is performed, time went backward to t, a different action might originate from the same circumstances.) So, even though the action A is actually caused, nothing, or nobody, can *control* its happening, in contrast to the possible happening of the other potential actions. And without control, we have seen, there cannot be any free actions, but only mere accidents.[33]

Therefore, like causal determinism, causal indeterminism seems to leave no space for freedom. However, we *do* have the intuition that sometimes we act and choose freely. Moreover, the content of this intuition— that is, our freedom—seems to be a fundamental basis for our moral judgment, for making sense of activities like pondering and deliberating, for fundamental social practices like praise and punishment, and even for the attribution of rationality to agents.[34] Van Inwagen takes the intuition of freedom very seriously: "Whether or not we are all, as the existentialists said, condemned to freedom, we are certainly condemned to *believe in* freedom—and, in fact, condemned to believe that we *know* that we are free."[35]

Thus, on the one side, we have the strong intuition that we enjoy freedom; on the other side, the combination of the arguments against compatibilism and libertarianism seemingly prove that freedom is chimerical. According to van Inwagen, if this is not a mystery, nothing is: "Free will seems . . . to be impossible. But free will also seems to exist. The impossible therefore seems to exist."[36]

In principle, says van Inwagen, there are only two possible ways out from this predicament. Either we prove that something is wrong with the anticompatibilist and/or the antilibertarian argument or we accept both of them, and consequently dismiss our trust in the intuition about freedom. However, many philosophers—who share van Inwagen's diagnosis up to this point—think that the former option is not practicable, since both the arguments are sound; for this reason, they bite the bullet, and opt for the latter option. Our idea that we are free is only grounded on an intuition—these philosophers maintain—but intuitions *may* be wrong, and not infrequently in fact are (do not we have the intuition that the earth is at rest?). Thus, according to such a line of reasoning, there is no genuine doubt here: having to choose between two sound arguments and an intuition, we should certainly dismiss the intuition. Therefore, they conclude, freedom is a mere illusion.

The defenders of the illusion-view split as to the weight of the illusion of freedom in our lives. Some of the advocates of this view think that this illusion is indispensable, and cannot be eradicated (Paul Smilansky, for instance, writes: "Humanity is fortunately deceived on the free will issue, and this seems to be a condition of civilized morality and personal sense of value").[37] Others, such as many "hard determinists," think that the awareness of our lack of freedom cannot affect our lives in any relevant way.[38] What is important here, however, is that all the defenders of the illusion view assume that the alleged mystery of freedom fades away when we realize that the intuition of free will is entirely deceptive.

IV. Nature and Freedom

Nobody doubts that from a *practical* point of view the intuition of our freedom plays a very relevant role. However, from a *theoretical* point of view, the situation looks very different, since such an intuition seems refuted by the skeptical arguments considered above, and many think that nothing will ever be able to revive it. Should we admit, then, that Dr. Johnson was right in saying that "all theory [is] against freedom of the will," even if "all practice [is] for it"?[39]

Perhaps not. As we have seen, the mystery view and the illusion view share the idea that the anticompatibilist argument and antilibertarian argument, taken together, show that freedom is not possible (while these two views diverge with respect to the credit that should be respectively given to those arguments and to our intuition of freedom). However, to reach such a skeptical conclusion one has to assume not only that these two arguments are valid, but also that this way of arguing refutes *all* the sound conceptions of freedom. Therefore, if we found a conception of freedom unaffected by such arguments, a theoretical conflict would emerge, which would suggest that something might be wrong with the skeptical strategy.

In this light, some points deserve discussion. One could wonder, for example, if it is true that *all* theory shows that freedom is impossible, as both Samuel Johnson and the contemporary skeptics think. In other words, one should determine whether it is true that there is no way of *theoretically* justifying the possibility of freedom, notwithstanding its *intuitive* appeal.

In my opinion, this is not true. In fact, we *do* have *theoretical* reasons for thinking that in some cases we enjoy freedom. That is in fact an implicit but essential assumption of most of the theories of the human and social sciences that aim at explaining *agency*. More specifically, in most cases the attributions of rationality and autonomy to interpreted agents made by intentional psychology, sociology, history, and anthropology essentially require that such subjects choose and act *freely*. This Kantian point has been clearly expressed by G. H. von Wright:

> The concepts used for describing and explaining a man's action, such as motive, reason, intention, choice, deliberation *etc.*, are all of

them tied to the idea of "freedom." To deny that an *agent* is free is to commit a contradiction in terms. The "mystery" of freedom, if there is one, is the "mystery" of the fact that there *are* agents and actions.[40]

Acting because of a reason (deliberation, choice) is a process that intrinsically requires both the *self-determination* of the subject and the *possibility of doing otherwise*—that is, the two classic conditions of freedom (whatever freedom may be). Actions are the special kind of events they are exactly because of their essential connection with the agent's reasons and motives—that is, because they are *self*-determined. And "reason," "deliberation," and "choice" are notions that conceptually refer to the alternative between different courses of action (reasons, for example, make some actions preferable to others).

It is true that attempts have been frequently made to set the study of agency on a hard-determinist ground that, arguably, would not leave space for freedom (think of sociobiology, of some forms of eliminativism in psychology, etc.); so far, however, these attempts have been, if anything, only very partially successful. Therefore, one can confidently say that most of the *best* explanations offered by the human and social sciences look at the agents in the way suggested by von Wright, since they postulate that in many cases agents do choose and act *freely*. What are the most enlightening explanations one can offer in order to explain, let us say, the events of the French Revolution? Definitely, those given by the human and social sciences, which in most cases posit the freedom of agents (for example, by assuming that Danton and Robespierre made such and such rational plans, and chose some courses of actions instead of others after having weighed up their respective pros and cons—and *because of that* their behavior can be understood and rationally evaluated).[41]

From this point of view, freedom—far from being mysterious or illusory—has to be thought as an essential requirement for understanding human beings, as a fundamental precondition of our theories about agency. It is not true, then, that the idea of freedom has only an intuitive appeal, since *theoretical* support can be offered in its favor as well. In the light of this, since the best accounts of agency are typically offered by theories that presuppose the existence of freedom, one could think of a peculiar form of *inference to the best explanation*, in order to justify the belief that agents enjoy free will. What can support our ontological assumptions—including the ones that concern humans and their properties—more adequately than our *best* epistemic practices?[42]

If this is correct, we have an *argument* that justifies our intuitive beliefs about freedom. Since our best theories of agency presuppose that agents enjoy freedom, and we accept those theories, we should be committed to the idea that we are free as well. However, a typical objection can be raised to this line of reasoning. According to it, no genuine ontological commitment can be legitimately derived from the human and social sciences,[43] since, if this were possible, an irreconcilable fracture between the natural and the human world would immediately become evident, a fracture that surely could not be overcome using the linguistic trick of *stating* that the world of agency is just a part of the natural world. Jaegwon Kim expresses a related concern when he states that the failure of the "causal closure of the physical domain"—which is implied by that scenario—would amount to "an anachronistic retrogression to Cartesian interactionist dualism."[44]

In view of this objection, a sharp distinction is often drawn between seriously acceptable, "first-class" theories (that is, theories belonging to the natural sciences, particularly to physics) and "second-class" theories that make essential reference to intentional and normative notions (that is, the theories of the human and social sciences).[45] From this point of view, ontological implications are legitimately drawn only from first-class theories, but not from the theories of the human and social sciences—with regard to which, by the way, according to some philosophers, the term "science" is used in a very suspicious way.

Defenders of the skeptic view about freedom could actually appeal to arguments similar to this. The arguments against compatibilism and libertarianism—these skeptics argue—reflect the light that is shed on this matter by the natural sciences, particularly physics: the point of these arguments is precisely that they show that physical causation, whether deterministic or indeterministic, does not leave any room for freedom. If these arguments are correct, there is no possibility of saving freedom, in spite of what the human and social sciences may say in that respect.

However, this argument is open to objections. First, one could doubt that the skeptical arguments against freedom really express the point of view of the natural sciences on the issue. Second, and more generally, one could challenge the idea of a rigid separation between "first-class" (ontologically relevant) theories and "second-class" (ontologically irrelevant) theories.

As to the first point, it could be objected, following Davidson, that the skeptical arguments are centered on the analysis of causation, whereas the more a science is advanced the less it appeals to causal notions—to the point that contemporary physics tends to expel them altogether.[46] If this is true, it is wrong to think that the above-mentioned arguments against freedom, which are based on analyses of causation, offer the last word on this matter *because of* their alleged privileged relation with the account of nature given by physics.[47]

But even if one grants that causation is a kosher physical notion, it is not obvious that these arguments simply reflect the light of contemporary science upon the freewill issue—and that, *consequently*, we should consider such arguments as the last word as regards that issue. On the contrary, there are good reasons to think that, in essence, those arguments are highly metaphysical or even ideological.

Consider, for example, the idea of the "causal closure of the physical domain." As a *methodological* assumption for the physicists, it works very well;[48] but why should we interpret it as an *ontological* postulate?[49] What reasons do we have for being sure that *every* event has a *sufficient* physical cause? Even if for many events we have found out such causes, obviously induction cannot suffice for justifying the universal quantification at stake here.[50] And notoriously attempts to support this point by referring to the notion of an "ideal physics"—which would give the monolithically *true* description of the world—besides being a clear expression of an extreme metaphysical realism, are deeply unsatisfactory.[51] Finally, as has been well explained by Hilary Putnam, it is reasonable to think that the notion of causation is interdependent with the notion of explanation, and that different explanations generalize to different classes of cases (there are "as many kinds of cause as there are senses of 'because' ").[52] If this is true, the causal closure of the physical domain, conceived as an ontological principle, is evidently false.

One should wonder, then, whether the refusal of the ontological (physicalist) unity of the world really implies the "retrogression" to Cartesianism feared by Kim. Indeed, this is true only if one assumes that Cartesianism and physicalism are exhaustive. As to this, Kim himself has offered good reasons to think that *nonreductive physicalism* is an untenable position;[53] but why should one think that physicalism altogether is the *only* alternative to the intolerably obsolete ontological views of Cartesianism?

Recently some interesting forms of ontological pluralism that are very different from Cartesianism have been defended. John Dupré, in particular, has interestingly argued in favor of an antiessentialist and antireductionist pluralistic view, which is *not* Cartesian either, for it explicitly denies the existence of purely mental entities.[54] Even if this is not the place for analyzing the prospects of this view in detail, one remark may be useful. In a pluralistic scenario of this kind, the idea of a distinction in principle between "first-class" and "second-class" theories loses its appeal, since the ontological relevance of a theory cannot be defined a priori (as it happens when it is limited by definition to physical theories), but depends on empirical and pragmatic reasons.[55] In such a perspective, *there is* room for thinking that the human and social sciences can contribute to shaping our ontology—so that rational agents, societies, political parties, and revolutions may have the same ontological dignity as atoms and molecules. In the same light, since the attribution of freedom to agents plays, as we have seen, an essential role in most of the theories of these sciences, we should be inclined to think that we are also *committed* to thinking that we are free.

Therefore, besides intuition and common sense, a theoretical argument also supports the idea of freedom; so *there is* some ground for being optimistic about the possibility of saving the idea of freedom from the destructive fury of the skeptics. But there is a price for this, of course: one has to give up the assumptions of the "restricted" or "scientific" naturalism that inspire the skeptical approaches. However, considering the strong metaphysical realist flavor of this conception, and its many weaknesses, one should not worry too much about this.

On the other hand, as an ontological alternative to "restricted naturalism," non-Cartesian pluralism would certainly deserve to be held in higher esteem than it usually is because it makes the intuitive idea that we are free seem much less mysterious or illusory. And, considering how much we care about our freedom, this is a virtue that should not be ignored.[56]

∼ *11*

Subjectivity and the Agential Perspective

STEPHEN L. WHITE

The Passive Subject

Imagine that you and a friend have planned a trip whose success depends on an early start. You are dismayed to discover, then, when you arrive at the appointed time, that he is still in bed. You remind him that your plan requires leaving right away, and you point out that if he moves quickly there will still be time to do so. Your friend readily agrees, but makes no move to get out of bed. Your patience nearly exhausted, you suggest in no uncertain terms that he get up. To your amazement, he calmly responds that he understands perfectly well that the trip depends on his being up soon and expresses the sincere hope that he will be. Suppose that in response to your evident consternation he hastens to explain. While he understands the necessity of his being up and mobile, he finds incomprehensible your suggestion that he bring this about. It is not, he says, that there is any disagreement between you where the language of happenings is concerned. But he goes on to explain that although he went to bed a normal subject, he discovered on awakening that the language of action had become unintelligible. By way of support for his new perspective, he points out that whereas you both agree in viewing the past as fixed, he is consistent in seeing the future (quantum indeterminacies aside) in the same light. As he warms to the topic of the incoherence of the conceptual scheme that includes doings as well as happenings,

201

you remind him that speaking is an action—on hearing which, and after some signs of struggle, he lapses into silence.

As the remarks of the passive subject suggest, this story can be told in such a way that there are no factual disagreements between the passive subject and us.[1] If so, then what distinguishes the passive subject from the normal subject? Is the passive subject missing something that we get? And if so, what? Or, if there is nothing that we get and he doesn't, is he responding irrationally or unreasonably to the facts upon which we all agree? Or are *we* in some way out of touch or irrational?

Suppose we ask whether this example raises a problem for a scientific realism or scientific naturalism. Many, no doubt, would claim that it doesn't. The thought would be that there is a straightforwardly naturalistic explanation of the difference between the passive subject and us. There are two obvious forms this response might take. It might be suggested that what the passive subject lacks is simply a causal connection (or the right kind of causal connection) between his desires (for example, the desire to be out of bed) and bodily movements. The suggestion then would be that his beliefs and desires, construed as physical states of the brain, lack the causal efficacy of ours. Alternatively, it might be suggested that there are many compatibilist accounts of action, agency, free will, and freedom available and that whichever one is correct will tell us what the crucial difference between us and the passive subject consists in.

In the remainder of this section, I shall argue that neither of these responses is adequate. I shall begin by addressing the two responses directly and then go on to characterize the kind of problem I am raising in more general terms. The problem to which I am pointing, however, is not one that has been generally recognized in this context. Thus the characterization of the problem in its full generality will be postponed until later, where I shall point to its analogies to a problem in another philosophical domain whose depth and significance has been far more widely appreciated.

The claim that the passive subject differs from us in that our beliefs and desires lead to bodily movements whereas his do not is clearly true. But equally clearly, this is not the only difference. Nor is it the most important one. Simply adding a causal connection between the passive subject's desires and his motor systems so the desires produce bodily movements will not make the passive subject an agent. Such an addition would, in an obvious sense, leave the connection between the desires and the movements *opaque.* For consider an analogy: In certain works of art a mysterious stranger acts so as to satisfy a character's desires that that character would never act to satisfy or to satisfy in that way. (Examples include the recent film *With a Friend Like Harry*, the Patricia Highsmith novel and the Hitchcock film *Strangers on a Train*, and the Curtis Hanson film *Bad Influence*.) In the case under consideration, the passive subject's relation to his own bodily movements would be no closer than such a character's relation to the actions of the Mephistophelian stranger. Nor would it suffice to give the passive subject reliable advance knowledge of the movements in question. For even clairvoyance about how one's body will move as a causal result of one's desires is not the same as one's actually *moving* it. Indeed, that his body should move in ways that satisfy his desires, and that he should have advance knowledge of what the movement will be, is something the passive subject can fully understand. What he lacks is the concept of a *doing* as opposed to a happening. And nothing we have provided so far takes him out of his passive condition.

A similar point applies to the suggestion that we can address the problem raised by the passive subject by an appeal to one of the contemporary and naturalistic accounts of the compatibility of free will and determinism. Certainly it *seems* that such accounts would have to address this problem squarely, since they purport to say how action is possible in the face of a future that is fixed. In fact, however, this is not the case. In part this is because such accounts focus on determinism, whereas the real problem is *objectivism*. It is just as difficult to reconcile genuine agency with indeterminism or randomness as with its opposite. Indeed, any objective metaphysics—that is, one expressible without psychological, agential, or normative concepts—raises the same problem.[2]

Of course this point has not gone completely unnoticed. Galen Strawson has appealed to points of this kind to ground an essentially skeptical treatment of freedom and free will.[3] But even Strawson's skepticism fails to address the real problem raised by the passive subject. Strawson suggests that freedom is really a kind of necessary illusion but fails to ask the genuinely deep question—namely, what the illusion is an illusion *of*. If freedom and agency are incoherent on the assumption of determinism and, equally, are incoherent on the assumption of randomness and on any other assumption about the objective metaphysical facts, then from an objectivist metaphysical perspective the notion is incoherent. It is then a mystery *what* people *think* they have when they think they have free will. If so, then far from providing an answer to the passive subject, accounts like Strawson's, when their implications are spelled out, simply raise the same problem in an equally acute form.

Strawson's is, of course, a skeptical account of freedom and agency. It says, in effect, that determinism rules out freedom and agency and that every other objectivist account does so as well. But the problem for

Strawson is not by itself a problem for (naturalistic) compatibilist accounts that say that determinism is *not* a problem for freedom and agency and that there could well be *non*determinist accounts that would be equally unproblematic. But having seen the problem for Strawson's skepticism, we can easily see where such accounts will fail. The problem is one of *meaning:* The passive subject purports not to understand "action." Strawson provides no account of the *content* of the illusion of freedom, and prima facie both the idea that the future is completely fixed and the idea that there are random events make the idea of action *incoherent.* We can, then, for any alleged compatibilist analysis of freedom and agency consider an analogue of Moore's open question argument: It seems that for any such analysis of his performing an action, the passive subject can say that he hopes that the conditions specified in the analysis comes to pass or are obtained soon. Since this is an inappropriate attitude to take to a possible action of one's own, it points up the inadequacy of the analysis, at least if it is understood as a priori or conceptual in character.[4]

Meaning and Agency

It will help to clarify what I am calling the problem of the meaningfulness of such terms as "action" if we compare it to an analogous problem in another domain—one that has been generally recognized and is, by comparison, relatively well understood. In a highly influential account of our evaluative discourse and practices, *Ethics: Inventing Right and Wrong* (New York: Penguin, 1977), J. L. Mackie has argued that our ordinary evaluative claims are false. Mackie's position can be summarized in three points:

1. Our ordinary moral discourse commits us to the existence of objective values or objective goods[5]—things that are objectively and intrinsically prescriptive in the sense that they are "action-directing absolutely, not contingently . . . upon the agent's desires and inclinations" (p. 29). "An objective good would be sought by anyone who was acquainted with it, not because of any contingent fact that this person, or every person, is so constituted that he desires this end, but just because the end has to-be-pursuedness somehow built into it" (p. 40).
2. There are no such objective values or goods (pp. 29, 35).
3. The denial of the existence of objective values or goods is not a conceptual or analytic or a priori truth, but an a posteriori and empirical one (pp. 35, 40).

These three theses, however, are difficult to reconcile. It is not easy to see, for example, how values could be both "a very central structural element in the fabric of the world" and such that "just knowing them or 'seeing' them will not merely tell men what to do but will ensure that they do it, overruling any contrary inclinations" (p. 23). The reason that this is difficult to imagine is that it is not enough that objective values should have their prescriptive and motivating force independently of agents' contingent desires. They must also have their force independently of agents' contingent vulnerabilities to persuasion. (An automobile would not become objectively valuable, for example, merely because it had a mechanism for projecting subliminal images on the windshield that were extremely effective in getting people to buy it regardless of their contingent motivational makeups prior to the experience.) Thus objective values would have to have their prescriptive and motivational force for all rational subjects merely in virtue of that rationality. But it seems that for anything that was genuinely a part of the fabric of the universe, we could imagine a rational creature capable of apprehending it while remaining indifferent to it.[6] And if in fact this is always possible to imagine, then the objection to objective values is not contingent, a posteriori, and empirical but a priori and conceptual.

It seems, then, that Mackie's endorsement of 3) was ill-considered. Was this, then, just a lapse on Mackie's part? The answer, of course, is no. For, as Mackie was perfectly well aware, there must be an explanation of our evaluative discourse. That is, even if we are error theorists—even if, like Mackie, we hold that ordinary evaluative beliefs are false—there must be an account of what the world would be like if such beliefs were true. And Mackie's own view, implausible as it seems, at least provides an answer. Since on his view there are possible worlds at which objective values exist, for our evaluative beliefs to be true would be for us to inhabit such a world.

Of course, this is merely the semblance of an answer, since Mackie provides no substantive account of what such a world would be like—nothing beyond what follows trivially from his definition of objective value (together with the assumptions that values are extramental and that evaluative statements are genuinely true and false). Mackie may seem to gesture in this direction when he discusses Hume's conception of the mind's "propensity to spread itself on external objects," and his own conception of "the projection or objectification of moral attitudes and its relation to the 'pathetic fallacy.' "[7] But these are suggestions about the *subpersonal mechanisms* whereby the illusion of objective value is produced, not about its content—that is, not about what the illusion is an illusion of.

It might be suggested at this point that the demand for an answer to this latter question is misguided. It might be held, that is, that the illusion of objective value is a shallow illusion—one that we can see through with minimal effort. This suggestion is desperate but, in the realm of values, one that cannot be dismissed out of hand. But this is what makes the comparison between the problem of meaning for our evaluative notions and the problem of meaning for our agential notions useful. On the one hand, the problem itself is better understood in the evaluative domain. Michael Smith's well-known analysis of what he calls "the moral problem" essentially follows Mackie's, without Mackie's commitment to the contingency of the nonexistence of objective values. Smith identifies the following three theses as forming an apparently inconsistent triad:

1. Cognitivism for evaluative claims. (They express beliefs, not attitudes.)
2. Intrinsic objective prescriptivity and motivational force for such claims.
3. Humean moral psychology according to which beliefs and desires are separate and independent existences.[8]

Thus for Smith there is an apparent inconsistency between the idea of objective values and a Humean moral psychology, and he regards the latter as justified on conceptual grounds or a priori. On the other hand, confidence that we *have* something more than a shallow illusion of a coherent discourse and practice (and hence that there is something to be explained) is far more likely in the agential domain. No one is likely to maintain seriously that our agential discourse and practice is based on a shallow illusion, if for no other reason than that the difference between us and the passive subject is not a shallow difference.[9] Both Mackie and Strawson, as error theorists in their own domains, are vulnerable to the same objection: that they have failed to tell us what the content of the error is or what the illusion is an illusion of. In the next section I shall sketch the outlines of a positive account.

Since the problem raised by the passive subject is one of meaning, we can distinguish two subproblems. We need, first, an account of the inferential or conceptual role of the terms in our agential vocabulary. Second we need an account of the way in which those terms are grounded in our perceptual experience. In other words, we need an account of their meaning in terms both of their word-to-word and their word-to-world connections.

Since it figures prominently in Mackie's skepticism about value, I shall begin with the second aspect. Mackie's claim that there are no objective values hinges on two related arguments, which make up the metaphysical and the epistemological parts of what he calls the "argument from queerness." According to the epistemological argument, "if we were aware of [objective values] it would have to be by some special faculty of moral perception or intuition, utterly different from our ordinary ways of knowing everything else."[10] And he goes on to add that

> when we ask the awkward question, how we can be aware of . . .
> authoritative prescriptivity. . . . None of our ordinary accounts of
> sensory perception or introspection or the framing and confirming
> of explanatory hypotheses or inference or logical construction or
> conceptual analysis, or any combination of these, will provide a sat-
> isfactory answer; "a special sort of intuition" is a lame answer, but
> it is the one to which the clear-headed objectivist is compelled to
> resort. (pp. 38–39)

He specifically rejects the idea of "a power of immediately perceiving right and wrong, which yet are real characters of actions" (p. 39).

Mackie makes it clear that his rejection of moral intuition or moral perception is based on a Humean conception of perceptual experience. And although Mackie's rejection purports to be grounded empirically, the point is far more plausibly construed as a priori—given a Humean conception of experience, particularly visual experience, how could "to-be-pursuedness" possibly *get into* what is given to visual perception? As we shall see, a similar point applies to whatever we take as paradigmatically agential properties.

The conception of perceptual experience, particularly visual experience, according to which this objection to moral perception seems irrefutable, is based on an analogy between the character of the given in visual experience and the image produced by a camera, or in a so-called realistic painting, or by light on the retina. But this analogy, natural as it seems, is a false one. I shall argue that what we are given is in some ways much richer and in other ways much more impoverished than the analogy implies. I shall refer to the phenomenology of visual experience that will emerge as an *inflationary and deflationary phenomenology.*

Deflationary Phenomenology of Experience

It will help to reposition some of our intuitions, some of which are deeply entrenched, if we start with the deflationary side of the argument. Begin by distinguishing two theses:

1. Our perceptual experience of the world is like a photograph or a "realistic" painting.

2. Our perceptual experience of the world is like our perceptual *experience* of a photograph or a realistic painting.

Thesis 2) is plausible in at least those cases in which we mistake our experience of a photograph or painting for an experience of the world itself (for example, in the case of a trompe l'oeil painting). And it is thesis 2) that Gombrich expresses when he characterizes our response to realistic pictures as "something akin to visual hallucination."[11] On this account, the similarity of a picture to the thing it represents is not an *intrinsic* similarity, such as the similarity of an original to a copy, but "it is the similarity between the mental activities that both can arouse."[12] (One might think in this context of painted stage scenery that can look extremely realistic from one's location in the audience and virtually unrecognizable from the stage.) It is thesis 1), however, with which we are concerned.

Thesis 1) derives much of its plausibility from the analogy between the camera and the human eye. But the thesis is not that the *retinal image* is like a photograph or painting. It is that conscious visual experience— experience as it is given to the subject from the first person perspective— is, in relevant respects, like a photograph. What does this mean?

The essential idea is that a subject's visual field, construed as something consciously and fully available to the subject, has properties analogous to those of a photograph—or analogous to those of the image that the scene before the subject projects on the retina. This second thesis is expressed in Leon Battista Alberti's *De Pictura:*

> For Alberti, a painter is able to represent what he sees because the elements of vision and the rules for their comparison are themselves pictorial. Once this principle is established, Alberti identifies what he sees as a constructed picture, analyzes it, and uses the product of the analysis for the artificial and correct representation of the perceived image.[13]

Such a conception runs through the empiricism and rationalism of the seventeenth and eighteenth centuries and the phenomenalist and sense-data theories of the nineteenth and twentieth centuries. An even more recent version has been defended by Christopher Peacocke:

> Suppose you are standing on a road which stretches from you in a straight line to the horizon. There are two trees at the roadside, one

a hundred yards from you, the other two hundred. Your experience presents these objects as being of the same physical height and other dimensions. . . . Yet there is also some sense in which the nearest tree occupies more of your visual field than the more distant tree. . . . It is a feature which makes Rock say that the greater size of the retinal image of the nearer tree is not without some reflection in consciousness.[14]

According to Peacocke, the properties of our conscious visual perceptual experience are not exhausted by its representational properties, such as the property in virtue of which the two trees are represented as being the same size. In addition, there are nonrepresentational or "sensational" properties, such as the property in virtue of which the closer of the two trees is represented in a larger area of the visual field—a property analogous to that in virtue of which it would be represented in a larger portion of the surface of a photograph of the same scene from the same point of view. Such a model of visual perception, I shall say, is based on the *camera analogy*. Such models have strong similarities to so-called sense-data theories. According to such theories, what is most directly given in visual perception are colored areas of various shapes in a visual field, in virtue of which the visual experience has the representational properties that it does.[15] According to these theories, the actual shapes, sizes, and colors of the areas of the visual field are the apparent shapes, sizes, and colors of the external objects of our visual perception. On such theories, the portion of the visual field that represents a plate viewed at an angle, for example, will be elliptical, and theorists of this persuasion speak in such cases of an elliptical sense-datum.

I shall argue that the camera analogy is badly flawed as a way of thinking about out visual perception. And I shall claim that the flaws undermine arguments like Mackie's against the possibility of objective value, as well as the possibility of such agential properties as being an action or being an agent. (We can now see that the terms "inflationary" and "deflationary" are used relative to phenomenologies that exploit the camera analogy—specifically as explicated by thesis 1) and by such expository remarks as Ayer's and Peacocke's.) Consider first the deflationary claim. There are good reasons to think that although we have access to some of the apparent shapes, sizes, and colors that the theory requires, such access, except in very easy and obvious cases (for example, to the fact that the apparent shape of a rectangle viewed at an angle is a trapezoid or trapezium), is extremely limited.

It is not difficult to construct thought experiments that support this suggestion, and such experiments play an important role in loosening the grip in which the camera analogy continues to hold our thinking. Here is one such experiment. Try to approximate the apparent shape of your car windshield from the driver's seat using four straight lines. (It is worth actually trying this exercise before going on.) The naive response is a trapezoid with its base wider than its top and with interior base angles of approximately 60°. A moment's reflection, however, shows that this cannot be right. Since one sits closer to the left side than the right, the top and bottom must converge in the latter direction. But it is not easy, through reflection alone, to complete the construction. Counting the convergence of the top and bottom, there are, in fact, three significant departures from the naive response.[16] Among the responses I have received, the majority are essentially the naive response, though a significant minority incorporate one of the departures from this trapezoidal shape. Only very rarely does a response incorporate two departures, and no one in my experience has produced all three on a first exposure to the problem.

It is sometimes objected, however, that this example merely reveals the limits of our memory for shapes and so has no relevance to a theory of perception. Consider, then, the following experiment. While standing straight with your hand four inches from your eye, estimate the ratio of the apparent distance from your wrist to the end of your middle finger to the apparent width of your foot. Typical responses are off by a factor of five, and many are even less accurate.[17]

Such experiments, of course, are not conducted with the apparatus and formality of contemporary experimental practice in psychology. To dismiss them on this ground, however, would be to miss the point. The experiments are not primarily intended as proto-psychological exercises that report the responses of experimental subjects. Rather they are exercises that the reader can reenact with a minimum of difficulty to provide subjective experiences with the potential to undermine the influence that a certain rhetorical tradition and a certain picture exercise on our thinking about perception. As such, they are not intended as conclusive refutations of the camera analogy but as ways of making intelligible to ourselves the possibility that it is wrong. I shall now outline a distinct argument that it is *in fact* wrong. In the absence of such preliminary exercises, however, the degree to which we are gripped by the analogy is likely to prevent any argument from being effective.

I shall call the argument that the camera analogy is fundamentally misguided the *wide-angle lens argument*. The conclusion is a consequence of two facts, well known to anyone familiar with photography and, indeed, in a somewhat different formulation, recognized by theorists of perspective representation since the fifteenth century. Stated in terms of modern camera terminology, we can say that among 35mm camera lenses the ones that produce the most natural looking shapes and distances have a focal length of approximately 50mm and that such lenses produce an angle of vision of approximately 45°. Our perceptual experience, on the other hand, seems to give us an angle of vision of roughly 150°. And since a lens capable of taking in such a wide angle produces extreme distortion of shape at the periphery, as well as very significant distortion of apparent distance, our photographs cannot reproduce the apparent shapes and distances we seem to be given over the wide angle of vision we seem to enjoy. The problem becomes even more acute when one considers movie cameras, since in panning across a scene with an even moderately wide-angle lens, shapes and objects seem to change—a very apparent dynamic distortion that has no counterpart in our ordinary visual experience.

It hardly needs to be said that the point is not one about current lens technology but about the possible ways of mapping three-dimensional space onto a two-dimensional plane. As such it has been recognized explicitly since the late 1400s.

> When Alberti first described a system of single point perspective in his treatise *De Pictura*, he stressed that the artist should find the appropriate point and angle of the visual pyramid. . . . When Marolois described the process he described far more specific guidelines. He maintained that the angle of vision should be more than 60° but less than 90°. . . . Marolois derived these limitations from earlier sources. The idea can be traced back to the 1480's when it appeared in Piero della Francesca's *De prospectiva pingendi*. Such limitations upon the angle of vision were central to the traditional Renaissance concept that perspective gave scientific validity to painting. It was a concept shared by Alberti. He, however, does not seem to have considered the consequences of an artist who consciously chose to view his subject at an abnormally large angle. Piero realized that such a painting would appear distorted. An artist could thus create a distorted image of reality while strictly adhering to the laws of perspective. This situation was unacceptable to theorists who argued for the scientific validity of perspective. *Consequently an important element in Piero's theory was that wide angle vision, where distortions are most visible, should be forbidden* [italics added].[18]

That this result is fatal to our tendency to think of our visual experience as literally like a picture (that is, to thesis 1)) has not generally been recognized. And this, I conjecture, is for several different reasons. On the philosophical side, the distinction between thesis 1), which the wide angle lens argument undermines, and thesis 2), which it leaves intact, is rarely made as clearly as it should be.[19] On the nonphilosophical side, there are considerations in the sociology of knowledge that explain why a camera-analogue conception of visual perception would have appealed to artists since the Renaissance and to early modern scientists.[20]

Why, though, couldn't we advance a modified version of thesis 1): that having a visual experience is like an image projected on a curved surface? Actually, as I shall go on to point out, there is an important truth in this thesis. But it is not a line open to the proponent of 1). For it suggests (quite correctly on the view that I shall develop) that we are given depth as a primitive property. And once this is acknowledged, the motivation for describing our experience as imagelike in any sense is undermined. We are, in fact, given objects at an indefinite variety of distances from us, not just those distances that fall on a smooth curve of any particular shape. And, as I shall argue, this visual experience of multiple depths is basic: these depths are not inferred on the basis of depth cues contained in some more primitive visual experience of a different sort. In particular they are not inferred on the basis of a visual experience as conceived in thesis 1).

The Inflationary Phenomenology of Experience

As the preceding claims suggest, the deflationary argument—that in visual experience we are, in important respects, not given as much as the camera analogy requires—goes hand in hand with an inflationary argument—that in equally important respects we are given a great deal more than the analogy allows. And, as is also apparent, the best case for this claim lies in the visual perception of surface depth—the distances from us of the various surfaces that reflect the light that falls on our retinas. It is virtually impossible to deny that we see things at different distances from ourselves; we do not infer (at the personal level) these distances on the basis of cues contained in an experience as of a flat plane (or, as we have seen, a curved surface).

Given the undeniability of this fact, we might wonder how the camera analogy could have exercised the influence it has and does. In addition to the two points already made—that we confuse theses 1) and 2) and that a belief in thesis 1) had significant payoffs for early modern theorists of perception—I shall mention two more points in passing. First, sense-data theories as developed by Locke, Berkeley, Hume, Russell, and Ayer, among others, which were the natural developments of thesis 1), had natural epistemological and semantic advantages, some of which are still not fully appreciated. Although philosophers have focused on the importance of sense-data in providing an incorrigible epistemological foundation in perception, their semantic advantages are, I would argue, far more significant. Visual sense-data—mental entities whose actual properties are the properties that ordinary objects seem to have in visual perception—allegedly bear a natural, or nonlinguistic and nonconventional relation (typically resemblance, higher-order isomorphism, and so on, at least where spatial properties are concerned), to the world. Thus they are well suited to *ground* our uses of language. Though linguistic meaning is constituted in part by word-to-word connections, unless these are grounded in something nonlinguistic—something outside the circle of word-to-word relations—we never get beyond a formal calculus to the possession of a meaningful language.[21]

Of course it might be suggested that this role is played by real causal connections to external objects. But these connections cannot satisfy either the principle of charity or Frege's constraint. The former says that in the interpretive task of giving meaning to a subject's utterances and ascribing content to his or her intentional states, we must reveal the subject as rational and do full justice to that rationality. The latter says that we must ascribe contents in such a way as to explain differences in the cognitive significance of linguistic expressions.[22] For example, there would be a difference in the content ascribed to "Hesperus" and to "Phosphorus" for a speaker who did not know that the terms are coreferential, because such a speaker could be rational in believing what he or she would express by saying "Hesperus is inhabited" and in not believing what he or she would express by saying "Phosphorus is inhabited." In this case the content would very likely take the form of different descriptions associated with the two expressions.

Now a theory that ascribes only linguistic descriptive content grounded in causal relations to external objects involves a vicious circle. We ascribe unmediated connections (that is, unmediated by descriptive content) between referential expressions and objects in the world in order to break the circle of language-to-language (and word-to-word) connections, and we ascribe linguistic descriptions that mediate these connections in order to satisfy Frege's constraint. Thus if the resources available to us include only linguistic-referring expressions, linguistic descriptive content, and bare causal connections (connections unmediated by any sort of intentional content) between linguistic expressions and objects in the world, the attempt to satisfy the requirement that language be grounded while Frege's constraint is simultaneously satisfied generates a vicious circle.

Adding sense-data to our stock of available theoretical resources is one way of dissolving this apparent dilemma. Sense-data satisfy Frege's constraint precisely in virtue of their pictorial character. Like images, they have no hidden sides. Hence there is no possibility of being given the same sense-datum without recognizing that fact. Sense-data, then, in virtue of being perceptual and nonlinguistic, halt the regress of language to language connections. But unlike ordinary objects, sense-data generate no Frege problems of their own. (The postulation of relations of direct reference between linguistic items—logically proper names—and sense-data introduces no violations of Frege's constraint.) Thus the introduction allows us to avoid the vicious circle just described. The upshot is that without sense-data, or something capable of playing the same role, we cannot simultaneously satisfy the constraint that requires a connection between language and the world unmediated by linguistic descriptive content on the one hand and Frege's constraint on the other. And in neither case is the constraint one that we could seriously contemplate giving up.

There is one final reason why the obvious fact that we perceive depth directly has not undermined thesis 1). There is a pervasive tendency to confuse directness at the personal level with directness at the level of subpersonal mechanisms. Clearly at the latter level our perception of depth is indirect and involves depth cues in the retinal image as well as processes that we might well describe as unconscious inferences. None of these obvious points, however, undermines the claim that depth is perceived directly at the *personal* level—that it is perceived and that it is not perceived on the basis of anything else that is *perceived by*, or *given to*, the subject.

The question then is how much more we are given in visual perception than is allowed by the camera analogy. In what follows I shall argue that both the philosophical arguments and the experimental literature suggest that we are given at least some kind of causal relations and some sort of third-person agential activities and capacities, as well as real human possibilities in the form of opportunities for action.

Perception as Availability to Basic Action Capacities

In what follows I can sketch only the broadest outlines of a more phenomenologically adequate account of perception. Some aspects of the account have been developed more fully elsewhere.

As an alternative to the sense-datum account and to the account in terms of the descriptive linguistic content of belief, we can think of our visual perceptual experience in terms of our access to objects (what will, on this account, be the objects of those experiences) in virtue of our basic action capacities—particularly our demonstrative capacities. Take, for example, objects we can see. We have the capacity to point to them, indicate their extent, trace their outlines, move toward or away from them, find spots, if they exist, from which the view of the object is not occluded (or from which it is), and so on. We know how to bring an object at the periphery of our visual fields into the center and how to detect and bring into view sources of movement outside the field in which we can see objects. We can shift our focus and we can shift our attention from one aspect of our visual world to another. And we have the capacity to recognize not only how we might move within the available spaces of a fixed spatial configuration but how we could change the configuration, either by modifying objects or by rearranging them. If we have linguistic capacities we can answer questions about shapes, colors, and so forth.

These capacities are not to be thought of as things we do on the basis of a visual experience that exists independently of them. For it seems that the idea that we might have all the first-order capacities of a normal subject but lack any visual experience is incoherent. This may not be immediately apparent in the light of the blindsight examples. Some subjects who report that they have no visual experience in an area of their visual field can, with prompting, answer questions about the visual properties of visual images that fall within that area.[23] But it is important to note that the discriminative capacities of such subjects where visual properties are concerned never begin to approach those of a normal subject. And it is precisely the subject who has exactly the *same* first-order capacities as the normal subject while lacking any visual experience—whom we may call the *perfect blindsight subject*—whose intelligibility is in question. Imagine looking at the keyboard of your word processor. Is it really intelligible to suppose that you could have all the same first-order capacities regarding the keyboard—for example, to answer the same questions about the visual properties of the keyboard spontaneously and with complete confidence and to exercise all the same demonstrative skills and more generally all of the same nonverbal pragmatic capacities while having no visual experience where the keyboard was concerned? Or, consider a more dynamic example. Can you imagine driving in downtown Boston with the same degree of skill and confidence, avoiding pedestrians, erratic drivers, and new construction, reading signs, and scanning the street for parking spaces, while being completely blind?

Notice that we can assume that in having all the first-order capacities of a normal subject you have the capacity to report on which things are visible from particular locations and in particular circumstances. For example, you can report that from a particular location the no-parking sign is hidden by the moving van, or that the piece of cardboard located perpendicular to your line of sight that would obscure your view of the plate seen at an oblique angle and not obscure your view of anything else would be elliptical. Thus it seems that as someone with all the first-order capacities of a normal subject you would have all the (most important) information about apparent shapes with which sense-data theorists can justifiably credit us. And the same applies to apparent colors. A white cup illuminated by red light (say a spotlight) would be indistinguishable in color from a red cup in normal light right beside it. Thus it seems that as such a subject you could learn to construct the (most important) sorts of descriptions that sense-data theorists regard as paradigmatically expressive of our first-person access to the subjective character of our visual experience.[24] Thus given all the relevant capacities of a normal subject, it seems impossible to say what blindness could consist in.

On the proposed account of visual perception, then, according to which it is a matter of our basic action capacities, visual experience is intentional, and so, by definition, has content. But in being essentially tied to action capacities, this content is neither linguistic nor pictorial. Rather, we should think of it as providing semantic grounding in virtue of the constitutive connection between meaning and use. And since the uses in question involve actions, there is a sense in which the account is nonreductive. Visual perceptual content grounds language by taking us outside the circle of linguistic descriptions. But since it itself is intentional, it does not take us outside the intentional circle.

The A Priori Argument for an Inflationary Phenomenology

What is the connection between this general approach to perceptual experience via action capacities and an inflationary phenomenology? That is, what is the connection between this approach and a phenomenology according to which we literally perceive such things as causal connections, the intentional activity of others, and the threats and promises as well as the opportunities for action—the real human possibilities—that our surroundings present us? The a priori argument for such a phenomenology stems from the claim that perception is what makes action possible by providing our demonstrative connection to the world. This is to say that there is a gap between our descriptive-linguistic beliefs about the world and our capacity for action. Indeed, it is precisely the point of the example of the passive subject that it makes manifest one aspect of this gap. The passive subject agrees with us about all the objective facts—those that can be expressed in the language of the natural sciences without demonstratives or indexicals—and yet finds our talk of action unintelligible. Since the passive subject also understands the inferential relations between the various elements of the agential vocabulary, what he lacks, as I shall suggest below, is something perceptual; he lacks the perception of opportunities for action that are genuine opportunities for him, or, in Gibson's terms, he lacks *affordances*.[25]

As this suggests, however, another aspect of the gap between our descriptive-linguistic beliefs and our capacity for action lies in the irreducibility of demonstrative to descriptive content. In fact, it is the upshot of the criticisms of Stephen Schiffer's position in "The Basis of Reference" by Brian Loar, Gareth Evans, and others that demonstrative content is irreducible to descriptive content even as supplemented by the "essential indexicals" "I," "here," and "now."[26] Indeed, this is just another aspect of the fact that our system of descriptive representations requires semantic grounding—grounding in a relation to things in our surroundings that is nondescriptive and nonlinguistic: in other words, in a relation that is irreducibly demonstrative or ostensive.

According to the account of perception and consciousness outlined in the last section, however, the perceptual and the demonstrative *are* the agential. Being in a perceptual relation to the objects in one's environment is a matter of those objects being accessible to a wide range of one's basic action capacities—particularly those capacities that go to make up one's demonstrative skills. Thus being in a perceptual relation to the objects in question is being in a demonstrative relation, and this in turn is being in an agential relation to them.

How, then, do we get the result that we perceive affordances? Our capacities for basic actions require that we be given things as doable—that we be presented not just with threats and promises (to use Gilbert Ryle's expression), but with *opportunities*. Moreover, the capacity for action requires that we be able to identify demonstratively what we might call the "environmental levers of action"—that we know, for example, that in order to leave the room we have to turn *that* handle.

The a priori argument, then, is that whatever else it is or is not, perception is our demonstrative link to the world. This link provides semantic grounding for our language and for the linguistic-descriptive content of our beliefs and is constituted by our basic action capacities. And our capacity for action presupposes that affordances are a part of our perceptual experience—the perceptual experience that separates us from the passive subject with whom we share all of our objective, descriptive beliefs. But this argument is abstract—largely because it appeals to interrelations among the referents of a small circle of expressions ("perceptual experience," "demonstrative relation," "basic action capacities," "demonstrative skills," "semantic grounding," "perception of affordances"). Because the account is explicitly nonreductive, circularity is not the issue. But an account that involves an extremely *small* circle risks being less informative than we might have hoped. To address this problem, I shall give another argument that we do in fact perceive affordances. Besides expanding the circle involved in the analysis, this has the added advantage of loosening the grip of the camera analogy on our visual perception.

The Slippery Slope Argument for an Inflationary Phenomenology

That we perceive depth directly—that it is not, at the personal level, inferred on the basis of something that is given more directly, such as apparent shapes—is unlikely to be denied by many. Moreover, where the passive subject is concerned, we have seen strong reasons for believing that the difference between such a subject and a normal subject cannot be explained simply in terms of descriptive belief content. Nor could it be a matter of sense-data alone, since on the classical understanding, there should be no relevant difference in the sense-data available to the passive subject and his closest normal counterpart (a normal subject situated in the same position, with eyes open and working normally during the same period of time, and so on). These two examples alone should be sufficient to undermine the camera analogy conception of visual perception. In addition to providing semantic grounding compatible with Frege's constraint, however, that conception has a further advantage—it provides a noncircular way of saying what our visual experience is *like*, a way that is independent of saying what it represents. We can talk, for example, about the layout of apparent shapes in a visual field in a way that seems independent of what they are the apparent shapes of. (Think of an unpainted paint-by-numbers canvas and note that while one may recognize all the shapes, one may completely fail to recognize the subject depicted.) And because we can do so, and do so in a way that is independent of the concepts normally used to characterize the objects and events that the perceptual experience represents, this conception of experience seems to give us a vivid sense, not only that our experience grounds our linguistic representations, but of *how* it does so. And because the conception has this advantage, it is unlikely that any one or two examples will make much headway against it. It will be useful, then, to see something of the variety of ways in which this conception is violated by our visual experience.

1) *Orientation in Space.* Along with the claim that we perceive depth directly, the analogous claim regarding many forms of orientation in space is relatively uncontroversial. As Peacocke puts it:

> the experience of being in a tilted room is different from that of being in the same room when it is upright and the experiencer's body is tilted. Or again, a visual experience as of everything around one swinging to one's left can be distinguished from the visual experience as of oneself revolving rightwards on one's vertical axis.[27]

Of course, it is clear that the experiential difference is largely a causal result of events in the inner ear, as well as other nonvisual orientational cues. But this is quite compatible with the experiences (and the differences between the experiences) being *visual*. (We may simply be aware of a visual difference and unaware of anything going on in the inner ear.)

2) *Personal Orientation.* Imagine waking up in a room and not remembering or having any idea where you are. If the memories of your surroundings now come flooding back, there is an overwhelming inclination to say that when one has finally come to recognize the room, it *looks* different. This inclination, I would suggest, should be taken at face value: the room really does look different in the same way in which a city square or small park may look very different when one is thoroughly familiar with the surrounding city, from the way it looked on a first encounter. Again it might be suggested that there is a causal explanation: in these cases, perhaps, that all one's unconscious habits of looking (that is, the unconscious eye movements used to scan the scene, which is viewed in a single direction with one's head still in both experiences being compared) have changed from the earlier to the later experience. This is not an implausible suggestion, but again it misses the point. At the personal level it may be that no such difference is apparent. It may simply be the

case that the same scene viewed from the same point in the same direction *looks* different on the two occasions.

3) *Gestalt Phenomena.* The same pattern of shapes on a page may look very different depending on how it is organized as a figure and ground—for example, the familiar figure that may be seen as two profiles separated by empty space on the one hand or as a goblet or vase on the other. The same point could be made about figures that from the perspective of gestalt principles can be organized into a number of equally good patterns. In this case too the point might be made that the different figures involve different unconscious habits of looking and again it is irrelevant. At the personal level there is a visual difference that has no camera-analogue counterpart.

4) *Aspects.* In the case of the duck-rabbit or the Necker Cube, different aspects produce different visual experiences, even though the subject is perfectly well aware that the difference has no camera-analogue explanation. In other words, there is no difference that could be described in terms of a difference in the layout of apparent shapes, sizes, and colors in a visual field.

5) *Mechanical Causality.* Michotte's experiments in the perception of causality suggest that under well-defined circumstances a sequence of images on a screen (of the sort that might be produced by a two-dimensional animated film) can produce a visual impression of causality that is distinct from the visual impression of the pattern of movement itself.[28] Taken at face value, these experiments suggest that there is an aspect of our visual experience that is irreducible to a pattern of shapes in motion within a visual field—and hence an aspect that is incompatible with the camera-analogue account. Indeed, it is the camera analogy that seems to have led Hume to claim that there is no impression of a causal connection: and Michotte is normally interpreted as having provided strong evidence that Hume was wrong.[29]

6) *Intentional Causality.* Current research in this area, like Michotte's, is based on patterns of movements among shapes on a screen. Interpreted at face value, it indicates that there is a visual impression or experience of intentional causality or third-person agency. (Some shapes, for example, are seen as "helping" or "hindering" other shapes in the latter's attempts to bring about some goal or end state.)[30]

7) *Affordances.* J. J. Gibson argued that we perceive affordances, or objects of use—things that will support us or shelter us, that will provide escape routes or hide us from danger, or the routes or means to desired goals—*directly.*[31] Although Gibson's claims are not always easy to interpret, it is natural to take him as saying at least that we are not given a

visual impression or experience of pragmatically neutral objects or situations on the basis of which we impose an interpretation or infer a description that entails their utility. Rather, at the person level, their usefulness is given to us *directly* in visual perception. As Sartre puts it:

> When I run after a streetcar ... there is consciousness *of-the-streetcar-having-to-be overtaken*. ... I am then plunged into the world of objects. ... It is they which present themselves ... with attractive and repellent qualities.[32]

And to say that such pragmatic qualities are given directly is simply to say that there is nothing given in our visual perception that is given *more* directly and on the basis of which the utility of such objects and situations is given. And we can understand this claim by analogy with the claim that (normally) one's raising one's arm is a basic action. To make the latter claim is not to deny the existence of causal processes that mediate between the occurrence of the intentions to raise one's arm and one's arm going up. Rather, it is to say that there is nothing one *does*—no other *action* one *performs*—in virtue of which one raises one's arm.

Conclusion

If none of these things is essential to perception, what is? And is there no sense in which perception necessarily provides a given element in experience? In fact there are a number of senses all closely related:

1. Perception is necessarily given in the sense of a) providing an element that is nonlinguistic and nondescriptive, b) being *prior* to language and descriptive content, c) grounding language and descriptive content subject to Frege's constraint—in other words providing semantic grounding.
2. Perception is necessarily given in the sense of being intimately tied to our capacity for demonstration and demonstrative reference. Some would say that our perceptual experience makes perceptual demonstratives available,[33] but this would at least *seem* to presuppose a prior and completely independent account of the content of perceptual demonstratives, and it is unclear where such an account would come from. I would prefer to say that perceptual experience puts us into a demonstrative relation to the object of the perception (an actual relation to an actual object if "perception" is being used as a success term, and if not, then at least a

virtual relation to an actual or virtual object). Another way to put this is to say that perception makes it possible for us to act in the world on the basis of our beliefs (beliefs that are about the world) when we are in an appropriate perceptual relation to it.

3. Perception is necessarily given in the sense of there being something it is like from the subjective point of view to have a conscious perceptual experience.

These three claims, though they come from very different areas of contemporary philosophy, are closely related. The first point, that language must be grounded, is, as we have seen, an extremely general one in the theory of meaning. It is implicit in Russell's contention that the logically proper names refer to sense-data and, arguably, in the entire empiricist tradition. It is mentioned explicitly in epistemological contexts by Ayer, as we have seen, and by Anthony Quinton among others, and should hardly be controversial. As Ayer puts it:

> It is necessary that, besides the rules which correlate symbols with other symbols, our language should also contain rules of meaning, which correlate symbols with observable facts.[34]

The point that language must be grounded while simultaneously satisfying Frege's constraint is perhaps more controversial. (Actually, the point is not one that is vigorously denied on the basis of cogent arguments. Rather, it is one with regard to which the profession is currently in denial.) It is nonetheless also implicit in Russell's choice of sense-data as the referents of logically proper names. Any solution to what I have called elsewhere the problem of perspectival grounding[35] must do at least as much as Russell's theory does and do so without the (by now) all too evident drawbacks of a sense-datum theory. Theories like Pitcher's or Armstrong's that make perceptual experience a matter of belief acquisition or a disposition toward belief acquisition, far from doing more than Russell's theory, do less—they provide no account at all of perspectival grounding.[36]

The second point comes out of more recent work in the philosophy of language: work on essential indexicals, de re and de se thought, and demonstratives.[37] Perry's point that our ability to act in the world depends on our ability to deploy propositions couched in essential indexicals such as "I," "here," and "now" has been widely assimilated. One's belief that the department meeting starts at noon and one's desire to arrive on time can produce (in the appropriate way) action only if one is capable of recognizing something that can only be expressed in terms of such an indexical—for example, it is *now* (almost) noon. The same point, however, applies to demonstratives. One cannot leave the room as a basic action unless one can recognize something couched in demonstrative terms such as that *that* is the exit. And like our capacity to recognize what would be expressed through the use of essential indexicals, our capacity to recognize what would be expressed through the use of demonstratives is basic. As we have seen, it is irreducible to any of our capacities for linguistic-descriptive understanding. But as the last example suggests, such a demonstrative capacity depends on our perceptual capacities. (The claim is not that every basic action requires our perceptual contact with the object of the action. One might reach for, and move, something such as a gear shift lever in the dark. The claim is simply that our agential capacities and our demonstrative capacities depend on *some* perceptual capacities.)

The final point comes out of the study of consciousness in the philosophy of mind. As we have seen, *the perfect blindsight argument* undercuts the plausibility of analyses of conscious perceptual experience in terms of second-order representation. This is because, as I have argued, it seems inconceivable that we could have all the first-order capacities of a normal subject and lack conscious visual perceptual experience. The alternative, as I have argued elsewhere, is to recognize that what the normal blindsight subject lacks is not the second-order representation of first-order (unconscious) perceptual states. Rather it is the accessibility of the objects of his or her first-order states (for example, the images flashed on the screen in the experimental set up) to a wide range of basic action capacities, including particularly demonstrative and phenomenal capacities.[38]

If this last point is correct, then we have completed the circle of conceptual dependencies. Action (in the world) requires demonstrative capacities, which require (conscious) perceptual capacities, which require agential capacities (particularly those that I have called demonstrative and phenomenal). The conclusion is that these capacities form a tightly connected domain of mutual dependencies. This domain grounds our linguistic descriptive capacities in the sense that it takes us outside the circle of language to language or symbol to symbol connections (recall Ayer) and it does so in accordance with Frege's constraint.

Suppose then that we take seriously the claim that the positive "essence" of perception is to ground language subject to Frege's constraint by (roughly) putting us in a demonstrative relation to objects in the world. Then there seems to be nothing to rule out our being given af-

fordances—opportunities for action—directly. We have seen too many
difficulties with arguments based on the camera analogy to suppose that
they could block such a suggestion. Nor, as we have seen, is it ruled out
by any considerations of what perception must be like if creatures like
us are to have states with content and contact with their world. And
certainly phenomenology—that is, considerations of how our perceptual
experience seems to us from the first-person perspective that we can be,
and very often are, given directly not simply the shapes and colors of the
objects with which we interact. As the slippery slope argument suggests,
we seem to be given depth, gestalt properties, aspects, meaning properties, causal properties, and some intentional properties *directly*. And the
arguments we have been considering suggest that there is no reason not
to take this apparent fact at face value.

The foregoing considerations suggest that nothing *rules out* our perceiving affordances directly. I shall now argue that in fact we *must* do so.
For the passive subject is like us as far as all the contents of our intentional states are concerned that can be expressed without an essential use
of any specifically agential concepts (the nonagential concepts, for
short).[39] Indeed, we can tell the story of the passive subject so that not
only does he share all of our nonagential beliefs, but having been an
active subject, he has a perfectly competent grasp of all the inferential
roles associated with our agential concepts. Here is an analogy. At the
end of Louis Malle's *Damage*, the main character recalls meeting, after
several years of separation, the woman for whom his obsession has destroyed his career and family and says: "She looked like anyone else."
We can assume that in this state of incomprehension of the actions of
his earlier self, the character would remain capable of applying all the
predicates to the former object of his love that did not imply the special
character of his relation to her. But further, we can imagine that he recalls
all too well the characterizations with these implications that he applied
in the past and that he can trace their conceptual connections and inferential roles with the same facility and competence as his former self.
Indeed we can even imagine that he remains competent to say with regard to counterfactual situations that he could have experienced but
didn't, what it would have been appropriate to say and believe. What we
can imagine him lacking in this disenchanted state is no part of the inferential roles of the concepts that expressed his obsessive love, but any
sense of what in his experience made it reasonable to apply them.

Like the disenchanted lover, the passive subject lacks nothing of the
conceptual roles of our agential vocabulary but their experiential grounding. This presupposes, of course, that there is no inferential route from

an understanding of our nonagential conceptual scheme to a genuine understanding and appreciation of agency. That this is so is made clear by the fact that for any objective characterization that purports to locate his agency as an objective feature of the world, we can imagine the passive subject saying that he hopes that feature will come to characterize him. We have, in other words, as we have seen, an analogue of Moore's argument. The passive subject says, in effect, that he understands full well the advantage it would be to him if events in his brain caused (in certain appropriate ways) his limbs to move. But we can nonetheless imagine that despite this appreciation, the utter incomprehensibility of our suggestions that he *do* something remains unchanged.

It is this inferential insulation of the agential and nonagential perspectives that forces us to accept the direct apprehension of affordances to explain what we have and the passive subject lacks, as well as to explain how our agential concepts are to be grounded. Indeed it is no exaggeration to say that we inhabit a different world from the passive subject or that our conceptual schemes are incommensurable—where both of these claims are understood in the sense in which comparable claims regarding theorists guided by different paradigms have been ascribed to Kuhn.[40] In both cases the richness that allegedly characterizes perceptual experience plays a crucial role in generating the incommensurability. In the Kuhnian case, the inability of theorists in the grip of different paradigms to understand fully each other's theories stems from two sources. First, the concepts of neither theory can be definitionally reduced to the concepts of the other. (And, needless to say, there is no third theory in which they can be defined.) Second, since each theory generates its own theory-laden perceptual experience, there is no neutral basis for comparison. Similarly, in the case of the normal subject and the passive subject, there is no definitional reduction of the normal subject's agential concepts in terms of the objectivist notions in terms that the passive subject understands. And because the passive subject lacks our agency-laden experiences, there is no way in which he can simply learn our agential concepts ostensively.

If this analysis is roughly correct, then it follows that there could not be a *completely* passive subject—at least not if subjectivity requires intentional states. For according to the analysis, conscious perceptual experience requires the accessibility of the objects of perception to a wide range of basic actions, particularly of the demonstrative and phenomenal variety. And since (it has been claimed) intentional states have genuine content in virtue of their ties to perceptual states, a completely passive subject should be, on this analysis, a conceptual impossibility.[41] But this is really just to reemphasize what has already been said—that perception, a capacity for demonstration, and a capacity for basic action form a tightly connected domain of mutually supporting relations.

It is not simply for dramatic effect, then, that the example is one of a slowly encroaching passivity. If we imagine the stages of the subject's progress toward passivity prior to those of the example, we should perhaps suppose that what is first lost is the capacity for deliberate action based on explicit practical reasoning—that Hamlet-like the subject loses the connection between reason and action—indeed that the process of reasoning becomes antithetic to action. This is consistent, of course, with the persistence of relatively well entrenched routines, the performance of which we can suppose to cease at a later stage. Even then, however, we can imagine that the subject remains capable of spontaneous responses to exceptionally strong stimuli—the subject hears what sounds like a riot in the street and leaps up to look out the window or sees you about to drink what he takes to be a poisoned glass of wine and leaps up to knock it out of your hand. And as the example is described, we are certainly imagining that the subject finds verbal stimuli so powerful that he responds spontaneously—at least until the spontaneity of his speech has been undermined.

By this stage, however, or at least by the stage at which the subject's verbal responses have become somewhat more laconic, we can well believe his claim not to find action genuinely intelligible. But we can still imagine, I think, that if full-blown affordances are gone—except perhaps at the brief moment at which spontaneous actions are performed—there are nonetheless attenuated counterparts—memories of things "done," hopes for a "normal" future—sufficiently anthropomorphic and agential in character to generate a domain of perceptual, demonstrative, and agential connections rich enough to ground the content of intentional states.

Indeed we know that this must be possible because we know that in cases of extreme depression the domain of agency and of the self shrinks. All that remains is that we describe the experience of a subject for whom this has occurred with devastating effect:

> I saw things, smooth as metal, so cut off, so detached from each other, so illuminated and tense that they filled me with terror. When, for example, I looked at a chair or jug, I thought not of their use or function—a jug not as something to hold water and milk, a chair not as something to sit in—but as having lost their names, their functions and meanings; they became things.[42] . . . Living in an

environment empty, artificial and apathetic, an invisible, insuperable wall divided me from people and things.[43]

And after such an experience the return of agency has the force of revelation:

> With the astonishment that one views a miracle, I devoured with my eyes everything that happened. . . . They were useful things, having sense, capable of giving pleasure. Here was an automobile to take me to the hospital, cushions I could rest on. . . . And to the stupefaction of the nurse, for the first time I dared to handle the chairs, to change the arrangement of the furniture. . . . What unknown joy, to have an influence on things; to do with them what I liked and especially to have the pleasure of wanting the change.[44]

IV
ETHICAL AND
AESTHETIC
NORMATIVITY

12

A Nonnaturalist Account of
Personal Identity

CAROL ROVANE

*I*F IT SHOULD TURN out that personal identity is, broadly speaking, a product of effort and will, then that would put into doubt the success of efforts that philosophers have made to give naturalistic accounts of personal identity where it turns out, broadly speaking again, to be a metaphysical given. In arguing that it is a product of effort and will, therefore, this paper will be proposing a nonnaturalist account of personal identity, an account that implies that it is within the power of persons literally to redraw the boundaries that mark them off one from another.

Locke's famous distinction between personal identity and animal identity set much of the agenda for discussions of personal identity among philosophers, dividing them to this day between neo-Lockeans and animalists. But on the subject of the present paper—naturalism—there has tended to be accord on both sides. Neo-Lockeans are just as committed to providing a naturalistic account of personhood and personal identity as their animalist opponents. Section 1 of the paper will be devoted to showing how this naturalism currently prevails on both sides of the philosophical dispute about personal identity, among those who embrace, as well as among those who reject, Locke's distinction.

Section 2 will sketch the nonnaturalist alternative I'm advocating.[1] I will be arguing, in particular, that human-size persons can by will and effort integrate with others in order to generate group persons who are composed of many human beings and, also, they can similarly choose and strive to fragment in order to generate multiple persons within the same human being. In arguing for the possibility of group and multiple persons I am arguing for a version of Locke's distinction between personal identity and animal identity. But these are not the possibilities that contemporary neo-Lockeans have in mind when they defend Locke's distinction. They have in mind the possibility that a person's consciousness (and other psychological attributes) could be switched from one animal body to another. This is not a possibility that has ever been realized in fact. Neo-Lockeans (and Locke before them) have, therefore, had to rely on thought experiments in order to establish it. In contrast, the possibilities I have in mind, of group and multiple personhood, are much closer to being realized in fact. For I'm claiming that it is within our power, exactly as we are here and now, to make them real if we should choose to do so. I'm also claiming that there already exist real phenomena, in the form of joint endeavors and fragmented human lives, that realize these possibilities in degree. So, in more than one sense, I will be sticking closer to actual cases.

In section 3, I will reexamine dissociative identity disorder in the light of nonnaturalism about personal identity. This is a disorder in which individual human beings may manifest more than one distinct personality. Often, it is possible to treat such alter personalities as separate subjects of address in conversation and argument and, when this is so, interacting with them is uncannily like interacting with individual persons. It will emerge that there is no purely metaphysical reason why we should not regard them as persons in their own rights and, hence, as instantiating my thesis that there can be multiple persons within a single human being. However, this is not the only issue that nonnaturalism about personal identity raises for our understanding of dissociative identity disorder. There is another, more fundamental issue concerning what unifies the self, and why unity is absent in those human beings who suffer from dissociative identity disorder. I am claiming that the unity is in every case—even in the paradigmatic case of the normal adult human being—the product of effort and will. If this claim is correct, then we shall have to rethink how we should represent to ourselves the dissociated state, the therapeutic goal of integration, and the available means to achieving that goal.

The reexamination of dissociative identity disorder that I propose to carry out in section 3 will not restrict itself to the abstract questions that philosophers are bound to raise about the self and its unity. I want to show what happens when we bring philosophical ideas to bear in real life, in a particular life, the life of someone I have come to know very well, for whom the project of self-understanding has been poignantly difficult due to the fact that she suffers from a dissociative disorder. The biographical details that I will be discussing demonstrate that philosophical ideas about what we are can be brought to bear in such a way as to alter the reality of what we are. This fact is of a piece with my central thesis that persons are, in an important sense, nonnatural.

The final section of the paper will further clarify this nonnaturalism by contrasting it with Ian Hacking's Foucaultian perspective on dissociative identity disorder (or, really, its precursor, multiple personality disorder). He agrees that our ideas about what we are can, and generally are, brought to bear in such a way as to alter the reality of what we are. But we shall see that he means something quite different from what I mean when I say that we have the power to alter the facts of personal identity.

1. Naturalism Currently Prevails on Both Sides of the Philosophical Dispute About Personal Identity

The contemporary philosophical dispute about personal identity was inaugurated by Locke when he argued that personal identity is not the same as animal identity.[2] He defined the person as "a thinking, intelligent Being, that has reason and reflection, and can consider it self as it self, the same thinking thing, in different times and places."[3] He took this definition to entail that a person is an agent and, hence, a locus of will, responsibility, and self-concern. He also took the definition to entail that the condition of personal identity must coincide with the condition in which there is a single consciousness. And he offered a thought experiment in order to demonstrate that this condition need not coincide with the biological identity of a human animal. The experiment first asks us to imagine that the consciousnesses of a prince and a cobbler are switched, each into the other's body; then it asks us to conclude that the prince and the cobbler each continue to exist as the same person by virtue of retaining the same consciousness even after they have been switched to new bodies.

Neo-Lockeans embrace Locke's distinction between personal and animal identity on similar grounds.[4] They share roughly the same conception of the person, as a reflective rational agent. However, they don't typically emphasize consciousness per se in their accounts of personal identity over time, incorporating instead a wider range of psychological relations such as memory, similarity, and the relation that obtains between an intention and its subsequent execution. But this difference doesn't prevent them from agreeing with Locke that a person's identity can diverge from the life of a given animal. And they typically defend this conclusion by invoking thought experiments modeled on his original, in which the psychological life of the same person continues despite switching bodies. Only their experiments are updated to reflect current theories about the mind and the mind-body relation. So, for example, functionalists might portray body-switching as the result of "brain reprogramming," whereas those who conceive the mind-body relation as a weaker supervenience relation might portray body-switching as the result of physical duplication, as in teletransportation.

Animalists, of course, reject Locke's distinction between personal and animal identity. This is not because they disagree with him about whether a person is a reflective rational agent. Like neo-Lockeans—and, indeed, virtually everyone—they recognize that the capacity for reflective rationality, along with some related practical and social capacities, are distinctive to persons. But they see these distinctive capacities of persons as part of the natural biological endowment of certain species of animals, the only known case of which is *Homo sapien*. And just as they see the capacities of persons as provided for by biological nature, likewise they see personal identity in the same way. In their view, a person *just is* a suitably endowed animal and, in consequence, its life cannot possibly diverge from the biological life of a given animal in the ways suggested by Locke and neo-Lockeans.[5]

It is obvious that animalists are committed to giving a naturalistic account of personal identity. They explicitly conceive the existence of a person as a natural occurrence within the biological order on a par with all other animals. However, it may be less obvious that neo-Lockeans are also committed to giving a naturalistic account of personal identity. One reason why it may be less obvious is that their thought experiments do not portray body-switching as the outcome of a natural process. That is, they do not ask us to imagine that nature itself produces persons who travel from body to body. Body-switching is generally portrayed as the result of *technological* processes like brain reprogramming and teletransportation, the results of which could hardly be called natural. Yet it would be quite wrong to infer that neo-Lockeans are not committed to giving a naturalistic account of personal identity. Their thought experiments do not aim to describe miracles that contravene the laws of nature altogether. They aim to describe possibilities that accord with those laws. Otherwise, they would not demonstrate that the life of a person can *really* come apart from the life of a given human being. They would no more demonstrate this than the story of Peter Pan demonstrates that human children can really fly. Admittedly, many of the thought experiments that neo-Lockeans have put forward read like bad science fiction and, as a result, do seem to be a bit like Peter Pan stories. But all the same, it's clear that even the most far-fetched thought experiments do not aim to describe miracles. And the more sober neo-Lockeans actually invoke specific theories of the mind in order to vindicate their idea that the life of a person can come apart from the life of a given animal. The favored theory is functionalism. And this stands to reason. A functional process or system is just the sort of thing that could be realized in a succession of different material circumstances and yet remain the same thing, just as Locke argued is true of persons.[6] I hope it is clear, then, that neo-Lockeans share with animalists a broad commitment to accounting for personal identity within a naturalistic framework.

In addition to sharing this broad commitment to naturalism, neo-Lockeans and animalists also share many *specific* assumptions about *human nature* and its role in the lives of actual persons. Both parties assume that the distinctive capacities of persons, such as reflective rationality, belong by nature to human beings—that is, they are part of a human being's native biological endowment. Both parties also assume that the normal biological development of a human being will culminate in the existence of an individual person, one who does not move from body to body and who will not survive the death of the human being that gave it life. Animalists infer from these assumptions that the life of a person is, therefore, inextricably tied to the life of a given human being. All that divides neo-Lockeans from animalists is that they do not draw this inference, but instead affirm the possibility that the same person could in principle persist in different animal bodies. As I've already explained, the thought experiments that neo-Lockeans offer in order to demonstrate this possibility do not rewrite the laws of nature, and this includes the laws of human nature. That is why the experiments always portray body-switching as the result of technological processes like brain reprogramming and teletransportation. It is because neo-Lockeans agree with animalists that body-switching is not, strictly speaking, a natural occurrence. It follows that when neo-Lockeans envisage the life of a person as involving body-switching they are envisaging something that is, strictly speaking, nonnatural. But it does not follow that neo-Lockeans generally envisage the actual facts of personal identity as we know them as nonnatural facts. An analogy will help to bring out why. Consider human bodies that have been given organ transplants or prosthetic limbs. Here too the results are not entirely natural. Yet it is perfectly correct to view most human bodies—the ones that have not undergone these technological transformations—as entirely natural, in the sense of being natural outcomes of normal human biological development. And this is precisely how neo-Lockeans view actual persons who have not undergone the sorts of technologically induced transformations that they envisage in their thought experiments. They view all such actual persons as the natural outcomes of normal human biological development.

It is this picture of actual persons that I will be calling into question— the picture that animalists and neo-Lockeans share, according to which the existence of a person is a metaphysical given of nature that typically arises as the normal outcome of the biological development of a human being.

2. Nonnaturalist Account of Personal Identity

Let me begin by registering two points of agreement with the two main parties to the philosophical dispute about personal identity. First, Locke was right to make the capacity for reflective rationality central in his definition of the person. Here is why. Agents who have this capacity have a related social capacity to engage one another in distinctively interpersonal ways. In all such interpersonal engagement, one person addresses and aims to influence another by engaging the other's rational point of view. This involves a very complicated sort of mutual recognition among self-knowing subjects. The subject of address must conceive itself as being addressed by something that conceives itself as addressing something that conceives itself as being addressed. Because these forms of engagement involve these complicated forms of mutual recognition, you cannot have the capacity for such engagement without knowing that you do. And in knowing this about yourself, you know something about what distinguishes you and others like you from all other things and, hence, as forming a single kind, which I'm proposing to call "person."

You could know you are a member of this kind even if you wouldn't use the term "person" in order to express your knowledge. All that such knowledge requires is a) going in for distinctively interpersonal forms of engagement and b) recognizing that there are some things you can engage in these ways and other things you can't engage in these ways, such as your pet. You can love your pet; you can need it; you can lose games to it; you can even lose battles of will to it. But you can't lose an argument to it. And you know that. Thus you know you have a nature that you don't share with your pet, but do share with other things whom you can engage in distinctively interpersonal ways. This amounts to knowledge that you are a person, whether or not you would put it that way.

And I want to propose that we do put it that way. I propose that we apply the term "person" to all and only those things that can be engaged in distinctively interpersonal ways. This amounts to a *pragmatic criterion of personhood*, according to which something *is* a person just in case it can be *treated as* a person.[7]

The second point of agreement I want to register with both neo-Lockeans and animalists is this: the capacity for reflective rationality, along with the related practical and social capacities that distinguish persons from all other things, belongs to the native biological endowment of human beings. It might be wondered why an animalist conclusion doesn't directly follow. After all, if a human being by nature has the capacities that distinguish persons from all other things, doesn't it follow that a human being *is* a person? We've seen why neo-Lockeans think it doesn't automatically follow. They offer thought experiments designed to show that the psychological continuity of a reflective rational agent— and hence its identity—could in principle be preserved in a succession of different animal bodies. I'm going to offer quite different reasons for supposing that personal identity can come apart from animal identity. They are not derived from thought experiments, but from sustained reflection on certain practical and social capacities of persons, all of which are bound up with the capacity for reflective rationality by virtue of which persons can be treated specifically as persons.

Let's consider more carefully the condition in which something can be treated as a person, through distinctively interpersonal forms of engagement. The first thing to note is that all such engagement aims at rational response, and this presupposes that persons are, in some minimal way, responsive to the normative requirements of rationality. I won't try to give an exhaustive specification of the normative requirements of rationality that a person must be committed to satisfying. I'll make do with a few examples and an observation about their common goal. The most general normative requirement that rationality imposes on a person is that the person should arrive at and act upon all-things-considered judgments about what it would be best to do in the light of all of its beliefs, desires, and other attitudes. Such judgments presuppose a variety of rational activities that together comprise a person's deliberations, such as the following: resolving contradictions among one's beliefs, working out the implications of one's beliefs and other attitudes, ranking one's preferences in a transitive ordering. Each of these rational activities is directed at meeting a specific normative requirement of rationality—the requirements of consistency, closure, and transitivity of preferences, re-spectively. Deliberation involves many more rational activities, each of which is similarly directed at meeting some specific normative require-ment of rationality. But it doesn't matter for my argument here what they might happen to be. What matters is that all of these rational ac-tivities have a common purpose, which is to contribute to the overarching rational goal of arriving at and acting upon all-things-considered judg-ments. If it is not evident to you that the more specific normative re-quirements of rationality do contribute to this overarching rational goal, try to imagine what it would be like to arrive at all-things-considered judgments without satisfying them. If you refused to resolve contradic-tions among your beliefs, for example, there might be no such thing as what it was best for you to do in the light of your beliefs. One belief might direct you to perform a certain action while its contrary (which you also believe) directed you not to perform it. Similar problems would arise if you refused to work out the relevant implications of your atti-tudes, or to rank your preferences transitively. You would be refusing to consider all things in the sense required for deliberation; you would be refusing to consider their rational import. I'm going to call the state that would be achieved if a person were to succeed in this endeavor, of arriv-ing at and acting upon all-things-considered judgments, the state of *over-all rational unity*. And I'm going to suppose that there is one overarching normative requirement of rationality on persons that incorporates all of the other, more specific requirements like consistency, closure, and the like, namely the normative requirement to achieve overall rational unity.

I am now in a position to lay down the two crucial planks of my positive account of personal identity. First, a person is *subject* to the nor-mative requirement to achieve overall rational unity within itself. This follows directly from Locke's definition of the person as a reflective ra-tional being, along with the conception of the normative requirements of rationality I outlined in the preceding paragraph. Second, a person is not only subject to the normative requirement to achieve overall rational unity; a person must also be *committed* to satisfying that normative re-quirement. This follows from my pragmatic criterion of personhood, which adds to Locke's definition the condition that a person be capable of distinctively interpersonal forms of engagement. Any attempt at such engagement necessarily appeals to this commitment on the part of per-sons, to achieving overall rational unity within themselves. For, as I said earlier, the aim of such engagement is always to prompt a rational re-sponse. This already means that such engagement must, therefore, appeal to a person's commitment to being rational. And we can now see that this is precisely a commitment to achieving overall rational unity, by arriving at and acting upon all-things-considered judgments. Even lies and threats appeal to this normative commitment. Their point is not to get a person to go in for rational failure; their point is rather to get a person to judge that it is best, all things considered, to believe the lie or comply with the threat.[8] And so it is with all attempts at interpersonal engagement, in which persons treat one another specifically as persons. They must all appeal, however implicitly, to the commitment that persons have to achieve overall rational unity within themselves.

This account of what sort of thing a person is—a reflective rational being who is committed to achieving overall rational unity and who can, therefore, be engaged in distinctively interpersonal ways—incorporates an implicit reference to personal *identity*. For the normative requirement to achieve overall rational unity *defines* what it is for an *individual* person to be fully or ideally rational. This can be seen from the fact that there is no failure of rationality when a group of persons fails to meet this ideal, but only when an individual fails to meet it. So, for example, if I have inconsistent beliefs, I am guilty of rational failure; but my beliefs may be inconsistent with yours without there being any rational failure on either of our parts.

One promising way to approach the problem of personal identity, then, is to investigate the condition in which the normative requirement to achieve overall rational unity applies—or, rather, the condition in which a *commitment* to meeting it arises. For that is the condition in which we have something that meets the pragmatic criterion of personhood, as something that can be treated as a person.

Prima facie, it might seem that this commitment should arise wherever something both has and exercises the capacity for reflective rationality. If this were true, then it would follow that personal identity is a metaphysical given of biological nature, in much the way that animalists insist must always be true and neo-Lockeans grant is generally true in actual cases. For it surely belongs to human nature both to have and to exercise the capacity for reflective rationality. And it may be hard to see why this doesn't suffice to generate in human beings a commitment to achieving overall rational unity within themselves, thereby qualifying them as individual persons.

Here is why it doesn't suffice. Although rational capacities must always be directed at achieving rational unity *somewhere*, they needn't be directed at achieving rational unity within the biological boundaries by which nature marks one human being off from another (or the phenomenological boundaries by which nature marks one consciousness off from another). Human beings can exercise their native rational capacities in order to achieve different levels of rational unity within different boundaries. They can exercise their rational capacities together so as to achieve rational unity within groups that are larger than a single human being, and they can also exercise their rational capacities in more restricted ways so as to achieve rational unity within parts that are smaller than a single human being. When this happens, it is not individual human beings but, rather, groups and parts of them that can be treated specifically *as persons*.

These claims are bound to meet with some skepticism. Unfortunately, I can't give a full defense of them here. What I can do is indicate the kinds of considerations that support them and, in doing so, further elaborate their meaning.[9]

I'll start with the case of group persons. It is well known that when human beings engage in group activities, their joint efforts can take on the characteristics of individual rationality. Think, for example, of marital partners who deliberate together about how to manage their homes and families and other joint concerns. They may in the course of such joint deliberations do as a pair all of the things that individuals characteristically do in order to be rational: they may pool their information, resolve conflicts between them, rank their preferences together, and even arrive at all-things-considered judgments together about what they should together think and do—where the "all" in question comprises all of their pooled deliberative considerations. The same can also happen in a less thoroughgoing way when colleagues coauthor papers, or when teams of scientists design and run experiments together, or when corporations set up and follow corporate plans. We tend to assume that such joint endeavors leave human beings intact as individual persons in their own rights. Insofar as that is so, it should be possible to engage those human beings separately in conversation, argument, and other distinctively interpersonal relations. But sometimes this is not possible. Sometimes, marital partners won't speak for themselves. Their commitment to deliberating together is so thoroughgoing and so effective that everything they say and do reflects their joint deliberations and never reflects their separate points of view. The same can happen to coauthors, team members, and bureaucrats. The kind of case I have in mind is not one in which human participants simply wish to give voice to the larger viewpoint of the groups to which they belong. The kind of case I have in mind is one in which the human constituents of the group are not committed to having separate viewpoints of their own. That is, these human beings are not committed to achieving overall rational unity separately within their individual lives. Yet it is not because they lack rational capacities. It is because those rational capacities are directed in a different way, so as to help fulfill a larger commitment on the part of a whole group to achieve overall rational unity within it.

If this seems implausible, just think about two different attitudes you might bring to a department meeting. You might bring your own separate viewpoint to the table with the aim of convincing your colleagues to agree with you. This attitude takes for granted the status of each colleague as an individual person in its own right with its own separate point of view. The attitude also *perpetuates* that status. For the effect of adopting it will be that you maintain the separateness of your point of view by deliberating on your own, with the aim of achieving rational unity just within your own self. Even when you are moved by what your colleagues say, the reason why is not that you want to resolve disagreements with them, or do anything else that would help you to achieve rational unity as a group. You will be moved by your colleagues only insofar as what they say bears on your personal project of achieving such unity by yourself—by showing you that you have internal reasons, from your own point of view, to accept what they are saying. But you might bring a quite different attitude to a department meeting, one that would not perpetuate your separateness from your colleagues. You might bring to the table all you have thought of with respect to the issues the department faces, with a view to pooling your thoughts with your colleague's thoughts, so that you can together discover the all-things-considered significance of the whole group's thinking. If your colleagues do the same, then it won't be true that each of you is committed to achieving overall rational unity on your own; you will be jointly committed to achieving such unity within the department. And, for this reason, it will be possible for others to engage the department itself in conversation, argument, and other distinctively interpersonal relations. The department could be asked, for example, why you did such and such, and there will be a coherent answer that reflects the department's joint deliberations. I'm not saying that departments of philosophy typically have the commitment that would render them sufficiently unified to be engaged in this way. But I am saying it is possible. It is possible for human-size philosophy professors to undertake a commitment to achieve rational unity together. And, if they were to live up to that commitment, then the lines that divide one person off from another would have shifted. They would no longer follow the biological divisions that mark off different human animals, or the phenomenological divisions that mark off different centers of consciousness. They would follow nothing else than the commitment to rational unity that is characteristic of the individual person. To say that these lines can be redrawn in these ways is to say that the facts of personal identity are matters of choice and, hence, nonnatural.

Many objections could be raised at this point, more than can be addressed in a single article. I'll briefly take up two before moving on to the case of multiple persons. These objections do not call into question whether human beings can coordinate their deliberative and practical efforts in the ways I've been suggesting. What they call into question is whether such group endeavors could ever undermine the status of individual human beings as persons in their own rights. The common thought behind these objections is that the facts of personal identity in these human cases are not the products of effort and will but are metaphysical givens of human nature, contrary to my suggestion.

The first objection notes that my own descriptions of group persons referred at certain crucial points to the thoughts and choices of their individual human participants. For example, I referred to two different attitudes that an individual philosophy professor might bring to a department meeting. One would maintain its internal rational unity and, thereby, the separateness of its point of view, while the other would contribute to the overall unity of the department and, thereby, help to constitute the department's more inclusive point of view. I also described two marital partners as each being committed to engaging in joint deliberations. My language may have given the impression that the unity of the group person is in each case actively maintained through individual commitments and efforts on the part of its human members, the philosophy professors and marital partners, respectively. And that seems to imply that the human members themselves must remain individual persons in their own rights even in the context of a group endeavor, since otherwise they could not possibly maintain group unity through their *individual* commitments and efforts. But my language was misleading. What is true is that a group person may *initially* be brought into existence through the individual decisions and actions of smaller persons, typically of human size. But if these initial efforts have been successful, then a group person will have been brought into existence. And, thereafter, at least some of the intentional episodes that occur within the human organisms involved will be episodes in the life of a group person rather than in the separate lives of human-size persons. Going back to the case of a philosophy department, when I bring to the table the aim of joining in a departmental deliberation, then, insofar as my aim is shared by others and is efficacious, the result will be that the subsequent deliberations *around* the table are carried out from a new, emergent group point of view that can't be equated with my point of view or any other human-size point of view. This is not to say that there is no sense at all in which separate, human-size points of view would be left intact. All of the human beings involved would still have separate centers of consciousness and, hence, separate *phenomenological* points of view. But it is important not to confuse a phenomenological point of view with the sort of point of view that each individual person has, by virtue of which it can be engaged in distinctively interpersonal relations. The latter is a *rational* point of view that can be engaged in distinctively interpersonal ways, by virtue of its commitment to achieving overall rational unity within itself. And, in the case under discussion, the separate phenomenological points of view of the human members of a unified philosophy department do not qualify as separate rational points of view in this sense. Such centers of consciousness are not centers of rational activity aimed at achieving rational unity within them. They are sites of rational activity aimed at achieving rational unity within the larger boundaries of the department. When this happens, the human members of a group can no longer be engaged as individual persons in their own rights. And, so, the fact that they remain intact as individual animals with separate phenomenological points of view does not suffice to show that they also remain individual persons, as the objection alleges.

The second objection insists that it is always possible to describe the phenomena associated with group endeavors in methodological individualist terms—that is, in terms of thoughts and actions that belong to their human participants. It concludes that there is no reason to grant my claim that group endeavors may literally alter the boundaries between persons. My response to this objection is that it may be carried even further, further than its proponents intend. If it is possible to describe group endeavors in methodological individualist terms, it is equally possible to describe human endeavors in homuncular terms. And, so, if it is supposed to follow in the one case that human activity cannot produce group persons, it should follow in the other case that homuncular activity cannot produce persons of human size. But certainly, the latter inference does not go through. Homuncular activity can be directed in such a way as to yield overall rational unity within the larger human being. Indeed, this had better be so. Otherwise, the homuncular theory would not be consistent with known facts about human social interactions, which typically take the form of interpersonal relations in which one human-size person actively engages the rational point of view of another human-size person. This would not be possible unless homuncular activity could be directed at achieving overall rational unity within the whole human being. And, if this can happen among homunculi, it can also happen among human beings; their rational activities can be directed at achieving overall rational unity within a whole group. It may seem unfair to have saddled the proponents of methodological individualism with homuncular theory. But it is not unfair insofar as methodological individualism is supposed to follow from the fact that it is always *possible* to describe group endeavors in methodological individualist terms. For then it is relevant that it is *also* possible to describe human endeavors in homuncular terms. Now, it is often observed that references to homunculi are not *necessary* in adequate descriptions of human psychology. And that may be the spirit in which methodological individualists want to rule out the existence of group persons. They may be claiming that references to group persons are not necessary in adequate descriptions of human psychology, any more than homunculi are. And, so, by Ockham's razor the only persons left standing are persons of human size—nothing larger or smaller need be posited. But this reasoning begs the question in favor of the basicness of human beings. From the point of view of homuncular theory, references to human-size persons might seem just as unnecessary as references to homunculi might seem from the point of view of a humanistic theory. We can easily avoid this impasse by adopting the pragmatic criterion of personhood according to which anything that can effectively be treated as a person is a person. Homunculi don't pass this test. Many human beings do. And the latter should not be disqualified from the status of persons just by virtue of the fact that clever theorists can describe their mental lives in homuncular terms. Similar remarks apply to group persons. They qualify as persons insofar as they pass the test of being treatable as persons. And they should not be disqualified from the status of persons just because clever theorists can describe their intentional activities in methodological individualist terms. All that matters in either case is whether there is a requisite commitment to rational unity by virtue of which it is possible to engage them in distinctively interpersonal ways.

Multiple persons are distinguished from homunculi precisely by the fact that they satisfy the pragmatic criterion of personhood; they can be treated as individual persons in their own rights despite the fact that they cohabit the same human body. Let me now outline the considerations that I think support the idea that such multiple persons are possible.

The considerations are really generalizations from the case of group persons. That is, I propose to model *all* cases of rational unity on the unity of a group. My suggestion is that rational unity doesn't *just happen* as the inevitable product of some natural process, such as the natural biological development of a human being. Rational unity is something that is *deliberately achieved* for the sake of some *further end.* There are things that a philosophy department can do as a unified group person that no human-size person can do on its own. And that may constitute a *reason* why such human-size persons might initially decide to pool their efforts in a joint endeavor. If they implement their decision, they no longer maintain separate rational points of view. So, what perpetuates the group person once it has been brought into existence is not separate commitments on the part of its human constituents; it is up to the group itself to maintain its existence by continuing to strive for overall rational unity within it. When we view the unity of a human-size person along these lines, we must see it as deliberately achieved for the sake of some further end that couldn't be achieved without it. The appropriate contrast here is with an impulsive human being who doesn't strive for rational unity—who doesn't deliberate at all but simply follows current desires unreflectively and uncritically. Since the capacity to deliberate belongs to human nature, perhaps it is fair to say that such a human being is acting against its nature. But that doesn't harm my point, which is that when human beings do exercise their rational capacities, they are *generating* rational unity through their intentional efforts. And it is part of this same point that these capacities can be directed at the achievement of rational unity within different boundaries. An initially impulsive human being might come to strive for rational unity within each day, or week, or month, or year, or even a whole lifetime. The last goal was celebrated by Plato as part of the just life and by Aristotle as part of the virtuous life. In a less high-minded way, we now typically pursue the project of living a unified human life for the sake of other more specific projects such as life-long personal relationships (friendships, marriages, families) and, also, careers. But what I want to emphasize is that these are *projects* and they are *optional.* It is possible for human beings to strive for much *less* rational unity than these projects require and still be striving for rational unity. And, sometimes, the result may be relatively independent spheres of rational unity with a significant degree of segregation. Such segregation is evident in degree in the lives of many human beings whom we find it possible to treat for the most part as roughly human-size persons. We may find, for example, that when we visit the corporation our friend "becomes" a bureaucrat who cannot recognize the demands of friendship at all. What this means is that our friend's life actually takes up a bit less than the whole human being we are faced with, the rest of which literally belongs to the life of the corporation. According to the nonnaturalist account of personal identity that I'm now elaborating, this would not be aptly characterized as "role playing." It would be better

characterized as a fragmentation of the human being into relatively independent spheres of rational activity, so as to generate separate rational
points of view that can be separately engaged. Of course, group endeavors do not necessarily result in such fragmentation; in principle, they can
completely absorb the human lives that they involve (this may actually
happen in the armed forces and certain very intense marriages). But when
a group endeavor does *not* completely absorb the human lives that it
involves, there is a consequent split in those lives. And I propose to
conceive multiple persons along precisely these lines. The only difference
is that the separate rational points of view of multiple persons need not
be imposed by involvements in group projects but, rather, by involvements in other sorts of projects that it is not possible for a single human
being to pursue in a wholehearted and unified way. When a human being's projects are numerous, and when they have nothing to do with one
another, this may make it pointless to strive to achieve overall rational
unity within that human life. And it may be a rational response to let go
of the commitment to achieving such overall rational unity within that
human life and to strive instead for as many pockets of rational unity as
are required for the pursuit of those relatively independent projects. So,
just as a group person may dissolve itself for the sake of human-size
projects that would otherwise have to be forsaken for the sake of the
group's overall unity, a human-size person may dissolve itself for the sake
of even smaller projects that would otherwise have to be forsaken for the
sake of the human being's overall unity. In such conditions, we will find
the emergence of multiple persons within that human being, each of
whom can be treated as a person in its own right.

I don't want to suggest that this is typically how persons come into
existence, through the breakdown of some larger unity. I think it usually
occurs in the reverse direction, when it is noticed that there is something
worth doing for the sake of which more unity needs to be achieved. That
is certainly how group persons would typically come to be. And I'm
suggesting that the same holds for human-size persons.

In conclusion, it is not nature, but intentional activity and the undertaking of appropriate projects, that yields the commitment to rational
unity characteristic of the individual person, and that transforms a human
being into a human-size person. There is no law of nature that precludes
a less ambitious transformation into multiple persons instead. To a certain extent, this happens when human-size persons give over portions of
their lives to group endeavors. And, to a certain extent, this happens in
all human lives. Qua reflective rational agents, human beings are less
separate from one another, and less whole within themselves, than is

ordinarily assumed. What individuality human beings manage to achieve, qua reflective rational agents, is truly an achievement. So it is with every case of rational unity, whether it be in whole human beings, or groups of them or parts of them. That is why the facts of personal identity are nonnatural.

3. Dissociative Identity Disorder

Dissociative identity disorder is a disorder in which individual human beings manifest two or more distinct personalities, each of which is dominant at a particular time. It is generally agreed that alter personalities develop in response to child abuse, usually sexual in nature. But it is less clear whether certain defining characteristics of alter personalities should be regarded as necessary. For example, alter personalities are often divided by amnesia barriers and yet this is not always so. Sometimes, they are "co-conscious," which is to say, they have direct introspective access to one another's thoughts. Such co-conscious alters can nevertheless emerge as being both highly integrated within themselves and quite separate from one another—so much so that they can engage in independent and, indeed, incompatible practical pursuits. When alters meet this last condition, they typically also satisfy the pragmatic criterion of personhood. That is, they can be separately engaged in distinctively interpersonal ways, from what seem to be separate points of view. Many such alters are childish and in various ways dysfunctional or incompetent. But many are not. Some have even satisfied the standards of legal competence in some states.

It should be obvious why the nonnaturalist account of personal identity I elaborated in the last section puts pressure on me to conclude that some alters might really be persons in their own rights. This will seem especially clear if you bear in mind that I allowed that something can be a person and, moreover, know that it is a person, even if it would not use the language of personhood in order to express it. For my claim was that a person can display such self-knowledge simply by engaging in distinctively interpersonal relations. And this, it seems, is something that some alters can and do, even if they are not prepared to *say* that they are persons in their own rights. However, it is not my primary aim to defend the conclusion that alter personalities should be counted as persons in their own rights.[10] My primary aim is to reexamine dissociative identity disorder in the light of nonnaturalism about personal identity.

Most discussions of dissociative identity disorder implicitly presuppose the sort of naturalistic perspective that I am challenging. Rational unity is conceived as a natural state of the human being that arises in the course of normal human development. And, so, any form of multiplicity, such as we find in dissociative identity disorder, must be regarded as an abnormal departure from the natural state, a pathology. Thus, multiplicity is something to avoid and to cure. And in our efforts to avoid and cure it, we are directed to look for its causes. We seek to learn what it is about some human beings that deflects the course of their development away from its natural state of unity to the abnormal state of multiplicity. Early child abuse has been identified as one such cause, though it may be that certain background conditions must also be in place, such as a predisposition to dissociation, which appears to be linked to a high susceptibility to hypnosis.

I don't want to suggest that there is nothing abnormal about dissociative identity disorder. Nor do I want to suggest that it is somehow inappropriate to look for natural causes of multiplicity. But we need to take care how we conceive those causes and the background conditions in which they operate. If I'm right, the state of rational unity is not a natural state. It is not the inevitable and involuntary deliverance of normal human biological development. It is something that human beings deliberately achieve for the sake of further ends, the limiting case of which is just living a unified human life. So if we want to portray dissociation and multiplicity as departures from some *natural* state of the human being, the state of overall rational unity is not the right candidate. Furthermore, we can't assume that every failure to achieve such unity must be pathological or even involuntary. Multiplicity is one of the possible states at which human rational activity could be deliberately and coherently directed. When such activity is so directed, it is not, of course, carried out from one human-size point of view but from multiple points of view, each of which has separate ends for the sake of which it is striving to achieve rational unity within itself instead of striving for rational unity within the whole human being.

Even though the origins of alter personalities are pathological, their functioning resembles the functioning of such multiple persons. That is, once alters have come into existence, they have separate points of view from which to think about the relative merits of their separate projects and even their own existence. The fact that alters might have been caused by early child abuse does nothing to undermine this fact about them. A child can need and love their parents (or other adults in their lives) and yet, if they are abusive, also resent and hate them. In the confusion of these conflicted attitudes toward the parental figure one can also develop very different senses of oneself, of what makes one good or bad, lovable or unlovable, and so forth. One can also develop very different social tendencies, based on the ability or inability to trust. These different attitudes may lead to very different sorts of relationships and other "life projects" that are not coherently pursuable together. And that is precisely the condition in which it would make sense that rational and practical efforts be divided, thereby providing reasons for the existence of multiple persons rather than a human-size person. Thus, involuntary origins can give way to a willed state of being, in which alters direct their effort and will at maintaining their separate existence, rather than integrating into a single human-size person. If this is right, then merely discovering the natural causes of multiplicity won't get us very far in our efforts to understand and cope with it. This is confirmed by a conversation I had with a therapist in Boston long ago, before I ever thought I would write about this subject. She worked with multiples. And she reported that very little of her therapeutic attention could be directed to the project of integration because of the ways in which it was resisted by alters. The more pressing issue for them concerned how to share the body they inhabited more harmoniously. She found that the best way to approach this issue was by analogy with territorial disputes in politics—an explicit concession to the separateness and independence of the alters' points of view.

Now consider two different messages such alters could be given if the aim was to persuade them of the merits of integrating. Presuming a naturalistic perspective, they could be told that their very existence is a sign of abnormality and pathology and ill health, and that they need to fix what is wrong by integrating so as to become like other, healthy human beings. Or, presuming a nonnaturalist perspective, they could be told that the reason why other human beings are unified is not merely that they are normal and healthy; the reason why is that they have life projects—friendships, marriages, families, careers—for the sake of which they have chosen to strive to achieve overall rational unity. Given this nonnaturalist perspective, one thing that alters would need to consider are the relative merits of the sorts of projects they can pursue in their independent ways and the sorts of projects that will remain foreclosed to them so long as they remain separate.

It's not yet known what the differential effects of these two messages would be, since the second has not, to my knowledge, been tried in the therapeutic context—or even recognized as an option. Yet I can report something about one particular case in which the second, nonnaturalist message did become available outside the therapeutic context. I'll now describe my encounter with a real person, for whom questions about the unity of the self are not merely abstract philosophical questions, nor even questions of theoretical psychology, but living issues that she must sort out in order to make sense of herself.

I came to know this person through her psychiatrist. He had been attending a seminar of mine, in which I argued for the possibility of multiple and group persons. At certain points, my arguments involved a philosophical interpretation of certain quasi-empirical facts about dissociative identity disorder. Although he was not overtly unsympathetic to my philosophical point, he did register that he had never encountered a case of the disorder. He also told me that he had a patient who would definitely be so diagnosed by certain other psychiatrists whom he could name, and with whom he would not agree on the diagnosis. He thought it might be interesting for me to talk to her. And he thought she might oblige me if I would talk about philosophy with her, which she did. We have talked at length over the years and are now friends.

She feels that she is very different from other people in several respects. The first respect concerns her secret life as an intellectual. She has markedly high mathematical abilities, which she tends to use in metaphysical speculations about the nature of the whole universe, including both its outer limits and its smallest workings. She is especially interested in how life and consciousness fit into the universe and, ultimately, how this bears on the meaning of life. Her favored patterns of thinking involve infinite iterations accompanied by attempts at reduction, so as to facilitate nothing less than the contemplation of an infinite and complex totality all at once.

You might wonder, why should a penchant for such metaphysical reflection make this person feel that she is different from other people? Largely because for her it has always been a solitary and, moreover, an isolating enterprise. Her reflections—she simply calls it "thinking"—started in very early childhood. She was clearly a precocious and, also, a neglected child. Her main impression of her childhood is of a kind of solitary confinement on a porch behind the house in which she grew up. She also reports that her psychiatrist believes that she was a victim of child abuse. He believes this on the basis of some phobias that strongly indicate to him that she was forced to have oral sex as a very young child. But she claims to remember nothing more than one inappropriately sexual kiss from her father. In any case, whatever happened in her house with her parents, her solitary confinement on the porch was the physical and emotional place from which her thinking proceeded. Socially, there seems to have been nothing but her family and the Catholic Church. Both were completely intolerant of her intellectual efforts. So when she reached adolescence she abandoned them, and focused on becoming socially and romantically adept. This continued into adulthood. She had a long affair involving a kind of high life with a married man. She hasn't wanted to tell me more about this period of her life, except to indicate that she thought it might shock me. Eventually, she married a profoundly anti-intellectual man and bore him a child. It didn't seem to matter that her husband is anti-intellectual until after she began seeing her psychiatrist. By then she was in her mid-forties.

She marks the real beginning of her therapeutic progress with an intellectual reawakening that resulted from reading, upon her psychiatrist's recommendation, Bertrand Russell's *Problems of Philosophy*. After reading it, she read Russell's *History of Western Philosophy*, and then went on to devour the history of philosophy on her own. She continues to read widely in philosophy, and in physics and biology and cognitive science. In the course of all this reading, she has come to know for the very first time in her life that others think in something like the way she does. But this discovery has not sufficed to remove her sense of isolation and difference. After all, she will never meet the authors with whom she feels like-minded. Nor does she feel entirely like them. They do not and did not live where she lives, not in any sense. She is home with an anti-intellectual husband who does not know anything about her inner life. He does not know she is seeing a psychiatrist, and he would rather she didn't read or write except to keep the accounts in his business. Of course, it is not such a rare thing to feel as this woman does. Many intellectuals have found themselves in circumstances that left them no natural social outlet for their intellectual urges—and hence feeling different from other people.

But there is another, much less common, reason why she feels she is different from others. She does not really feel like *one* person, at least not always. I cannot say that in the course of our relationship she has appeared to me as many persons as opposed to one. Rather, she has appeared to me as one person with several disparate sets of yearnings and skills. Many of these disparate commitments I know about only through her testimony. What I know directly is her deep commitment to what she calls thinking. She tends to present this part of herself as what is best and truest in her. But she also insists that she did no thinking at all for decades. And this led to one of the most poignant moments in our early philosophical conversations. She stared into my eyes and asked: "If this is really me, then where the hell was I all those years when no thinking was going on?" My honest, but not very reassuring, answer was that from a philosophical perspective there are a number of possibilities to consider.

This is not the only kind of disunity from which she suffers. She has also reported the experience of "switching." It surprised me that she used this term. For it is commonly used in biographical and autobiographical accounts of dissociative identity disorder, and she claimed to have kept away from all such literature. She doesn't want to regard herself as a multiple, and her psychiatrist supports her in this. In any event, compared to what we find in the popular accounts of such celebrated figures as Sybil, this woman's experiences of switching do not seem all that dramatic. She reports that during a stressful interview with her son's principal she switched into a small child. On another occasion, she reports having felt exposed in her psychiatrist's office because a neighbor was able to spy her from the waiting room and, in response, she switched into an aggressive and lewd woman who easily severs personal ties—on this occasion her ties with her psychiatrist. Frankly, these experiences seem like not very distant relatives of fairly common experiences. Many of us have watched ourselves exhibit regressive or passive-aggressive behavior, wishing all the while that it was not going on.

For most of us, these experiences of disunity involve a recognition that we are not always in control of the thoughts and actions we observe in motion. But we don't generally feel tempted to attribute those thoughts and actions to somebody else. That's why they are a source of regret: they're *ours*, despite the fact that they don't reflect our choices. Thus for most of us, the experience of disunity is not also an experience of multiplicity. But I think this woman does sometimes experience multiplicity. There is first of all the fact that she cannot view her intellectual self as the same person who did no thinking for decades. She also keeps a journal in which she finds it necessary to employ many names for herself, through which she tracks quite different personae or senses of self. Several times she found it necessary to use a different name in her e-mail correspondence with me. The first time she was telling me about a medical emergency she had just had, and before signing off she confessed that she didn't understand why she thinks at all since, really, she is a very simple person—and she just couldn't bring herself to sign her usual name to that confession. She also has wardrobe issues of the sort that typically characterize dissociative identity disorder. On at least one occasion that I know of, these wardrobe issues have correlated with the sort of amnesia barriers that also characterize the disorder. On this occasion, she confessed to having difficulty remembering how she had spent Saturday, except for a dim recollection of wearing black leather clothes and being addressed as "Sir" in the library.

These signs of multiplicity, especially when taken in conjunction with a history of child abuse, would suffice in the eyes of many psychiatrists to establish that this woman does indeed suffer from dissociative identity disorder. But, as I said, her psychiatrist rejects that diagnosis. I did not ask him what his diagnosis is, because I didn't want to be forming my own impressions in the light of it. So what I have come to know of his views derives mainly from her own account of them and, to a lesser extent, his remarks in the seminar of mine he had attended. According to her, he always wants to emphasize her oneness over her apparent multiplicity. He has advised her to accept all of the different thoughts, feelings, and actions of which she has conscious awareness as her own, because a failure of such acceptance would amount to an abdication of responsibility for self. Thus, in his view, she is not free at any time, no matter what her circumstance or mood, to discount any episodes of regression, or passive-aggression, or cross-dressing, as not really hers; nor is she free when she is feeling identified with her domestic life as wife and mother to discount her intellectual aspirations as not really hers.

In advising her to take responsibility for all of these aspects of herself, her psychiatrist was manifesting a commitment to something like the naturalist perspective I said is implicit in most discussions of dissociative identity disorder, according to which overall rational unity is the natural and normal state of the human being and any departure from such unity is a sign of ill psychic health. Despite my philosophical reservations about this naturalist perspective, I wasn't at all sure that it would be wise to dispute the advice that flowed from it. For it wasn't clear to me that it would be wrong or bad for this woman to strive to achieve overall rational unity. So imagine my trepidation when she broached the subject of my own work. I could see that she would, inevitably, sit down and read the book in which I had defended the possibility of multiple and group persons. And, I could also see that she might come to think differently, both about what her own multiplicity might mean, and about what reasons there might be (or fail to be) to prefer unity instead.

I did manage to gain some impression of her self-conception before she read my book. I can't say that she explicitly endorsed the view that rational unity is a metaphysical given of human nature. But she certainly regarded such unity as a normal state that for some reason occurs in most human beings but not in her. In consequence, she regarded herself as unwell. She wanted to know why she is unwell in this way, but had never made much progress toward figuring it out. This caused her anxiety. I'm quite sure that it wouldn't have given her any help to accept an official diagnosis of dissociative identity disorder. It would have led her to attribute to herself a kind and degree of abnormality that she abhors.

What is worse, it wouldn't have left her with any clear instruction about what to do. In contrast, her psychiatrist's view was instructive in the ways I described above: she must not dissociate or distance herself from any of her thoughts and actions, but rather take responsibility for all of them.

I suppose that the instruction was meant to be empowering. It leaves it up to her to take responsibility for her whole self. But it also creates anxiety. Why, she has repeatedly asked me, is it so much harder for her to achieve rational unity than it is for others? And why is it that she so often doesn't feel like one person?

The fact that she has these questions and can't answer them is part of what makes her feel so isolated and different from other people. I'm not sure that her psychiatrist's instruction has helped to mitigate these feelings. If anything, I think it may have exacerbated them. It gave her another dimension along which to feel different from others. Besides her intellectual isolation, and her secrecy about her experiences of multiplicity, there is her sense that what is hard for her with respect to the project of achieving unity comes easily to others—indeed, for them it is not a project at all but, as I've said, a state that nature gave them.

When she read my book, she said things began to look different. And the difference was provided by what was on offer—a nonnaturalist perspective on personal identity, according to which the rational unity of a person is never a metaphysical given of human nature but always a product of effort and will. This means that when she looks for an explanation of her own disunity and/or multiplicity, she is not directed to view herself as an abnormal specimen of the human species. She is directed instead to look for conflicting values and projects within her that might stand in the way of leading a unified human life. And she isn't under quite the same pressure that her psychiatrist has applied, to view all of these conflicting values and projects as hers in a sense that presupposes that she is, au fond, one person. For you simply don't have one person unless there is one point of view that can be addressed in the course of interpersonal engagement—and this condition of personal identity cannot be met by a human being that houses too many conflicts and divisions. On the other hand, this does not mean that she cannot, through effort, become one person. She can. Moreover, she needn't view such an effort in the way her psychiatrist does, as a response to a quasi-moral imperative to take responsibility for her whole self. Instead, she can view the goal of overall unity as something that she *might* find reason to embrace, *provided* that she has *other* projects that would require it. Since she is now a mother she does have at least one such project.

She claims to have found this way of seeing things—I mean, herself—

salutary. I can't say I am sure that it is all to her good to see things this way. For it is clear that my metaphysical picture gives her no particular strength with which to address her past, which very probably included severe child abuse. But it does give her a way of seeing herself as less different from others, less weird. And it gives me an opportunity to think of metaphysics as potentially making a difference to a life—all because persons are, in an important sense, a function of what they think of themselves.

4. Knowledge and Reality

In this last section I want to clarify the metaphysical status of persons as nonnatural objects, partly by way of contrast with the sort of nonnaturalism that Ian Hacking espouses. In many ways, the section is an exploration of what is and is not within the power of persons to bring about with respect to their own reality.

I first need to make clear that the account of personal identity that I'm offering is explicitly revisionist. Whenever philosophers offer a revisionist account of something, they are presupposing that it is within our power to change our concepts. But, in addition, the particular conceptual revisions I'm proposing may also change lived human reality. That was meant to come through as more than an abstract possibility via the case study I presented above.

There are actually a number of different respects in which the account I'm offering is revisionist. First of all, our commonsense thinking about persons is inconsistent. For some purposes, it is animalist. We count persons by counting human beings, and we mark the beginnings and ends of their lives by the biological events of birth (or conception) and death. Yet, for other purposes, it concedes much to the opposed Lockean view, insofar as it accommodates religious accounts of reincarnation and life after death. (I'm supposing it would be going too far to say that the religious lack common sense.) Any consistent account of personal identity must select from these inconsistent strands in our commonsense thinking and, to that extent, revise it. The strand I'm proposing to select actually runs through both sides of the philosophical dispute about personal identity. It is the conception of the person as a reflective rational agent who is capable of distinctively interpersonal forms of engagement.

But I'm not proposing merely to select one or other strand in our common sense thinking. The particular strand I've selected has also led me to identify a mistake that runs through much of commonsense thinking, and most philosophical discussions as well. The mistake is precisely to think of personal identity as a metaphysical given of nature. So, the second respect in which my account is revisionist is that it *corrects* this mistake.

The mistake comes into view once we understand the third respect in which the account is revisionist, insofar as it brings to light *new conceptions* and, therewith, *new practical possibilities* in the form of group and multiple persons. Once we conceive and accept these as genuine practical possibilities for us human-size persons, we can see why it was a mistake to conceive our identities as metaphysical givens of nature to begin with. For there is a sense in which it has always been within our power to realize these alternative possibilities. Although we may have been prevented from realizing them by failing to conceive them, they are nevertheless provided for by the very nature of human rational and practical capacities. Indeed, once we understand the nature of these capacities, we can see that we must already have exercised them in order to achieve whatever levels of rational unity we have achieved within human lives.

At this point, it may seem that nonnaturalism can't be right as an account of actually existing human-size persons. After all, most actually existing persons do not have the idea that it is possible for them to alter the boundaries of their existence by integrating into group persons or fragmenting into multiple persons. This means that they don't think that they have to *do* anything in order to maintain themselves as individual persons. They make the usual mistake of conceiving their identities as metaphysical givens of nature. But how can it be that their very existence is the product of effort and will—as per nonnaturalism—if they don't even have the idea that it *could* be the product of effort and will? In answer, I want to insist that actually existing persons do have the idea that their *rational unity* is the product of effort and will. They know that it is up to them to frame life projects and pursue them in a unified way, rather than living from moment to moment. Indeed, the Socratic question, how shall I live? and its contemporary equivalent, what shall I do with my life? both signal that human persons have long been preoccupied with the goal of achieving rational unity within a human lifetime. It is a goal that human persons were able to conceive and strive for prior to being exposed to my revisionist suggestions. What these suggestions add is a proper understanding of how that conception and striving—in other words, the commitment to overall rational unity—in fact underpins the identity of a person, at least insofar as persons are conceived as things that can be engaged in distinctively interpersonal ways. The suggestions also bring into view the unnoticed fact that there are alternatives for human beings, besides living as individual human-size persons who are unified within themselves and separate from the rest. It is within their power to redraw the boundaries of their very existence.

From Hacking's Foucaultian perspective, a philosopher who makes revisionist suggestions is bound to appear benighted. This is not because he thinks lived human reality is unresponsive to new conceptions. He regards it as an important fact about human phenomena that they are responsive to new conceptions and, in that sense, nonnatural. But, in his view, the processes by which this happens are not always intentional. They are often driven by large historical, social, and institutional forces. And, although such historically driven processes always *involve* human intentional activity, they characteristically deliver outcomes that were never intended by anyone. These processes deliver up new concepts by which we can classify and interpret human phenomena and, somehow, the end result is that we begin to live in new ways that answer to those concepts without expressly intending to do so.

Hacking takes multiple personality disorder as a case in point.[11] According to him, the disorder emerged in this century in the wake of certain scientific, medical and psychological fascinations of the nineteenth century. Thus, although human beings did exhibit a capacity for various forms of dissociation before the nineteenth century, they did not and could not suffer specifically from multiple personality disorder before then. The same goes for its successor, dissociative identity disorder. These disorders became possible only after we came to conceive them—in fact, only after we named and defined them in our official diagnostic manuals. But this is not because people started choosing to have the disorder once it had been named and defined. Given its official definition, it's not the sort of state that could be chosen.

In many ways, Hacking's Foucaultian point of view is plausible. It is undeniable that our concepts are the products of large historical, social, and institutional forces that lie beyond anyone's intentional control. One reason why these forces are beyond such control is that they generally remain hidden from our view until well after they have done their work—that is, wrought their conceptual changes and, along with them, the lived reality that corresponds to them. As I've already emphasized, it is very important to the Foucaultian point of view that human beings can be responsive to new concepts, in the sense of coming to realize or instantiate them, without expressly intending to do so. I have to confess that I find it a bit mysterious how or why this should be so. But Hacking's discussion of multiple personality disorder has at least helped to convince me *that* it is so.

Beyond seeming plausible, I suspect that the Foucaultian point of view is irrefutable. It is hard to imagine *any* significant human phenomenon that is not the product of large historical, social, and institutional forces and that could not, therefore, be illuminated by Foucaultian analysis. That includes the phenomenon of a philosopher offering revisionist suggestions about personhood and personal identity. No doubt, there are sociohistorical reasons why it became possible, at this particular time and place, for a philosopher to conceive the possibilities of group and multiple persons and to infer from these possibilities, as I have done, that the facts of personal identity are in every case nonnatural—where the inference requires a revision of our current naturalist assumptions.

But, in closing, I want to emphasize that the possibility of a Foucaultian analysis here should not blind us to the fact that the sort of nonnaturalism about personal identity for which I have argued is *not* the Foucaultian sort. I am appealing to a kind of dependence of reality on our concepts that actually presupposes *direct intentional control* at the level of the individual person. If I am right, human beings could never have become (roughly) human-size persons without exerting effort and will for the express sake of achieving overall rational unity within their human lives. That is the only condition in which they could qualify as individual reflective agents who can be engaged in distinctively interpersonal ways, which is the hallmark of personhood. This fact has been obscured to us for reasons that a Foucaultian analysis would undoubtedly shed light on. But the fact itself is not to be conceived along Foucaultian lines. If it is a fact, the fact derives from the metaphysically given nature of the rational and practical capacities that human beings typically possess as part of their native biological endowment. Those capacities are such that they can be exercised in order to achieve rational unity within different boundaries—a whole human life or something less or something more. This has always been true, even before it was noticed. And it has always been partly understood, insofar as human-size persons have always understood that the unity of their lives is not a metaphysical given but a project—the project of leading a unified human life. We can now get clearer about the nature and the merits of that project, by setting it alongside alternative projects that we might pursue instead, as group or multiple persons. To recognize that there are such alternative projects is to recognize that the facts of personal identity are indeed nonnatural. And this nonnaturalism can be recognized without embracing the controversial elements of Foucaultian nonnaturalism, though I daresay it has controversial elements of its own.

~ 13

Against Naturalism in Ethics[1]

ERIN I. KELLY

I

This paper explores a certain class of "reductive" moral philosophies. Generally speaking, reductive accounts attempt to analyze the nature and content of morality without relying on evaluative concepts, or at least none other than those employed in the natural and social sciences. The aim is to describe what people are doing when they engage in moral evaluation and what would give them reason to accept a set of norms as justified. At the same time, the hope is to avoid endorsing any substantive position within ethics. Moral philosophy thus attempts to be less controversial and more objective. Jürgen Habermas, for instance, criticizes John Rawls's aim of elaborating an idea of a just society that citizens could use to evaluate existing political arrangements and policies. Habermas proposes instead "that philosophy limit itself to the clarification of the moral point of view and the procedure of democratic legitimation, to the analysis of the conditions of rational discourses and negotiations. . . . It leaves substantial questions that must be answered here and now to the more or less enlightened engagement of participants, which does not mean that philosophers may not also participate in the public debate, though in the role of intellectuals, not of experts."[2]

Habermas's concern is that philosophy not encroach into the province of democracy, but his conclusion is echoed by developments in analytic

259

meta-ethics that have been motivated by other considerations. Analytic moral philosophers have emphasized a division between the project of clarifying the logic and meaning of our moral concepts, on the one hand, and the task of a moral theory that draws on and attempts to systematize our substantive moral intuitions, on the other. The division makes possible disinterested inquiry within the former domain, or so it has been thought. The enterprise of meta-ethics came to be identified with this ambition and is characterized by several prominent positions. In response to G. E. Moore's open question argument and in view of the development of causal theories of meaning and reference, Richard Boyd and others formulated a variety of moral naturalism that they refer to as "moral realism."[3] Moore argued that naturalistic definitions of ethical concepts will fail to be adequate since questions about the normative significance of any set of natural properties remain open.[4] Boyd argues that our normative notions may refer to natural properties that help to explain our moral practices and conclusions whether or not we identify our notions with those properties. Thus empirically identifiable properties may constitute moral facts even though questions about whether those properties are normatively significant seem open.

Emotivists and other reductive noncognitivists took a different approach in response to Moore. They disputed the apparently cognitive content of our evaluative judgments by maintaining that moral judgment consists not in a cognitive state but in the expression of a feeling or of a person's disposition to have certain feelings.[5] This finding bodes well for the prospects of an objective meta-ethical analysis, since the relevant feelings and dispositions can be described from an evaluatively neutral stance, or so these philosophers have maintained. Moral philosophers could then inform and expand their analysis by utilizing research in psychology and evolutionary biology.

Emotivists have notoriously had trouble analyzing moral disagreement and understanding how disagreement may be addressed through an exchange of reasons. Allan Gibbard's expressivism is more sophisticated. He proposes that moral judgments express our acceptance of certain norms, norms that we consult to determine whether certain reactive feelings are warranted. Norms can be discussed and critically evaluated. Nevertheless, it is not clear, on Gibbard's account, how fully the grounds for our acceptance of norms could be evaluated for their reasonableness or how disagreement about which norms we ought to accept could be rationally resolved. The ultimate ground for a claim of rationality, on Gibbard's analysis, is our disposition to accept a norm that supports it, and this is largely a matter of feelings we in fact experience.[6] What seems to be missing is an analysis of the ethical importance of responding to moral disagreement by offering considerations we think others have reason to accept. We want to know what counts as a plausible basis for arguing that mutual acceptance of proposed norms would be reasonable.[7] The relevant question may be posed in various ways. We want to know what reasons we have to accept norms we would be disposed to accept, why we ought to accept them, or why our acceptance of them is justified. Christine Korsgaard calls this the normative question.[8]

Moral realists might seem better equipped to engage the normative question and, in particular, to understand how it is that moral deliberation could issue in justifiable results. They can affirm that parties in disagreement address a common question and may reason together about it. Furthermore, they maintain that we can describe the cognitive activity of moral deliberation without employing evaluative concepts and entering the debate. We can instead position ourselves to draw upon the resources of the natural and social sciences in order to identify the causes and effects of this activity. Using empirical methods we may arrive at the content of justifiable norms. In this way, the relevant natural and social facts would serve to clarify and to demystify the requirements of morality without having to explain away its apparently cognitive character. Appreciation of the relevant empirical facts could provide us with, as Jeremy Bentham put it, a "clew to the labyrinth."[9]

In order to engage the normative question, moral philosophers must offer a plausible description of the normative activity of moral reasoning and defend its criteria of justification. Throughout this paper I will understand moral reasoning as an activity that aims to arrive at mutually acceptable norms to govern social life. Persons who care about morality are concerned to establish the interpersonal justification of shared norms: each person should take the interests of others into account in order to arrive at principles that could be accepted by all. The reductive accounts that I will be concerned with all aim to provide a naturalistic understanding of what people would think and how they would proceed when engaged in this sort of mutual task. My disagreement with them is thus framed by some common assumptions about the aims of morality.

I have chosen to focus on a number of views that all characterize morality as involved with the aim of establishing mutually acceptable social norms both because this is a compelling account of the practical nature and social role of morality and because it gives naturalism a good run for its money. The idea that morality is concerned with interpersonal justification acknowledges and analyzes our reasoned response to moral disagreement. It allows us to abstract from the possible distortions and biases of actual negotiations and instead to propose conditions under which agreement would ideally be reached. Yet it still appears to describe an empirically identifiable social activity and role for moral norms. This makes it attractive to naturalists. The activity of moral evaluation takes place in a social context within which a claim about justifiable norms could apparently be appraised for its psychological and sociological plausibility. Justifiable norms could it seems be appealed to in order to explain how we would feel and act in certain kinds of situations. If the activity of finding mutually acceptable norms is in this way open to empirical inquiry, the prospects for using the methods of natural and social science to discover the content of morality appears promising. If, on the other hand, this practical and contextual conception of morality cannot be understood naturalistically, the promise of naturalism in ethics more generally may appear to be dim.

This paper argues that naturalistic approaches come up short. They fail to appreciate the normative content of ethics. An adequate account of the nature of our morally legitimate interests and of the norms compatible with due respect for those interests must rely upon substantive moral judgments. These are judgments that in effect take a normative position in ethics. They employ rather than simply describe or reference our evaluative concepts. An empirical reduction of these judgments cannot fully be carried out and thus no empirical reduction of the justification of moral norms can ultimately be given.

II

The first attempt at reduction we will consider identifies the content of moral norms by reference to certain idealized responses of rational agents. One of the most prominent accounts of this kind is found in Peter Railton's interpretation of moral realism.[10] Specifically, Railton defends the claim that moral norms are norms that reflect "what would be rationally approved of were the interests of potentially affected individuals counted equally under circumstances of full and vivid information."[11] Railton maintains that his approach is reductive because the relevant facts about people's responses pick out properties that can be described without using evaluative concepts. It is naturalistic because these properties are natural properties that figure into causal accounts of our behavior given by the natural and social sciences.

Railton arrives at his idealized response criterion of moral rightness by aiming to identify a criterion that would be supported by reference to sociological, physiological, and psychological accounts of our moral dispositions and conduct. For example, when social arrangements fail to satisfy the relevant criterion, this might help to explain why people get angry, organize and protest, or become depressed. A criterion of moral rightness that has this kind of support is one that facilitates "criterial explanation" of our behavior. Because the criterion is reductive and naturalistic, the behavioral explanations that Railton thinks are supported by reference to moral rightness are explanations that will refer only to natural (as opposed to nonnatural) facts. He refers to these natural facts as "moral facts." They might include, for example, psychological facts about what distribution of scarce resources we would be disposed to approve of when we aim for consensus on questions about the distribution of social goods. Like Boyd, Railton believes that reference to moral facts could help to explain our behavior, whether or not we believe those facts ought to guide our behavior, that is, independently of our beliefs about what is morally right. Because the moral facts do not depend on what we believe they are, he thinks we may understand the view he sets forth as a form of moral realism.

Railton launches his analysis of moral norms with a brief account of when the assessment and regulation of behavior should be thought, generally speaking, to take place on moral grounds. Here he appeals to some convergence among moral philosophers on the idea that moral norms concern the assessment of conduct or character where the interests of more than one individual are at stake. In adjudicating the interests of many persons, morality would appear to aim for impartiality and to be equally concerned with all those potentially affected.[12] Railton thinks these are the aims of a form of social rationality and that the substance of moral realism emerges in the analysis it gives of the nature and content of social rationality, for instance, in its treatment of "equal concern." As we have seen, central to the account Railton defends is the idea that the content of moral norms is a matter of what would be approved of by persons who are symmetrically situated and fully informed about the nature of each other's interests.

The strength of this account, according to Railton, and the source of its validity lies in its explanatory potential. He argues that moral facts about what is socially rational could help to explain the dissatisfaction and unrest that may characterize social arrangements that significantly discount the interests of a particular group.[13] It may also be the case that social arrangements that are nonoptimal with respect to social rationality display "a tendency toward certain religious or ideological doctrines, or toward certain sorts of repressive apparatus; they may be less productive in some ways (for example, by failing to develop certain human resources) and more productive in others (for example, by extracting greater labor from some group at less cost)."[14] Causal connections between these tendencies and failures of social rationality would be empirically significant. Furthermore, such an account may help us to understand how persons acquire the belief that their society is unjust and to explain why their society may come to develop norms that better approximate social rationality.[15] Although Railton hesitates to endorse a general thesis of historical moral progress, he does identify certain historical trends that he thinks are amenable to criterial explanation by reference to moral rightness.[16] These include a growing tendency in moral theory to draw a connection between normative principles and human interests.

The terms of this conception of moral rightness are appealing in several respects. A concern with our idealized responses would seem to acknowledge the importance within morality of giving the interests of all equal consideration and, ultimately, of reaching agreement. It is relevant to abstract from the epistemic limitations of our actual circumstances and to consider instead the ideal circumstances in which rational agreement on the content of moral norms could be worked out. These would seem to be core aspects of moral reasoning. Yet the finer details of the account, designed to enable us to identify people's idealized responses, are less convincing. This significantly compromises the potential of Railton's account to illuminate our moral practices.

On Railton's approach, identifying moral norms will depend on our understanding of what count as people's interests. To address this need he formulates what is, despite some counterfactual idealization, a reductive, psychological description of people's interests. He thinks my interests can be understood in terms of what I would want my nonidealized self to want, with a view only to self-interest and not to the interests of other persons. Specifically, my interests are a matter of what I would want my nonidealized self to want were I to consider the matter from a position in which I have unqualified cognitive and imaginative powers and full factual and nomological information about my physical and psychological constitution, capacities, circumstances, history, and so on.[17] More simply put, "a person's interests are a matter of what he would want himself to seek if he knew what he were doing."[18]

This stance for identifying an agent's interests is meant to be predictive. It orients us to natural facts relevant to predicting what a person would approve of, given full information, et cetera. Railton's reference to "unqualified cognitive and imaginative powers" is supposed to be normatively thin; he rejects anything but an instrumental conception of rationality. We may think of his understanding of an agent's objective interests as fitting within Bernard Williams's understanding of internal reasons. Williams claims that what a person has reason to do must have the support of his or her present motives or of reasoning that supports those motives.[19]

Railton thinks that once we have identified all the interests that members of a given social group have, we can formulate moral norms for that group that set the standard of right action for it. We do this by predicting which norms would be judged to be of instrumental value by persons who count each other's interests equally under certain counterfactual circumstances: circumstances in which persons have full and vivid information about the consequences for their interests of compliance with the proposed norms. Railton thinks this points us toward norms that would maximize the overall satisfaction of interests, but this is, on his approach, an empirical matter.[20]

I will focus on three problems with this approach. The first two concern the status of Railton's definitions. It is not clear that his analysis provides an empirical reduction after all. The reference to "full and vivid information," for instance, would appear to involve evaluative concepts and appeal to "rational approval"; while normatively thin, this is still nonreductively normative. I will not pursue this criticism in any detail, however, and will simply accept Railton's view as minimally normative.

Second, even if what Railton offers as the relevant notion of interests is nonreductively normative, it appears to be insufficiently normative. I turn briefly to an account of normative reasons developed by Michael Smith in order to make out this criticism. Smith endorses an analysis that overlaps with Railton's in important respects. Like Railton, he argues that "what it is desirable for us to do in our actual circumstances is what our more rational selves, looking down on ourselves as we actually are from their more privileged position, would want us to do in our actual circumstances."[21] He claims that a fully rational agent is one who suffers no psychological disorders, has no false beliefs, has all relevant true beliefs, and engages in sound means-ends reasoning. Nevertheless, Smith thinks the satisfaction of these conditions does not entail that a person's preference is fully rational, for they do not capture an important respect in which rational reflection can lead us to revise our current aims. This concerns whether our current aims are "systematically justifiable."[22] Our desires and aims are systematically justified when they fit together in a coherent and unified way. The process of achieving coherence and unity may lead us to give up certain desires and to acquire others. Making

adjustments in our overall set of desires and values for the sake of coherence is the process Rawls has described as attaining "reflective equilibrium." This is a plausible requirement of moral reasoning, especially
in view of the role within morality that principles play. We could supplement Railton's account of the relevant understanding of people's interests by adding to his criteria of rationality the requirement of reflective
equilibrium described by Smith.[23]

Even when it is supplemented by this aspect of Smith's general account
of normative reasons, however, Railton's analysis is inadequate. The
problem is that Railton treats the content of persons' morally relevant
interests as fixed prior to moral reasoning. In fact, he identifies them as
aspects of a person's "non-moral good."[24] He does not attempt to characterize moral criteria for determining what to count as legitimate interests, and thus he gives us no sense of why and to what extent we
should expect others, if they are reasonable, to accept claims based upon
our individual interests. As we have seen, morality must posit a set of
fundamental interests as a justifiable basis of claims, but if morality is to
have the interpersonal role I have imputed to it, this set of interests can
not include all the interests that persons may affirm.[25] There is no reason
to think that all the interests that a person would affirm under conditions
of full information and in reflective equilibrium would help to comprise
an acceptable basis for identifying social norms of right action.[26] Railton
concedes that some persons may turn out to have objective interests in
things we find harmful or repulsive and that we may well judge these
interests to be morally wrong.[27] Why, then, should such interests be
counted equally along with morally unobjectionable interests when it
comes to determining which norms are socially rational? It is not enough
for Railton to argue that objectionable interests will get "overruled": they
simply should not count.[28] Other interests, while perhaps not morally
repugnant, presuppose ideas about what is good that are the subject of
genuine and not unreasonable disagreement. Interests rooted in the endorsement of a particular religious doctrine or ethnic identity, for instance, are not generally shared. If such interests are to ground legitimate
moral claims, say, for a distributive claim to a share of social goods or to
special rights, they must be reinterpreted in terms of values that persons
more generally have reason to care about, such as the value of freedom
of conscience and freedom of association or the moral importance of
rectifying an injustice. This is because such distributive claims impose
costs on other persons and it is objectionable to impose costs on persons
in order to advance values they could not reasonably be expected to
recognize. Interests that cannot be generalized in the way I have de-

scribed should drop out of consideration as a reasonable basis for making demands on other people.

Although Railton's account of social rationality is constructed in accordance with a requirement of interpersonal agreement, it seems inadequate as an account of the reasoning that makes agreement possible and underwrites its validity. As we have seen, we need an account of the reasoning that could plausibly narrow the class of relevant interests. Without this kind of filtering, we could not expect to reach agreement, at least not for the right reasons. Our morally legitimate interests must have the support of values that all relevant participants to moral deliberation could reasonably be expected to recognize, in full view of the burdens that realization of those values may impose.[29] This characterization of morally relevant interests does not attempt to fix their content prior to moral reasoning, but would use moral reasoning to understand them. It will rule out certain interests, for example, state-sponsored religion in a religiously pluralistic society or school prayer in a society that contains nonbelievers.

In terms of the notion of reflective equilibrium to which Smith appeals we might say: morality requires that reflective equilibrium be not only wide but also general.[30] Interests that provide a reasonable basis for making moral claims on other people must fit into a moral conception that could be the object of wide and general reflective equilibrium. Wide reflective equilibrium is attained when a moral agent achieves coherence in her moral judgments, not just through making minimal adjustments to fit the closest approximating theory but after more wide-ranging reflection about possible alternatives. Reflective equilibrium is general when different persons affirm the same moral theory, or as Rawls puts it, "the same conception is affirmed in everyone's considered judgments."[31] He continues, "In such a society not only is there a public point of view from which all citizens can adjudicate their claims, but also this point of view is mutually recognized as affirmed by them all in full [that is, wide and general] reflective equilibrium."[32] What this means is that our understanding of other people's basic interests must fit into a conception of morality that we may reasonably think could be affirmed from their perspective as well as our own. Railton has not provided a reductive analysis of these judgments. Indeed, he has not attempted to, since he appears not to acknowledge the importance of establishing that a person's morally relevant interests should meet the requirements of wide and general reflective equilibrium.

I have considered two problems with Railton's account. The first concerned whether Railton's account provides an empirical reduction after all. The second concerned whether his account of people's morally relevant interests is sufficiently normative. Finally, I turn to a third problem with Railton's account. This is a problem with Railton's claim that the interests of all be counted equally. As I have indicated, Railton suggests that equal consideration of the interests of all would lead us to aggregate and to maximize the overall satisfaction of interests.[33] But why is this so? Why should it not instead lead us to affirm a conception of equal rights? Or the value of equal outcomes? Or the importance of equal opportunity for all? The basis for predicting that we would adopt an aggregative and maximizing interpretation of "equal consideration of interests" is not obvious. In any case, we want to know why we ought to accept an aggregative and maximizing approach. Missing from Railton's description of the standards of moral deliberation is a normative criterion and analysis of reasonable moral judgment.

III

Let us now turn to a prominent attempt by Jürgen Habermas to analyze the requirement of interpersonal justification.[34] His approach interests me because it appears to include an analysis of moral reasoning that aims, among other things, to narrow the class of relevant interests. At the same time, the analysis of moral reasoning he offers is reductive. In particular, Habermas claims that his principles of discourse ethics can be represented procedurally without reference to the normative content of the particular outcomes compatible with these principles.

Habermas's principles of discourse ethics hold that justifiable moral norms are those that would be affirmed by free and symmetrically situated participants in ideal discourse. Participants in ideal discourse attempt to determine whether all persons affected by a proposed norm could accept the intended consequences and side effects that the general observation of the norm could be expected to have for the interests of each person. This criterion of legitimacy for ideal discourse is expressed by a "Universalization Principle" that Habermas refers to as Principle U. Principle U states, "A norm is valid when the foreseeable consequences and side effects of its general observance for the interests and value-orientations of *each individual* could be *jointly* accepted by *all* concerned without coercion."[35]

Principle U bears some similarity to Railton's criterion of social rationality. Recall that Railton proposed that moral norms are norms that reflect what would be rationally approved of were the interests of all counted equally under circumstances of full and vivid information. Both approaches aim for ideal agreement, abstracting from morally distorting features of actual negotiations, such as the influence of ignorance, an imbalance of power, or disproportionate attention to self-interest. In two ways, however, U appears to capture the requirement of interpersonal justification better than Railton's criterion of social rationality does. First of all, Railton believes that counting the interests of each person equally supports the idea that we ought to aggregate and to maximize the overall satisfaction of interests. By contrast, Habermas affirms the equal status of other persons by having us take up their perspective and determine whether the proposed norms are acceptable in view of their interests. This reciprocal perspective-taking would seem to block Railton's move toward aggregation. Moral norms must represent what all consider fair to and in the best interests of each person, and this means that the basic interests of each person must be protected; the violation of some persons' basic interests cannot be outweighed by greater gains to others. This gives good sense to the idea of justification to all.

Second, as Habermas understands Principle U, the content of people's fundamental interests is not fixed prior to moral discourse but rather is subject to negotiation and agreement. Principle U governs our reasoning about which interests are morally relevant as well as which norms ought to guide us in acting. Relevant interests must be "generalizable": they must be interests whose legitimacy can be affirmed from all points of view.[36] Interests are relevant only when they meet a requirement of interpersonal justification.

The reductive aspect of Habermas's account relates to his claim that the moral content of Principle U can be represented procedurally via formal constraints on the ideal discourse situation. These formal constraints are captured by a set of "general symmetry conditions." Following Robert Alexy, Habermas states these conditions as follows:

1. Every subject with the competence to speak and act is allowed to take part in a discourse.
2. a. Everyone is allowed to question any assertion whatever.
   b. Everyone is allowed to introduce any assertion whatever into the discourse.
   c. Everyone is allowed to express his attitudes, desires, and needs.
3. No speaker may be prevented, by internal or external coercion, from exercising his rights as laid down in 1 and 2.[37]

The reason Habermas thinks Principle U can be represented procedurally by way of these symmetry conditions on discourse is that he thinks these conditions represent the formal or structural features of discursive practices per se and that U in fact derives from the formal features of practical discourse.[38] Practical discourse is the discursive context within which we evaluate reasons for accepting possible action-guiding norms.[39] Drawing upon a general theory of argumentation, Habermas claims that when we advance arguments that aim for agreement on action-guiding norms, we commit ourselves to the idea that an argument can rationally be accepted as valid only when the context of discussion guarantees in principle freedom of access, equal rights to participate, truthfulness on the part of participants, and the absence of coercion in adopting positions.[40] These are the presuppositions captured by the general symmetry conditions listed above. Arguments that depend on violating any of these conditions fall short of being rationally convincing, and thus must fail to demonstrate the validity of principles or other claims put forth. Since the above presuppositions are unavoidable and rationally necessary constraints on argumentation, or so Habermas claims, any attempts to jettison them will be inconsistent. Consider the following statement: "By excluding questions that slowed down the discussion, we demonstrated that a proposed ethical norm is rationally defensible." Such a statement, argues Habermas, involves a "performative contradiction."[41] Argumentation that claims to establish the validity of a norm implies that a mutual agreement on that norm by way of the full discursive participation of rational and relevantly situated persons could be worked out. In this example, however, it is claimed that validity has been established under conditions that preclude the free and full participation of all. This is inconsistent.

Habermas's argument, then, is that a set of general symmetry conditions, together with a weakly normative understanding of what it means to justify norms, entail Principle U.[42] In other words, if one engages in argumentation with the aim of establishing that certain norms of right action ought to be adopted, the presuppositions of discourse (captured by the general symmetry conditions) entail that one also presupposes Principle U. Habermas thus takes the position that justifiable norms must have the support of an agreement that would emerge from free and full discussion, the conditions of which appear to be empirically verifiable. This proposal is appealing for its simple, democratic, and naturalistic character.[43] Let us now evaluate its plausibility.

In claiming that the principles of discourse ethics can be represented as purely formal constraints on deliberation, Habermas is claiming that the discourse ethical principles do not restrict the content of norms that can be proposed in ideal discourse, only the conditions under which discourse proceeds. This means that whatever rational persons agree to under those conditions would be justified. Habermas does not attempt to eliminate references to rationality, but he believes that its noninstrumental requirements can be represented formally.[44] Hence the justification of particular norms or principles, such as principles of justice, can be understood in terms of instrumentally rational agreement under the formal constraints on joint deliberation represented by the general symmetry conditions. Provided that we can establish that the symmetry conditions and the (weak) requirements of instrumental reason are satisfied, determining which norms would be the object of interpersonal agreement becomes an empirical matter.

I do not find this account plausible. The reason is that Principle *U* appears to convey substantive moral content not contained in the general symmetry conditions Habermas elaborates. It would appear to be derived on the basis of premises not represented in those conditions and to act as a more substantive guide to deliberation. Principle *U* formulates an idea of the aims it is reasonable for participants to ideal discourse to attempt to advance: participants should propose as valid only principles they believe express equal respect for and consideration of the interests and value-orientations of all. Thus, if participants do not conform to this requirement, they violate the conditions of ideal discourse. This narrows the range of considerations participants to ideal discourse could put forth, increasing the likelihood of convergence. In this way, *U* articulates substantive normative constraints on proposals that are worth taking seriously. What count as legitimate reasons within discourse must be compatible with a certain ideal of equality and mutual respect.[45] But then it would appear no longer to be true that in ideal discourse, "anyone can advance any claims whatever." Certain sorts of proposals will be discounted, even though they may generally be compatible with the communicative aim of persuading others on the basis of reasons. Such proposals could be those that fail to draw upon shared values and interests, appealing instead, for instance, to private experience and anecdotal evidence, the value of particular aesthetic or religious conceptions, or the importance to the majority of an established way of life.[46]

Habermas might reply that objectionable proposals would be filtered out in practice as they fail to generate agreement. But this may not be true. It seems possible that group consensus about what constitutes a reasonable proposal could be distorted in significant ways even when participants to discourse are not obviously unreasonable. The possibility of collective yet unreasonable agreement could be traced to the ways in which people's life experience and social position may distort their judgment. Some persons have low self-esteem and underestimate the value of their claims. Others are overconfident and self-important and press their claims too far. These distortions are not psychological disorders but common and sometimes subtle biases. A group as a whole could over-estimate the value of austere measures of self-sacrifice, for example, or be overly invested in punishing offenders due to collective guilt for the misdeeds of previous generations. These factors may lead a group to agree on principles that are not entirely fair and responsive to the needs and interests of all persons. The idea that satisfying the general symmetry conditions is incompatible with these biases is not plausible unless those conditions contain normative content that Habermas does not analyze.

The question that moral theory should try to answer is what would guide us to reasonable agreement. Once we understand how the sub-stantive requirements of moral reasoning extend beyond the general sym-metry conditions Habermas elaborates, we are in a position to see that those conditions do not provide us with any real guidance in determining which claims we have moral reasons to take seriously. Principle U tells us that the claims people advance in practical discourse need to be as-sessed for their moral content in order to determine their relevance: we need to assess whether proposals express due consideration for the in-terests and value-orientations of all and thus could be affirmed in a pro-cedure of universal perspective-taking. The mere fact that somebody has freely advanced a claim in discourse carries no weight. There would even appear to be some tension between promoting Habermas's symmetry conditions and the discriminatory judgment required by U.

An advantage of what we might think of as the reductive interpretation of U—which more or less equates the content of U with the alleged formal features of discourse elaborated by the general symmetry condi-tions—is that it makes it easier to envisage what would be involved in the realization of practical discourse procedurally governed by U. This could put us in a position to study the activity of moral justification empirically and to identify its results. But read as a substantive moral principle, U cannot be implemented as straightforwardly as the general symmetry conditions could be. The implementation of U requires the subtle and discriminatory judgment required in perspective-taking and the conduct of fair play. The moral sensitivities of those persons capable of making use of U as a regulative principle must already be considerably developed.[47] Participants in discourse must understand the difference be-tween what is respectful and what is inconsiderate or exploitative, for instance, if they are to succeed in implementing U.[48] They must maintain a sense of fairness and goodwill toward one another, and be capable of discerning which proposals fall short of demonstrating full commitment to the aims of practical discourse. Also, they must be able to make out clear and cogent arguments that are responsive to the relevant information and be careful in addressing matters that are commonly the subject of disagreement. Discourse ethics must rely irreducibly on reasonable judgments about the moral relevance of various sorts of considerations, judgments that Habermas's procedural reduction does not analyze.

IV

The notion of what is reasonable plays a larger role in moral deliberation than either Habermas or Railton would seem to admit.[49] It characterizes not only the symmetrical situation of participants to moral discourse and the information on the basis of which their deliberation proceeds, but also their orientation and judgment within deliberation. The fact that an agreement emerges from discourse characterized by Habermas's general symmetry conditions or meeting Railton's criterion of social rationality is not sufficient to ensure its reasonableness; it must also be supported by the right reasons, say, by reasonable judgments of the legitimacy and relative urgency of the needs and interests of affected persons.[50]

The notion of the reasonable is not itself fundamental. The normative force and content of the reasonable judgments derives from arguments about the relevance to moral deliberation of invoking particular values. Moral principles to govern social life will be justified by reference to the values of fairness, respect, equality, reciprocity, and so on. Various values together help to explicate the requirement of interpersonal justification because they each provide compelling and rationally defensible grounds for preferring some proposed principles to others. For example, as T. M. Scanlon puts it, we have reason to reject principles when they arbitrarily favor the claims of some persons over the identical claims of others: that is to say, because they are unfair.[51] The same may be true about principles that are incompatible with the reasons we have to want to live our lives in ways that realize important values such as friendship.[52]

The point is that in analyzing the justifiability of possible action-guiding norms we must look beyond the psychological and sociological fact that persons take certain reasons to provide compelling and rationally defensible grounds for preferring some moral norms and rejecting others. We must look to why, if at all, these reasons should play this role. The clue to the labyrinth of our moral notions lies in evaluating the normative force of the moral arguments into which they figure.[53] Only doing this will enable us to understand what will have made it possible to reach reasonable agreement on moral norms and to correct distortions in judgments, when agreement has provisionally been attained. It is not just the relevant notion of interests that resists reduction, but a whole family of moral reasons and the arguments upon which they rest for their relevance.

We should reject reductive accounts of how the work of moral reasoning is done. When norms that satisfy naturalistic criteria of moral rightness fail to square with our settled moral convictions, there is reason to doubt that these criteria illuminate the nature of morally defensible norms and practices or that they are adequate to guide us in deliberating about which social norms are justifiable. The requirements of reason in morality cannot be codified by a list of formal constraints on a procedure of reasoning or by a causal account of the content of our moral judgments. In order to illuminate the nature of our moral aims and judgments, a moral philosopher must engage in substantive moral reasoning, however indeterminate and fallible it might be—that is, she must engage as a participant in moral discourse. There is, philosophically, no shortcut around practical reasoning itself. We identify morally justifiable norms on the basis of compelling reasons to think that a proposed position reasonably takes everyone's interests into account. No set of social, psychological, or historical facts can replace the role that good arguments play in the enterprise of identifying justifiable moral norms.[54]

This does not mean that our moral notions could not figure into empirical theories. Our normative notions may well have explanatory value. Let's hope they do. But unless empirical explanations of social behavior incorporate our reasonable judgments, and not just the nonnormative fact that we have and regard as reasonable such judgments, those explanations will not count as moral explanations, that is, explanations that rest on "moral facts," as relative and relational as those facts may be.

Postscript (2002) to "The Investigations' Everyday Aesthetics of Itself"

STANLEY CAVELL

$\mathcal{T}$HESE BRIEF REMARKS were composed, at the invitation of the editors, to accompany the proposed reprinting in this volume of an essay of mine entitled "The *Investigations'* Everyday Aesthetics of Itself." When this reprinting became unfeasible, they wished to retain the remarks, since, if less conveniently, the essay they supplement is available in *The Cavell Reader.*[1] I yield to the editors' conviction that even in this unattached state these remarks strike a note worth preserving for the volume. My understanding of the conviction is that my writing over the years on Wittgenstein's *Philosophical Investigations*[2] has so stressed the recurrence in that text to various registrations of the concept of nature (from the idea of forms of life, to ideas of the natural reactions of human beings, to considerations of applying the concept of pain to a wriggling fly, or that of simulation to a dog) that it may be said to propose Wittgenstein's work there as a naturalizing of philosophy, but one that of course no more assumes that what it says about a chair or a stone is of interest to physics than it assumes validation by psychology for its use of the concepts of, for example, expectation or hope or pain; nor, of course, does it await the rebuff of these sciences. Stressing in this way the differences of naturalization in the *Investigations* from that proposed in the established program of naturalization in the theory of knowledge (if that is indeed what my reading of Wittgenstein suggests) has assembled thoughts for me in a way that I feel I have benefited from. The following paragraphs attempt to specify the benefit.

My essay on the aesthetics in and of *Philosophical Investigations* at one stage elicits a set of traits of what I call the modern subject, and which suggest in effect a portrait of the imagined reader of that work. The traits I name (or claim the text implies, each on the basis of specific passages of Wittgenstein's text) are torment, strangeness, perverseness, exile, disappointment, suffocation, and so on. Thinking of this portrait in the context of thoughts invoking the idea of naturalizing philosophy forces the question of the status of these traits. Are they, and their con-junction, reflections of a historical period, call it the modern, or are they natural to the human at any time? (This is a question I have asked myself about skepticism, or modern skepticism, in the form[s] taken, or taken up, in Descartes and Hume and Kant.)

If I said I would like to answer that these traits are part of the natural history of the human, would that seem an evasion, an effort to have it both ways? Wittgenstein both affirms and denies that thoughts of his amount to contributions to a natural history of the human. At § 425 Wittgenstein writes: "What we are supplying are really remarks on the natural history of human beings; . . . observations . . . which have escaped remark only because they are always before our eyes." (At § 25 he notes: "Commanding, questioning, recounting, chatting, are as much a part of our natural history as walking, eating, drinking, playing.") But on p. 230 we find this: "Our interest certainly includes the correspondence between concepts and very general facts of nature. . . . But . . . we are not doing natural science; nor yet natural history since we can invent fictitious natural history for our purposes." The purpose, for example, may be that of making intelligible "the formation of concepts different from the usual ones" (ibid.). Would the following count as examples here?: If for some reason human beings became constitutionally by nature or by, let us say, something regarded as religion limited to a small number of spoken words each day, or males avoided approaching females closer than a dis-tance of seven meters except for the purpose of procreation, then our usual concept of chatting would become obsolete, or would not apply to exchanges between males and females.

The equal possibilities of observed or imagined natural history suggest that since the features from Wittgenstein's texts I identified as of the modern subject may also be imagined as abnormal, even as unnatural (compared with their opposites, or binary partners, for example, peace-fulness, familiarity, domesticity, satisfaction, and fluency), we might also wish to say that what is natural to the human is precisely the unnatural, as when we perceive that what the human calls ordinary is extraordinary, what extraordinary, ordinary, as when we call what is historical natural (for example, poverty) or what is natural historical (for example, aggression). These ambiguities are perhaps most concisely registered in my distinguishing what I have called two directions in Wittgenstein's invocation of "forms of life," namely a social or conventional or horizontal direction (where differences between dining and snacking may be significant) and a biological or natural or vertical direction (where differences between eating and feeding, or between tables and troughs, are to the point).

The distinction between conceptual directions of forms of life suggests to me that my usual distinction between the actual ordinary (from which philosophy begins, as in Plato's Cave, in which we are lost, disoriented) and the eventual ordinary (to which Wittgenstein says his philosophizing is to "return" us, though we have never lived there in consciousness, and which we will chronically attempt to "leave" again), might be recast as a return from the unnatural to the natural, emphasizing that the human is that creature who has to *discover* (one might even say invent) what is natural to him/her. The idea of the natural thus brings to the situation (in which we are lost and found in or by philosophy) the sense of normativity in human judgment as grounded in the idea that *this* is (what we call) having a chat, or taking a walk, because this *is* having a chat, taking a walk, and so forth. (In what became the opening and title essay of my first book, *Must We Mean What We Say?*³ I was pointing to this connection in saying: "The normativeness which Mates felt [in the so-called ordinary language philosopher's appeal to what can and cannot be said], and which is certainly present, does not lie in the ordinary language philosopher's assertions about ordinary use; what is normative is exactly ordinary use itself.")⁴ It is a normative that is in principle not unchanging and in which the claim to exemplify the normative is inherently contestable. Such remarks are in service of an idea of the normative not dependent upon the possession of rules but, I might say, on the capacity and willingness of each to follow another and of each to initiate change.

I should add, with perhaps undue provocativeness, that I am not willing to concede that *Philosophical Investigations* is opposed to ideas of naturalizing philosophy even when that means taking philosophy as a chapter of science, so long as we can still wonder what makes a study science, and be curious about what has happened to the idea of nature and of the philosophy of nature. Here is a quote from a review by Stephen Jay Gould of *The Map That Changed the World: William Smith and the Birth of Modern Geology* by Simon Winchester:⁵

Observational studies of nature's broad expanse—Hyman's full range
of taxonomic order, or Smith's full panoply of geological time—have
taken second place in both popular and professional regard, to the
experimental and quantitative approaches of astronomy or classical
physics . . . based on predictive statements and law-like structure.
The natural history of taxonomic diversity or temporal change, by
contrast, strikes many people as a simple, if admittedly compendious,
description of theoretically uninteresting uniqueness. . . . Yet Smith
and his colleagues achieved one of the greatest and most practically
important renderings of knowledge and perception in all our history.

Out of this alternative picture of what can constitute science, I might say
that what disturbs me in the accepted idea of naturalization, as I understand it, is no more the exhaustion of philosophy by (the philosophy of)
science than the resultant conventionalizing of experience, its stylization
as "checkpoints" of predictions.

Projecting the image of science from the region of nonexperimental,
nonquantitative science does not bring philosophy, as conceived in *Philosophical Investigations*, any closer to becoming part of science, since "[i]t
is of the essence of our investigation that we do not seek to learn anything
new by it" (§ 89). But it seems to encourage me in my wish to become
or remain interested in my experience of the natural (as much as in the
social) world, to remain to this degree an empiricist, which is to say,
interested in the full panoply of things that my language has thought to
mark, and is prepared to mark further, for example (to take instances in
Philosophical Investigations not usually found in modern philosophical
texts), the child, and, beyond the occasional dog and fly, the cow and hen
and beetle and lion and goose, and the capacity or necessity to have one's
eyes shut before certain possibilities (p. 224) and the condition of possibility of a smile (§ 583). But at the same time, these possibilities would
not exist as interests but for the conceptual powers articulated in grammar and criteria, which could be said to exist "before" these discoveries
("[o]ne might also give the name 'philosophy' to what is possible before
all new discoveries and inventions" [§ 127]), which seems to confirm my
wish to remain to this degree a rationalist, at home in the a priori.

Stressing the sense of competing directions in the human life-form is
meant to caution against what I believe is the more common over-
conventionalized reception of Wittgenstein's thinking, shown for example in emphasizing our capacity to construct language-games more than
our chronic disappointments with our constructions. Disappointment
within science is a spur to further investigation of a sort that will over-

come disappointment; whereas in philosophy it is of interest to investigate the disappointment itself as of revelatory value, part of human natural history. The perennial interest science has for philosophy is not likely to be forgotten by philosophers (in my part of the philosophical forest); unlike the interest that, for example, the arts, great and small, have, or have had, for philosophy. I do not say this explains my career-long emphasis on the arts as spur and competitor of philosophy, but since both knowing and shaping are parts of the natural history of humans, equally primordial routes of human aspiration and accommodation, I hope I may be forgiven for the emphasis.

Notes

Introduction: The Nature of Naturalism

1. Of course, besides the scientific naturalism discussed here, there have been many other forms of naturalism in the history of philosophy, of which Aristotelean, Spinozistic, and Scottish are some of the best known examples.

2. The term "ethical naturalism," like the term "naturalism" itself, has been employed in various different ways. Very commonly, however, ethical naturalists argue that moral values can be fitted into the natural world as it is understood by the natural sciences either by denying that moral discourse is cognitive or by reducing moral properties to naturalistic properties. Similar versions of ethical naturalism that fit within the scientific naturalist paradigm can be found in the writings of Peter Railton, Gil Harman, David Lewis, Richard Boyd, Simon Blackburn, and Allan Gibbard, among others. Erin I. Kelly's paper in this anthology discusses some of these views.

A few versions of ethical naturalism are not forms of scientific naturalism. They include *theological ethical naturalism* as defended by R. M. Adams—really a form of supernaturalism—and *neo-Aristotelian ethical naturalism* as defended by, for example, P. T. Geach and Mary Midgley. See C. R. Pidgen, "Naturalism," in Peter Singer, ed., *A Companion to Ethics* (Oxford: Blackwell, 1991), pp. 421–431.

3. See, for example, Kai Nielsen, *Naturalism and Religion* (Amherst: Prometheus, 2001).

4. In the late 1970s Dennett could report that "it is widely granted these days that dualism is not a serious view to contend with, but rather a cliff over which to push one's opponents." Daniel Dennett, "Current Issues in the Philosophy of Mind," *American Philosophical Quarterly* 15 (1978): 249–261. Two rare exceptions to this antidualist unanimity include John Foster, *The Immaterial Mind: A Defence of the Cartesian Dualist Conception of the Mind* (London: Routledge, 1997), and K. R. Popper and John Eccles, *The Self and Its Brain* (New York: New Springer Verlag, 1977).

5. Lawrence Sklar, "Naturalism and the Interpretation of Theories," *Proceedings*

and Addresses of the American Philosophical Association 75 (2001): 1–9, quotation from p. 1 (pagination refers to APA website).

6. See Tom Sorell, *Scientism and the Infatuation with Science* (London: Routledge, 1991).

7. Wilfred Sellars, "Empiricism and the Philosophy of Mind," in *Science Perception and Reality* (London: Routledge, 1963), pp. 127–196, quotation from p. 173.

8. For two important attempts to naturalize mathematical properties, see Hartry Field, *Science Without Numbers: A Defense of Nominalism* (Princeton: Princeton University Press, 1980), and Penelope Maddy, *Realism in Mathematics* (Oxford: Clarendon, 1990).

9. Note that if one were *very* liberal in what one counts as a science, so that *all* rational inquiry counts as scientific, the idea that our concepts must refer to, or pick out, some aspect of the world-as-studied-by-the-sciences carries no real bite.

10. See, for example, Stephen Stich, "Naturalism, Positivism, and Pluralism," in *Deconstructing the Mind* (New York: Oxford University Press, 1996), p. 196. This point is also raised by Jennifer Hornsby in *Simple Mindedness: In Defense of Naïve Naturalism in the Philosophy of Mind* (Cambridge: Harvard University Press, 1997), p. 9.

11. D. M. Armstrong, "Naturalism, Materialism, and First Philosophy," in *The Nature of Mind and Other Essays* (St. Lucia: University of Queensland Press, 1980), pp. 149–165, quotation from p. 156.

12. Hartry Field, for example, writes: "when faced with a body of doctrine (or a body of purported causal explanations) that we are convinced can have no physical foundation, we tend to reject that body of doctrine (or of purported causal explanations)." Hartry Field, "Physicalism," in John Earman, ed., *Inference, Explanations, and Other Frustrations: Essays in the Philosophy of Science* (Berkeley: University of California Press, 1992), pp. 271–291, quotation from p. 271. This is not to say that physics is the only true science. It is to indicate that anything deserving the title of a natural science must be similar enough to physics. That, of course, leaves room for dispute about what counts as similar enough, and in what respects.

13. Physicalism may be regarded as an ontological scientific naturalism according to which the only genuine and irreducible natural science is physics. Recent critical assessments of physicalist naturalism include Howard Robinson, ed., *Objections to Physicalism* (Oxford: Clarendon, 1993), and Carl Gillet and Barry Loewer, eds., *Physicalism and Its Discontents* (Cambridge: Cambridge University Press, 2001). For some sharp criticisms of physicalism, see Tim Crane and D. H. Mellor, "There Is No Question of Physicalism," *Mind* 99 (1990): 185–206.

14. A recent collection on this topic is Elias Savellos and Umit Yalcin, eds., *Supervenience: New Essays* (Cambridge: Cambridge University Press, 1995).

15. For example, John Haugeland has influentially argued in favor of the weak supervenience claim "that nothing could have been otherwise without something physical being otherwise." Part of the attraction of this position is that, with regard to the relation of the mental to the physical, this weak supervenience claim can be accepted without having to accept either type- or token-identity theory. John Haugeland, *Having Thought: Essays in the Metaphysics of Mind* (Cambridge: Harvard University Press, 1998), p. 95.

16. An excellent book-length discussion of this and related issues is Jaegwon Kim, *Supervenience and Mind* (Cambridge: Cambridge University Press, 1993).

17. On the issue of the autonomy of the human and social sciences with respect

to the natural sciences, the debate is long-standing and the literature is immense. Two excellent examples of the two ends of the spectrum, the monist and the pluralist, are respectively represented by A. R. Damasio, Anne Harrington, and Jerome Kagan, eds., *Unity of Knowledge: The Convergence of Natural and Human Science* (New York: New York Academy of Sciences, 2001), and Charles Taylor, *Philosophical Papers*, vol. 2, *Philosophy and the Human Sciences* (Cambridge: Cambridge University Press, 1985).

18. Kant, *Critique of Pure Reason*, trans. Norman Kemp Smith (London: MacMillan, 1929). While he speaks of placing metaphysics on the path of a science (B xiv), believes that pure reason can discover a priori its own conditions and possibility.

19. David Hume, *A Treatise of Human Nature*, 2nd ed., rev. and ed. P. H. Nidditch (Oxford: Clarendon, 1978), introd., p. xv.

20. This is not to say that Hume fully achieved this vision. In particular, his "Bundle Theory" of the mind retains a vestigial allegiance to elements of Cartesian dualism.

21. W. V. Quine, *Theories and Things* (Cambridge: Harvard University Press, 1981), p. 67. More fully, he speaks of naturalism as "the recognition that it is within science itself, and not in some prior philosophy, that reality is to be identified and described" (p. 21).

22. P. K. Moser and J. D. Trout, eds., *Materialism: A Reader* (London: Routledge, 1995), p. 9.

23. For a defense of ontological naturalism, see, for example, D. M. Armstrong, *Universals and Scientific Realism*, 2 vols. (Cambridge: Cambridge University Press, 1978).

24. Of course, we might speak *as if* there were entities that do not, in fact, exist.

25. Mackie famously described objective moral values as "queer" entities. See John Mackie, *Ethics: Inventing Right and Wrong* (New York: Penguin, 1977), pp. 38–42.

26. For a defense of methodological (or epistemological) naturalism, see Quine, *Theories and Things*; Philip Kitcher, "Naturalists Return," *Philosophical Review* 101 (1992): 53–114; and Hilary Kornblith, ed., *Naturalizing Epistemology* (Cambridge: MIT Press, 1994).

27. For a discussion of semantic naturalism, see, for example, Barry Loewer, "A Guide to Naturalizing Semantics," in Bob Hale and Crispin Wright, eds., *A Companion to the Philosophy of Language* (Oxford: Blackwell, 1997), pp. 108–126. See also Peter Railton, "What the Non-cognitivist Helps Us to See the Naturalist Must Help Us to Explain" and "Reply to David Wiggins," in John Haldane and Crispin Wright, eds., *Reality, Representation, and Projection* (Oxford: Oxford University Press, 1993), pp. 279–299, 315–328.

28. See, for example, Frank Jackson's defense of a modest conception of the a priori in *From Metaphysics to Ethics: A Defence of Conceptual Analysis* (Oxford: Clarendon, 1998). For a useful discussion of the notion of the a priori in light of Quine's work, see Hilary Putnam, "Analyticity and Apriority: Beyond Wittgenstein and Quine," *Philosophical Papers*, vol. 3, *Realism and Reason* (Cambridge: Cambridge University Press, 1983).

29. Philosophers in the spirit of Quine will want to reject even this vestigial a priorism. See, for example, Michael Devitt, *Realism and Truth*, 2nd ed. (Oxford: Blackwell, 1991).

30. Ludwig Wittgenstein, *Tractatus Logico-Philosophicus* [1922], trans. D. F. Pears and B. F. McGuiness (London: Routledge, 1961), 4.112. Today, Michael Dummett still defends the view that the aim of philosophy is the clarification of thought, with

the proviso (with which he thinks both Frege and Wittgenstein would agree) that this goal can only be achieved through the clarification of language. See Michael Dummett, *The Origins of Analytical Philosophy* (London: Duckworth, 1993).

31. Peter Hylton, *Russell, Idealism, and the Emergence of Analytic Philosophy* (Oxford: Clarendon, 1990), pp. 14–15.

32. Ibid., p. 388.

33. See, in particular, W. V. Quine, "Two Dogmas of Empiricism," in *From a Logical Point of View* (Cambridge: Harvard University Press, 1953), pp. 20–46, and W. V. Quine, *World and Object* (Cambridge: MIT Press, 1960).

34. See, especially, W. V. Quine, "Epistemology Naturalized," in *Ontological Relativity and Other Essays* (New York: Columbia University Press, 1969), pp. 69–90.

35. A representative comment is this: "I admit to naturalism and even glory in it. This means banishing the dream of a first philosophy and pursuing philosophy rather as a part of one's system of the world, continuous with the rest of science." W. V. Quine, "Reply to Putnam," in L. E. Hahn and P. A. Schillp, eds., *The Philosophy of W. V. Quine* (La Salle: Open Court, 1986), quotation from pp. 430–431.

36. Kitcher, "Naturalists Return."

37. Stich speaks, instead, of "puritanical naturalism." See Stich, "Naturalism, Positivism, and Pluralism," chap. 6.

38. Dewey, for example, remarks that "the naturalist is one who has respect for the conclusions of natural science." Y. H. Krikorian, ed., *Naturalism and the Human Spirit* (New York: Columbia University Press, 1944), p. 2.

39. Richard Rorty, *Rorty and Pragmatism: The Philosopher Responds to His Critics*, ed. H. J. Saatkamp Jr. (Nashville: Vanderbilt University Press, 1995), p. 201.

40. Hornsby, *Simple Mindedness*.

41. See his "Naturalism in the Philosophy of Mind" in the present volume.

42. See his "The Charm of Naturalism" in the present volume.

43. Stanley Cavell, "The *Investigations'* Everyday Aesthetics of Itself," in Stephen Mulhall, ed., *The Cavell Reader* (Cambridge: Blackwell, 1996), pp. 369–389.

44. Although the majority of scientific naturalists continue to subscribe to a restrictive conception of the sciences even in spite of these difficulties, it has to be admitted that *some* scientific naturalists (e.g. Stephen Stich) are happy to acknowledge the diversity and plurality of the sciences.

45. The inspiration for the suggestion is Ludwig Wittgenstein's discussion of aesthetics as reported by G. E. Moore in "Wittgenstein's Lectures in 1930–33" in his *Philosophical Papers* (London: Allen and Unwin, 1959). Cavell's conception of philosophy, as exemplified in his practice, represents an elaboration and extension of this suggestion.

46. Here it is worth considering Rush Rhees's remark about Wittgenstein's writing, "If you do not see how style or force of expression are important you cannot see how Wittgenstein thought of philosophical difficulties and of philosophical method." Rush Rhees, "The Philosophy of Wittgenstein," *Ratio* 8 (1966): 180–193.

47. This is something that analytic philosophy, and its typical self-effacing mode of presentation in essays modeled on scientific papers, does its best to deny.

48. These reflections are indebted to Stanley Cavell's discussion of the relation between aesthetic judgment and the claims of ordinary language philosophers in "Aesthetic Problems of Modern Philosophy," in *Must We Mean What We Say* (Cambridge: Cambridge University Press, 1969).

49. We would like to thank Mark Colyvan, Erin Kelly, Peter Menzies, and Stephen White for their comments on earlier drafts of this Introduction.

1. The Charm of Naturalism

1. See W. V. Quine, "Epistemology Naturalized," in *Ontological Relativity and Other Essays* (New York: Columbia University Press, 1969), pp. 69–90.

2. Fred Dretske, *Naturalizing the Mind* (Cambridge: MIT Press, 1995).

3. Alvin Plantinga, *Warrant and Proper Function* (New York: Oxford University Press, 1993), p. 46.

4. Ibid., p. 237.

5. For this description of naturalized epistemology, see "Introduction: What Is Naturalistic Epistemology?" in Hilary Kornblith, ed., *Naturalizing Epistemology* (Cambridge: MIT Press, 1985), pp. 1–14.

6. Quine, "Epistemology Naturalized," p. 75.

7. Ibid., p. 78.

8. Ibid., p. 26.

9. Ibid., p. 87.

10. See Casimir Lewy, "G. E. Moore on the Naturalistic Fallacy," in P. F. Strawson, ed., *Studies in the Philosophy of Thought and Action* (Oxford: Oxford University Press, 1968), pp. 134–146, quotation from p. 137.

2. The Miracle of Monism

1. Barry Stroud, "The Charm of Naturalism," *Proceedings and Addresses of the American Philosophical Association* 70 (1996): 43–55.

2. See Ian Hacking, *Representing and Intervening* (Cambridge: Cambridge University Press, 1983).

3. The locus classicus for the general rejection of any account of scientific method is of course Paul Feyerabend's *Against Method* (London: New Left Books, 1975).

4. Indeed, enthusiasts for Popper's work will no doubt object, quite rightly, that I have presented no more than a caricature of Popper's most sophisticated development of his views. My response is that the kinds of ways that crude falsificationism misrepresents these various practices are highly diverse, and attempts to conform them to sophisticated falsificationism would take the theory in diverse directions that would not leave anything like a unified account of scientific method.

5. An interesting speculation here is that the term "transmission genetics" already carries the seeds of error. The development of genetics as a science involving hypothetical factors capable of transmitting traits, and the emphasis on experiments such as Mendel's and later work on Drosophila involving traits that did indeed vary in systematic response to different genes, led to the assumption that inheritance was to be explained in terms of genes. When the molecular structure of genes was subsequently elucidated it became natural to think of this as the discovery of the molecular basis of inheritance. But while there is no question that genes play a fundamental role in inheritance, it is essential to realize that this is only an essential contribution to a very complex process.

6. A good example of this view of biology is Alexander Rosenberg, *Instrumental Biology or the Disunity of Science* (Chicago: University of Chicago Press, 1994). In the philosophy of mind such a view has led, among other oddities, to the bizarre but widely discussed panpsychist dualism of David Chalmers, *The Conscious Mind: In Search of a Fundamental Theory* (Oxford: Oxford University Press, 1996).

7. Nancy Cartwright, *How the Laws of Physics Lie* (Oxford: Oxford University Press, 1983).

8. Peter Galison, *How Experiments End* (Chicago: Chicago University Press, 1987).

9. This point is developed at length in my recent book *Human Nature and the Limits of Science* (Oxford: Oxford University Press, 2001). There I try to show both the defects of some questionable scientific projects, most especially evolutionary psychology, and also how the motivation for much bad science draws on the mythology of unity.

10. It is no coincidence that John Tooby and Leda Cosmides begin what has become a classic defense of the unity of science with a discussion of this very topic. John Tooby and Leda Cosmides, "The Psychological Foundations of Culture," in Jerome Barkow, Leda Cosmides, and John Tooby, eds., *The Adapted Mind* (New York: Oxford University Press, 1992), pp. 19–136.

11. C. P. Snow, *The Two Cultures* (Cambridge: Cambridge University Press, 1959).

12. The broadest theme of my recent book, *Human Nature and the Limits of Science*, is that human nature is a topic that can only be adequately addressed from such a plurality of perspectives.

13. Thomas Kuhn, *The Structure of Scientific Revolutions*, 2nd ed. (Chicago: University of Chicago Press, 1970).

3. The Content and Appeal of "Naturalism"

1. There is a different use, due to John McDowell, characterized by the idea—which McDowell draws from Aristotle—that, although we are indeed animals, and thus part of nature, we acquire a "second nature" as we become sharers of a culture. John McDowell, *Mind and World* (Cambridge: Harvard University Press, 1994). My subject in the present essay isn't this sort of naturalism, which I agree with, but which is either ignored or actually scorned by the "naturalists" I shall be talking about.

2. Richard Boyd, Philip Gasper, and J. D. Trout, eds., *The Philosophy of Science* (Cambridge: MIT Press, 1991).

3. The history of the term is no help. Dewey gave it currency, and he certainly insisted that "the methods of the natural sciences" are applicable in every area of inquiry, but for Dewey what that meant was that one should be *fallibilistic* and *experimental* in every area of inquiry (including when one is painting or criticizing a picture—see his *Art as Experience*, vol. 10 of *John Dewey: The Later Works*, ed. Jo Ann Boydston [Carbondale: Southern Illinois University Press, ca. 1981–1990]). It also meant that one should see the "scientific method," in his sense, as presupposing the interpenetration of fact and value (including aesthetic value)—the interpenetration of problems of use and enjoyment and abstract scientific problems. But this is not what philosophers who talk about "the methods of the natural sciences" mean by that expression today.

4. W. V. Quine, *Ontological Relativity and Other Essays* (New York: Columbia University Press, 1969), p. 24.

5. In *The Cement of the Universe* (Oxford: Clarendon, 1974), John Mackie described the ordinary notion of causality as a New Stone Age ("neolithic") notion. He tried to provide a substitute, but, as I argued in "The Causal Structure of the Physical," collected in my *Realism with a Human Face* (Cambridge: Harvard University Press, 1990), he did not succeed (see pp. 93–95).

6. James Conant, "Wittgenstein's Philosophy of Mathematics," *Proceedings of the Aristotelian Society* 97, no. 2 (1997): 195–222, quotation from p. 202. The passage reads: "Putnam wants . . . to hang on to . . . the idea that ethical and mathematical

propositions are *bona fide* instances of assertoric discourse: ethical and mathematical thought represent forms of reflection that are as fully governed by norms of truth and validity as any other form of cognitive activity. But he is not friendly to the idea that, in order to safeguard the cognitive credentials of ethics and mathematics, one must therefore suppose that ethical and mathematical talk bear on reality *in the same way* as ordinary empirical thought, so that in order to safeguard the truth of such propositions as 'it is wrong to break a promise' or '2 + 2 = 4,' one must suppose that, like ordinary empirical propositions, such propositions, in each sort of case, 'describe' their own peculiar states of affairs. There is an assumption at work here that Putnam wants to reject—one which underlies Blackburn's way of distinguishing realism and antirealism—the assumption that there are just two ways to go: either (i) we accept a general philosophical account of the relation between language and reality according to which all indicative sentences are to be classified equally as 'descriptions of reality'; or, (ii) we accept an alternative account of the relation between language and reality which rests on a metaphysically-grounded distinction between those sentences which do genuinely describe reality (and whose cognitive credentials are therefore to be taken at face value) and those which merely purport to describe reality (and whose claims to truth are therefore to be taken as chimerical)." Of course (as Conant is aware) there are other statements that Blackburn and some others would reject as not fully worthy of being taken cognitively seriously—statements about what *refers* to what, statements about what *caused* what, for example—that I would regard as *bona fide* statements *and* as (when true) "descriptions of reality." The point is that the claim that the supposedly "second-grade" statements are *bona fida* in the sense of being governed by norms of truth and validity must not be confused with the claim that *all* of them are "descriptions of reality." This is the error that Conant accuses Sabina Lovibond of making. This point will be returned to in the final paragraph of the present essay.

7. Simon Blackburn, *Spreading the Word* (Oxford: Clarendon, 1984); Bernard Williams, *Descartes: The Project of Pure Enquiry* (Harmondsworth: Penguin, 1978); and Bernard Williams, *Ethics and the Limits of Philosophy* (Cambridge: Harvard University Press, 1985).

8. Quine wrote, "The quest for a simplest clearest overall pattern of canonical notation is not to be distinguished from a quest of ultimate categories, a limning of the most general traits of reality," in *Word and Object* (Cambridge: MIT Press, 1960), p. 161.

9. Richard Boyd, "How to Be a Moral Realist," in Geoffrey Sayre-McCord, ed., *Essays in Moral Realism* (Ithaca: Cornell University Press, 1988), pp. 181–228; Peter Railton, "Moral Realism," *Philosophical Review* 95 (1986): 163–207.

10. Jerry Fodor, "Meaning and the World Order," *Psychosemantics* (Cambridge: MIT Press, 1987), pp. 97–127; and Jerry Fodor, *A Theory of Content* (Cambridge: MIT Press, 1990). For some criticisms, see the chapter on Fodor (chap. 3) in my *Renewing Philosophy* (Cambridge: Harvard University Press, 1992), pp. 35–59.

11. The classic formulation of the problem is Paul Benacerraf's "Mathematical Truth," *Journal of Philosophy* 70 (1973): 661–679. For a recent attempt to deny that the problem is genuine while defending naturalism, see Jody Azzouni, *Metaphysical Myths, Mathematical Practice* (Cambridge: Cambridge University Press, 1994). For my own view, see my "Was Wittgenstein *Really* an Antirealist About Mathematics?" in Peter Winch and T. G. McCarthy, eds., *Wittgenstein in America* (Oxford: Oxford University Press, 2001).

12. Quine, *Word and Object*, p. 221.

13. W. V. Quine, *The Pursuit of Truth* (Cambridge: Harvard University Press, 1990), p. 33.

14. Stephen Leeds, "Brains in Vats Revisited," *Pacific Philosophical Quarterly* (June 1996): 108–131. Leeds's earlier paper, "Theories of Reference and Truth," *Erkenntnis* 13 (1978): 11–127, is one of the most widely cited statements of the "deflationist" position on truth and reference. A similar view was defended by Hartry Field in a paper about my book *Reason, Truth, and History* titled "Realism and Relativism," *Journal of Philosophy* 79, no. 10 (1982): 553–567. I replied to Field in "A Defense of Internal Realism," *Realism with a Human Face* (Cambridge: Harvard University Press, 1990).

15. Quine speaks in terms of "proxy functions" rather than models, but the point is unaffected.

16. At a discussion between us in Cerisy (June 25, 1995), Rorty chided me for calling myself a "commonsense realist," saying "commonsense realism is as bad as metaphysical realism: one leads to the other." Nor is this the only occasion on which he has virtually equated being a "realist" and being a "metaphysician"—the latter term being clearly pejorative.

17. "The fallacy comes in thinking that the relationship between vocable and reality has to be piecemeal (like the relation between individual kicks and individual rocks), a matter of discrete component capacities to get in touch with discrete hunks of reality." Richard Rorty, "Pragmatism, Davidson, and Truth," in Ernie Lepore, ed., *Truth and Interpretation* (Oxford: Blackwell, 1986), pp. 145–146.

18. I develop an account along these lines in *The Threefold Cord: Mind, Body, and World* (New York: Columbia University Press, 1999).

19. David Lewis, "Radical Interpretation," *Synthèse* 23 (1974): 331–344; collected in his *Philosophical Papers*, vol. 1 (Oxford: Oxford University Press, 1983).

20. At the most fundamental level, present-day physics does *not* say the entities of which the world consists are *either* particles (not if "particles" are supposed to be objects one can assign number and determinate identity to through time) *or* (*pace* Quine) fields with real number values or ordinary vector values at points in a space-time, which is supposed to be "there" independently of the fields. It is curious how many philosophers who praise modern physics as first philosophy don't trouble to learn it.

21. Here I use "positivist" in the sense it had before Logical Positivism appeared on the scene, the sense introduced by Auguste Comte. In this older sense, "naturalism" seems to be precisely the late-twentieth/early-twenty-first century form of "positivism."

22. That the failure of reductionism in cases like that of geology is perfectly acceptable to a "naturalist" is made clear in Jerry Fodor, "Special Sciences (or the Disunity of Science as a Working Hypothesis)," *Synthèse* 28 (1974): 97–115; at the same time, Fodor tries very hard to explain the notion of reference reductively with the aid of the notion of "causation" precisely because he supposes—wrongly, in my opinion—that there are no intentional (or "semantic") elements in the latter notion. Hence the revealing statement in *Psychosemantics*, pp. 126–127, that Fodor has "wasted a lot of time that I could have put in sailing" if "the cause" is indeed intentional/semantic.

23. Quine preferred to take the basic entities to be space-time points, which he identified with *quadruples of real numbers*, and regions, which he identified with *sets of quadruples of real numbers*, but I do not know any philosopher who followed him in this (self-styled) "Pythagoreanism."

24. The physics is fictitious because in our most fundamental physical theory, quantum field theory, "what there is" isn't fields and particles in the classical sense at all. What is associated with each space-time point (or rather, with each point in a postulated background space-time, which is not the same as physical space-time!) is not a field vector, but a "___-function," a vector in an infinite-dimensional space (a Hilbert Space or some other abstract space), and there are no definite particles and no definite field intensities at all, in the general case.

25. Saul Kripke, *Naming and Necessity* (Cambridge: Harvard University Press, 1980).

26. Kripke does not discuss mereological sums as such in *Naming and Necessity*, but his rejection of "counterpart theory" (ibid., lecture 1, especially p. 45) turns on the claim that when I say *I* would have done such and such if I had eaten different food, I mean precisely that; I am not saying that an X that isn't identical with me would have done such and such. Moreover, my statement may well be *true*.

27. I agree with this much, but in addition I am attracted to an idea that I know Kripke does not like, the idea of "sortal" identity: that is, the idea that things can be *identical in a respect but not in another respect*. For example, I am inclined to say (still idealizing the physics, by the way) that a certain mereological sum of time-slices of atoms *is*, as things actually stand (I didn't have pot roast for dinner last night), *identical with me qua physical system,* but *not identical with me qua person*. This doesn't rescue the ontology of basic physical entities and mereological sums thereof, at least as usually understood, because as usually understood the identity of formalized ontology isn't sortal identity. And if we do allow sortal identity, then the ontology only tells us what there is *in a respect* (say what there is, *qua* physical objects); sortal identity is essentially *pluralistic*, and unless we postulate that the number of *sorts* can be limited in advance—which I would deny—sortal identity *subverts* the question "What is there?" by countering: "What is there in *which respect?*"

28. See my forthcoming Hermes Lectures (given in Perugia, October 2001), *Ethics Without Ontology*. The English version will be published by Harvard University Press.

29. In *Methods of Logic* Quine defines validity—for first-order logic only (he rules that second-order logic isn't logic but "mathematics")—thus: a sentence is valid if and only if it is a substitution-instance of at least one valid schema, and a schema is valid if and only if all its substitution-instances are *true*. The inadequacies of these definitions that I refer to in the text include the following: (1) In the Tarskian semantics that Quine accepts, "true" is defined for only one formalized language at a time. In other words, given the conceptual resources Quine is willing to accept, there is, strictly speaking, *no such predicate as "true,"* but only a potentially infinite number of particular predicates "True-in-L_0," "True-in-L_1," "True-in-L_2," . . . corresponding to a potential infinity of formalized (and interpreted) languages $L_0, L_1, L_2, \ldots$ (Note that the names "L_0," "L_1," "L_2" . . . do not, from a logical point of view, occur as *meaningful* parts in the expressions "True-in-L_0," "True-in-L_1," "True-in-L_2," . . . any more than the English word "cat" occurs as a *meaningful* part in the English word "cattle," and similarly the word "True" does not occur as a *meaningful* part in the names "True-in-L_0," "True-in-L_1," "True-in-L_2" . . . ; "True-in-L_0" and its mates are all, from a logical point of view, arbitrary and *undecomposable* names. [That Truth is not *relative* to a language but rather *defined one language at a time* if one follows Tarski is something that Donald Davidson seems to me to be confused about, and perhaps other people share this confusion.] If we follow Quine, then, *validity* will likewise not be *relative* to a language but rather defined one language at a time.) (2) Pending

success in the process of completely formalizing a natural language, Quinian validity is only defined for *formalized* languages. In no natural language do the foregoing definitions "work." Moreover, according to Quine himself, formalizing a natural language is not discovering a preexisting content (if it were, a notion of *correct translation* would be presupposed, contradicting Quine's indeterminacy thesis). This means that for a strict Quinian, the failure of the definitions of validity in the case of natural languages could not be repaired even by formalizing them—formalizing a language is just deciding to use a different language altogether. (3) The *modal* character of the notion of validity—the fact that substitution instances of a valid schema are not just true but *necessarily* true—is ignored. (Quine, famously, rejects modal concepts altogether, but those who don't follow him in this should be bothered by this fact.)

4. Naturalism Without Representationalism

1. I am grateful for help with ancestors of this paper from audiences at Edinburgh, ANU, Sydney, San Diego, and King's College, London, and the Mind and Language Seminar at NYU. Thanks also to David Macarthur, for insightful comments on the penultimate version, and many conversations on related issues over several years.

2. It is a nice issue whether there is any deep difference between these two versions of the view, but an issue I'll ignore for present purposes.

3. Both attributions call for some qualification. As a parent of empiricism, for one thing, Hume certainly bears some responsibility for the object naturalist's conception of the nature of knowledge.

4. W. V. Quine, *Philosophy of Logic* (Englewood Cliffs, N.J.: Prentice-Hall, 1970), p. 12.

5. The fallacy turns on the fact that on the disquotational view, an expression of the form " 'Snow is white' is true" contains a use masquerading as a mention. If it were a genuine mention, to call "Snow is white" true would not be "to call snow white," as Quine puts it. If we term this disquotational mention a *formal* mention, then formal mention is effective use, and the fallacy here involves a confusion between genuine and formal mention, or true mention and effective use.

6. Paul Boghossian, "The Status of Content," *Philosophical Review* 99 (1990): 157–184; Paul Boghossian, "The Rule-Following Considerations," *Mind* 98 (1989): 507–549.

7. In a more detailed examination of these issues, it would be interesting to consider the connection between this kind of consideration (and indeed Boghossian's argument) and Putnam's "just more theory" concerns about the metaphysical use of a theory of reference. Hilary Putnam, *Meaning and the Moral Sciences* (Boston: Routledge, 1978); Hilary Putnam, *Reason, Truth, and History* (New York: Cambridge University Press, 1981).

8. That is to say, it doesn't arise as a question driven by naturalism. Such questions arise in many other contexts, of course—"What is justice?" "What is irony?" "What is choux pastry?" for example. If more or less commonplace questions of these kinds do give rise to puzzles of an object naturalist sort, the subject naturalist recommends a dose of linguistic therapy: Think carefully about what you are assuming about language, before you allow yourself to be convinced that there's a genuine ontological puzzle.

9. David Lewis, "Psychophysical and Theoretical Identifications," *Australasian Journal of Philosophy* 50 (1972): 249–258; David Lewis, "How to Define Theoretical Terms," *Journal of Philosophy* 67 (1970): 427–446.

10. See especially Frank Jackson, *From Metaphysics to Ethics* (Oxford: Clarendon, 1998).

11. The claim that metaphysics extends beyond the causal realm is perhaps more controversial than I here allow. Someone who rejects it will be inclined to say that where causation stops, nonmetaphysical modes of philosophy begin: formalism, perhaps, in the case of mathematics, noncognitivism in the case of value, and so on. For present purposes, it is enough to point out that such a view is thereby committed to a linguistic conception of the placement issue, for the latter views are linguistic in nature. However, it is worth noting that in a causally grounded metaphysics of this kind, the notion of causation is likely to be problematic, in a way analogous to the semantic notions in a linguistically grounded object naturalism. It will be a primitive notion, inaccessible to the program's own professed methods.

12. David Lewis, "An Argument for the Identity Theory," *Journal of Philosophy* 63 (1966): 17–25.

13. This kind of linguistic pluralism is very Wittgensteinian in spirit, of course. One of Wittgenstein's main themes in the early sections of the *Investigations* is that philosophy misses important distinctions about the uses of language, distinctions that are hidden from us by "the uniform appearances of words" (§11). The view proposed here may be too naturalistic for some contemporary Wittgensteinians, but would Wittgenstein himself have objected to it? (He might have thought that it is science, not philosophy, but that's a different matter.)

14. Or more likely, I think, "several things among many," in the sense that scientific language itself is not monofunctional. I think that causal and modal talk has distinct functions in this sense, and, while essential to any interesting science, is not the whole of it. If so, this is enough to show that there is functional plurality within scientific language, as well as outside it. For more on this theme, and the program here envisaged, see my "Naturalism and the Fate of the M-worlds," *Proceedings of the Aristotelian Society* supp. 71 (1997): 247–267, and "Metaphysical Pluralism," *Journal of Philosophy* 89 (1992): 387–409.

5. Naturalism in the Philosophy of Mind

1. Wilfred Sellars, "Empiricism and the Philosophy of Mind," in Herbert Feigl and Michael Scriven, eds., *Minnesota Studies in the Philosophy of Science*, vol. 1 (Minneapolis: University of Minnesota Press, 1956), pp. 253–329, quotation from pp. 298–299. Richard Rorty quotes the remark *twice* in *Philosophy and the Mirror of Nature* (Oxford: Blackwell, 1980), pp. 141, 389.

2. See p. 257 of Sellars, "Empiricism and the Philosophy of Mind," for a formulation on these lines.

3. See Rorty, *Philosophy and the Mirror of Nature*, p. 157, where Rorty sharply separates "what Sellars calls 'the logical space of reasons' " from "that of causal relations to objects."

4. I am suggesting that we can appeal to the idea of laws of nature in order to express the contrast Sellars insists on, while urging that the contrast is essentially modern. I am not thereby flying in the face of the plain fact that the concept of a law of nature predates modernity, just as the concept of nature does. The phrase

itself obviously traces back to a time when the idea of laws of nature did not stand in contrast with the idea of a normative organization of a subject matter. This does not undermine the point I exploit, which is one about what the idea of a law of nature has become.

5. See especially Donald Davidson, "Mental Events," *Essays on Actions and Events* (Oxford: Clarendon, 1980), pp. 207–225; the phrase I have quoted is from p. 223.

6. See Daniel Dennett, *The Intentional Stance* (Cambridge: MIT Press, 1987).

7. See the discussion of "the Normative Principle" at pp. 342–343 of ibid.

8. Some people think sentience is quite another matter, but I do not believe that is right (though I cannot discuss the matter here). For some hints, see my "One Strand in the Private Language Argument," *Grazer Philosophische Studien* 33–34 (1989): 285–303. In any case, sapience is enough for my present purpose.

9. I have exploited a suggestive parallel between Sellars's talk of "the logical space of reasons" and Davidson's talk of "the constitutive ideal of rationality." But we should note a difference between Sellars's point about knowledge and its generalization. A state or episode counts as one of knowing only if it comes up to scratch in the light of norms of justification. If we extrapolate mechanically from that, we shall suppose, quite wrongly, that "space of reasons" understanding of thought and action is unavailable where rationality is less than perfect.

10. This is connected with a fact that I noted earlier: Rorty has causation, just as such, on the opposite side of the Sellarsian divide from the considerations about justification or warrant that are the proper environment for classifying states or episodes as cases of knowledge. That means that Rorty lacks a resource that would surely be needed if we tried to put detail into the thought that capacities to acquire knowledge are natural powers.

11. Compare Kant's remark about Locke, *Critique of Pure Reason*, preface, A ed., p. ix, cited in Rorty, *Philosophy and the Mirror of Nature*, p. 126.

12. See Rorty, *Philosophy and the Mirror of Nature*, chap. 5.

13. Saul Kripke's Wittgenstein would be a case. See Saul Kripke, *Wittgenstein on Rules and Private Language* (Oxford: Blackwell, 1982). But I was looking for an actual occupant of the position, not a fictional character.

14. Consider, for example, such claims as that "beliefs . . . are attributed in statements that are true only if we exempt them from a certain familiar standard of literality." Dennett, *Intentional Stance*, p. 72. Compare the suggestion that the subject to whom things are said to seem thus and so is "just a theorist's fiction." Daniel Dennett, *Consciousness Explained* (Boston: Little, Brown, 1991), p. 128.

15. The qualification matters. I make no claims about the historical Descartes in this paper. The reading is that given currency by Gilbert Ryle, *The Concept of Mind* (London: Hutchinson, 1949).

16. I do not mean to suggest that a wish to disburden oneself of responsibility is anything but central to a proper understanding of the genesis of modern philosophy. But I do not believe a supposedly autonomous obsession with certainty is the right context in which to understand such a wish.

17. For a formulation on these lines, see p. 232 of Colin McGinn, "The Structure of Content," in Andrew Woodfield, *Thought and Object* (Oxford: Clarendon, 1982), pp. 207–258.

18. Examples include John Perry, "Frege on Demonstratives," *Philosophical Review* 86 (1977): 74–97; and McGinn, "Structure of Content."

19. See in particular Ruth Millikan, "Perceptual Content and Fregean Myth,"

Mind C (1991): 439–459; and Ruth Millikan, "White Queen Psychology," in *White Queen Psychology and Other Essays for Alice* (Cambridge: MIT Press, 1993). Similar assumptions seem to me to vitiate pp. 570–571 of Robert Brandom, *Making It Explicit: Reasoning, Representing, and Discursive Commitment* (Cambridge: Harvard University Press, 1994).

20. Millikan, "White Queen Psychology," pp. 286–287, esp. p. 287: "Of these . . . claims, the givenness of meaning identity is the most central."

21. See Gareth Evans, "Understanding Demonstratives," in Herman Parret and Jacques Bouveresse, eds., *Meaning and Understanding* (New York: De Gruyter, 1981), pp. 280–303. Millikan blurs this point by a strange reading of the principle Evans calls "Russell's Principle" (see chap. 4 of Gareth Evans, *The Varieties of Reference* [Oxford: Clarendon, 1982])—the principle that "in order to be thinking about an object one must know which object is in question—one must know which object it is that one is thinking about" (p. 65). Evans shows how this principle fits in a Fregean framework, and Millikan ("White Queen Psychology," pp. 287–288) reads the principle as requiring that a thinker be able to tell when she is thinking of the same object again (or, in a weaker form, that she be able to tell when the object figures in her thoughts later under the same mode of presentation). But contrary to what Millikan's citations imply, the requirement that a thinker be able to tell when she is thinking of the same object again is no part of what Evans means by "Russell's Principle." And even the weaker version, in terms of modes of presentation, goes far beyond Frege's principle, with its "at the same time" qualification.

22. It is remarkable how many philosophers suppose that Frege has a problem with thoughts such as the one that Rip Van Winkle might express, on waking after his twenty-year sleep, by saying, "Today is the day I fell asleep."

23. Transparency is really a red herring. At pp. 121–130 of *Intentional Stance*, Dennett rehearses the usual case against a putatively Fregean construal of propositional attitudes. (Though Frege's *Gedanken* do not actually figure in his catalogue of possible things to mean by "propositions" [p. 121].) Dennett casts the argument as a problem for the idea of "grasping senses"—or, as one might say, knowing what one thinks—posed by the fact that one can lose track, be deceived by ringers, and so forth. Would Dennett argue that my claim to know, on a suitable occasion, that it is Dennett whom I see before me is undermined if I could be deceived by a ringer (as I surely could)? Why is knowledge of what one thinks held to a higher standard? (At p. 129 Dennett writes: "One could sum up the case . . . thus: propositions are not *graspable* because they can elude us." Are live chickens not graspable? They can surely elude us.) In the same spirit, at p. 200 Dennett offers another strange reading of Russell's Principle, as expressing the idea "that we can define a kind of aboutness that is *both* a real relation to something in the world *and* something to which the believer's access is perfect." Why must the access be perfect (that is, proof against ringers, losing track, and the like)? This is not Russell's Principle as Evans uses it, which is what Dennett claims to be talking about. It would be an interesting exercise to work out how the strikingly Cartesian conception of self-knowledge that Dennett here foists on Fregeans is connected with Dennett's psychologistic (though certainly nondualistic) conception of what it would be for something to be otherwise than "psychologically inert" (p. 130).

24. Millikan, "White Queen Psychology," p. 290.

25. Ibid., p. 289.

26. I have shifted from a focus on the transparency of samenesses and differences

in sense to a focus on the capacity of a concept of sense to cater for directedness at objects (which is part of the semanticity of singular thoughts) at all. Millikan's basic point against Frege is still formulable in this context: grasping senses would have to be an exercise of "mechanical rationality," and sense and reference could hang together in Frege's way only if "mechanical rationality" sufficed for semanticity, which it does not. The advantage of the shift is that it obviates any need to set foot in the morass of cases like Kripke's Pierre (which Millikan exploits in "White Queen Psychology," pp. 290–291). Just for the record, let me say that Kripke's Pierre poses no problem for a Fregean view; as Frege's principle requires us to say, he has two different modes of presentation for London. It is a gross misconception to suppose this involves segregating a putative notion of rationality from directedness at the objective world ("a relocation of rationality into some inner, purer, safer realm" ["White Queen Psychology," p. 348]).

27. That is, rational enough to count as a thinker (and it would be silly to ask, "How rational is that?"). Formulations like the one in the text do not imply that the conceptual apparatus I am talking about becomes unavailable if a subject shows less than perfect rationality.

28. The point is the same as the one that Dennett makes by saying that "the brain . . . is just a *syntactic engine*" (*Intentional Stance*, p. 61). It is because this is a way of putting Millikan's own thought that I can classify her naturalism about "the intact mind" as a case of restrictive rather than liberal naturalism. She argues that "the biological sciences, including physiology and psychology, are distinguished from the physical sciences by their interest not in lawful happenings . . . but in biologically proper happenings" ("White Queen Psychology," p. 362). But this does not remove the biological, as she conceives it, from what I introduced as the realm of law: it is just that the relevant laws are underwritten by considerations about proper function, rather than inductively based on what actually happens. We still have the contrast with the space of reasons.

29. See an extraordinary passage in Millikan, "Perceptual Content and Fregean Myth," p. 442, in which she takes the idea of "grasping senses" to be a case of "postulating intermediaries," with a view to theorizing about "the underlying nature of the vehicle of thought."

30. Perhaps expressing skepticism about whether there must be any such internal mechanics. Consider, for example, Wittgenstein's notorious remarks about "the prejudice of psychophysical parallelism" (§ 611) at §§ 608 of *Zettel* (Oxford: Blackwell, 1967/1981).

31. Millikan, "Perceptual Content and Fregean Myth," p. 442.

32. Millikan, "White Queen Psychology," p. 280.

33. Is it a difficulty that the "head-world system" is itself only a syntactic engine? Millikan must hope that if we describe it in a way that is suitably organized in terms of biological function, we shall be describing it in a way that reveals it as genuinely instantiating rationality—as a semantic engine. This strikes me as a fantasy, but I need not substantiate that impression; my present point is that even if we allow Millikan what she must hope for, it does not yield a satisfactory answer to the question "What thinks (what exercises semantic rationality)?"

34. John Searle is unique among contemporary neo-Cartesians in thinking he can both deimmaterialize the Cartesian *res cogitans* and keep its remarkable powers.

35. See my "Putnam on Mind and Meaning," *Meaning, Knowledge, and Reality* (Cambridge: Harvard University Press, 1998).

36. Dennett's thinking shows this blemish in parts. He endorses Millikan's attack on Frege. And consider this passage from Dennett, *Consciousness Explained*, p. 41: "Dualism, the idea that a brain cannot be a thinking thing so a thinking thing cannot be a brain, is tempting for a variety of reasons, but we must resist temptation. . . . Somehow the brain must be the mind." But a brain *cannot* be a thinking thing (it is, as Dennett himself remarks, just a syntactic engine). Dualism resides not in the perfectly correct thought that a brain is not a thinking thing, but in postulating something immaterial to be the thinking thing that the brain is not, instead of realizing that the thinking thing is the rational animal. Dennett can be comfortable with the thought that the brain must be the mind, in combination with his own awareness that the brain is just a syntactic engine, only because he thinks that in the sense in which the brain is not *really* a thinking thing, nothing is: the status of possessor of intentional states is conferred by adoption of the intentional stance toward it, and that is no more correct for animals than for brains, or indeed thermostats. But this is a gratuitous addition to the real insight embodied in the invocation of the intentional stance. Rational animals genuinely are "semantic engines." (It is irrelevant to this claim that the intentionality of rational animals is a product of evolution, a causal outcome of "intentionality" on the part of "Mother Nature"; compare pp. 287–321 of Dennett, *Intentional Stance*.) The blemish is detachable: much of the material in, say, *Consciousness Explained* is illuminating independently of Dennett's neo-Cartesian thought that the brain must be the mind. It makes a contribution to the study of "the mechanics of consciousness" in an acceptable sense, not parallel to the sense in which Millikan supposes that Frege must have been concerned with the mechanics of intentionality.

6. Naturalism and Skepticism

1. Thanks to Jody Azzouni, Mario De Caro, and Peter Menzies for comments on an earlier draft of this essay. I have also benefited from many stimulating conversations with Stephen L. White.

2. Immanuel Kant, *Critique of Pure Reason*, trans. Norman Kemp Smith (London: Macmillan, 1929), B ed., p. xl.

3. René Descartes, *Meditations on First Philosophy*, trans. John Cottingham (Cambridge: Cambridge University Press, 1986).

4. I shall also speak of this as *answering* the skeptic. Note that it is a condition of a successful refutation (or answer) that it not beg the question against the skeptic. This has proved to be a very demanding condition to meet.

5. Descartes, *Meditations*.

6. Kant, *Critique of Pure Reason*.

7. G. E. Moore, "Proof of an External World," *Philosophical Papers* (London: George, Allen & Unwin, 1959).

8. Gilbert Harman, *Skepticism and the Definition of Knowledge* (New York: Garland, 1990).

9. Stewart Cohen, "How To Be a Fallibilist," in James Tomberlin, ed., *Philosophical Perspectives* 2 (1988): 91–123.

10. Ted Warfield, "A Priori Knowledge of the World: Knowing the World by Knowing Our Minds," *Philosophical Studies* 92 (1998): 127–147.

11. See Barry Stroud, preface to *The Significance of Philosophical Skepticism* (Oxford: Clarendon, 1984).

12. Scientific naturalism involves methodological (or epistemological) and onto-logical elements that are, in principle, distinguishable though they are often con-joined in practice. For the purposes of this paper I leave aside the semantic version of scientific naturalism that attempts to provide a reductive account of "problematic" concepts in terms of naturalistic concepts.

13. Richard Fumerton, "Skepticism and Naturalistic Epistemology," in P. A. French, T. E. Uehling, and H. K. Wettstein, eds., *Midwest Studies in Philosophy*, vol. 19, *Philosophical Naturalism* (Notre Dame: University of Notre Dame Press, 1994), pp. 321–340, quotation from p. 324.

14. David Hume, *A Treatise of Human Nature*, 2nd ed., rev. and ed. P. H. Nidditch (Oxford: Clarendon, 1978), bk. 1, pt. 4, sec. 1.

15. W. V. Quine, "The Nature of Natural Knowledge," in Samuel Guttenplan, ed., *Mind and Language* (Oxford: Oxford University Press, 1975), pp. 67–81, quota-tion from p. 68.

16. The distinction I draw between refutation and quietism is similar to Michael Williams's distinction between constructive and diagnostic responses to skepticism. See Michael Williams, *Unnatural Doubts* (Oxford: Blackwell, 1991), preface, pp. xv–xvii.

17. Compare McDowell's characterization: "my move is <u>not well cast as an *answer*</u> <u>to skeptical challenges</u>; it is more like <u>a justification of a refusal to bother with them.</u>" John McDowell, "Knowledge and the Internal," *Philosophy and Phenomenological Re-search* 55 (1995): 877–893, fn. 19.

18. As we shall see, I want to allow for the possibility that contemporary natural-ism diverges from Hume's position in various respects.

19. W. V. Quine, *Theories and Things* (Cambridge: Harvard University Press, 1981), p. 21. Elsewhere he explains naturalism simply as "abandonment of the goal of first philosophy" (p. 72).

20. D. M. Armstrong, "Naturalism, Materialism, and First Philosophy," *The Na-ture of Mind and Other Essays* (St. Lucia: University of Queensland Press, 1980), pp. 149–165. Cynthia MacDonald captures the spirit of this position in remarking, "What unifies physicalist-naturalists and biological naturalists is the belief that all natural processes are causal processes." Cynthia MacDonald, "What Is Empiricism? Part 2: Nativism, Naturalism, and Evolutionary Theory," *Proceedings of the Aristotelian Society* supp. 64 (1990): 81–92.

21. Naturalists identify causation with a mind- and context-independent structure of efficient, lawlike, causal relations. At most, context only enters the account in helping to pick out "the cause" from "background causal factors." This view of cau-sation leads naturalists to reject or overlook the possibility of other kinds of causation (for example, singular causation and formal causation), and to deny that the concept of causation has intentional or occasion-sensitive elements. For a recent defense of a contextualist view of causation, see Peter Menzies, "Difference-Making in Context," in John Collins et al., eds., *Counterfactuals and Causation* (forthcoming from MIT Press, 2004).

22. As Strawson observes, the notion of mechanical transaction, and the related ideas of links or chains of causation, are fundamental to the concept of efficient causation. See Peter Strawson, *Analysis and Metaphysics* (Oxford: Oxford University Press, 1992), pp. 118–119.

23. See David Armstrong, *What Is a Law of Nature?* (Cambridge: Cambridge Uni-versity Press, 1989).

24. For both a good summary of the issues and a contribution to the debate, see Mark Colyvan, *The Indispensability of Mathematics* (Oxford: Oxford University Press, 2001).

25. Bundle dualism is committed to a dualism of perceptions (impressions and ideas) and the body as an external existence. Hume, *Treatise*, bk. 1, pt. 4, sec. 6.

26. This was, until recently, the standard reading of Hume. See David Fate Norton, "Introduction to Hume's Thought," in David Fate Norton, ed., *The Cambridge Companion to Hume* (Cambridge: Cambridge University Press, 1993), p. 7.

27. Certainly, if we assume that in experience we are confronted not with ordinary things such as trees, cars, and people but with an array of discontinuous mind-dependent "sensory ideas" or "impressions" then there is an obvious gap between what is immediately given in experience and the external world we believe on the basis of it. The moral to be drawn from the history of unsuccessful attempts to bridge this gap is that classical empiricism is inherently skeptical.

28. This misinterpretation of the relation between naturalism and skepticism arises because Hume's causal account of the belief in the external world, in which its origin is traced to the imagination, is widely supposed to be a challenge to the skeptic's insistence that this belief stands in need of rational justification. Notwithstanding, Hume did not think of naturalism as a philosophically adequate response to skepticism. Naturalism merely *replaces* skepticism as a matter of fact whenever we leave the study. See, for example, David Hume, *Enquiries Concerning Human Understanding*, 3rd ed., rev. and ed. P. H. Nidditch (Oxford: Clarendon, 1777/1975), sec. 22, pt. 1 (119). This reading has been convincingly defended by Janet Broughton, "Skepticism and Naturalization in Book One of Hume's *Treatise*" (unpublished manuscript).

29. The independence of (subjective) experience from the external world is suggested by perceptual errors in which appearance and reality come apart.

30. Note that on either the intentionalist or the adverbialist construals, subjective experience is not the object of perception but its means. That is enough to show that the causal model need not be understood as a version of what McDowell calls the highest common factor model of experience. Indeed, a skeptic could happily accept a disjunctive account of subjective experience. What he could not accept, of course, is content externalism. See John McDowell, "Criteria, Defeasibility, and Knowledge," *Proceedings of the British Academy* 68 (1982): 455–479.

31. Hume, *Enquiries*, sec. 22, pt. 1 (119).

32. Note that this argument does not presuppose any commitment to dualism of any variety. Since we are posing the argument as a challenge to naturalists we can grant, for the sake of argument, that the mind is realized in the brain or, perhaps, in some other material form. The inner-outer distinction will still be drawn in terms of subjective experiences and the external world. However, there will now be a further distinction between the matter in which the mind is realized and the matter that lies outside the mind, if there is such.

For a further defense of the claim that the skeptical problem can arise within various nondualist conceptions of mind (for example, behaviorism, identity theory, and functionalism), given a commitment to the autonomy or self-containedness of mind, see Gregory McCulloch, *The Mind and Its World* (London: Routledge, 1995). McCulloch seems to think that the motivation for a commitment to the autonomy of mind is Descartes' conceivability argument for the real distinction between mind and body. My claim is that a more powerful motivation arises from first-person reflection upon the causal model of experience.

33. I agree with Tyler Burge in reading Descartes "as capitalizing on the causal gap that we tend to assume there is between the world and its effects on us: different causes could have produced 'the same' effects." Tyler Burge, "Cartesian Error and Perception," in John McDowell and Philip Pettit, eds., *Subject, Thought, and Context* (Oxford: Clarendon, 1986), pp. 117–136, quotation from pp. 120–121.

However, I contest Burge's further contention that "[t]he causal elements by themselves do not support the individualist position," especially if we consider these elements in the context of the inner-outer distinction from the first-person perspective. Contra Burge, individualism is strongly suggested by the thought that different external causes would bring about the same mental effects. Burge rejects this on the ground that it begs the question against anti-individualism. But if we are concerned with those considerations that intuitively lead us to embrace individualism, this response is beside the point.

34. I have followed McDowell in connecting the attraction of "the idea of the inner realm as self-standing . . . [to] a plausible aspiration to accommodate psychology within a pattern of explanation characteristic of the natural sciences." John McDowell, "Singular Thought and the Extent of Inner Space," in McDowell and Pettit, *Subject, Thought, and Context*, pp. 137–168, quotation from p. 152.

35. See Burge, "Cartesian Error and Perception," for a more careful and elaborate account of individualism.

36. Wilfred Sellars, *Science, Perception, and Reality* (London: Routledge, 1963). My characterization of the manifest image is a modification of Sellars's.

37. One well-known application of this general idea concerns the ontological status of colors. Insofar as colors are not posited by the natural sciences, the naturalist must either ontologically reduce them to scientifically respectable properties or else deny their apparent status as objective properties of material objects. Given the difficulties in finding a plausible physicalist reduction of colors, colors come to be thought of as mere "projections" of mind at best correlated with some disjunction of physical properties (for example, reflectance properties). See C. L. Hardin, *Color for Philosophers: Unweaving the Rainbow* (Indianapolis: Hackett, 1988). Similar considerations point to a projectivism about value.

38. One case that may be worth mentioning is the naturalist who blocks the skeptical argument by presupposing content externalism. Brian McLaughlin has recently argued that externalist theories of content are, even if a priori, empirically defeasible, so that any warrant they provide for an antiskeptical thesis inevitably begs the question against the skeptic. See Brian McLaughlin, "Self-Knowledge, Externalism, and Skepticism—Part I," *Proceedings of the Aristotelian Society* supp. 74 (2000): 93–117.

39. In conversation, I have heard naturalists suggest that their position is clearly rationally preferable to skepticism simply because it is antiskeptical!

40. In its strongest form, skepticism "threatens our conceptual system from the inside," as Putnam has put it. Hilary Putnam, "Skepticism," in *Festschrift für Dieter Heinrich* (Frankfurt am Main: Suhrkamp, 2000), p. 40.

41. Peter Strawson, *Skepticism and Naturalism: Some Varieties* (New York: Columbia University Press, 1985), p. 20.

42. This view has also been defended by Williams, *Unnatural Doubts*, pp. 54–55, and James Pryor, "How To Be a Reasonable Dogmatist" (Ph.D. diss., Princeton University, 1996), pp. 57–61.

43. In showing that the inference to the best explanation fails in the context of an answer to the skeptic, I have not, of course, demonstrated that there is no way of

refuting the skeptic. But I believe that this does show that the hope of their being such a refutation is rather dim—especially in light of the long history of unconvincing "refutations."

44. See Richard Rorty, *Philosophy and the Mirror of Nature* (Oxford: Blackwell, 1980).

45. For a recent example of such a response, see Hilary Putnam, "Strawson and Skepticism," in L. E. Hahn, ed., *The Philosophy of P. F. Strawson* (Chicago: Open Court, 1998).

46. In "Epistemology Naturalized," *Ontological Relativity and Other Essays* (New York: Columbia University Press, 1969), pp. 69–90, Quine can be read as refusing to engage with the skeptic's question of rational justification, shifting instead to the genetic question of how observations, physicalistically described, can give rise to science. But even here Quine speaks of naturalism as a continuation of traditional epistemology. And in "The Nature of Natural Knowledge," Quine is clearly appealing to naturalism as a response, but not an answer, to skepticism.

47. In "Epistemology Naturalized," Quine's understanding of "sensory evidence" in terms of "the stimulation of his sensory receptors" (p. 75) and "certain patterns of irradiation" (p. 83) is carefully designed to avoid any reference to conscious awareness.

48. The naturalist tendency to deny subjective awareness is noted by Peter Strawson in *Skepticism and Naturalism*, p. 67.

49. Quine, "Nature of Natural Knowledge," p. 67.

50. W. V. Quine, "Reply to Stroud," in *Midwest Studies in Philosophy*, vol. 6 (Minneapolis: University of Minnesota Press, 1981), pp. 473–475, quotation from p. 475.

51. Quine, "Nature of Natural Knowledge," p. 67.

52. Quine, "Epistemology Naturalized," p. 82.

53. See Alvin Goldman, *Epistemology and Cognition* (Cambridge: Harvard University Press, 1986), pp. 36, 55.

54. In the modern period, skepticism tends to be viewed as primarily concerned with demonstrating that knowledge is not possible. See Bernard Williams, *Descartes: The Project of Pure Enquiry* (New York: Penguin, 1978), p. 62.

55. Ancient Pyrrhonian skeptics used arguments to show that for any belief that-P one might be committed to, there is equal reason to believe not-P, so that one ought to suspend judgment on the matter. They did not argue that justified belief or knowledge is not possible, but simply that, all things considered, we find that we do not have any as a matter of fact. See Gisela Striker, "Skepticism as a Kind of Philosophy" (unpublished manuscript).

56. Goldman makes a substantial concession to skepticism when he notes that his analysis of knowledge in terms of reliability "cannot be expected to entail that we *do* know, or that we know very much or very often." Goldman, *Epistemology and Cognition*, p. 55. However, he goes on to offer a question-begging appeal to psychology as the science that can determine whether our cognitive processes are reliable.

57. Strawson, *Skepticism and Naturalism*, p. 51.

58. Hume, *Treatise*, bk. 1, pt. 4, sec. 1.

59. Strawson endorses the position of many philosophers in holding that "the skeptical challenge is perfectly intelligible, perfectly meaningful." Strawson, *Skepticism and Naturalism*, p. 7.

60. Strawson admits that if you want a reason to believe in the existence of the external world you may be able to find one. However, his point is that your belief

will not be *based* on this reason; it will not be explained by the availability of this reason should you discover it.

61. Ludwig Wittgenstein, *On Certainty* (Oxford: Blackwell, 1969).

62. See, for example, Ludwig Wittgenstein, *Philosophical Investigations* (Oxford: Blackwell, 1958), §§ 109, 128. I have argued elsewhere that Strawson's attribution of the foundationalist theory of hinge propositions to Wittgenstein is based on a familiar misreading; and that Wittgenstein is concerned to undermine the attractions of the view that there are particular beliefs, assumptions, or presuppositions that frame any and every operation of our rational capacities. See David Macarthur, "Skeptical Reason and Inner Experience" (Ph.D. diss., Harvard University, 1999), chap. 4.

63. See W. V. Quine, *From a Logical Point of View* (Cambridge: Harvard University Press, 1964), chap. 2.

64. The matter of unrevisability has to be handled carefully, since there is a question whether we can even understand what it would be to revise some a priori propositions (for example, basic truths of mathematics and logic). We might formulate the point better by saying that there is no guarantee that what we currently regard as a priori truths will not be revised in the future. See Hilary Putnam, "Re-thinking Mathematical Necessity," *Words and Life* (Cambridge: Harvard University Press, 1994).

65. David Velleman, "The Guise of the Good," *Noûs* 26, no. 1 (1992): 3–26, quotation from p. 14.

66. This has been aptly described as reason's "transpersonal function of presenting true thoughts and guiding thought to truth, regardless of individual perspective and interest." Tyler Burge, "Reason and the First-Person," in Cynthia MacDonald, Barry Smith, and Crispin Wright, eds., *Knowing Our Own Minds* (Oxford: Oxford University Press, 1998), pp. 243–270, quotation from p. 254.

67. Strawson's account suggests that the skeptical threat is to our continuing to hold the belief in the external world. But this is a mistake. The skeptical challenge is meta-level, challenging whether we have good enough or sufficient reason to believe as we do. The skeptic need not dispute the tenacity of our beliefs.

68. This is closely related to what some philosophers conceive of as a clash between what are called the subjective and objective points of view. See, notably, Thomas Nagel, "The Absurd," in *Mortal Questions* (Cambridge: Cambridge University Press, 1979).

7. Intentionality and Norms

1. The subject of the normative nature of our intentional states is a very large subject, one of the largest in philosophy, and one that needs a whole book to discuss what I will be cramming into one short paper. Fuller expositions and arguments are attempted in a longer work presently under way, tentatively titled *The Value in Reason*. I should like to thank Carol Rovane, Isaac Levi, Stephen White, and Philip Kitcher for very helpful comments on this paper.

2. Saul Kripke, *Wittgenstein on Rules and Private Languages* (Cambridge: Harvard University Press, 1982).

3. Akeel Bilgrami, *Belief and Meaning* (Oxford: Basil Blackwell, 1992). For a more specific and pointed discussion of just this point, see my "Precis of 'Belief and Meaning' " in the symposium on the book in *Philosophy and Phenomenological Research* 58

(1998): 595–606, and in "Norms and Meaning," in Ralph Stoecker, ed., *Reflecting Davidson* (Berlin: De Gruyter, 1993), pp. 121–144. For a very plausible and congenial discussion of this point, see the discussion of rules and norms of meaning by Noam Chomsky in his *Knowledge of Language* (New York: Praeger, 1986), and the discussion of conventions in Donald Davidson's "A Nice Derangement of Epitaphs," in Ernest Lepore, ed., *Perspectives on Truth and Interpretation* (Oxford: Blackwell, 1986).

4. See Kripke, *Wittgenstein on Rules and Private Languages,* pp. 35–37.

5. Donald Davidson, "Mental Events," in *Essays on Actions and Events* (Oxford: Oxford University Press, 1980), pp. 207–227.

6. The Moorean nature of Kripke's points are never made explicit by him, but they are clearly assumed in his arguments, and I will draw them out in this paper. For Moore, see the first two chapters of his *Principia Ethica* (Cambridge: Cambridge University Press, 1903).

7. It is not clear actually that something like inductive logic is constitutive of beliefs as commitments, and it may be more sensible to restrict the normative principles constituting our beliefs qua commitments to something as minimal as the codifications of deductive rationality.

8. When one says a belief qua commitment is a state that is characterized in terms of the other beliefs that it entails and to which one is committed to believing, one is using the notion of belief to characterize a belief. But there is no great harm in this, since the goal is not to give something like an explicit definition of belief.

9. The first philosopher to have systematically treated intentional states as "commitments" is Isaac Levi. See his *Enterprise of Knowledge* (Cambridge: MIT Press, 1983). I differ from Levi on issues having to do with the extent of what count as commitments, and these differences issue from the fact that our interest in the notion seems to come from different contexts. Levi's primary use of the notion is situated in his interest in belief revision. He is skeptical of my interest in situating the idea in a notion of intentionality as commitment derived in part from a modified Strawsonian notion of agency in terms of the reactive attitudes. Despite these differences, I have been much influenced by his general stress on commitments in the study of intentionality. Robert Brandom in his *Making It Explicit* (Cambridge: Harvard University Press, 1994) also makes elaborate and interesting use of the notion of commitment.

10. The locus classicus is of course "Naming and Necessity" by Kripke himself, in Donald Davidson and Gilbert Harman, eds., *Semantics for Natural Language* (Boston: Reidl, 1972). Also Putnam's "The Meaning of Meaning," in Keith Gunderson, ed., *Language, Mind, and Knowledge: Minnesota Studies in the Philosophy of Language,* vol. 7 (Minneapolis: Minnesota University Press, 1975). It is mildly ironic that causal theories of reference formulated by Kripke might be relevant in this way to recent versions of naturalism about value, a naturalism that Kripke opposes. The irony will get a little less mild just below in the text, when I actually exploit a Fregean argument of the sort Kripke has deeply opposed in his writings on reference, in order to support Kripke's Moorean antinaturalism about intentionality and value.

11. Recent work by Richard Boyd is a good example of this second and more recent strain of naturalism about value. See his "How To Be a Moral Realist," in G. Sayre-McCord, ed., *Essays on Moral Realism* (New York: Cornell University Press, 1980). Sturgeon, Railton, and Brink are other philosophers writing within this broadly characterized form of ethical naturalism, despite the detailed differences among their positions.

12. See Gottlob Frege, "On Sense and Reference," in Peter Geach and Max Black, eds., *Philosophical Writings* (Oxford: Blackwell, 1952).

13. This Fregean argument is of course a perfectly general one and I have been deploying it for various ends against naturalist and certain forms of externalist accounts of mind in a number of my writings on the subject of intentionality. With somewhat other purposes in mind, Brian Loar used Fregean arguments of this kind very instructively and in detail in a paper titled "Social Content and Psychological Content," which I commented on at the Oberlin Colloquium, subsequently published as an exchange in Patrick Grimm et al., eds., *Contents of Thought* (Tucson: University of Arizona Press, 1985). But, following Loar, I have restricted my use of it to the study of intentional states. For a skillful use of it to resist materialist theories of phenomenal states such as pain, see Stephen White's paper "The Property Dualism Argument," forthcoming in the *Journal of Philosophy*.

14. Michael Devitt, for example, in his *Designation* (New York: Columbia University Press, 1981) explicitly says that this view is what is entailed by any workable causal-theoretic notion of the reference of terms. Kripke himself, to whom we owe the causal view of reference, treaded much more carefully on this and various other matters about which philosophers like Devitt have rushed in on his behalf.

15. For a carefully worked out and illuminating statement of this view, see P. Kyle Stanford and Philip Kitcher, "Refining the Causal Theory of Reference for Natural Kind Terms," *Philosophical Studies* 97 (1999): 99–129.

16. I guardedly say this because terms like "sky," "city," and "ocean" themselves will not figure in the ultimate scientific description of the world either, but for many there is an assumption regarding their relation to the terms that will figure in that description, an assumption that, it is being claimed by me, does not hold of evaluative terms on grounds of principle. For a forceful expression of a quite plausible view that denies that the very notion of reference has any role to play in any scientific study of language precisely because terms like "sky," "city," and the like are not assimilable into a genuinely scientific vocabulary, see various essays by Chomsky in his *New Horizons in the Study of Language and Mind* (Cambridge: Cambridge University Press, 2000).

17. What I am saying here is intended to be sympathetic to something that John McDowell has said in response to John Mackie's claim that evaluative facts would be a "queer" sort of facts. McDowell, as is well known, compares evaluative terms to terms describing secondary qualities. Of course we would find evaluative facts "queer" if we modeled them on primary qualities, he argues, but we need not find them queer if we modeled them on secondary qualities. It is his further claim that terms like "red" and "good" describe something just as real as "square" even if terms like "red" and "good" do not figure in the conceptual vocabulary of fundamental science. To deny this last claim is to express the same prejudice as the one I am inveighing against when I say that my naturalist opponent is working with a criterion for property existence that is scientistic when he says that the senses I have shown to be necessary by my argument do not describe anything real, they do not describe any evaluative properties.

18. For example, David Lewis in his "Dispositional Theories of Value," *Proceedings of the Aristotelian Society* supp. 62 (1989): 113–137.

19. In my book *Self-Knowledge and Resentment* (forthcoming from Harvard University Press in 2004) I argue that things are in fact much more general than that since the irreducible normativity of value is of a piece with the uniqueness of the

first-person perspective of agency that an agent has on his or her own intentional states; and I do so by developing the normative notion of agency found in P. F. Strawson's seminal paper "Freedom and Resentment," in *Freedom and Resentment and Other Essays* (London: Methuen, 1972).

20. I say "sometimes" because they clearly don't always have to be absent whenever there is a failure. They can be present but the failure is due to some other factor.

21. In making this point I have restricted the discussion to the second-order disposition underlying the preparedness to accept criticism, but the same point apples equally to the second-order disposition underlying the preparedness to cultivate the relevant first-order dispositions. Here too there is no way to characterize the second-order dispositions, except as the disposition to cultivate the first-order disposition to live up to the commitment that p, the disposition to cultivate the first-order disposition to live up to the commitment that q, the disposition to cultivate the first-order disposition to live up to the commitment that r.

22. In the work mentioned in note 1, I elaborate on this point much more fully, responding to objections. In it, I also look at the possibility of reading the preparedness as itself being a commitment, a second-order commitment, and not a second-order disposition. This raises difficulties having to do with regress, and other possibly deeper difficulties, which are discussed there at length.

23. Ryle did when he talked of dispositions merely as inference tickets. When it came to mental dispositions, he was in fact quite skeptical of the psychologistic, naturalistic underpinning of dispositions in causal terms. That development of giving it that underpinning came only with philosophers much later who developed the doctrine of functionalism along non-Rylean lines, even though Dennett among them is in some ways a functionalist who has kept faith with some aspects of Ryle in an interesting attempt at a hybrid position, whether in the end successful or not.

24. References to this principle can be found in many papers of his both in the philosophy of language and in the theory of action. They are pervasive and too numerous to mention. See the essays in his two volumes *Essays on Actions and Events* and *Inquiries into Truth and Interpretation* (Oxford: Oxford University Press, 1980 and 1984).

25. In fact because Davidson is convinced that we cannot but be living up to the principles of rationality (necessary charity, as he thinks of it), he does not even feel much pressure to think that we have a minimal commitment to the principles of rationality, leave alone beliefs and desires being commitments.

26. It is doubtful since it is always possible that we fail to live up to our commitments.

27. A. I. Melden, R. S. Peters, and Peter Winch are three among other authors in that series, which expressed some suspicion of the idea that reasons are causes.

8. Could There Be a Science of Rationality?

1. Ludwig Wittgenstein, *Philosophical Investigations* (Oxford: Oxford University Press, 1953), pt. 2, p. xiv.

2. Gilbert Ryle, *The Concept of Mind* (New York: Barnes & Noble, 1949), pp. 324–325.

3. W. V. Quine, "Mind and Verbal Dispositions," in Samuel Guttenplan, ed., *Mind and Language* (Oxford: Oxford University Press, 1975), pp. 83–95, quotation from p. 92.

4. W. V. Quine, *Word and Object* (Cambridge: MIT Press, 1960), p. 221.

5. The quoted passages are on pp. 87–91 and p. 84.

6. Quine, "Mind and Verbal Dispositions," p. 92.

7. Quine, *Word and Object*, p. 17.

8. The quotations are from W. V. Quine, *The Roots of Reference* (La Salle: Open Court, 1974), pp. 3, 36, 12, 33–34.

9. I introduced the phrase and the idea in "Mental Events" (1970), reprinted in *Actions and Events* (Oxford: Oxford University Press, 1980).

10. See, for example, "Mental Events" and "Three Varieties of Knowledge," in A. Phillips Griffiths ed., *A. J. Ayer: Memorial Essays: Royal Institute of Philosophy*, supp. 30 (Cambridge: Cambridge University Press, 1991), pp. 153–166.

11. I draw on Richard Jeffrey's version in *The Logic of Decision*, 2nd ed. (Chicago: University of Chicago Press, 1983). F. M. Ramsey's original theory is reprinted in *Philosophical Papers*, ed. D. H. Mellor (Cambridge: Cambridge University Press, 1990).

12. These remarks about the relevant scales apply strictly to Ramsey's theory; Jeffrey's theory is marginally different.

13. For some details, see my "The Structure and Content of Truth," *Journal of Philosophy* 87 (1990): 279–328.

14. The following discussion abbreviates a more detailed treatment of Fodor's criticism in my "Interpreting Radical Interpretation," in James Tomberlin, ed., *Philosophical Perspectives* 8, *Logic and Language* (1994): 121–128. Also printed in Ralf Stoecker, ed., *Reflecting Davidson: Donald Davidson Responding to an International Forum of Philosophers* (Berlin: De Gruyter, 1993), pp. 77–84. Both these sources print the article by Jerry Fodor and Ernest Lepore, "Is Radical Interpretation Possible?" (respectively, pp. 101–119 and pp. 56–76) to which I am replying. The passages quoted from Chomsky come from John Earman, ed., *Inference, Explanation, and Other Frustrations: Essays in the Philosophy of Science* (Berkeley: University of California Press, 1992), pp. 108–109.

15. "A Nice Derangement of Epitaphs," in R. E. Grandy and Richard Warner, eds., *Philosophical Grounds of Rationality* (Oxford: Oxford University Press, 1986), pp. 156–174. Reprinted in Ernest Lepore, ed., *Truth and Interpretation: Perspectives on the Philosophy of Donald Davidson* (Oxford: Blackwell, 1986), pp. 433–446.

9. Agency and Alienation

1. David Velleman, "What Happens When Someone Acts?" *Mind* 101 (1992): 461–481. Reprinted at pp. 123–143 in David Velleman, *The Possibility of Practical Reason* (Oxford: Oxford University Press, 2000), to which page references here refer. Quotation from p. 131.

2. The "standard causal story" of action is widely credited to Davidson. Certainly Davidson's work has done a great deal to ensure that the thesis that explanation of what people do that proceeds by giving their reasons is *causal* explanation; and a certain understanding of this thesis gives rise to the standard story (see § 6). But I think that Davidson's claims of the mental's irreducibility ought to discourage the picture of action that I criticize here (and that it would discourage it if a particular view of causality, also Davidsonian, weren't in play). There is further elaboration of the standard story in §§ 5 and 6.

3. Velleman's introduction to *The Possibility of Practical Reason* may not be such an obvious target for my remarks, as I acknowledge in a closing note. (Velleman is

not alone in allowing his naturalistic thinking to lead to very implausible accounts of ourselves as agents. In Jennifer Hornsby, "Agency and Actions," in a volume based on the 2002 Royal Institute of Philosophy Conference: Agency and Action, to be edited by John Hyman and Helen Stewart for Cambridge University Press, I pick on Michael Bratman.)

4. Thomas Nagel, *The View from Nowhere* (Oxford: Oxford University Press, 1986), p. 113.

5. David Hume, *Enquiry Concerning Human Understanding* (London, 1748; repr. Oxford: Clarendon, 1975), § 7, pt. 1.

6. At this stage in the *Enquiry*, Hume is in the process of arguing that we have no impression of causal power. He aims to refute someone who says that such an impression can be obtained from reflection on the influence of our volitions on bits of our bodies that we can move.

7. Velleman, "What Happens When Someone Acts?" p. 124.

8. The claim that one tries to do what one intentionally does may be denied. But this claim introduces nothing that is especially likely to be rejected by those whose style of causal theory I dispute. Indeed the claim can be quite welcome to my opponents: making mention of an event of the agent's trying to do something provides them with an item of a sort that may seem to them to be suited to belong among bodily movements' causal antecedents as they conceive these.

9. Mele aims to provide informative sufficient conditions for an event's being an action in order to win an argument with an opponent who is an "anticausalist teleologist." Alfred Mele, "Goal-Directed Action: Teleological Explanations, Causal Theories, and Deviance," *Philosophical Perspectives* 14 (2000): 279–300. I think that Mele's assumption that anyone who is opposed to "anticausalism" must provide such conditions has prevented philosophers from seeing that there is a more modest causalism than that espoused by those who tell the standard story. (Mele persists with the standard causal story when he responds to Velleman, "What Happens When Someone Acts?" in Alfred Mele, *Motivation and Agency* [Oxford: Oxford University Press, forthcoming], chap. 10. But Mele and I are in agreement (a) that there is no single state of mind corresponding to Velleman's agency *par excellence*, and (b) that some of Velleman's problems about locating agents go away when one acknowledges that an agent is a human being who acts.)

10. Anarchic hand syndrome is a rare condition, owed to injuries to the motor area of the brain and *corpus callosum*, from which Dr. Strangelove (the Peter Sellers character in the Kubrick film of that name) suffered.

11. My way of telling the story assumes that Davidson is right about actions' individuation. There are naturalists who think that Davidson is wrong about that. My claims would need to be recast to count against them.

12. Of course there is a use of "state" such that a person's desiring something or believing something (not to mention having a capacity to move her arm) is a state of hers. But in this use of "state," states don't belong in a category of particulars which includes events—or, as Velleman says, "occurrences, the basic elements of explanation in general . . . in terms of which any explanation of human action will speak." Velleman, "What Happens When Someone Acts?" p. 130. Helen Steward's *The Ontology of Mind: Events, States, and Processes* (Oxford: Oxford University Press, 1997) contains very effective criticism both of the way that "state" has come to be used in philosophy of mind, and of the model of causality that is brought to the subject with a "naturalistic conception of explanation" such as Velleman's.

13. My own claim has been that a bit of a person's body's moving may be causally

dependent on her trying to do something. With the notion of "trying to" introduced, then, it can be all right to speak of "bodily movements." But this is not to say that it is all right to speak of actions themselves as bodily movements—to speak as if a person's doing something were a bit of her body's moving.

14. Velleman, "What Happens When Someone Acts?" p. 129.

15. Ibid., n. 5, p. 128.

16. Cf. § 3.

17. Velleman, "What Happens When Someone Acts?" p. 131.

18. The idea that an agent can be more or less fully identified with what she does is one of the things that leads to Velleman's talk of the agent/action relation as coming in degrees. The language of *identification* crops up sometimes in the personal identity literature, and there it sometimes leads, as it sometimes does in the present case, to an unwarranted reductionism.

19. Velleman, "What Happens When Someone Acts?" p. 128.

20. The picture from Nagel's external perspective in which only events and states are visible extrudes nonhuman animals along with human beings. For something about how human beings may be accommodated into a different picture as, as it were, a special sort of animal, see John McDowell, *Mind and World* (Cambridge: Harvard University Press, 1994), pp. 114–119; and Marie McGinn, "Real Things and the Mind-Body Problem," *Proceedings of the Aristotelian Society* 100 (2000): 303–317, esp. pp. 309–315.

21. Michael Bratman argued this, and demonstrated the shortage in the kinds of mental state that the standard story trades in, in his *Intention, Plans, and Practical Reason* (Cambridge: Harvard University Press, 1987).

22. I quote more or less from Bernard Williams's description of the ingredients in a person's "motivational set" in his "Internal and External Reasons," in *Moral Luck* (Cambridge: Cambridge University Press, 1981), pp. 101–113. Williams's "Voluntary Acts and Responsible Agents," in *Making Sense of Humanity and Other Philosophical Papers* (Cambridge: Cambridge University Press, 1995), is a good antidote for those who are apt to think that there is some one, significant line to be drawn between agency that is genuine/full-blooded/par excellence and agency of a defective sort. But beware: Williams means something different both by "naturalism" and by "action" from what I use these to mean for the purposes of the present paper (see § 1 and parenthetic paragraph in § 3 above).

23. There is much more to be said against the psychological reductionism to which Velleman thinks we are obviously entitled. See, for example, John Dupré, *The Disorder of Things* (Cambridge: Harvard University Press, 1993), esp. chaps. 4 and 7. For those who have joined the naturalists in their habits of thought, it might help to point out that even when one contends that there are facts that are not part of the world defined by their naturalism, plenty of materialist intuitions can be retained. See, for example, John Haugeland, "Ontological Supervenience," *Southern Journal of Philosophy* 22 (1984): 1–12.

24. Velleman, "What Happens When Someone Acts?" p. 130.

25. In his introduction to *The Possibility of Practical Reason* (Oxford University Press, 2000), Velleman no longer wants to draw exactly the line that he aimed at in the paper first published in 1992 discussed above. And Velleman no longer speaks directly to the question of whether states of agents' minds that are introduced to characterize different kinds of agency must belong within an account that subscribes to only a naturalistic conception of explanation. But some of my criticisms still apply,

I think. In the introduction, Velleman retains the idea that there is some *one* property of agents that we must uncover to characterize autonomous action. And he carries on with the idea of "adding to the standard model" (pp. 10–12). His thoughts about "a mechanism modifying the motivational forces [already] at work" in a creature not endowed with practical reason also show him as captive still to the conception under attack in the present paper, I think.

The distinction that Velleman wants to capture in the introduction is between autonomous action and mere activity (as opposed to the 1992 distinction between agency *par excellence* and something relatively defective). Mere activities include so-called subintentional cases (along with the cases of defective agency of concern in "What Happens When Someone Acts?"). This means that the category within which the new distinction is to be made is not the category of actions as I have characterized these here, using "intentionally." Still, the crucial line on which I should insist is that between cases where the agent belongs in the story and cases where she does not. Thus I would agree with Velleman that one could find fault with the standard story for its assumption that the only important line to be drawn comes between actions (as characterized here) and other events. (This doesn't come to the surface in the present paper, but it will have repercussions for how one thinks of the "personal level" of explanation.)

Velleman has been a suitable person for me to single out for criticism because a naturalistic metaphysics informs his work even though the questions he addresses are not stock questions in theory of action. Certainly his work on agency in the last decade (see papers in *The Possibility of Practical Reason* and subsequent papers) contains much that is of immense interest and that can be disentangled from the naturalistic thinking that I have criticized here.

10. Is Freedom Really a Mystery?

1. As it has been noticed (for example by Robert Kane, *The Significance of Free Will* [Oxford: Oxford University Press, 1996], pp. 12–14), the term "problem of free will" covers different issues. Here I will discuss in particular the possibility of justifying the intuition of freedom, and the compatibility of freedom with causal determinism and indeterminism.

2. On this point, see Peter van Inwagen, *Metaphysics* (Boulder: Westview Press, 1993), p. 187: "the majority of twentieth-century English-speaking philosophers have been compatibilists." Indeed, the fortune of compatibilism (in its many different versions) during the early decades of the twentieth century was limited to the analytic world, since traditionally most continental philosophers sympathize with the opposite view of "incompatibilism," according to which freedom and causal determinism are incompatible. (Customarily, incompatibilists who believe in human freedom are called "libertarians"; those who deny it, and hold causal determinism, are called "hard determinists.") For an analysis of these views, see L. W. Ekstrom, *Free Will: A Philosophical Study* (Boulder: Westview, 2000).

3. See, for instance, Moritz Schlick, "When a Man Is Responsible," English translation in Bernard Berofsky, ed., *Free Will and Determinism* (New York: Harper and Row, 1966), pp. 54–63; R. E. Hobart, "Free Will as Involving Determinism and Inconceivable Without It," in Berofsky, *Free Will and Determinism*, pp. 63–95; and Alfred Ayer, "Freedom and Necessity," in Gary Watson, ed., *Free Will* (Oxford: Oxford University Press, 1982), pp. 15–23. Actually these authors, and many others,

affirm (following Hume) that freedom is not only compatible with causal determinism, but actually *requires* it; this position is sometimes called "supercompatibilism." For a contemporary version of compatibilism that is not supercompatibilist, see D. C. Dennett, *Elbow Room* (Cambridge: MIT Press, 1984).

4. Schlick, "When a Man Is Responsible," p. 54.

5. Donald Davidson, "Freedom to Act," in *Essays on Actions and Events* (Oxford: Clarendon, 1980), pp. 63–81, quotation from p. 63.

6. W. V. Quine, "Things and Their Place in Theories," in *Theories and Things* (Cambridge: Harvard University Press), pp. 1–23, quotation from p. 11.

7. Watson, *Free Will*; Timothy O'Connor, ed., *Agents, Causes, and Events: The Metaphysics of Free Will* (Oxford: Oxford University Press, 1995); *Philosophical Topics* 24 (1996), special issue; Laura W. Ekstrom, ed., *Agency and Responsibility: Essays on the Metaphysics of Freedom* (Boulder: Westview, 2001); Robert Kane, ed., *Free Will* (Oxford: Blackwell, 2002); Robert Kane, ed., *The Oxford Handbook of Free Will* (Oxford: Oxford University Press, 2002).

8. I take the term "restricted naturalism" from Barry Stroud's "The Charm of Naturalism" (reprinted in this volume); for the term "scientific naturalism," see the Introduction to this volume. Both these terms refer to views that attribute absolute epistemological and ontological primacy to the sciences—in particular to the natural sciences, and very often to physics only. With regard to this, I agree with Jennifer Hornsby, who sees continuity between contemporary orthodox naturalism—what can be called "restricted" or "scientific"—and the physicalism of the 1960s and 1970s. See her *Simple Mindedness: In Defense of Naive Naturalism in the Philosophy of Mind* (Cambridge: Harvard University Press, 1997), p. 9; see also Putnam's essay in this volume. This, of course, cannot be said of the sorts of naturalism defended by Hornsby herself or by John McDowell in *Mind and World* (Cambridge: Harvard University Press, 1994).

9. T. S. Kuhn, *The Structure of Scientific Revolutions* (Chicago: University of Chicago Press, 1962), chap. 8.

10. Ibid., p. 84.

11. Peter van Inwagen, *Metaphysics* (Boulder: Westview, 1993), p. 33.

12. Thomas Nagel, *The View from Nowhere* (Oxford: Oxford University Press, 1985), p. 112.

13. Ibid., pp. 119–120.

14. Peter van Inwagen, "The Mystery of Metaphysical Freedom," in Peter van Inwagen and David Zimmerman, eds., *Metaphysics: The Big Questions* (Oxford: Blackwell 1998), pp. 365–374; Peter van Inwagen, "Free Will Remains a Mystery," *Philosophical Perspectives* 12 (2000): 1–19.

15. Van Inwagen, "Mystery of Metaphysical Freedom," p. 374.

16. Colin McGinn, *The Mysterious Flame: Conscious Minds in a Material World* (New York: Basic Books, 1999), p. 168.

17. See van Inwagen, "Mystery of Metaphysical Freedom," p. 373.

18. Richard Double, *The Non-Reality of Free Will* (Oxford: Oxford University Press, 1991); Saul Smilansky, *Free Will and Illusion* (Oxford: Oxford University Press, 2000) (in this book, Smilansky [who labels his conception "Illusionism"] recognizes the relevance of the idea of freedom, even though he thinks that it is nothing more than an illusion: "Humanity is fortunately deceived on the free will issue, and this seems to be a condition of civilized morality and personal success" [p. 6]); Derk Pereboom, *Living Without Free Will* (Cambridge: Cambridge University Press, 2001); D. M. Wegner, *The Illusion of Conscious Will* (Cambridge: MIT Press, 2002).

19. See, for example, Ted Honderich, *A Theory of Determinism*, 2 vols. (Oxford: Oxford University Press, 1988); Galen Strawson, *Freedom and Belief* (Oxford: Oxford University Press, 1986); and Richard Double, *Metaphilosophy and Free Will* (Oxford: Oxford University Press, 1996).

20. For example, Harry Frankfurt ("Alternate Possibilities and Moral Responsibility," *Journal of Philosophy* 66 [1969]: 829–839) argues that moral responsibility does not require the "possibility to do otherwise," which many consider an essential component of freedom together with some form of "self-determination" or "control." On this point, see J. M. Fischer, "Frankfurt-Style Examples, Responsibility, and Semi-Compatibilism," in Kane, *Free Will*, pp. 95–109, and here, para. 3. Similar theses are defended by P. F. Strawson ("Freedom and Resentment," *Proceedings of the British Academy* 48 [1962]: 1–25) and Dennett (*Elbow Room*, chap. 8).

21. See Kane, *Significance of Free Will*, chap. 3; and Ekstrom, *Free Will*, pp. 139–214.

22. Double, *Metaphilosophy and Free Will*, p. 156.

23. See Kane, *Oxford Handbook of Free Will*, for a discussion of many contemporary libertarian and compatibilist views.

24. Lorenzo Valla, C. S. Peirce, and William James, for example, were skeptical about the possibility of *knowing* that we are free, whereas (from different hard-determinist perspectives) Luther, Diderot, La Mettrie, Holbach, Schopenhauer, and Laplace were skeptical about freedom altogether.

25. See David Macarthur's essay in this anthology for a defense of the idea that naturalism (or rather what we call "scientific naturalism") has similar skeptical implications also with regard to beliefs about the external world.

26. "Any adequate conception of free agency must provide for possibility and autonomy in some sense." Gary Watson, "Free Action and Free Will," *Mind* 96 (1987): 145–172, quotation from p. 145.

27. On this debate, see Bernard Berofsky, "Ifs, Cans, and Free Will: The Issues," in Kane, *Oxford Handbook of Free Will*, pp. 181–201.

28. See Tomis Kapitan, "A Master Argument for Incompatibilism?" in Kane, *Oxford Handbook of Free Will*, pp. 127–157; and Kane, *Significance of Free Will*, pp. 44–52.

29. See David Johnson and Thomas McKay, "A Reconsideration of an Argument Against Compatibilism," *Philosophical Topics* 24 (1996): 113–122; Alicia Finch and Ted Warfield, "The *Mind* Argument and Libertarianism," *Mind* 107 (1998): 515–528; Ekstrom, *Free Will*, chap. 2; and van Inwagen, "Free Will Remains a Mystery."

30. On this issue, see Ayer, "Freedom and Necessity"; and van Inwagen, *An Essay on Free Will* (Oxford: Oxford University Press, 1983), pp. 126–152.

31. See, for example, Carl Ginet, *On Action* (Cambridge: Cambridge University Press, 1990).

32. Philippa Foot, "Free Will as Involving Determinism," *Philosophical Review* 56 (1957): 429–450; John Austin, "Ifs and Cans," in *Philosophical Papers* (Oxford, Clarendon, 1961), pp. 153–180; G. E. Anscombe, *Causality and Determination: An Inaugural Lecture* (Cambridge: Cambridge University Press, 1971); Hilary Putnam, "The Place of Facts in a World of Values," in *Realism with a Human Face* (Cambridge: Harvard University Press, 1976), pp. 151–156; Ekstrom, *Free Will*, chap. 4. Libertarian views that appeal to indeterministic causation are presented in Robert Nozick, *Philosophical Explanations* (Cambridge: Harvard University Press, 1981), pp. 291–316; and Kane, *Significance of Free Will*.

33. The defenders of the so-called "agent causation"—a version of libertarianism

inspired by Thomas Reid—attempt to bypass this problem by saying that agents can *originate* new causal chains. See Roderick Chisholm, "Human Freedom and the Self," in Watson, *Free Will*, pp. 24–35; Richard Taylor, *Action and Purpose* (Englewood Cliffs, N.J.: Prentice Hall, 1966); and Timothy O'Connor, *Persons and Causes* (Oxford: Oxford University Press, 2000). According to these authors, *agent causation* differs from *event causation*, and is logically prior to it. Such a conception, however, has never been very popular, mostly because it looks metaphysically obscure, and according to many it is conceived *ad hoc* to solve the difficulties of libertarianism. Moreover, van Inwagen, in "Free Will Remains a Mystery," has persuasively argued that this view cannot even offer an answer to the antilibertarian argument mentioned above. In my opinion, the latter difficulty depends on the fact that the defenders of agent-causation simply acquiesce in the metaphysical realism of indeterministic libertarianism, and merely *add* to it a preternatural form of causation—for which they do not offer any convincing independent reasons.

34. On this point, see Thomas Nagel, *The View from Nowhere* (Oxford: Oxford University Press, 1986), chap. 7; and Christine Korsgaard, *The Sources of Normativity* (Cambridge: Cambridge University Press, 1996). For a different point of view about the relevance of the freewill issue, see Susan Wolf, "The Importance of Free Will," *Mind* 90 (1991): 386–405.

35. Van Inwagen, "Mystery of Metaphysical Freedom," p. 373. For a defense of the thesis that the negation of free will is contradictory, see van Inwagen, *Essay on Free Will*, p. 160–161.

36. Van Inwagen, "Free Will Remains a Mystery," p. 11.

37. Smilansky, *Free Will and Illusion*, p. 6.

38. For two recent defenses of hard determinism, see Honderich, *Theory of Determinism*, and Pereboom, *Living Without Free Will*. As it is well known, from a hard-determinist point of view, if we became aware of our lack of freedom, the *justification* of some of our social practices would be affected, but not the practices themselves: prisons would continue to exist, even though they would be justified only by utilitarian reasons, and not by appealing to notions like responsibility, desert, and retribution.

39. Quoted from Boswell's biography of Samuel Johnson in W. L. Rowe, "Two Concepts of Freedom," in O'Connor, *Agents, Causes, and Events*, pp. 151–171, quotation from p. 151.

40. G. H. von Wright, *Freedom and Determination* (Amsterdam: North-Holland, 1980), pp. 78–79. See also the introduction to Rosaria Egidi, ed., *In Search of a New Humanism: The Philosophy of Georg Henrik von Wright* (Dordrecht: Kluwer, 1999).

41. Hilary Putnam, "Reductionism and the Nature of Psychology," *Cognition* 2 (1973): 131–146, offers some persuasive reasons for thinking that *in principle* the explanations of the human and social sciences cannot be reduced to those of natural sciences.

42. Of course, what is in question here is not whether human and social scientists actually draw the ontological consequences implicit in their theories, or whether they should. The point is a strictly *philosophical* one, since it concerns the strategies that should be used in trying to outline the general ontological structures of reality.

43. I call "genuine" the ontological commitments of a theory that are accepted only insofar as they do not conflict with the ontological commitments of other theories that are considered more basic (such as the theories of physics).

44. Jaegwon Kim, "Dretske on How Reasons Explain Behavior," in *Supervenience*

and Mind: Selected Philosophical Essays (Cambridge: Cambridge University Press, 1993), pp. 285–308, quotation from p. 290.

45. W. V. Quine, *Word and Object* (Cambridge: MIT Press, 1960) and *Ontological Relativity and Other Essays* (New York: Columbia University Press, 1969). For some critical remarks on this view, see S. J. Wagner, "Truth, Physicalism, and Ultimate Theory," in Howard Robinson, ed., *Objections to Physicalism* (Oxford: Clarendon, 1993), pp. 127–158.

46. Donald Davidson, "Problems in the Explanations of Actions," in Philip Pettit, Richard Sylvan, Jean Norman, eds., *Metaphysics and Morality: Essays in Honour of J. J. C. Smart* (Oxford: Blackwell, 1987), pp. 35–49.

47. One should remember that Davidson connects the thesis that mature physics does not appeal to causal notions with the idea that any causal relation instantiates a law of physics (see "Mental Events," in *Essays on Actions and Events*, pp. 207–227; and "Laws and Causes," *Dialectica* 49 [1994]: 264–279). However, since the two theses are logically independent, one can hold the former without accepting the latter.

48. Max Planck, for example, wrote that the law of causality is a "heuristic principle, a signpost and in my opinion the most valuable signpost we possess, to guide us through the motley disorder of events and to indicate the direction in which scientific inquiry must proceed in order to attain fruitful results." Quoted in John Earman, "Determinism in the Physical Sciences," in M. H. Salmon et al., eds., *Introduction to the Philosophy of Science* (Englewood Cliffs, N.J.: Prentice Hall, 1992), p. 234.

49. See John Dupré, *The Disorder of Things: Metaphysical Foundations of the Disunity of Science* (Cambridge: Harvard University Press, 1993), pp. 229–233, where it is argued that the methodological ideal of unification is very different from, and much more justified than, the ontological principle of the unity of the world (to which the principle of the causal closure of the physical domain is strictly connected). On this, see also Hornsby, *Simple Mindedness*, pt. 1; and Dupré's essay in this volume.

50. In *The Dappled World: A Study of the Boundaries of Science* (Cambridge: Cambridge University Press, 1999), Nancy Cartwright maintains convincingly that "the impressive empirical successes of our best physics theories may argue for the truth of these theories, but not for their universality" (p. 4).

51. See Tim Crane and D. H. Mellor, "There Is No Question of Physicalism," *Mind* 99 (1990): 185–206. A strenuous critic of physicalism is Hilary Putnam: see his "Reflections on Goodman's *Ways of Worldmaking*," in *Philosophical Papers*, vol. 3, *Realism and Reason* (Cambridge: Cambridge University Press, 1983), pp. 155–169; "Is the Causal Structure of the Physical Itself Something Physical?" in James Conant, ed., *Realism with a Human Face* (Cambridge: Harvard University Press, 1990), pp. 80–95; *Renewing Philosophy* (Cambridge: Harvard University Press, 1992), chap. 5; "Three Kinds of Scientific Realism," in James Conant, ed., *Words and Life* (Cambridge: Harvard University Press, 1994), pp. 492–499; and his essay in this volume.

52. Hilary Putnam, *The Threefold Cord: Mind, Body, and World* (Cambridge: Harvard University Press), pp. 137–150; the quotation, taken from John Haldane, is at p. 137.

53. Jaegwon Kim, "The Myth of Nonreductive Materialism," in *Supervenience and Mind*, pp. 265–284. Typically, nonreductive physicalists believe that even if all the individuals are physical, they can have nonphysical properties that *supervene* on physical properties.

54. See Dupré, *Disorder of Things*. Dupré's pluralism is non-Cartesian both because

it is based "not on different kinds of stuff but on irreducibly different kinds of things" (p. 92), and because, in his view, the mental does not have any special ontological status ("Minds are no more nor less anomalous than cells, societies, or weather systems" [p. 90]). It should be noticed that Dupré, differently from the nonreductive physicalists, does not believe that nonphysical properties supervene on physical ones. See also Cartwright, *Dappled World*, pp. 31–33.

55. In criticizing the old criterion of the unity of science, Dupré (*Disorder of Things*, p. 11) lists some epistemic virtues to which we should refer for deciding what theories we should accept: "empirical accountability, consistency with common sense and other well-grounded scientific belief, and perhaps the more aesthetic virtues such as elegance and simplicity . . . [and] more straightforwardly normative virtues . . . [such as] a fundamental desideratum of democratic inclusion and accountability." If one accepts pluralism in ontology, there is no reason not to be committed to the ontology of any theory that satisfyingly fulfills these criteria. On this issue, see also Putnam's essay in this volume.

56. I am specially grateful to Stephen White for some very useful conversations concerning the issues treated here. Rosaria Egidi, Erin Kelly, David Macarthur, Giacomo Marramao, and Portia Prebys provided some valuable comments on a previous version of this essay.

11. Subjectivity and the Agential Perspective

1. We can take factual here to include anything expressible in a nonagential— and for reasons that will become clear later, nonnormative—vocabulary. These necessary omissions aside, there is no drawback in construing the domain of the factual as widely as possible.

2. Accounts of agent causation are clearly not objective in this sense, since the concept of an agent is ineliminable. An account that simply yokes agential and objectivist concepts together without explanation, however, is hardly illuminating.

3. Galen Strawson, *Freedom and Belief* (New York: Oxford University Press, 1986); see esp. chap. 2.

4. Most such analyses *have* been understood in this way. If, however, the analysis is a posteriori, then the argument against it would have to appeal to what I have called the property dualism argument. See "Curse of the Qualia," in *The Unity of the Self* (Cambridge: MIT Press, 1991); and "Why the Property Dualism Argument Will Not Go Away," read at the New York University Language and Mind Colloquium, April 4, 2000. We needn't address these issues here, however, since an a posteriori argument would not address the problem of the *meaningfulness* of the agential vocabulary.

5. J. L. Mackie, *Ethics: Inventing Right and Wrong* (New York: Penguin, 1977), pp. 31, 35, 40, 42.

6. Compare this to Smith's claim about beliefs and desires being independent existences. Michael Smith, *The Moral Problem* (Oxford: Blackwell, 1994), p. 12.

7. Mackie, *Ethics*, p. 42.

8. Smith, *Moral Problem*, p. 12.

9. The radical difference between the perspective of a normal subject and the perspective of a subject in the grip of a pathology that approaches that of the passive subject has been extensively documented in both literature and clinical psychology. I address this further in the conclusion.

10. Mackie, *Ethics*, p. 38.

11. E. H. Gombrich, "Illusion and Art," in R. L. Gregory and E. H. Gombrich, eds., *Illusion in Nature and Art* (London: Duckworth, 1973), pp. 193–243, quotation from p. 208, quoted in Joel Snyder, "Picturing Vision," *Critical Inquiry* (Spring 1980): 499–526, quotation from p. 500.

12. Gombrich, "Illusion and Art," p. 240, quoted in Snyder, "Picturing Vision," p. 501.

13. Snyder, "Picturing Vision," p. 515.

14. Christopher Peacocke, *Sense and Content* (New York: Oxford University Press, 1993), p. 12.

15. Bertrand Russell, *Problems of Philosophy* (New York: Oxford University Press, 1959); A. J. Ayer, *The Foundations of Empirical Knowledge* (London: Macmillan, 1962); R. J. Swartz, ed., *Perceiving, Sensing, and Knowing* (New York: Doubleday, 1965), sec. 2.

16. The correct shape is wider at the top than at the base and has interior base angles of approximately 105° on the left and 135° on the right. Thus the three departures from the trapezoid are the convergence of the top and base, the greater width at the top, and the very significant difference in the base angles.

17. If the distance from the foot to the eye is 5'4", then the hand is 15 times closer to the eye than the foot. If the real ratio is 11/2 to 1, the ratio of the apparent lengths is 24 to 1. For taller subjects the ratio will be significantly higher. Typical responses are in the neighborhood of 5 to 1.

18. A. K. Wheelock Jr., *Perspective, Optics, and Delft Artists Around 1650* (New York: Garland, 1977), pp. 70–71.

19. To see the point on the philosophical side, consider the problem that in viewing a row of columns perpendicular to the line of sight, the projections of the end columns on a transparent plane between the row and the viewer will be wider than the projection of the middle columns. It is sometimes thought that the problem is addressed by pointing to the curvature of the retina or the claim that what determines the character of our visual perception is a matter of the size of the angle and not the projection of that angle on a transparent plane between the object and the eye. But to say that the character of our conscious perceptual experience is a matter of the visual angle and not the projection on an appropriate plane is just to say that such experience is not pictorial in character—that no picture corresponds to the way in which the world is given to us in visual experience. And the same applies to the point about the curvature of the retina. The question is not what mechanism produces our experience but what it is like to have that experience.

This distinction is recognized by E. H. Gombrich, "Standards of Truth: The Arrested Image and the Moving Eye," *Critical Inquiry* (Winter 1980): 237–273; see esp. pp. 266–273.

20. Such sociological considerations range from the increased status accorded to artists as the ideology of perspective representation developed to the increased significance attached to visual observation and the consequences of this development for early modern science. See Wheelock Jr., *Perspective, Optics, and Delft Artists Around 1650*, pp. 85–86; and Snyder, "Picturing Vision," p. 523.

21. Ayer, *Foundations of Empirical Knowledge*, pp. 87–88, 107.

22. For example, referring expressions 'N' and 'M' differ in their cognitive significance if and only if there is some predicate expression 'F' such that the subject could be rational in believing what he or she would express by saying 'N is F' and not believing what he or she would express by saying 'M is F'.

23. See Lawrence Weiskrantz, *Blindsight* (Oxford: Oxford University Press, 1986).

24. See note 15.

25. J. J. Gibson, *The Ecological Approach to Visual Perception* (Hillsdale, N.J.: Laurence Erlbaum, 1986), pp. 127–128, 134.

26. Stephen Schiffer, "The Basis of Reference," *Erkenntnis* 13 (1978): 171–206; Brian Loar, *Mind and Meaning* (Cambridge: Cambridge University Press, 1981), p. 99, n. 1; Gareth Evans, *The Varieties of Reference* (New York: Oxford University Press, 1982), p. 173, n. 44; David Austin, *What's the Meaning of "This"?* (Ithaca: Cornell University Press, 1980), chap. 3.

27. Peacocke, *Sense and Content*, p. 9.

28. Albert Michotte, *The Perception of Causality* (New York: Basic Books, 1963).

29. See T. R. Miles, "Commentary," in Michotte, *Perception of Causality*, pp. 410–415.

30. *Causal Cognition*, ed. Dan Sperber, David Premack, and A. J. Premack (New York: Oxford University Press, 1995), pt. 3.

31. Gibson, *Ecological Approach to Visual Perception*, pp. 127–128, 134.

32. J. P. Sartre, *The Transcendence of the Ego* (New York: Farrar, Straus, and Giroux, 1992), pp. 48–49.

33. Christopher Peacocke, "Does Perception Have a Nonconceptual Content?" *Journal of Philosophy* 98 (2001): 244.

34. Ayer, *Foundations of Empirical Knowledge*, p. 112; Anthony Quinton, *The Nature of Things* (London: Routledge and Kegan Paul, 1973), pp. 126–130. Ayer's claim is discussed in Michael Williams, *Groundless Belief* (New Haven: Yale University Press, 1977), pp. 46–56; Quinton's is discussed in Laurence BonJour, *The Structure of Empirical Knowledge* (Cambridge: Harvard University Press, 1985), pp. 65–72.

35. "Consciousness and the Problem of Perspectival Grounding," paper read at the Workshop on Consciousness Naturalized, Certosa di Pontignano, Siena, May 28, 1999.

36. George Pitcher, *A Theory of Perception* (Princeton: Princeton University Press, 1971); David Armstrong, "Perception and Belief," in Jonathan Dancy, ed., *Perceptual Knowledge* (New York: Oxford University Press, 1988).

37. Schiffer, "Basis of Reference"; John Perry, "The Problem of the Essential Indexical," *Noûs* 13 (1979): 3–21; Loar, *Mind and Meaning*; Evans, *Varieties of Reference*; David Lewis, "Attitudes De Re and De Se," reprinted with a postscript in *Philosophical Papers*, vol. 1 (New York: Oxford University Press, 1983), pp. 133–159; Austin, *What's the Meaning of "This"?*

38. In "Consciousness and Perspectival Grounding." For a theory according to which consciousness is a matter of second-order representation (thought), see David Rosenthal, "Two Concepts of Consciousness," in *The Nature of Mind* (New York: Oxford University Press, 1991), pp. 462–477.

39. The passive subject could, for example, accept logical laws embodying agential notions—for instance: For every x, if x is an agent then either x is an agent or x is a prime number.

40. Thomas Kuhn, *The Structure of Scientific Revolutions* (Chicago: University of Chicago Press, 1962).

41. Indeed the analysis suggests that strictly we should not say that we see affordances, since conscious visual perception of any kind presupposes a capacity for action, and the capacity for action presupposes the perception of affordances. It might be better, I think, to say that we have conscious visual perceptual experience and a capacity for action as a result of our being *given* affordances directly.

42. *Autobiography of a Schizophrenic Girl* (New York: Penguin, 1951), p. 55.
43. Ibid., p. 83.
44. Ibid., p. 106.

12. A Nonnaturalist Account of Personal Identity

1. The section summarizes some of my previous writing, most especially *The Bounds of Agency: An Essay in Revisionary Metaphysics* (Princeton: Princeton University Press, 1998).

2. See John Locke, *Essay Concerning Human Understanding*, ed. P. H. Nidditch (Oxford: Oxford University Press, 1975), bk. 2, chap. 27.

3. Ibid., sec. 9.

4. For a good introduction to the neo-Lockean view, see Sydney Shoemaker's contribution to Sydney Shoemaker and Richard Swinburne, eds., *Personal Identity* (Oxford: Blackwell, 1984).

5. For defenses of animalism, see David Wiggins, *Sameness and Substance* (New York: Oxford University Press, 1980); and Eric Olson, *The Human Animal: Personal Identity Without Psychology* (New York: Oxford University Press, 1997).

6. Locke's own commitment to naturalism is less obvious, at least to me. For all I know, he may have been quite happy to allow that the divergence between a person's life and a particular animal's life could come about only through a miraculous intervention by God in an otherwise natural order.

7. In *Bounds of Agency*, I defend an equivalent criterion of personhood, which is that something is a person just in case it can engage in agency-regarding relations. There I call it an ethical criterion because I defend it on ethical grounds. The switch in labels doesn't indicate any change of view on my part. I just don't have the space here to explain why it is an ethical as well as a pragmatic criterion of personhood.

8. Thus, those who lie and threaten are not trying to get their victims to be irrational, as in weakness of will, nor even to engage in faulty reasoning. They do, of course, aim to take advantage of their victims in one way or another. The liar aims to take advantage of what she takes to be her victim's ignorance. The maker of a threat aims to take advantage of desires that she takes her victim to hold dear. But, in both cases, they aim to take advantage of this by relying on their victims' ability to reason correctly from their current points of view. (This is not to say that persons never try to take advantage of the fact that others are disposed to rational failure of one kind or another. It is only to say that this is not the canonical form of a lie or a threat. Forms of influence that aim to induce rational failure would be better classified as manipulation of quite another kind.)

9. See Rovane, *Bounds of Agency*, for a more complete defense of them, as well as an explicit formulation of the analysis of personal identity that goes together with them, which I call there the "normative" analysis of personal identity.

10. For a thorough discussion of the various pros and cons with respect to this issue, of whether to recognize alters as persons in their own rights, see Jennifer Radden, *Divided Minds and Successive Selves: Ethical Issues in Disorders of Identity and Personality* (Cambridge: MIT Press, 1996).

11. See Ian Hacking, *Rewriting the Soul: Multiple Personality and the Sciences of Memory* (Princeton: Princeton University Press, 1995).

13. Against Naturalism in Ethics

1. For helpful criticism and suggestions, I am indebted to Faviola Rivera Castro, Leonard Katz, Lionel McPherson, Angela Smith, Kok-Chor Tan, and Stephen White.

2. Jürgen Habermas, "Reconciliation Through the Public Use of Reason: Remarks on John Rawls's *Political Liberalism,*" *Journal of Philosophy* 92 (March 1995): 131.

3. Richard Boyd, "Fundamental Moral Realism," in Geoffrey Sayre-McCord, ed., *Essays on Moral Realism* (Ithaca: Cornell University Press, 1988). See also Peter Railton, "Moral Realism," *Philosophical Review* 95 (April 1986): 163–207; Nicholas Sturgeon, "Moral Explanations," in David Copp and David Zimmerman, eds., *Morality, Reason, and Truth* (Totowa, N.J.: Rowman and Allanheld, 1985); and David O. Brink, *Moral Realism and the Foundations of Ethics* (New York: Cambridge University Press, 1989). For a helpful discussion of Boyd, see Stephen L. White, *The Unity of the Self* (Cambridge: MIT Press, 1991), pp. 360–366.

4. G. E. Moore, *Principia Ethica* (Cambridge: Cambridge University Press, 1903), chap. 1.

5. This formulation is taken from Stephen Darwall, Allan Gibbard, and Peter Railton, "Toward *Fin de Siècle* Ethics: Some Trends," *Philosophical Review* 101 (January 1992): 149. See A. J. Ayer, *Language, Truth, and Logic* (London: Gollancz: 1946); and C. L. Stevenson, "The Emotive Meaning of Ethical Terms," *Mind* 46 (1937): 14–31.

6. Allan Gibbard, *Wise Choices, Apt Feelings: A Theory of Normative Judgment* (Cambridge: Harvard University Press, 1990), p. 46. Gibbard argues that these feelings tend to serve a coordinating function that can be explained by evolution. See pp. 64–80, 293–300.

7. Gibbard argues that we seem to accept a requirement of consistency and that we tend, in fact, to be influenced to accept norms that other people affirm. See *Wise Choices, Apt Feelings,* pp. 71–82. But these observations would seem to fall short of describing reasonable requirements on moral argumentation that I am claiming moral theory should aim to describe.

8. Christine M. Korsgaard, *The Sources of Normativity* (Cambridge: Cambridge University Press, 1996), chap. 1, esp. pp. 10–16.

9. See Jeremy Bentham, *Bentham Manuscripts,* University College London, 27.172. Quoted in Ross Harrison, *Bentham* (London: Routledge, 1983), p. 47. In searching for a clue to the labyrinth, Bentham was speaking of the labyrinth of jurisprudence: "the whole of jurisprudence a labyrinth without a clew." I am speaking, more generally, of the labyrinth of our normative concepts. Bentham aimed to formulate a metaphysics that could help to clarify the nature of law and provide a basis for reform. He thought that an aspect of what was confusing in the morass of legal language was the place occupied in it by the "fictions" of rights, duties, obligations, and the like, which he thought could be clarified by reference to certain facts. See, for example, *The Works of Jeremy Bentham,* ed. John Bowring (New York: Russell and Russell, 1962), vol. 3, p. 160, and vol. 8, p. 247. See also discussion by H.L.A. Hart, "Legal Duty and Obligation," *Essays on Bentham* (Oxford: Oxford University Press, 1982), pp. 131–132.

10. See also R. B. Brandt, *The Theory of the Good and the Right* (New York: Oxford University Press, 1979); Gilbert Harman, *The Nature of Morality* (New York: Oxford

University Press, 1977), pp. 125–133; and David Lewis, "Dispositional Theories of Value," *Proceedings of the Aristotelian Society* supp. 63 (1989): 113–137.

11. Railton, "Moral Realism," p. 190. Compare Harman, who argues that "something X is good to the extent that it adequately answers to the relevant interests." *Nature of Morality*, pp. 15–16. This analysis, Harman argues, suggests that evaluative facts might be constructed out of observable facts.

12. Railton, "Moral Realism," p. 189.

13. Ibid., p. 191.

14. Ibid., pp. 191–192.

15. Ibid., p. 193.

16. Ibid., pp. 195–199.

17. Ibid., pp. 174–175. For critical discussion, see Don Loeb, "Full-Information Theories of Individual Good," *Social Theory and Practice* 21 (Spring 1995): 1–30.

18. Railton, "Moral Realism," p. 177. See also Brandt, *Theory of the Good and the Right*, chap. 6.

19. See Bernard Williams, "Internal and External Reasons," in *Moral Luck* (Cambridge: Cambridge University Press, 1982).

20. Railton, "Moral Realism," pp. 190–191, n. 31.

21. Michael Smith, *The Moral Problem* (Oxford: Blackwell, 1994), pp. 151–152.

22. Ibid., pp. 158–160.

23. Railton's view may be able to accommodate this criticism. He could claim that one could become more instrumentally rational by making one's desires and aims more coherent. That is, it is instrumentally rational to eliminate aims and desires that are not consistent with and may even frustrate other aims and desires. It is also instrumentally rational to acquire aims and desires that will facilitate the aims and desires one already has. I thank Angela Smith for this point.

24. Compare Harman, who says that "the source of moral reasons is the aims and goals of the person involved." *Nature of Morality*, p. 133.

25. See T. M. Scanlon, "Preference and Urgency," *Journal of Philosophy* 72 (1975): 655–669. See also Thomas Nagel, *The View from Nowhere* (New York: Oxford University Press, 1986), pp. 166–171.

26. Smith agrees that his general account of normative reasons does not isolate what are, specifically, moral reasons. To do that, he argues, an analysis of the nature of rational reflection must be applied to the proper subject matter of morality, one that captures relevant platitudes about the content of morality. These are platitudes such as, "Right acts are in some way expressive of equal concern and respect." *Moral Problem*, p. 184; see also pp. 39–41, 183, and his "Response-Dependence Without Reduction," *European Review of Philosophy: Response Dependence* 3 (Stanford: CSLI, 1998): 85–108.

27. Railton, "Moral Realism," p. 177, n. 20.

28. I am indebted to Angela Smith for suggestions on this point.

29. The imposition of burdens upon some persons will be justifiable only when there are no alternatives that are less costly for them without imposing comparable burdens on others. See T. M. Scanlon, *What We Owe to Each Other* (Cambridge: Harvard University Press, 1998), p. 205. See also T. M. Scanlon, "Contractualism and Utilitarianism," in Amartya Sen and Bernard Williams, eds., *Utilitarianism and Beyond* (Cambridge: Cambridge University Press, 1982), p. 113.

30. John Rawls, *Justice as Fairness: A Restatement*, ed. Erin Kelly (Cambridge: Harvard University Press, 2001), p. 31.

31. Ibid.

32. Ibid.

33. Railton, "Moral Realism," pp. 190–191, n. 31.

34. Some of the ideas in this section and the following are discussed in my paper "Habermas on Moral Justification," *Social Theory and Practice* 26 (2000): 223–249.

35. Jürgen Habermas, *Inclusion of the Other: Studies in Political Theory*, ed. Ciaran Cronin and Pablo De Greiff (Cambridge: MIT Press, 1998), p. 42. For alternative statements of the principle, see Jürgen Habermas, *Moral Consciousness and Communicative Action*, trans. Christian Lenhardt and Shierry Weber Nicholsen (Cambridge: MIT Press, 1990), pp. 65, 93.

36. See Jürgen Habermas, *Legitimation Crisis*, trans. Thomas McCarthy (Boston: Beacon Press, 1975), pp. 89, 113.

37. Habermas, *Moral Consciousness and Communicative Action*, p. 89. See also Robert Alexy, "A Theory of Practical Discourse," in Seyla Benhabib and Fred Dallmayr, eds., *The Communicative Ethics Controversy*, trans. David Frisby (Cambridge: MIT Press, 1990), pp. 166–167.

38. Habermas, *Inclusion of the Other*, pp. 40–41. Habermas claims that the derivation of U proceeds from the formal features of practical discourse together with some weak understanding of what it means to justify moral norms. In a recent work, Habermas suggests that this weak understanding of what it means to justify norms is expressed by the "Discourse Principle" (Principle *D*). Principle *D* states that "only those norms can claim validity that could meet with the acceptance of all concerned in practical discourse." *Inclusion of the Other*, p. 41. See also Habermas, *Moral Consciousness and Communicative Action*, pp. 66, 93.

39. Jürgen Habermas, *The Theory of Communicative Action*, vol. 1, trans. Thomas McCarthy (Boston: Beacon Press, 1974), p. 19.

40. Jürgen Habermas, *Justification and Application: Remarks on Discourse Ethics*, trans. Ciaran P. Cronin (Cambridge: MIT Press, 1993), p. 31.

41. Habermas, *Moral Consciousness and Communicative Action*, pp. 88–91.

42. As claimed in note 38, Habermas's recent work suggests that this weak understanding of what it means to justify norms is expressed by Principle *D*. Previously, he formulates this understanding more loosely as the idea that "moral justifications resolve disputes concerning rights and duties, that is, concerning the rightness of the corresponding normative statements," and that the resolution of such disputes takes place via rational deliberation (i.e., on the basis of reasons). *Justification and Application*, p. 32; see also p. 52 and *Moral Consciousness and Communicative Action*, pp. 92–93.

43. See also Frank Michelman, "Conceptions of Democracy in American Constitutional Argument: The Case of Pornography Regulation," *Tennessee Law Review* 56 (1989): 291–319; Frank Michelman, "The Supreme Court 1985 Term—Foreward: Traces of Self-Government," *Harvard Law Review* 100 (1985): 4–77; and Jon Elster, "The Market and the Forum: Three Varieties of Political Theory," in James Bohman and William Rehg, eds., *Deliberative Democracy: Essays on Reason and Politics* (Cambridge: MIT Press, 1997).

44. For Rawls's criticism of Habermas's idea that reasonable procedural constraints on discourse can be understood to be purely formal, see sec. 5 of John Rawls, "Reply to Habermas," *Journal of Philosophy* 92 (1995): 132–180. There may also be reason to doubt whether in Rawls's own theory of justice, the requirements of the reasonable

can fully be represented through the imposition of the formal constraint of a veil of ignorance on the parties in the original position. See my review of John Rawls's *Theory of Justice*, rev. ed., in *Philosophical Review* 110 (July 2001): 421–425.

45. As Joshua Cohen argues, constraints on reasons that can be advanced in a fair procedure limit the substantive outcomes of the process; procedural and substantive values cannot be separated. See his "Pluralism and Proceduralism," *Chicago-Kent Law Review* 69 (1994): 609–610.

46. Or they could be dogmatic about how to understand key concepts, the priority ranking of shared values, the appropriate weight of relevant considerations, or the ways in which experience supports value judgments. See Rawls's discussion of the "burdens of judgment" in *Political Liberalism* (New York: Columbia University Press, 1993), pp. 54–58.

47. For an interesting discussion of the moral sensitivity required to see the relevance of moral principle in concrete life situations and to frame maxims adequately for evaluation by moral principle, see Barbara Herman, "The Practice of Moral Judgment," in *The Practice of Moral Judgment* (Cambridge: Harvard University Press, 1993), pp. 73–93.

48. See Hilary Putnam, "Values and Norms," in *The Collapse of the Fact/Value Distinction* (Cambridge: Harvard University Press, 2002), chap. 7.

49. For discussion of the notion of the reasonable, see Rawls, *Political Liberalism*, pp. 48–54; Scanlon, *What We Owe to Each Other*, pp. 32–33, 191–197; Joshua Cohen, "Moral Pluralism and Political Consensus," in D. Copp, J. Hampton, and John Roemer, eds., *The Idea of Democracy* (Cambridge: Cambridge University Press, 1993), pp. 281–284; and Charles Larmore, *The Morals of Modernity* (Cambridge: Cambridge University Press, 1996), chap. 7.

50. Also relevant may be considerations of responsibility and fairness. See Scanlon, *What We Owe to Each Other*, chap. 5. For a discussion of the concept of moral urgency, see Scanlon, "Preference and Urgency."

51. Scanlon, *What We Owe to Each Other*, p. 216. Scanlon writes that an advantage of his contractualism is that it "can account for the significance of different moral notions, within a unified moral framework, without reducing all of them to a single idea." He continues, "What is necessary in order to do this is to show in each case why people would have reason to insist upon principles incorporating these notions." *What We Owe to Each Other*, p. 216.

52. Scanlon, *What We Owe to Each Other*, pp. 218–223.

53. This helps to make sense of what it would mean to take seriously the various platitudes about morality to which Smith refers (see note 26). It means that moral theory must analyze the normative content of these platitudes and the arguments that support them.

54. There is a certain resemblance between my argument and Moore's open question argument. For related discussion, see Darwall, Gibbard, and Railton, "Toward *Fin de Siècle* Ethics," p. 177.

14. *Postscript (2002) to "The* Investigations' *Everyday Aesthetics of Itself"*

1. Stanley Cavell, "The *Investigations*' Everyday Aesthetics of Itself," in Stephen Mulhall, ed., *The Cavell Reader* (Cambridge: Blackwell, 1996).

2. Ludwig Wittgenstein, *Philosophical Investigations* (Oxford: Oxford University Press, 1953).

3. Stanley Cavell, *Must We Mean What We Say* (Cambridge: Cambridge University Press, 1969/1976).

4. Ibid., p. 21.

5. S. J. Gould, *New York Review of Books*, October 4, 2001.

Bibliography

Anscombe, G. E. *Causality and Determination: An Inaugural Lecture.* Cambridge: Cambridge University Press, 1971.

Armstrong, D. M. *Belief, Truth, and Knowledge.* Cambridge: Cambridge University Press, 1973.

———. *Universal and Scientific Realism.* 2 vols. Cambridge: Cambridge University Press, 1978.

———. "Naturalism, Materialism, and First Philosophy." In *The Nature of Mind.* St. Lucia, Queensland: University of Queensland Press, 1980, pp. 149–165.

Audi, Robert. *The Structure of Justification.* Cambridge: Cambridge University Press, 1993.

Bhaskar, Roy, and Andrew Collier, eds. *The Possibility of Naturalism: A Philosophical Critique of the Contemporary Human Sciences.* London: Routledge, 1999.

Blackburn, Simon. *Being Good: An Introduction to Ethics.* Oxford: Oxford University Press, 2001.

Block, Ned, Owen Flanagan, and Güven Güzeldere, eds. *The Nature of Consciousness: Philosophical Debates.* Cambridge: MIT Press (Bradford Books), 1997.

Bonjour, Laurence. "Against Naturalized Epistemology." In P. A. French, T. E. Uehling, and H. K. Wettstein, eds., *Midwest Studies in Philosophy,* vol. 19, *Philosophical Naturalism.* Notre Dame: University of Notre Dame Press, 1994, pp. 283–300.

Boyd, Richard. "Scientific Realism and Naturalistic Epistemology." *Philosophy of Science Association Proceedings* 2, no. 80 (1982): 195–223.

Brandom, Robert. *Making It Explicit: Reasoning, Representing, and Discursive Commitment.* Cambridge: Harvard University Press, 1994.

Bratman, Michael. *Intention, Plans, and Practical Reason.* Cambridge: Harvard University Press, 1987.

———. "Reflection, Planning, and Temporally Extended Agency." *Philosophical Review* 109 (2000): 35–61.

————. "Two Problems About Human Agency." *Proceedings of the Aristotelian Society* 101 (2001): 309–326.

Cartwright, Nancy. *How the Laws of Physics Lie.* Oxford: Oxford University Press, 1983.

————. *The Dappled World: A Study of the Boundaries of Science.* Cambridge: Cambridge University Press, 1999.

Chalmers, D. J. *Conscious Mind: In Search of a Fundamental Theory.* Oxford: Oxford University Press, 1996.

Cherniak, Christopher. *Minimal Rationality.* Cambridge: MIT Press, 1986.

Chisholm, R. M. "Human Freedom and the Self." In *The Lindley Lecture.* Lawrence: University of Kansas Press, 1964, pp. 3–15. Reprinted in Gary Watson, ed., *Free Will.* Oxford: Oxford University Press, 1982, pp. 24–35.

Churchland, P. M. *A Neurocomputational Perspective.* Cambridge: MIT Press, 1989.

Churchland, P. S. *Neurophilosophy.* Cambridge: MIT Press, 1986.

Craig, W. L., and J. P. Moreland. *Naturalism: A Critical Analysis.* London: Routledge, 2000.

Crane, Tim, and D. H. Mellor. "There Is No Question of Physicalism." *Mind* 99 (1990): 185–206. Reprinted with a postscript in P. K. Moser and J. D. Trout, eds. *Contemporary Materialism: A Reader.* London: Routledge, 1995, pp. 65–89.

Damasio, A. R., Anne Harrington, and Jerome Kagan, eds. *Unity of Knowledge: The Convergence of Natural and Human Science.* New York: New York Academy of Sciences, 2001.

Darwall, Stephen, Allan Gibbard, and Peter Railton. "Toward Fin de Siécle Ethics: Some Trends." *Philosophical Review* 101 (1992): 115–189.

Davidson, Donald. *Essays on Actions and Events.* Oxford: Clarendon, 1980.

————. *Inquiries into Truth and Interpretation.* Oxford: Clarendon, 1984.

————. "Problems in the Explanations of Actions." In Philip Pettit, Richard Sylvan, and Jean Norman, eds., *Metaphysics and Morality: Essays in Honour of J. J. C. Smart.* Oxford: Blackwell, 1987, pp. 35–49.

————. "Laws and Causes." *Dialectica* 49 (1994): 264–279.

————. *Subjective, Intersubjective, Objective.* Oxford: Clarendon, 2001.

Dennett, Daniel. *The Elbow Room: The Varieties of Free Will Worth Wanting.* Cambridge: MIT Press, 1984.

————. *The Intentional Stance.* Cambridge: MIT Press, 1987.

————. *Consciousness Explained.* Boston: Little, Brown, 1991.

————. *Darwin's Dangerous Idea.* New York: Simon & Schuster, 1995.

Double, Richard. *The Non-reality of Free Will.* Oxford: Oxford University Press, 1991.

————. *Metaphilosophy and Free Will.* Oxford: Oxford University Press, 1996.

Dretske, Fred. *Knowledge and the Flow of Information.* Cambridge: MIT Press, 1981.

————. *Naturalizing the Mind.* Cambridge: MIT Press, 1995.

Dummett, Michael. *The Origins of Analytic Philosophy.* London: Duckworth, 1993.

Dupré, John. *The Disorder of Things: Metaphysical Foundations of the Disunity of Science.* Cambridge: Harvard University Press, 1993.

————. *Human Nature and the Limits of Science.* Oxford: Oxford University Press, 2001.

Egidi, Rosaria, ed. *In Search of a New Humanism: The Philosophy of Georg Henrik von Wright.* Dordrecht: Kluwer, 1999.

Ekstrom, Laura. *Free Will: A Philosophical Study.* Boulder: Westview Press, 2000.

Evans, Gareth. *The Varieties of Reference*. Oxford: Clarendon, 1982.

Feldman, Richard. "Methodological Naturalism in Epistemology." In John Greco and Ernest Sosa, eds., *The Blackwell Guide to Epistemology*. Oxford: Blackwell, 1999, pp. 170–186.

Feyerabend, P. K. *Against Method*. London: New Left Books, 1975.

Field, Hartry. *Science Without Numbers*. Oxford: Blackwell, 1980.

———. "Physicalism." In John Earman, ed., *Inference, Explanation, and Other Frustrations: Essays in the Philosophy of Science*. Berkeley: University of California Press, 1992, pp. 271–291.

Fodor, Jerry. "Special Sciences." *Synthèse* 28 (1974): 77–115.

Fogelin, R. J. "Quine Limited Naturalism." *Journal of Philosophy* 94 (1997): 543–563.

Foster, John. *The Immaterial Mind: A Defence of the Cartesian Dualist Conception of Mind*. London: Routledge, 1997.

French, P. A., T. E. Uehling, and H. K. Wettstein, eds. *Midwest Studies in Philosophy*. Vol. 19, *Philosophical Naturalism*. Notre Dame: University of Notre Dame Press, 1994.

Galison, Peter. *How Experiments End*. Chicago: University of Chicago Press, 1987.

Gibbard, Allan. *Wise Choices, Apt Feelings: A Theory of Normative Judgement*. Cambridge: Harvard University Press, 1990.

Giere, R. N. *Science Without Laws*. Chicago: University of Chicago Press, 1999.

Gillet, Carl, and Barry Loewer, eds. *Physicalism and Its Discontent*. Cambridge: Cambridge University Press, 2001.

Ginet, Carl. *On Action*. Cambridge: Cambridge University Press, 1990.

Goldman, Alvin. *Epistemology and Cognition*. Cambridge: Harvard University Press, 1986.

———. "Naturalistic Epistemology and Reliabilism." In P. A. French, T. E. Uehling, and H. K. Wettstein, eds., *Midwest Studies in Philosophy*, vol. 19, *Philosophical Naturalism*. Notre Dame: University of Notre Dame Press, 1994, pp. 301–320.

Haack, Susan. *Evidence and Inquiry*. Oxford: Oxford University Press, 1993.

Hacking, Ian. *Representing and Intervening*. Cambridge: Cambridge University Press, 1983.

Haldane, John and Crispin Wright, eds. *Reality, Representation and Projection*. Oxford: Oxford University Press, 1993.

Harman, Gilbert. *Change in View: Principle of Reasoning*. Cambridge: MIT Press, 1986.

Haugeland, John. "Ontological Supervenience." In *Having Thought: Essays in the Metaphysics of Mind*. Cambridge: Harvard University Press, 1998.

Heil, John, and Alfred Mele, eds. *Mental Causation*. Oxford: Clarendon, 1993.

Honderich, Ted. *A Theory of Determinism*. 2 vols. Oxford: Oxford University Press, 1988.

Hornsby, Jennifer. *Simple Mindedness: In Defense of Naive Naturalism in the Philosophy of Mind*. Cambridge: Harvard University Press, 1997.

Huemer, Michael. "Naturalism and the Problem of Moral Knowledge." *Southern Journal of Philosophy* 38 (2000): 575–597.

Hume, David. *A Treatise of Human Nature*. 2nd ed. Oxford: Clarendon, 1740/1978.

———. *An Enquiry Concerning Human Understanding*. 3rd ed. Oxford: Clarendon, 1748/1975.

Hylton, Peter. *Russell, Idealism, and the Emergence of Analytic Philosophy*. Oxford: Clarendon, 1990.

Kane, Robert. *The Oxford Handbook of Free Will.* Oxford: Oxford University Press, 2002.

Kim, Jaegwon. "What Is 'Naturalized Epistemology'?" In J. E. Tomberlin, ed., *Philosophical Perspectives,* vol. 2. Atascadero: Ridgeview 1988, pp. 381–405.

———. "The Myth of Nonreductive Materialism." *Proceedings and Addresses of the American Philosophical Association* 63 (1989): 31–47.

———. *Supervenience and Mind.* Cambridge: Cambridge University Press, 1993.

———. *Mind in a Physical World.* Cambridge: MIT Press, 1998.

Kitcher, Philip. "Mathematical Naturalism." In William Aspray and Philip Kitcher, eds., *Minnesota Studies in the Philosophy of Science,* vol. 11, *History and Philosophy of Modern Mathematics.* Minneapolis: University of Minnesota Press, 1988, pp. 293–325.

———. "The Naturalists Return." *Philosophical Review* 101 (1992): 53–114.

Kögler, H. H., and K. R. Stueber, eds. *Empathy and Agency: The Problem of Understanding in the Human Sciences.* Boulder: Westview Press, 2001.

Kornblith, Hilary. "The Psychological Turn." *Australasian Journal of Philosophy* 60 (1982): 238–253.

———. "Introduction: What Is Naturalistic Epistemology?" In Hilary Kornblith, ed., *Naturalizing Epistemology.* Cambridge: MIT Press, 1985, pp. 1–14.

———. "Naturalizing Epistemology and Its Critics." *Philosophical Topics* 23 (1995): 237–255.

———, ed. *Naturalizing Epistemology.* Cambridge: MIT Press, 1985.

Krikorian, Y. H., ed. *Naturalism and the Human Spirit.* New York: Columbia University Press, 1944.

Kripke, Saul. *Naming and Necessity.* Oxford: Blackwell, 1980.

———. *Wittgenstein on Rules and Private Language.* Oxford: Basil Blackwell, 1982.

Kuhn, T. S. *The Structure of Scientific Revolutions.* Chicago: Chicago University Press, 1962/1970.

Laudan, Larry. "Normative Naturalism." *Philosophy of Science* 57 (1990): 44–59.

Lewy, Casimir. "G. E. Moore on the Naturalistic Fallacy." In P. F. Strawson, ed., *Studies in the Philosophy of Thought and Action.* Oxford: Oxford University Press, 1968, pp. 134–146.

Libet, Benjamin, Anthony Freeman, and Keith Sutherland, eds. *The Volitional Brain: Towards a Neuroscience of Free Will.* Thoverton: Imprint Academic, 1999.

Loewer, Barry. "A Guide to Naturalizing Semantics." In Bob Hale and Crispin Wright, eds., *A Companion to the Philosophy of Language.* Oxford: Blackwell, 1997, pp. 108–126.

Lycan, W. G. *Judgement and Justification.* Cambridge: Cambridge University Press, 1988.

Mackie, John. *Ethics: Inventing Right and Wrong.* New York: Penguin, 1977.

Maddy, Penelope. *Realism in Mathematics.* Oxford: Clarendon, 1990.

McDowell, John. *Mind and World.* Cambridge: Harvard University Press, 1994.

McGinn, Colin. *Problems in Philosophy.* Oxford: Blackwell, 1993.

———. *The Mysterious Flame.* New York: Basic Books, 1999.

McGinn, Marie. "Real Things and the Mind-Body Marie Problem." *Proceedings of the Aristotelian Society* 100 (2000): 303–317.

Mele, Alfred. "Goal-Directed Action: Teleological Explanations, Causal Theories, and Deviance." *Philosophical Perspectives* 14 (2000): 279–300.

———. *Motivation and Agency.* Oxford: Oxford University Press, forthcoming.

Midgley, Mary. *Beast and Man.* Ithaca: Cornell University Press, 1978.

Millikan, R. G. *White Queen Psychology and Other Essays for Alice*. Cambridge: MIT Press, 1993.

Moser, P. K., and J. D. Trout, eds. *Contemporary Materialism: A Reader*. London: Routledge, 1995.

Nagel, Thomas. *The View from Nowhere*. Oxford: Oxford University Press, 1986.

Nannini, Sandro, and H. J. Sandkuhler, eds. *Naturalism in the Cognitive Sciences and the Philosophy of Mind*. Frankfurt am Main: Peter Lang, 2000.

Nielsen, Kai. *Naturalism and Religion*. Amherst, N.Y.: Prometheus, 2001.

Nozick, Robert. *Philosophical Explanations*. Cambridge: Harvard University Press, 1981.

———. *Invariances: The Structure of the Objective World*. Cambridge: Harvard University Press (Bradford Books), 2001.

O'Connor, Timothy, ed., *Agents, Causes, and Events: Essays on Indeterminism and Free Will*. Oxford: Oxford University Press, 1995.

———. *Persons and Causes*. Oxford: Oxford University Press, 2000.

Oppenheim, Paul, and Hilary Putnam. "The Unity of Science as a Working Hypothesis." In Herbert Fiegl, Michael Scriven, and Grover Maxwell, eds., *Minnesota Studies in the Philosophy of Science*, vol. 2, *Concepts, Memories, and the Mind-Body Problem*. Minneapolis: University of Minnesota Press, 1958, pp. 3–36.

Papineau, David. *Philosophical Naturalism*. Oxford: Blackwell, 1993.

Parfit, Derek. *Reasons and Persons*. Oxford: Oxford University Press, 1984.

Pereboom, Derk. *Living Without Free Will*. Cambridge: Cambridge University Press, 2001.

Pettit, Philip. "Naturalism." In Ernest Sosa and Jonathan Dancy, eds., *A Companion to Epistemology*. Oxford: Blackwell, 1992, pp. 296–297.

Pidgen, C. R. "Naturalism." In Peter Singer, ed., *A Companion to Ethics*. Oxford: Blackwell, 1991, pp. 421–431.

Pietroski, P. M. *Causing Actions*. Oxford: Oxford University Press, 2000.

Plantinga, Alvin. *Warrant and Proper Function*. New York: Oxford University Press, 1993.

Price, Huw. "Naturalism and the Fate of the M-Worlds." *Proceedings of the Aristotelian Society* supp. 71 (1997): 247–267.

Putnam, Hilary. "Reductionism and the Nature of Psychology." *Cognition* 2 (1973): 131–146.

———. "The Place of Facts in a World of Values." In *Realism with a Human Face*. Cambridge: Harvard University Press, 1976, pp. 151–156.

———. *Reason, Truth, and History*. Cambridge: Cambridge University Press, 1981.

———. *Philosophical Papers*, vol. 3, *Realism and Reason*. Cambridge: Cambridge University Press, 1983.

———. "Why Reason Cannot Be Naturalized." In *Philosophical Papers*, vol. 3, *Realism and Reason*. Cambridge: Cambridge University Press, 1983, pp. 229–247.

———. *Representation and Reality*. Cambridge: MIT Press (Bradford Books), 1988.

———. *Realism with a Human Face*. Cambridge: Blackwell, 1990.

———. *Renewing Philosophy*. Cambridge: Harvard University Press, 1992.

———. *Words and Life*. Cambridge: Harvard University Press, 1994.

———. *The Threefold Cord: Mind, Body, and World*. New York: Columbia University Press, 2000.

———. *The Collapse of the Fact/Value Dichotomy and Other Essays*. Cambridge: Harvard University Press, 2002.

Quine, W. V. *Word and Object*. Cambridge: MIT Press, 1960.

——. "Epistemology Naturalized." In *Ontological Relativity and Other Essays*. New York: Columbia University Press, 1969, pp. 69–90.

——. "The Nature of Natural Knowledge." In Samuel Guttenplan, ed., *Mind and Language: Wolfson College Lectures*. Oxford: Oxford University Press, 1975, pp. 67–81.

——. *Theories and Things*. Cambridge: Harvard University Press, 1981.

——. "Things and Their Place in Theories." In *Theories and Things*. Cambridge: Harvard University Press, 1981, pp. 1–23.

——. *Pursuit of Truth*. Cambridge: Harvard University Press, 1992.

——. *From Stimulus to Science*. Cambridge: Harvard University Press, 1995.

Railton, Peter. "Naturalism and Prescriptivity." *Social Philosophy and Policy* 7 (1989): 151–174.

Robinson, Howard, ed. *Objections to Physicalism*. Oxford: Clarendon, 1993.

Rorty, Richard. *Philosophy and the Mirror of Nature*. Oxford: Blackwell, 1980.

Rosenberg, Alexander. *Instrumental Biology or the Disunity of Science*. Chicago: University of Chicago Press, 1994.

Ryle, Gilbert. *The Concept of Mind*. London: Hutchinson, 1949.

Sayre-McCord, Geoffrey, ed. *Moral Realism*. Ithaca: Cornell University Press, 1988.

Schear, Jonathan, ed. *Explaining Consciousness: The Hard Problem*. Cambridge: MIT Press (Bradford Books), 1998.

Schmitt, F. F., ed. *Socializing Epistemology: The Social Dimensions of Knowledge*. Lanham, Md.: Rowman and Littlefield, 1994.

Searle, John. *The Rediscovery of Mind*. Cambridge: MIT Press, 1992.

Sellars, R. W. *Evolutionary Naturalism*. Chicago: Open Court, 1992.

Sellars, W. F. *Science, Perception, and Reality*. London: Routledge, 1963.

Siegel, Harvey. "Justification, Discovery, and the Naturalizing of Epistemology." *Philosophy of Science* 47 (1980): 297–321.

——. "Empirical Psychology, Naturalized Epistemology, and First Philosophy." *Philosophy of Science* 51 (1984): 667–676.

Sklar, Lawrence. "Naturalism and the Interpretation of Theories." *Proceedings and Addresses of the American Philosophical Association* 75 (2001).

Smart, J. J. C. *Philosophy and Scientific Realism*. London: Routledge, 1963.

Smilansky, Saul. *Free Will and Illusion*. Oxford: Oxford University Press, 2000.

Snow, C. P. *The Two Cultures*. Cambridge: Cambridge University Press, 1959.

Sorell, Tom. *Scientism and the Infatuation with Science*. London: Routledge, 1991.

Sosa, Ernest. *Knowledge in Perspective: Selected Essays in Epistemology*. Cambridge: Cambridge University Press, 1991.

Stein, Edward. *Without Good Reason: The Rationality Debate in Philosophy and Cognitive Science*. Oxford: Oxford University Press, 1996.

Steward, Helen. *The Ontology of Mind: Events, States, and Processes*. Oxford: Oxford University Press, 1997.

Stich, Stephen. *Deconstructing the Mind*. New York: Oxford Unviersity Press, 1996.

——. *The Fragmentation of Reason: Preface to a Pragmatic Theory of Cognitive Evaluation*. Cambridge: MIT Press, 1990.

Strawson, Galen. *Freedom and Belief*. Oxford: Oxford University Press, 1986.

——. *Mental Reality*. Cambridge: MIT Press (Bradford Books), 1994.

Strawson, Peter. "Freedom and Resentment." Reprinted in Gary Watson, ed., *Free Will*. Oxford: Oxford University Press, 1982, pp. 59–80.

——. *Skepticism and Naturalism: Some Varieties*. New York: Columbia University Press, 1985.

Stroud, Barry. "The Significance of Naturalized Epistemology." In P. A. French, T. E. Uehling, and H. K. Wettstein, eds., *Midwest Studies in Philosophy*, vol. 19, *Philosophical Naturalism*. Notre Dame: University of Notre Dame Press, 1994, pp. 455–471.

———. "The Charm of Naturalism." *Proceedings and Addresses of the American Philosophical Association* 70 (1996): 43–55. Reprinted here.

Swain, Marshall. "Epistemics and Epistemology." *Journal of Philosophy* 75 (1978): 523–525.

Taylor, Charles. "Understanding in Human Science." *Review of Metaphysics* 34 (1980): 25–38.

———. *Philosophy and the Human Sciences*. Philosophical Papers no 2. Cambridge: Cambridge University Press, 1985.

Taylor, Richard. *Action and Purpose*. Englewood Cliffs, N.J.: Prentice-Hall, 1966.

Traweek, Sharon. *Beamtimes and Lifetimes: The World of High Energy Physicists*. Cambridge: Harvard University Press, 1988.

Van Frassen, Bas. "Against Naturalized Epistemology." In Paolo Leonardi and Marco Santambrogio, eds., *On Quine: New Essay*. Cambridge: Cambridge University Press, 1995, pp. 68–88.

Van Inwagen, Peter. *An Essay on Free Will*. Oxford: Oxford University Press, 1983.

———. *Metaphysics*. Boulder: Westview Press, 1993.

———. "Free Will Remains a Mystery." *Philosophical Perspectives* 12 (2000): 1–19.

Velleman, David. "What Happens When Someone Acts?" *Mind* 101 (1992): 461–481.

———. *The Possibility of Practical Reason*. Oxford: Oxford University Press, 2000.

Villanueva, Enrique, ed. *Philosophical Issues*. Vol. 4, *Naturalism and Normativity*. Atascadero: Ridgeview, 1993.

Von Wright, G. H. *Explanation and Understanding*. London: Routledge, 1971.

———. *Freedom and Determination*. Amsterdam: North-Holland, 1980.

Wagner, S. J. "Truth, Physicalism, and Ultimate Theory." In Howard Robinson, ed., *Objections to Physicalism*. Oxford: Clarendon, 1993, pp. 127–158.

Wagner, S. J., and Richard Warner, eds., *Naturalism: A Critical Appraisal*. Notre Dame: University of Notre Dame Press, 1993.

Warner, Richard, and Tadeusz Szubka, eds. *The Mind–Body Problem: A Guide to the Current Debate*. Oxford: Blackwell, 1994.

Watson, Gary, ed. *Free Will*. Oxford: Oxford University Press, 1982.

———. "Free Action and Free Will." *Mind* 96 (1987): 145–172.

Wiggins, David. "Towards a Reasonable Libertarianism." In Ted Honderich, ed., *Essays on Freedom and Action*. London: Routledge, 1973, pp. 31–62.

Williams, Bernard. *Descartes: The Project of Pure Enquiry*. Harmondsworth: Penguin, 1978.

———. "Internal and External Reason." In *Moral Luck*. Cambridge: Cambridge University Press, 1981, pp. 101–113.

———. *Ethics and the Limits of Philosophy*. Cambridge: Harvard University Press, 1985.

Wittgenstein, Ludwig. *Philosophical Investigations*. Oxford: Oxford University Press, 1953.

———. *Tractatus Logico-Philosophicus*. London: Routledge, 1961.

Woodfield, Andrew, ed. *Thought and Object*. Oxford: Clarendon, 1982.

Worrall, John. "Philosophy and the Natural Sciences." In A. C. Grayling, ed., *Philosophy*, vol. 2. Oxford: Oxford University Press, 1988, pp. 199–266.

Contributors

Akeel Bilgrami is the Johnsonian Professor of Philosophy at Columbia University. He is the author of *Belief and Meaning* (1992) and *Self-Knowledge and Resentment* (forthcoming), and various articles on the philosophy of language and mind.

Stanley Cavell is Professor Emeritus at Harvard University, having formerly been the Walter M. Cabot Professor of Aesthetics and the General Theory of Value. He is the author of many books and articles, including *Must We Mean What We Say* (1969/1976), *The Claim of Reason* (1979), *A Pitch of Philosophy: Autobiographical Exercises* (1994), and *Contesting Tears: The Melodrama of the Unknown Woman* (1996). He is a past President of the American Philosophical Association.

Donald Davidson was Willis S. and Marion Slusser Professor of Philosophy at the University of California, Berkeley. His many publications include *Essays on Actions and Events* (1980), *Inquiries into Truth and Interpretation* (1984), and *Subjective, Intersubjective, Objective* (2001). Numerous books and anthologies have been dedicated to his philosophy, including a volume of *The Library of Living Philosophers* (1999).

Mario De Caro teaches at Università Roma Tre. He previously taught at Tufts University and Saint Mary's College (Notre Dame, Indiana), and was a visiting scholar at MIT and a Fulbright visiting scholar at Harvard University. He is the editor of *Interpretations and Causes: New Perspectives on Donald Davidson's Philosophy* (1999).

John Dupré is Professor of Philosophy of Science at the University of Exeter. He has formerly held positions at Stanford University and Birkbeck College, London. His publications include *The Disorder of Things: Metaphysical Foundations of the Disunity of Science* (1993), *Human Nature and the Limits of Science* (2001), and *Humans and Other Animals* (2002). His main area of research is the philosophy of biology.

Jennifer Hornsby is Professor of Philosophy at Birkbeck College, University of London. She is author of *Actions* (1980) and *Simple Mindedness: In Defense of Naive Naturalism in the Philosophy of Mind* (1997), and coeditor of two anthologies on feminist themes. Her published articles and current work concern the philosophy of mind, philosophy of language, metaphysics, and areas of social philosophy informed by feminist thinking.

Erin I. Kelly is Associate Professor of Philosophy at Tufts University. Her recent papers include "Personal Concern," published in the *Canadian Journal of Philosophy*, vol. 30, no. 1 (2000), and "Doing Without Desert," published in *Pacific Philosophical Quarterly*, vol. 83, no. 2 (2002). She is editor of John Rawls's *Justice as Fairness: A Restatement* (2001). Her research interests include moral and political philosophy.

David Macarthur is a Lecturer in Philosophy at the University of Sydney, having previously held a research fellowship in philosophy at Macquarie University and a teaching position at Tufts. His recent publications include "On Putnam's Return to Natural Realism," in Marie-Luise Raters and Marcus Willaschek, eds., *Hilary Putnam und die Tradition des Pragmatismus* (2002), and "McDowell, Skepticism, and the 'Veil of Perception,'" *Australasian Journal of Philosophy*, vol. 81, issue 2 (June 2003). His main areas of research are epistemology, philosophy of psychology, history of modern philosophy, and aesthetics.

John McDowell is a University Professor of Philosophy at the University of Pittsburgh. His books include *Mind and World* (1994/1996) and two volumes of collected papers, *Mind, Value, and Reality* (1998) and *Meaning, Knowledge, and Reality* (1998). He prepared for publication Gareth Evans's posthumous book *The Varieties of Reference* (1982); and he coedited, with Evans, *Truth and Meaning* (1974) and, with Philip Pettit, *Subject, Thought, and Context* (1986). He is a Fellow of the British Academy and of the American Academy of Arts and Sciences.

Huw Price is an ARC Federation Fellow and Challis Professor of Philosophy at the University of Sydney. He was formerly professor of Logic and Metaphysics at the University of Edinburgh. His publications include *Facts and the Function of Truth* (1988), *Time's Arrow and Archimedes' Point* (1996), and many articles on the philosophy of language, pragmatism, philosophy of physics, time asymmetry, and probability and decision theory. He is a fellow of the Australian Academy of the Humanities, and a past President of the Australasian Association of Philosophy.

Hilary Putnam is Cogan University Professor Emeritus at Harvard University. He is the author of many books and articles, including *Reason, Truth, and History* (1981), *Realism with a Human Face* (1990), *Renewing Philosophy* (1992), *Words and Life* (1994), *Pragmatism: An Open Question* (1995), and *The Threefold Cord: Mind, Body, and World* (2000). His collection *The Collapse of the Fact/Value Dichotomy and Other Essays* was published in 2002. He is a past president of the American Philosophical Association, a Fellow of the American Academy of Arts and Sciences, and a Corresponding Fellow of the British Academy.

Carol Rovane is an Associate Professor of Philosophy at Columbia University. Her publications include *The Bounds of Agency: An Essay in Revisionary Metaphysics* (1998), and articles on various subjects in metaphysics, philosophy of language, philosophy of mind, and ethics.

Barry Stroud is Mills Professor of Metaphysics and Epistemology at the University of California, Berkeley. He is the author of *Hume* (1977), *The Significance of Philosophical Scepticism* (1984), *The Quest for Reality* (1999), and two volumes of collected essays, *Understanding Human Knowledge* (2000) and *Meaning, Understanding, and Practice* (2000).

Stephen L. White is Associate Professor of Philosophy at Tufts University. He is the author of *The Unity of the Self* (1991) and of a number of papers on the philosophy of language, philosophy of mind, moral psychology, and moral theory. His research interests include narrow content, the subjective perspective, agency, value, and the self.

Index